CW01560501

# CLASSICAL PRESENCES

*General Editors*

Lorna Hardwick     James I. Porter

# CLASSICAL PRESENCES

The texts, ideas, images, and material culture of ancient Greece and Rome have always been crucial to attempts to appropriate the past in order to authenticate the present. They underlie the mapping of change and the assertion and challenging of values and identities, old and new. Classical Presences brings the latest scholarship to bear on the contexts, theory, and practice of such use, and abuse, of the classical past.

# Ted Hughes and
# the Classics

Edited by
ROGER REES

OXFORD
UNIVERSITY PRESS

# OXFORD
## UNIVERSITY PRESS

Great Clarendon Street, Oxford OX2 6DP

Oxford University Press is a department of the University of Oxford.
It furthers the University's objective of excellence in research, scholarship,
and education by publishing worldwide in

Oxford New York

Auckland Cape Town Dar es Salaam Hong Kong Karachi
Kuala Lumpur Madrid Melbourne Mexico City Nairobi
New Delhi Shanghai Taipei Toronto

With offices in

Argentina Austria Brazil Chile Czech Republic France Greece
Guatemala Hungary Italy Japan Poland Portugal Singapore
South Korea Switzerland Thailand Turkey Ukraine Vietnam

Oxford is a registered trade mark of Oxford University Press
in the UK and in certain other countries

Published in the United States
by Oxford University Press Inc., New York

© Oxford University Press 2009

The moral rights of the author have been asserted
Database right Oxford University Press (maker)

First published 2009

All rights reserved. No part of this publication may be reproduced,
stored in a retrieval system, or transmitted, in any form or by any means,
without the prior permission in writing of Oxford University Press,
or as expressly permitted by law, or under terms agreed with the appropriate
reprographics rights organization. Enquiries concerning reproduction
outside the scope of the above should be sent to the Rights Department,
Oxford University Press, at the address above

You must not circulate this book in any other binding or cover
and you must impose the same condition on any acquirer

British Library Cataloging in Publication Data

Data available

Library of Congress Cataloguing in Publication Data
Library of Congress Control Number: 2008943414

Typeset by SPI Publisher Services, Pondicherry, India
Printed in Great Britain
on acid-free paper by the
MPG Books Group, Bodmin and King's Lynn

ISBN 978–0–19–922971–0

3 5 7 9 10 8 6 4 2

# Preface

I don't have a particularly clear memory of going to a Ted Hughes recitation, as a sixth former, one dark evening in Birmingham. I can't even be sure of the year—1984 or 1985. The only memory that remains strong is that Hughes introduced and read 'February 17th', his extraordinary first-person narrative about saving a ewe in labour whose lamb, head out, had been strangled mid-birth; the narrator cuts off the head and succeeds in dragging the decapitated foetus out by forcing its vertebrae against the mother's pushes (originally from *Moortown Diary*, now in *Collected Poems* 518–19). The shocking poem made an enduring impression on me as a suburban teenager, but I lacked the critical imagination and experience to relate the poem to European traditions of pastoral poetry, despite the fact I was studying Vergil's *Eclogues* at school. In my mind, Ted Hughes and the classics were simply not on the same map.

So it remained for many years, my awareness of the controversies in Hughes's life (1930–98) and my enthusiasm for his poetry slowly aggregating, until the publication of *Tales from Ovid* (1997), the *Oresteia* (1999), and the *Alcestis* (1999) forced upon me the realization that 'Ted Hughes and the classics' was a very considerable topic, and as I discovered, hardly touched upon by scholars. Further, the study of the 'classical' in the work of Hughes promised to offer a new—and difficult—dimension to appreciation of a writer with little formal training in classical culture, widely if perhaps erroneously viewed as a radical nature poet, and who had even turned his back on academic literary criticism when changing degree topics at Cambridge from English to Archaeology and Anthropology.

After Keith Sagar's introductory chapter, the articles collected here seek to offer original and challenging perspectives on Hughes's engagement with classical culture, from his version of the storm scene from *Odyssey* 5 in 1960 to the posthumous publications nearly forty years later. Inevitably, given Hughes's prolific output, the articles cover a wide range of texts and genres, but recurrent themes include Hughes's competence in classical languages, his translation practices, his mythopoiesis, the types and quality of his allusion, his response to rationalism and its place in natural order, and his sense of a tradition redeployed. Together, I hope they work towards a better awareness both of the relationship between 'the classics' and Hughes's wider work and life, and of the place of Hughes's work in the field of classical reception in English literature of the late twentieth century.

The collection has its basis in a conference held at the School of History and Classics at Edinburgh University in November 2005, featuring specialists in the fields of classics, English literature, translation, reception, and theatre. My thanks are due to the School for financial support, and to the Classical Association and the Hellenic Society for their award of bursaries. I am also grateful to the School of Classics at St Andrews for help with publication expenses. For encouragement and help in various ways, I would like to thank Terry Gifford, Stuart Gillespie, Stephen Halliwell, Lorna Hardwick, Carol Hughes, Hilary O'Shea, Neil Roberts, Keith Sagar, Ann Skea, Jenny Wagstaffe, Daniel Weissbort, Colin Wilcockson, and the Press's anonymous reader. Michael Silk's article first appeared in *Arion* 14.3 (2007) 1–33.

I am also grateful for permissions to reproduce material: Bloodaxe Books for quotation of 'Final Remarks' by Peter Reading; Faber and Faber for quotations from T. S. Eliot, Seamus Heaney, Sylvia Plath, and Ted Hughes; Farrar, Strauss and Giroux, LLC for permission to reprint the excerpt from 'The Diviner' from *Opened Ground: Selected Poems 1966–1996* by Seamus Heaney, © 1998 by Seamus Heaney; 'Finale' from *Cave Birds*, 'Solomon's Dream', 'The Rabbit Catcher', 'Go Fishing', 'The Hidden Orestes', and excerpts from *Collected Poems* by Ted Hughes, © 2003 by The Estate of Ted Hughes; HarperCollins for 'The Rabbit Catcher' from *Winter Trees* by Sylvia Plath, copyright © 1972 by Ted Hughes, reprinted by permission of HarperCollins Publishers; Harcourt, Inc. for the excerpt from *Collected Poems 1909–1962* by T. S. Eliot, copyright 1936 by Harcourt, Inc., and renewed 1964 by T. S. Eliot, reprinted by permission of the publisher; Carol Hughes for quotation of unpublished material, and the sources of that material, the British Library and the Manuscript, Archives and Rare Books Library at Emory University; Jonathan Cape for 'A Bed of Leaves' from *Collected Poems* by Michael Longley, © Michael Longley 2006, reprinted by permission of The Random House

Group Ltd; for US permission for the same, Wake Forest University Press; and the National Portrait Gallery for the cover photograph of Ted Hughes (May 1970), © Edward Lucie-Smith/ National Portrait Gallery, London.

# Contents

# Notes on Contributors

**Professor Sarah Annes Brown** teaches at Anglia Ruskin University. She has worked extensively on various aspects of classical reception and her publications in this field include an edition of Nicholas Rowe's translation of Lucan's *Pharsalia* (Everyman 1997, co-edited with Charles Martindale) and *The Metamorphosis of Ovid: Chaucer to Ted Hughes* (Duckworth 1999). She edited a volume of essays for Blackwell, *Tragedy in Transition*, with Catherine Silverstone.

**Janne Stigen Drangsholt** is Research Fellow at the Department of English, University of Bergen. She is currently working on a Ph.D. on Hughes's mythopoeic metaphor. Her most recent publication is 'A Singular Encounter: Jean-Luc Nancy, Gayatri Spivak and the Others' (co-authored with Charles I. Armstrong) in *Postcolonial Dislocations: Travel, History and the Ironies of Narrative*.

**David Gervais** is Honorary Fellow in English at the University of Reading and has been editor of *The Cambridge Quarterly* since 1981. He is the author of *Flaubert and Henry James* (MacMillan 1978), *Literary Englands* (CUP 1993), *John Cooper Powys, T. S. Eliot and French Literature* (Cecil Woolf 2005) and numerous articles on English and French literature and painting. He has just completed a book on Shakespeare and Racine.

**Stuart Gillespie** is Reader in English Literature at the University of Glasgow. His research interests cover many aspects of the classical tradition and his relevant publications include *The Poets on the Classics: An Anthology of English Poets' Writings on the Classical Poets and Dramatists* (1988); he is editor of the journal *Translation and Literature* (Edinburgh University Press), of the five-volume *Oxford History of Literary Translation in English* (2005– ), and co-editor of *The Cambridge Companion to Lucretius*.

**Lorna Hardwick** teaches at the Open University where she is Professor of Classical Studies and Director of the Reception of Classical Texts Research Project. Her publications include *Translating Words*,

*Translating Cultures*, articles on the translation, performance, and mediation of tragedy and epic, and on their reception in post-colonial contexts. She is currently working on a monograph on the migration of classical texts.

**Jennifer Ingleheart** completed her doctorate, a commentary on Ovid's *Tristia* 2, at Oxford in 2004. A lecturer in Classics at the University of Durham, she is interested in the poetry of Ovid, its reception, and literary autobiography.

**Garrett Jacobsen** is an Associate Professor and Chair of the Department of Classics at Denison University in Granville, Ohio. He has published and presented papers on Ovid, as well as on the classical tradition, most recently 'Nought may endure but Mutability: Ovid's *Tristia* I.11', a study applying Gadamer's theories of language to Ovid's poetic reality of exile. A larger project on 'Art and Alienation in Ovid's *Metamorphoses*' is in progress.

**Genevieve Liveley** is a lecturer in Classics at Bristol. Her teaching and research interests are in Latin literature and culture, gender and sexuality, critical theory, and the classical tradition. She is author of *Ovid: Love Songs* (Duckworth, 2005), and co-editor with Patricia Salzman of *Elegy and Narrativity* (OSUP, forthcoming). She is currently working on two books: one on post-feminism and the classical tradition, and another on time and narrative in Roman elegy.

**Hallie Marshall** is a doctoral student in the Comparative Literature Program at the University of British Columbia. She is completing a doctoral thesis on the place of Tony Harrison's classical plays within the tradition of twentieth-century British drama.

**Roger Rees** has been Reader in Latin at St Andrews University since 2006. He has published variously on Latin literature and Roman history, including *Layers of Loyalty in Latin Panegyric 289–307*CE (OUP, 2002) and edited *Romane memento: Vergil in the Fourth Century* (Duckworth, 2004).

**Neil Roberts** is Professor of English Literature at University of Sheffield. He is co-author of *Ted Hughes: A Critical Study*. He has also written books on George Eliot, Peter Redgrove, George Meredith, D. H. Lawrence and *Narrative and Voice in Postwar Poetry*.

He was the editor of the *Blackwell Companion to Twentieth Century Poetry*. He has also written a literary life of Ted Hughes.

**Keith Sagar** has published over twenty books, most of them on D. H. Lawrence or on Ted Hughes, whose friendship he enjoyed for thirty years. His magnum opus, *Literature and the Crime Against Nature*, was published in 2005. He is currently a Special Professor in the School of English at Nottingham University.

**Michael Silk** is Professor of Greek Language and Literature at King's College, London. His main areas of academic interest are Greek poetry and drama, the theory of literature, comparative literature and the classical tradition. He is currently preparing *Poetic Language in Theory and Practice: Greek Archetypes and Modern Dilemmas*, for OUP, the outcome of his recent Leverhulme project, 'A Study of Greek Poetic Style in the Classical Age'.

**John Talbot** (Ph.D. Boston) teaches classical and modern literature at Brigham Young University. His publications, which focus on classical and English literary relations, appear in journals like *Studies in Philology, Arion, Essays in Criticism, Classical and Modern Literature,* and *The International Journal of the Classical Tradition*. He contributed a chapter to the *Oxford History of Literary Translation in English*, and is at work on a book-length study of the classical presence in Robert Frost.

**Anne-Marie Tatham** is currently working on a Ph.D. on the evolution of Ted Hughes's poetical writings. Since 2003 she has been lecturing on English Language and Literature at the University of Grenoble in France, where in 2006 she organized an international interdisciplinary conference on the concept of Metamorphosis.

**Vanda Zajko** is Senior Lecturer in Classics at the University of Bristol. She has wide-ranging interests in the reception of classical literature particularly in the twentieth century. Recent publications include 'Homer and Joyce' in *The Cambridge Companion to Homer* and 'Women and Myth' in the *Cambridge Companion to Greek Myth*. She is the co-editor of *Laughing with Medusa: Classical Myth and Feminist Thought* (OUP).

# 1

## Ted Hughes and the classics

*Keith Sagar*

Ted Hughes had a split psyche. In saying that I am not saying anything startling. Don't we all (or at least the males among us)? Perhaps the main difference between a major poet and the rest of us is that the poet is fully aware of the split, of its seriousness and consequences, and of the need to try to heal it.

Early in the twentieth century the South African naturalist Eugène Marais studied the soul, as he called it, of the ape. After living with wild baboons for many years, one of his conclusions was that the more intelligent a baboon was, the less able it was to live as a baboon. Intelligence seemed to develop at the expense of instinct, including the basic knowledge of how to live in the given world.[1] Hughes commented:

Marais had really defined the subconscious as the lost, natural Paradise, where the lack of intellectual inquiry and adaptive ingenuity coincided with a perfect awareness of being alive in the moment, and in reality (an awareness approaching, maybe, a state of blessedness) and an inborn understanding of 'how to live'. He had explained, in a sense, man's perplexed feeling of being everywhere an exile, everywhere separated from his true being. And without saying that his smarter baboons had suffered something like The Fall, he had brought zoological evidence to the argument that the free intelligence is man's original enemy.[2]

Hughes concluded that man is, by his very nature, split, tragic.

---

[1] Marais (1973).
[2] Hughes (1986: 164). See further Roberts in this volume.

It had been so for Nietzsche, who, in *The Birth of Tragedy*, identified the split as the main preoccupation of Greek myth and literature, the conflict within every man between the rival, often mutually exclusive, claims of Apollo (representing civilization, intelligence, science, culture, and the autonomy of man) and Dionysos (representing instinct, nature, and man's total dependence on the non-human world).

*

Ted Hughes's first acquaintance with the classics would have been his Latin lessons at Mexborough Grammar School. He would probably, like his sister two years ahead of him, have been introduced to works by Vergil, Ovid, and Seneca. It is tempting to imagine the teenage Hughes lapping up the story of Dido and Aeneas, and the first seeds being sown for his later work on Seneca and Ovid. Though he did not study Greek at school, at sixteen he was reading Greek translations to Edna Wholey. But it would be quite wrong to imagine Hughes at this stage of his life as a precocious student. He resented every moment he had to spend on school work, especially Latin. On the eve of his School Certificate exams he wrote:

All those books of Latin Grammer [*sic*], all the French I could but stammer,
All those notes on Europe (d . . . her) and of poets who now have wings.
Never, even 'neath the burning oil lamp had I turned to learning
All my five years notes, but spurning these I lived on lighter things.
Wise was I in ways of fishing; fast in noble arts of dishing
Loads of shot to rabbits, wishing even then that I could think.
But when evenings came for working where was I?—In some place lurking
In the woodlands, always shirking any thing that needed ink.[3]

There was always, however, a pencil and paper in his pocket for writing his own poems. By sixteen he had no thought of any career other than that of a poet. It was his poetry, not his exam results, that got him into Pembroke College, Cambridge.

Hughes's leaving present from his English teacher at Mexborough, John Fisher, was a copy of Robert Graves' *The White Goddess*. Though Graves there concentrates on Celtic rather than classical mythology, the book served to confirm Hughes's sense of poetry as

---

[3] From an unpublished poem 'Follow my footsteps not. Advice to 5th formers'.

a bardic, prophetic, shamanic calling. *The White Goddess* replaced Henry Williamson's *Tarka the Otter* (which had shown him that the poetic imagination can deepen one's understanding of the natural world) as his holy book. Unlike other subjects of academic study, poetry seemed to him to belong to Dionysos, not Apollo. His next holy book, which lasted him the rest of his life, was to be the *Bacchae*.

For the Greeks, Dionysos, god of the wild things, was closely associated with the animal world. He was frequently represented as panther or bull. Hughes's earliest books were to contain poems about a jaguar and a bull, but his personal totemic beasts became the more vulnerable and victimized wolf and fox. As in the *Bacchae*, to repress, to hunt down, to try to exterminate everything wild (like the cricket singing in Mount Zion chapel) is to guarantee that the repressed energies will become destructive, and, ultimately, self-destructive.[4] Animals are the archetypes of those energies in the human unconscious. To look at an animal is also to look backwards into the head. Animals bellow the evidence that we strive to hide.

Towards the end of his second year at Cambridge Hughes had worked for days on an essay on Dr Johnson, without getting beyond the first sentence. At two in the morning he gave up and went to bed. He dreamed that he was still sitting at his table when the door opened and an appalling creature entered, a fox, but the size of a man, on two legs, and smouldering all over as if it had just escaped from a furnace. It placed a bleeding hand on his almost blank page, leaving a bloody print, and said 'You are killing us'. Hughes interpreted the dream as his own deepest self telling him that the academic study of English was destroying his true selfhood and creativity. He changed, for his final year, to Archaeology and Anthropology.

The choice of these subjects was inspired. Hughes became an expert on myth and folklore, and was able to support himself and his children through the lean years of the Sixties by reviewing books in these fields regularly in the weeklies. More importantly, he could recycle this knowledge of how other cultures and times had tried to express and deal with the same problem through his own psyche and into his work. Here was no facile dipping into a myth-kitty for

[4] CP 481.

cheap portentousness, but a recognition that the ancients had already found virtually definitive symbolic expression for the essentials of the problem, as such modern psychologists as Freud and Jung freely admitted.

Yet the accusation of the burnt fox was not silenced. Hughes continued to feel that in choosing to go to university at all, to become an intellectual pursuing the literary life, to marry a writer geared to fame and success, to accept the responsibilities of a family man, he had continued the slow process of killing what Lawrence called 'the honourable beasts of our being'.[5] When in the middle of London he was offered a fox cub for a pound, and felt that he could not return to his wife Sylvia and their baby in their poky flat with a fox cub, he knew he had denied an essential part of himself: 'Then I walked on | As if out of my own life':

> If I had grasped that whatever comes with a fox
> Is what tests a marriage and proves it a marriage—
> I would not have failed the test.[6]

He failed because he was 'in the cooker' of the Apollonian aspirations of the women in his life: 'Otherwise | I'd be fishing off a rock | In Western Australia'.[7] The alternative would have been to follow the example of his elder brother Gerald, who on leaving school had cut loose, become a gamekeeper in Devon, and after the war emigrated to Australia, or of Henry Williamson, whom Hughes met: 'He was untamed: and he was free'.[8]

After the death of Sylvia Plath, Hughes's greatest healing resource was fishing, which was, for him, a religious experience. To enter water and become continuous through his rod and line with the holy life of that magical element was a form of atonement, of receiving the blessings of an unfallen, Dionysian world. All fish which were not eaten were returned unharmed to their element. And writing poems was a parallel activity, projecting the imagination into darkness and otherness, which is simultaneously the Great Outer Darkness (GOD) and the small inner darkness of his own unconscious. 'What we capture in the outer world is what has escaped from our inner world'.[9]

---

[5] (1936: 759).      [6] *CP* 1115–17.      [7] *CP* 1076–9.
[8] Hughes (1980*b*: 164).      [9] Hughes (1978).

*

Hughes's first collection, *The Hawk in the Rain* (1957) contains few, if any, overt references to the classics. But the split is everywhere apparent. The jaguar in his cage is like Dionysos in Pentheus's prison ('The Jaguar'); 'Egghead' is the hubristic Apollonian or Socratic man who pits his feeble intellect against the mysteries and energies of the natural world ('Egg-head'); so is the Faust-like protagonist of 'Meeting', whose narcissistic vanity cannot survive an encounter with another animal avatar of Dionysos, a goat.

Hughes's second book *Lupercal* (1960) takes its title from the Roman Lupercalia, a fertility festival in honour of the wolf.[10] Here the sacredness of the goat is spelled out:

> Yet that's no brute light
>
> And no merely mountain light—
> Their eyes' golden element.
>
> . . .
>
> . . . Spirit of the ivy,
> Stink of goat, of a rank thriving,
> O mountain listener.[11]

In the Roman ritual infertile women were lashed with 'fresh thongs of goat-skin' by the athletes as they passed. The book's second poem, 'Everyman's Odyssey', brilliantly condenses the story of Telemachus and in 1961 Hughes was to contribute a vivid rendering of the storm episode from Book 5 of *The Odyssey* for schools radio:

> Odysseus exulted at his glimpse of the land and its trees,
> And he drove through the waves to feel his feet upon earth.
> But within hail of the land, heard sea rending on rock,
> Eruption of the surge, whitening over the land-face,
> Bundling everything in spray. No harbour fit for a ship and no inlet,
> But thrust prows of crags and spines of reefs under hanging walls.[12]

Though genetic in origin, Hughes believed that the psychic split had been exacerbated by the acceptance and even cultivation of it in Western thought as dualism. In *The White Goddess* Graves had blamed Socrates and Plato for 'philosophical dualism with all the

---

[10] Talbot (2006: 139).     [11] *CP* 88.
[12] *CP* 93–6; Weissbort in *ST* 14–18; see Gillespie in this volume.

tragi-comic woes attendant on spiritual dichotomy'.[13] Hughes would have found confirmation of this in Nietzsche's *The Birth of Tragedy*, and in Yeats, who wrote: 'When [Plato] separates the Eternal Ideas from Nature and shows them self-sustained he prepares the Christian desert and the Stoic suicide'.[14] This is the theme of a difficult poem in *Lupercal* called 'The Perfect Forms', which mocks Socrates' complacency, and the gulf between his ideal notion of man and the 'six-day abortion of the Absolute', the 'monstrous-headed difficult child' that evolution actually produced. Socrates is to appear again as one of the embodiments of the criminal protagonist in *Cave Birds* (1978). Hughes described his crime in these words:

The whole abstraction of Socrates's discourse must inevitably, given enough time and enough applied intelligence, result in machine-guns . . . machine-guns descending directly from a mechanical, mechanistic development of logicality which grows from the abstraction of dialectical debate.[15]

Hughes's first play, written in 1959, was called *The House of Taurus*. According to Sylvia Plath it was a 'symbolic drama' based on the *Bacchae*.[16] Hughes 'scrapped' it in favour of *The House of Aries*, which was broadcast. Lucas Myers recalls Hughes's preoccupation at this time with dismemberment, as symbolizing the only cure for hubris, the ego death which must precede a reconstitution or rebirth.[17] His symbolic poetic drama *Gaudete* (1977), which began life as a film script in 1964, also draws on the *Bacchae*. It opens with the sacrifice of a bull, and ends with the dismemberment of the changeling Lumb.

Sylvia Plath died in 1963. After a two-year silence, Hughes began his vast, never-to-be finished project *The Life and Songs of the Crow*, fusing into a single loose narrative material from a vast range of myth and folklore. Crow, among other things, is a trickster figure, a role sometimes played by Hermes in Greek myth, but more prominent in other mythologies.

\*

In 1967 the National Theatre commissioned a new translation of Seneca's *Oedipus* from David Turner. It was to have been directed by

---

[13] Graves (1961: 465).    [14] Yeats (1962: 271).
[15] From a reading at Leeds University, 10 March 1979.
[16] Plath (1975: 355).    [17] Stevenson (1989: 320).

Sir Laurence Olivier, but because of illness, Olivier invited Peter Brook to take over. Turner's translation did not suit Brook's ideas about the play, and it was agreed that Hughes should be called in. Hughes was not a classical scholar. He was not fluent enough in any foreign language to translate from it unaided.[18] His method was to procure from someone else a crib—that is a straightforward literal prose translation, from which Hughes would then produce his 'version'. In this instance he went back to a translation by Frank Justus Miller in the Loeb edition. When David Turner attended Hughes's reading of his version to the assembled company, he responded with extraordinary generosity:

> It was obvious from the moment he spoke that improvement was too weak a word for what he had done. It was more like apotheosis. In place of good serviceable prose there was inspiration, elegance, fire, poetry. It was all magic. And all the magic was Ted's.[19]

Many of the reviews made no mention of Hughes's contribution to the production, but Sir John Gielgud, who played Oedipus, gave him most of the credit for its success:

> Hughes's reading, which only lasted about 40 minutes, was an electrifying experience, and we huddled together spellbound by the power of the play itself and especially by the poet's brilliant handling of the material. . . . I am so proud to have been involved in this Oedipus production and to have heard it liberated by Hughes's own unique personality.[20]

Irene Worth, who played Jocasta, went so far as to say that Hughes had taught her to act:

> He beat out short, hard phrases, stoic and strong. After Ted wrote Jocasta's death speech he read it to us. I don't ever want to lose that sound. He read with a skill that cracked open words as though he had just invented them. . . . He taught me to feel the freedom in words, not their enmity. Ted had made a mighty speech for Jocasta about birth which I simply wasn't up to. He guided me in the kindest, subtlest way, but I'm afraid I let him down.

---

[18] Weissbort in *ST* 59–61; Roberts (2006: 179–96).

[19] Turner (1969: 9). In spite of these words, Turner was humiliated by the treatment he received from the National Theatre and took legal action against it. His translation was later published in Corrigan (1990).

[20] Gielgud (1999: 155).

I should have been monumental and mammoth. Alas, I was only Whistler's Mother, but he set me on a search I have never abandoned. I hear John Gielgud's voice at the close of the play: harsh, volcanic, majestic and brave, 'Lead me'.[21]

The production opened at the Old Vic on 19 March 1968.

The experience could not have been more timely for Hughes. He recalled:

It gave me a very sharp sense of how the language had to be hardened or deepened so it could take the weight of the feeling running in the story. After a first draft I realized that all the language I had used in the story was too light. So there was another draft and then another one. And as I worked on it, it turned into a process of more and more simplifying, or in a way limiting the language. I ended up with something like three hundred words, the smallest vocabulary Gielgud had ever worked with. And that ran straight into *Crow*.[22]

Thematically, also, *Oedipus* ran straight into *Crow*. Hughes wrote:

Seneca hardly notices the intricate moral possibilities of his subject. Nevertheless, while he concentrates on tremendous rhetorical speeches and stoical epigrams, his imagination is quietly producing something else—a series of epic descriptions that contain the raw dream of Oedipus, the basic, poetic, mythical substance of the fable, and whatever may have happened to the rhetoric, this part has not dated at all. For everybody must answer the sphynx.[23]

And:

I was in complete sympathy with Peter Brook's guiding idea, which was to make a text that would release whatever inner power this story, in its plainest, bluntest form, still has, and to unearth, if we could, the ritual possibilities within it.[24]

In an interview on Australian radio in 1982, Hughes elaborated on Brook's 'guiding idea':

Under this enormously ornate temple of language there's a very primitive, raw shape of a drama. And this is what he responded to. And this is what he wanted to dig out from all that language. And from the start, it was my idea

---

[21] Worth (1999: 157).     [22] Hughes (1980*a*: 212).
[23] *SO* 8.     [24] *SO* 7–8; *ST* 60.

in the translation to do that—to find some way of discarding the ornateness and the stateliness (and in a way, there's a great majesty of the thing, because they're enormously, impressive, majestic pieces) and to bring out some quite thin but raw presentation of the real core of the play.[25]

This stripping and simplifying process was by no means limited to Seneca or collaboration with Brook; it became a fundamental method with regard to all Hughes's dealings with the classics. He believed that the ancient poets knew that the myths were bigger and deeper than they were themselves. Their achievement in the great plays and epics was to let the power and meaning of the myth flow through the wire of language, burning off in its surge the accretions of the poet's ego and the cultural accretions of his time and place. These texts were not, for Hughes, literary/historical monuments. All that mattered to him was 'what makes our own imagination jump'.[26]

The speech which Irene Worth claimed defeated her had in fact no equivalent in Seneca, but was close to Hughes's concerns in *Crow*. He wanted to make the connection between Jocasta and the Sphinx:

> I knew the future was waiting for him like a greedy god
>     a maneater in a cave . . .
> what was he what wasn't he
> the question was unasked
> and what was I what cauldron was I
> what doorway was I what cavemouth[27]

'The mythical substance of the fable' for Hughes was the killing of the sphinx, which he interpreted as a greater crime than murdering the father or marrying the mother, an attempt to destroy Nature herself in her role as universal mother, creatress, Great Goddess, by subjecting her to the murderousness of human intelligence.

\*

Crow, like the questing hero, fights with monsters, but most of these turn out to be projections of his own sickness onto the receptive form of Nature. His crime is to fail disastrously in all his relations with the female—the female in all its manifestations, actual women, but also his own anima, and mother Nature herself. Not until too late (like

---

[25] Transcribed by Ann Skea, <http://ann.skea.com/ABC1.htm>.
[26] *ST* 201.    [27] *SO* 17–18.

Heracles in his madness) does he recognize his victims as his own
mother, wife, and children. Crow recapitulates not only what Hughes
now sees as his own fatal mistakes, but also all the mistakes of
the race. He is Oedipus Crow, who, in his hubristic madness, can
see the Sphinx, actually a beautiful manifestation of great creating
Nature herself, only as a monster, a huge maw threatening to swallow
him, to obliterate his male autonomy. By killing the Sphinx he brings
the curse of sterility down on Thebes.

> Oedipus took an axe and split
>    The Sphynx from top to bottom
> The answers aren't in me, he cried
>    Maybe your guts have got em
>                     Mamma Mamma

Out of the split Sphinx comes his own mother:

> He split his Mammy like a melon
>    He was drenched with gore
> He found himself curled up inside
>    As if he had never been bore.
>                     Mamma Mamma

In poems such as this, 'Song for a Phallus', the classical source is
overt;[28] but there are many poems in which the recycling process has
gone so far that the classical reference is no longer detectable in the
final draft. In 'Actaeon', for example, from *Earth-Numb* (1979) only
the phrase 'those hounds' connects the poem to its title.[29] There
are probably hundreds of poems where classical references were in
Hughes's mind in the early stages of composition, but, like scaffolding, were removed before the poems were completed.

At the end of the abandoned story of Crow, Crow was to have been
gradually 'corrected', reconstituted, and married to his former victim.
The aborting of the Crow project was largely the result of the second
tragedy within six years to strike Hughes, the deaths of his partner,
Assia Wevill, and their daughter Shura.[30] Much of that material
found its way into *Cave Birds* (1978).[31]

---

[28] *CP* 248.     [29] *CP* 558–9.
[30] Feinstein (2001: 170–1).     [31] See Roberts in this volume.

*

In 1971 Hughes accompanied Peter Brook to the Shiraz festival in Persia. Since the audience would have no common language (nor did Brook's company) he decided to invent a new language called Orghast (which was also the name of the play), which everyone would (theoretically) understand.[32] From Hughes's own summary it is obvious that the play, starting from the Prometheus myth, developed further all the themes I have been discussing:

Part I is the story of the crime against material nature, the Creatress, source of life and light, by the Violator, the mental tyrant Holdfast, and her revenge.... [She] succeeds, transcending the conflict by creating a being which, like Prometheus (this is the story of how he survives), includes the elemental opposites, and in whom the collision and pain become illumination, because it is the true account.

　Part II is the story of the tyrant Holdfast in the Underworld, the decomposition of the fallen ego among the voices of its crimes, oversights and victims. Hercules, his son, descends to raise him up, back into the world, but death gives instead the vulture (the mystery of Prometheus's physical/spiritual dilemma) transformed into a woman.[33]

Hughes expands on the nature of Prometheus' dilemma (he is here called Pramanath) as follows:

Conscious in eternity, he has to live in time. And he cannot solve his dilemma. He hangs between heaven and earth, almost torn apart, an open wound, immortal. Krogon [a combination of Kronos and Zeus] is in the soul of Pramanath like a demon, who regards his own arrangement as the only one suited to this impossible situation. If Pramanath could abjure his mortal Moa nature, he would no longer be the victim of Krogon. But he remains loyal to his mortal human self. And if he foreswore his immortal nature, he would become one of Krogon's enslaved prisoners. To solve this demon of disunity within himself, Pramanath descends into the warfare within himself, repeatedly.[34]

What is new about this treatment of the dilemma is Hughes's claim that pain, symbolized by the vulture, can, if accepted, become illumination.

---

[32] *ST* 69–74.
[33] Smith (1972: 132–3).　　　　[34] Smith (1972: 94–5).

Throughout his stay in Persia Hughes carried in his breast pocket a notebook in which he jotted down many short poems, twenty-one of which he subsequently collected as *Prometheus on His Crag* (1973).[35] This is a much simpler and more subjective version of the story of Prometheus from his crucifixion by Zeus to his eventual release. Though Hughes described *Prometheus on His Crag* as 'a numb poem about numbness', it does end with Prometheus's agony bringing him to the realization in the final poem that the dreaded vulture which every day pecks out his liver, is in fact the Helper and midwife to his rebirth.[36] As with all his uses of mythology, folklore, and classical literature, Hughes is clearly using this ancient and universal material as a means of dealing with his most urgent and personal problems. *Prometheus on His Crag* is the story of how Hughes sought to survive the hammer blows of 1963 and 1969. This was even more obviously true of the beautiful radio play *Orpheus,* broadcast in 1971, to which I shall return, of *Gaudete* (1977), which he began to rewrite at this time, and of *Cave Birds* (1978, begun in 1974), for which he claimed, 'my starting point was the death of Socrates and his murder of the Mediterranean Goddess'.[37]

Though he did not change his views on the possibility of pain becoming bliss, an idea he developed at length in his essay on Baskin, 'The Hanged Man and the Dragonfly',[38] Hughes fortunately found a less painful way of reintegrating himself with the given world. In 1970 he had married a farmer's daughter, Carol Orchard, and in 1972 he bought Moortown Farm, and ran it with Carol and her father until Jack Orchard's death in 1976. Farming literally brought Hughes down to earth after his rather too Blake-like excursions into prophetic books. It proved, for all the frustrations and losses, extremely therapeutic. My most comprehensive essay on Hughes is called 'From World of Blood to World of Light'.[39] A more accurate title, had it not been too long, would have been 'From World of Blood through World of Mud to World of Light'. The world of mud was the world of farming, of life at its most grounded in the land, animal life, and the seasons. Without that experience I believe it unlikely that Hughes

[35] See Zajko in this volume.  [36] Letter to Keith Sagar, November 1973.
[37] Skea (2000: xxiv–xxv).  [38] Reprinted in *WP* 84–102.
[39] Sagar (2000: 104–69).

would have come through to write his finest poems in the years 1976–82, *Moortown Diaries, Remains of Elmet,* and *River.* These collections are relevant to the theme of this volume precisely because of the conspicuous absence of overt references to the classics or any other mythological or literary sources. They are poems of raw, unmediated experience, of being born again into a radiant world which has no need of such defensive distancing.

*

Through the 1980s Hughes began to spend less and less time writing poetry. He wasted a year 'in the coils of the Plath Journals', edited anthologies with Seamus Heaney, gave many readings, judged poetry competitions, helped the Arvon Foundation.[40] His appointment as Poet Laureate in 1984 much increased the demands on his time.[41] Most of what he did write in the next ten years was in prose, including major essays on Leonard Baskin, Eliot, and Coleridge.[42]

In 1971 Hughes had written an amazing introduction to his *Choice of Shakespeare's Verse.*[43] The crucial part was his interpretation of Shakespeare's *Venus and Adonis,* where he argues persuasively that the boar which kills Adonis is in fact Venus, transformed by Adonis's rejection of her into the bloody opposite of her true self—the Goddess of Complete Being. He went on to argue that virtually all Shakespeare's subsequent plays are variations on this 'tragic equation'. He equates Shakespeare's sense of the tragic condition with that of the Greeks:

Very much as in Ancient Greece, it was the moment for tragedy: the agonies of an ancient Dionysus in a world of hardening sceptical intellect and morality.[44]

In 1989 Hughes decided to expand his 1971 piece into a book: *Shakespeare and the Goddess of Complete Being.* He did not realize that it would take up most of his time for the next three years.

---

[40] Feinstein (2001: 211–12).

[41] Middlebrook (2003: 265–8); Roberts (2006: 152–66); Rees in this volume.

[42] 'The hanged man and the dragonfly', 'The Poetic Self: A centenary tribute to T. S. Eliot' and 'The snake in the oak', all reprinted in *WP.*

[43] Reprinted as 'The Great Theme: Notes on Shakespeare' in *WP* 103–21.

[44] *WP* 111.

This decade of prose culminated in his collaboration with William Scammell in collecting and editing his selected prose in *Winter Pollen* (1994). Hughes came to regret writing so much prose. When, in 1997, he began to be treated for cancer, he felt that his dereliction of poetry had been a betrayal of his creative energies which had turned against him and were now killing *him*. His last years were devoted to verse again, completing *Birthday Letters,* which dealt with his relationship with Sylvia Plath on the personal level, not transposed into myth (though there are, of course, some classical references, such as those to the Minotaur), and a number of translations from the classics, from which he derived great satisfaction.

In 1993 Hughes received an invitation from Michael Hoffman and James Lasdun to contribute to *After Ovid,* their collection of 'treatments' of the *Metamorphoses* by living poets. He submitted four stories. Not surprisingly, these included 'Bacchus and Pentheus' and 'Venus and Adonis'. But the passage he clearly relished most was the first, 'Creation/ Four Ages/Flood', to which he gave a highly contemporary resonance. Man has made such a mess of creation that God decides to delete him, with hurricane and tsunami:

> Now flood heaps out over flood.
> Orchards, crops, herds, farms, are scooped up
> And sucked down
> Into the overland maelstrom.
> Temples and their statues liquify
> Kneeling into the swirls.
> Whatever roof or spire or turret
> Resists the rip of currents
> Goes under the climbing levels.
> Till earth and sea seem one—a single sea
> Without a shore.
> A few crowds are squeezed on diminishing islets
> Of hill-tops.
> Men are rowing in circles aimlessly, crazed,
> Where they ploughed straight furrows or steered wagons.
> One pitches a sail over corn.
> Another steers his keel
> Over his own chimney.
>     . . .

Starvation picks off the survivors.
Drowned mankind, imploring limbs outspread,
Floats like a plague of dead frogs.[45]

Hughes so much enjoyed doing these translations ('like a holiday in a rest home') that he later added twenty-one more stories for *Tales from Ovid* (1997).[46]

*

Euripides' *Alcestis* was Hughes's only uncommissioned translation. Why should he have chosen this apparently undistinguished play? Why not rather the *Bacchae,* the play which had meant more to him than any other and come closest to his lifelong concerns?

Tony Harrison, attempting to explain why, in the Great Dionysia, every contestant had to follow his three tragedies with a satyr play writes:

This journey back into the service of the presiding god [Dionysos] seems to be paralleled by the release of the spirit back into the life of the senses at the end of the tragic journey.... The sensual relish for life and its affirmation must have been the spirit of the conclusion of the four plays. The satyrs are included in the wholeness of the tragic vision.[47]

It is this wholeness we find in Shakespeare's last plays, which subsume tragedy in a larger affirmation of miraculously recovered life. And there are Greek plays which attempt to reconcile the tragic vision with the capacity of life to continue. Harrison draws attention specifically to what he calls

the category-disturbing *Alcestis,* often termed proto-satyric because Euripides offered it in place of the satyr play as the fourth play of his competition entry. In this play Euripides introduced his 'satyr', in the shape of Heracles, into the very body of the tragedy: the celebrant admitted before the tragic section had come to an end. The playwright thus showed both elements intertwined: *at the same time* the reveler is hasting to his wine and Admetus is burying his wife.[48]

*Alcestis* strongly resembles *Helen,* a much later play of Euripides. Just as Shakespeare often handled very similar themes in tragedy, comedy,

---

[45] *CP* 879–80.
[46] See Jacobsen, Tatham, and Ingleheart in this volume.
[47] Harrison (1990: xi).  [48] Harrison (1990: xii).

and romance, so Euripides liked to work, until his last years, in an 'upbeat' mode. *Alcestis* and *Helen* are not only very like each other, they are also very like such Shakespearean romances as *Pericles* and *A Winter's Tale*. In *Helen*, Menelaus, miraculously preserved from death at sea, is equally miraculously restored to his lost, loving and long-suffering wife. In all four plays the lost wife appears to return from the dead. Only in the *Alcestis* does she actually do so.

*Alcestis*, however, is not one of the best-known or most admired and produced of Greek plays. This seems to me to be for the simple reason that it is not among the best. The plot and characters offer opportunities for broad comedy, for near tragedy, and for psychological probing of exactly the kind which was to be Euripides' forte. Yet he made little of it. The whole thing seems curiously bland. *Alcestis* may not be a play of the same order as the *Bacchae*, but Hughes cannot have failed to recognize in it disturbing echoes of his own story he was simultaneously telling in *Birthday Letters*. In the Vellacott translation, Admetus says of the death of his wife: 'I can never again take heart to touch my lyre'.[49] After the death of Sylvia Plath, Hughes entered a two-year silence. Later Admetus cries: 'What sharper stroke can shatter a man's heart | Than loss of his true wife?'.[50] The fact that *Alcestis* is a minor play allowed Hughes if not to appropriate it for his own purposes, at least to see himself as creative collaborator, filling out from bitter experience what Euripides only gestures towards.[51] Hughes's version is half as long again as the original.

Hughes's chorus says of Admetus in lines which might be from *Birthday Letters*:

> He does not know what loss is.
> When everything is too late
> Then he will know it.
> When he has to live in what has happened.[52]

Before lapsing into his two-year silence, Hughes had written two poems, 'The Howling of Wolves' and 'Song of a Rat'.[53] In *Alcestis* Hughes recapitulates the horror of 'Song of a Rat':

---

[49] Euripides, trans. Vellacott (1953: 132).
[50] Euripides, trans. Vellacott (1953: 149).
[51] See Brown in this volume.        [52] A 10–11.        [53] CP 180–1; 169–70.

The Admetos that brought Alcestis to the grave
Is like the body of a rat
Trapped with bones and sinews in the trap.
He is trying to chew it off—the whole body.
Admetos is trying to gnaw himself
Free from Admetos.[54]

Some of the most horrific poems in *Birthday Letters*, 'Suttee', for example, are recapitulated in *Alcestis*:

No refuge anywhere in me
From this fire, this huge dark single flame,
That caresses my whole body.[55]

In the Sixties, Hughes's vision had been of a word made of blood, entirely given over to death. At the beginning of *Alcestis* Death claims that life is 'paltry and precarious', 'the briefest concession', 'an aberration from the status quo—which is me'.[56] *Alcestis* is the summation of Hughes's lifelong wrestling with Death to prove him wrong.

Hughes's works are replete with suffering, often dealt with in ways which remind us of Greek tragedy. Like the Greeks he wanted to look at suffering and loss open-eyed, extenuating nothing. The danger was that he would become a nihilist or absurdist; that he would leave his readers feeling suicidal. He struggled to make his endings what he called 'upbeat'; but it was a struggle because he would admit no positives or affirmations or hopes which had not been fully paid for by a full look at the worst. What *Alcestis* offered Hughes was a more hopeful treatment than the unsparing *Birthday Letters* of the theme of the attempt to recover in some sense a dead wife. In a message read for him at the award ceremony of the Forward Poetry Prize, Hughes said that in writing *Birthday Letters* over about twenty-five years he had 'tried to open a direct, private, inner contact with my first wife, not thinking to make a poem, thinking mainly to evoke her presence to myself and feel her there listening'.[57] This clearly brings Hughes close to Orpheus striving to recover his dead wife. And indeed the Orpheus story was the first that occurred to Hughes after Sylvia Plath's death. He rejected it as 'too obvious an attempt to exploit

---

[54] *A* 47.    [55] *A* 66; *CP* 1138–40.    [56] *A* 5–6.
[57] *The Guardian*, 8 October 1998.

my situation'.[58] He did, however, write a version as a radio play for
children broadcast in 1971. Here Orpheus' music is the music of
happiness only, happiness deriving from Euridice.[59] It makes even
the trees and stones dance. But a voice in his ear, like the voice of a
spider, tells him that 'everything must be paid for'. When Eurydice
dies—'Her voice has been carried away to the land of the dead'—
'Orpheus' hand suddenly becomes numb'. (Hughes wrote no adult
poems for three years.) At last Orpheus decides to go to the underworld to attempt to recover his wife. He uses his guitar like a shaman
to make a road of sound to the bottom of the underworld, one note
insanely repeated, gathering volume and impetus, and lands at the
feet of Pluto, king of the kingdom of the dead. His wife, Pluto tells
him, was the payment for his music. Orpheus plays a new music, a
music not of beauty and happiness and life only, but of pain and all
the cycles of death and renewal. This music causes Persephone herself
to flower, the first time Pluto has seen her open since he snatched her
from the upper world. Orpheus demands his own wife in exchange.
Pluto cannot give him his wife: 'Your wife's body is crumbling to
dust', but gives him her soul: 'Return to the world. Your wife's soul
will be with you'. He returns, like so many of his heroes, 'a step, a step,
and a step'. He cannot see or touch his wife, but he can hear her.
She asks him to play for her:

The music was not the music of dancing
But of growing and withering,
Of the root in the earth and the leaf in the light,
The music of birth and of death.
And the stones did not dance. But the stones listened.
The music was not the music of happiness
But of everlasting, and the wearing away of the hills,
The music of the stillness of stones,
Of stones under frost, and stones under rain, and stones in the sun,
The music of the seabed drinking at the stones of the hills.
The music of the floating weight of the earth.
And the bears in their forest holes
Heard the music of bears in their forest holes.
The music of bones in the starlight,

---

[58] Letter to Keith Sagar, 18 July 1998.
[59] *CPC* 93–105.

The music of many a valley trodden by bears,
The music of bears listening on the earth for bears.
And the deer on the high hills heard the crying of wolves.
And the salmon in the deep pools heard the whisper of the snows,
And the traveller on the road
Heard the music of love coming and love going
And love lost forever,
The music of birth and of death.
The music of the earth, swaddled in heaven, kissed by its cloud and watched
by its ray.
And the ears that heard it were also of leaf and of stone.
The faces that listened were flesh of cliff and of river.
The hands that played it were fingers of snakes and a tangle of flowers.[60]

Hughes avoided the story for decades in his work for adults, but in
*Alcestis*, feeling perhaps that in the long agony recorded in *Birthday
Letters* he had finally paid for the right to lay claim to the story,
he expanded a passing reference to Orpheus, a single sentence in
Euripides, to a twenty-seven line recapitulation of the whole story (as
he had earlier inserted the story of Prometheus' release from the
torment of the vulture).

Admetus has lost his wife Alcestis, and is consumed with guilt. He had
mismanaged the situation. He had somehow let his wife's life slip
through his fingers. Like Orpheus he had taken his happiness for granted:

> So much confidence. So many blessings.
> So much time!
> So many decades ahead of us.[61]

He finds himself

> Thinking about Orpheus—in the thick of all this.
> Thinking of the impossible.
>
> How he went down there,
> Into the underworld, the dead land,
> With his guitar and his voice—
> He rode the dark road
> A horse of music.
>
> He wrapped himself in his voice,
> Death-proof, a voice of asbestos,

---

[60] *CPC* 105.    [61] *A* 68.

> He went
> Down and down and down.
>
> You remember—
>
>> He went for his dead wife
>> And he nearly got her.[62]

But for Admetus the impossible happens. 'What was beyond belief' is accomplished: Alcestis is returned to him. Heracles says 'She is yours. | All you thought you had lost—she is here'. Admetus' happiness is greater than ever, because now fully paid for:

> We have taken the full measure of grief
> And now we have found happiness even greater.
> We have found it and recognized it.[63]

Out of the sufferings of Prometheus and Orpheus, out of the decades of pain, Hughes finally distills this positive vision. The last words of *Alcestis* are: 'Let this give man hope'. The hope referred to is not, of course, the hope that if you lose a much-loved wife in her prime, some friendly superman might turn up, wrestle with death, and bring her back as good as new. It is rather the hope expressed in 'Red', the last poem in *Birthday Letters,* where the red of pain and loss is balanced by the blue of what can nevertheless be recovered (recovered in his case only by the full payment of half a lifetime and hundreds of poems)—the memories of joys, births, and indestructible love, a healing gift.

*

In June 1994 Hughes received a letter from John Durnin, Artistic Director of the Northcott Theatre in Exeter, inviting him to adapt Aeschylus' tragic trilogy the *Oresteia* for the theatre:

I am fairly certain in my own mind that these components—Aeschylus' story, your dramatized interpretation, a chorus of community performers, the Northcott's particular skill in realizing stories of epic proportions in an accessible form—would fuse together to create an outstanding theatrical experience.[64]

Hughes responded positively, and decided to postpone completion of *Alcestis* (only the Heracles interlude remained to be written) in

---

[62]  A 22–3.      [63]  A 83.
[64]  Published by kind permission of John Durnin.

favour of this project. I sent him a couple of translations he did not have, H. D. F. Kitto's *Greek Tragedy* (which, he said, 'strengthens my faith in Aeschylus's canniness') and my own essay on the *Oresteia* ('Pointed up certain things in just the right way').[65] In March 1995 he wrote to me:

Main problem in these plays is to give the active details of imagery etc. real dramatic life—projected, active leverage on the listener. To give each image the role of a sort of actor. If you can't do that, then the passages seem simply too long.

To Leonard Baskin he wrote in December: 'I tried to release the howl in every line'.[66]

Hughes interrupted his work on the *Oresteia* to do his version of Wedekind's *Spring Awakening*, ('powerful and relevant to modern youth'), which had been commissioned by the Royal Shakespeare Company, but returned to it in May.[67] In July 1995 financial constraints forced the Northcott to postpone the project until the following year. Hughes wrote that he had not really expected the theatre to be able to go through with it, but had gone ahead for his own purposes. He sent them his version of the trilogy's first play, the *Agamemnon*, in August and the other two parts in October. But by that time funding cuts had made it impossible for the Northcott to raise an adequate fee. For several months they pursued the possibility of sponsorship or a grant from the Arts Council or British Council, while Hughes looked into the possibility of a joint venture with the National Theatre or Shared Experience. Eventually he abandoned hope of involving the Northcott, and after fruitless negotiations with the Almeida and the Royal Court, signed a contract with the National Theatre in April 1997. Katie Mitchell's production opened in 1999, a year after Hughes's death.

Shortly before his death Hughes described the *Oresteia* as 'the best thing I have ever done. I read it and wonder how I ever did it'.[68] Here is the wonderful speech of Clytemnestra, when, after her murder of Agamemnon, the elders speak of banishing her:

---

[65] Later published in Sagar (2005: 15–27).    [66] *ST* 125.

[67] Sagar (2000: xxxii).    [68] Skea (2000: xxxi).

How ready you are, of a sudden,
To bleat about banishment.
The righteous curse of the public!
The sacred verdict of the mob.
Where were they, and where were you
When this monster here
Butchered his own daughter on the block?
He found it easier
Than sacrificing one of his precious cattle
To butcher my daughter—
Like somebody else's goat.
All to persuade the wind to shift a few points
And make some sailors happy,
He ripped my daughter's throat and shook the blood out of her.
To gratify his whimpering love-sick brother
And catch a runaway whore.[69]

Hughes's final encounter with the classics came when Jonathan Kent, then Joint Artistic Director of the Almeida Theatre, invited him, in August 1997, (Hughes having earlier declined his invitation to translate Euripides's *Medea*), to provide a version of Racine's *Phèdre* for Diana Rigg. Three months later Kent received the script:

I think it is absolutely remarkable. The hammer-blows of the short sentences echo with the compacted pain and rage of the original, like no other translation I know. What seems to me particularly remarkable is that you've retained your own voice while being true to the spirit of Racine. We're honoured and excited that the Almeida will do it.[70]

The Almeida production opened at the Malvern Festival on 6 August 1998. I did not know Racine's *Phèdre* before seeing this production. Though Hughes's translation was gripping and Diana Rigg's performance overwhelming, I was appalled by what Racine had done with his source material in Euripides' *Hippolytus*. His parents having died when he was young, Racine was brought up by his grandparents, who were Jansenists, a highly moralistic and puritanical Catholic sect. As a young man, despite the strong opposition of his family, he was seduced by the theatre, where he made his fame and fortune

---

[69] *O* 70–1.
[70] Published by kind permission of Jonathan Kent.

over the next dozen years. He also had a reputation as something of a rake. He wrote his last play, *Phèdre*, at the age of thirty-eight, and in his highly moralistic account of the myth there are signs of his subsequent sudden decision to renounce the theatre altogether and reconcile himself with Jansenism and his family. In Euripides' version, the fault is entirely in Hippolytus, Phaedra's stepson. He had abused Aphrodite, and sworn an oath of chastity to her rival Artemis. Like Adonis, he spurns love in favour of hunting and horsemanship. Everything in the play is engineered by Aphrodite in order to exact terrible punishment on Hippolytus. Both Phaedra and her husband Theseus are helpless puppets in her revenge. The inevitability of tragedy is symbolized from the start by the presence at each side of the stage of statues of the rival goddesses, Aphrodite and Artemis. Euripides has no interest in passing moral judgements: Racine reduces everything to moralizing.

Seneca was the first to shift the centre of gravity of the play away from Hippolytus, who becomes a fairly inert agent in Phaedra's tragedy. This was possibly because *hubris*, the prevailing tragic flaw in Greek drama, had become the prime virtue for the Romans. Racine acknowledged his debt to Euripides, but his version is much closer to Seneca, and shows little understanding of what Euripides was about. There is no sense of the determining power of the two goddesses, and no sense that Hippolytus' coldness is anything more than adolescent priggishness. Hippolytus' indifference to women is explained by the fact that he just had not met the right woman yet, and Racine provides just such a woman for him in the form of a beautiful imprisoned princess, Aricia, who does not exist in any earlier tellings of the story. Racine's Hippolytus has no tragic flaw, and his gruesome death is gratuitous. Phèdre is presented as degraded by sexual passion, and trivialized by making mere jealousy of a younger, prettier rival the motivation for her false accusation of rape against Hippolytus.

Apparently Hughes felt that Racine had unconsciously identified himself with Hippolytus and Phèdre with the temptation to a life of passion, especially sexual indulgence, which the theatre had come to seem to him. When I wrote to him about my dissatisfaction with the play, Hughes replied:

You were watching the wrong play. Racine's play is 5 universes away from the Euripides. I read it as a (subconscious) analysis and total dramatisation of his (Racine's) rejection of the theatre (Phèdre) and his reversion to the Jansenist brainwashing of his youth (against which the whole theatre adventure had been a defiant resistance and escape). Hence Aricia etc.[71]

Hughes's own 'theatre adventure' had brought his imagination into direct contact with the roots of Western consciousness and the fundamentals of human experience.

[71] Letter to Keith Sagar, 14 August 1998.

# 2

## Hughes's first translation: '*The Storm* from Homer, *Odyssey,* Book V'

*Stuart Gillespie*

Hughes is one of several poets of his generation to take a pronounced interest in translating, or if one prefers adapting, imitating, the Latin and Greek classics of dramatic and non-dramatic verse. Before his time this had not happened on any scale in English poetry for many years—in fact for most of the twentieth century. But as we head towards the second decade of the twenty-first century, verse translation in English, from post-classical as well as classical sources, could be said to have become a phenomenon which begins to resemble the English Renaissance translating tradition in its extent and scope. Not only does it connect senior figures such as Tony Harrison, Seamus Heaney, and Edwin Morgan; from a younger generation may be mentioned writers like Robert Crawford, Jamie McKendrick, Derek Mahon, Tom Paulin, and Peter Robinson. I am thinking here not of specialist translators, but of writers whose *original* verse is widely considered their principal work—though in the case of some of these figures, including Hughes, translation seems increasingly to have *become* the main thing as their careers went on.

The modest purpose of the present essay is to call attention to one extremely little-known product of this enduring interest of Hughes's, his translation of a 100-line excerpt from the *Odyssey*. This text, as far as is known, is Hughes's earliest translation of any kind, and it is certainly his only translation of Homer. It is a work that remains remarkably little noticed, owing entirely to its publication

history—or lack of one. The *Collected Poems* of 2003 made it readily
available, but following its reading on BBC radio's Third Programme
in 1960 there was no print publication either in Hughes's ensuing
collections (even though *Wodwo*, his next volume for adults, contains
other work for radio) nor at any other time during the following
forty-two years.

Because *The Storm* has so little 'prehistory' in what has been said
and written about Hughes and his work of this period, it will be
worth first outlining its immediate context.[1] Its ultimate origins are
obscurely connected with those of Christopher Logue's Homeric
imitations (fresh instalments of which continue to appear many
decades later, into the twenty-first century). In the late 1950s verse
by the young Logue (1926– ) was being broadcast on the Third
Programme, but he had no training in Greek. Donald Carne-Ross
and his partner Xanthe Wakefield, both classical scholars (and the
latter the daughter of a powerful Tory Member of Parliament) caused
Logue to acquire a commission which proved to be the beginning of
*War Music*.[2] Logue recalls events thus in his recent biographical
memoir *Prince Charming*:

Donald gave me lunch at Broadcasting House and, at Xanthe's bidding,
proposed I translated a sequence from Book XXI of the *Iliad*. To the question
of my knowing no Greek Donald answered: 'Read translations by those who
did. Follow the story. A translator must know one language well. Preferably
his own.'

. . .

When 'Achilles and the River' was transmitted in June 1959 it interested a
number of literary grandees. The broadcast was repeated; parts of it were
televised; then it was published by *Encounter*, a serious non-specialist maga-
zine. Finally, promoted by the grandees, I was given a grant by an American
foundation to do more of the same.[3]

It seems to have been the interest Logue's work attracted, together, no
doubt, with other factors, that led to a series of translations of Homer

---

[1] The principal source here is Daniel Weissbort's commentary on the translation
in *ST*, based on notes emanating originally from Anthony Thwaite. I am grateful
to Alistair Elliot for supplementary information drawn from his recollections of
participating in the series to which *The Storm* belongs (see below).

[2] Logue (1981).

[3] Logue (1999: 221, 224).

being specially commissioned by the BBC from contemporary poets immediately after this point: twelve verse renderings of twelve different episodes in the *Odyssey*. The editors responsible were Louis MacNeice and Anthony Thwaite, for the BBC Features Department. It was MacNeice who singled out the twelve episodes he felt would be most suitable. The translators, some with Greek and others, like Logue, without, included Alistair Elliot, Peter Green, and Rex Warner. Like the other contributions to the series, Hughes's work was read for the broadcast (10 November 1960) by Patrick Garland.[4]

The episodes seem to have been allotted in something like the way the chunks of the *Metamorphoses* were apportioned in that later Hughes-related collection of classical translations by several hands, *After Ovid*—as the editors of the more recent collection have described it.[5] In that case, the editors chose the writers and proposed the selection to them; the writers said yes or no. But things would seem to have been rather less flexible in the BBC venture. Alistair Elliot reports having had no choice about which episode to take on, whereas in *After Ovid* there was negotiation, and some of the contributors eventually supplied more passages than they were originally asked to translate.[6] With the BBC project there were doubtless certain other guidelines, but specific forms were not suggested—Alistair Elliot remembers agonizing about the range of verse options (metre, rhyme). There was never any plan for print publication; in fact Elliot possesses no copy of his own contribution. And contrary to what Anthony Thwaite seems to have suggested to Daniel Weissbort, there was no attempt to cover the whole of the *Odyssey*, to translate all parts, which indeed could hardly have been a realistic objective within twelve segments of anything like the size of Hughes's 100-line rendering.[7]

So much for the context of the BBC commission; what of the context in Hughes's own work? Just one obviously Homer-inspired

---

[4] The date is supplied by Paul Keegan, *CP* 1245. Weissbort provides the same date (*ST* 14), although the translation is wrongly assigned to 1961 in the contents list (v).

[5] Hofmann and Lasdun (1994: xii–xiii).

[6] Elliot's recollections on this and other points were in the form of personal communications to the present writer.

[7] *ST* 14.

poem, 'Everyman's Odyssey', had preceded it. Though not published until *Lupercal* (March 1960), this was written in 1957.[8] 'Everyman's Odyssey' relates to the story of Odysseus's son Telemachus, and his punishment of Penelope's suitors. It is about Telemachus's coming of age, metaphorically part of the 'odyssey' all men undergo.[9] Like *The Storm* it discerns in the experience of Homer's heroes the experience of mankind, but here the resemblance largely ends.

Pertinent also are Hughes's early ideas on the craft of translation. He wrote on this subject more than once in the 1960s, in editorials contributed to the (at that time) irregular journal *Modern Poetry in Translation*.[10] Perhaps his own experience of working on Homer itself helped him arrive at these views; in any case a fairly good fit can be claimed between his desiderata and the mode of the *Odyssey* translation. Hughes wrote in the first issue of *MPT* as an editor inviting contributions:

The type of translation we are seeking can be described as literal, though not literal in a strict or pedantic sense. Though this may seem at first suspect, it is more apposite to define our criteria negatively, as literalness can only be a deliberate tendency, not a dogma. We feel that as soon as devices extraneous to the original are employed for the purpose of recreating its 'spirit', the value of the whole enterprise is called in question.[11]

By the third issue of the journal Hughes was developing the view that literalism will in itself lead to new possibilities of thought and expression:

The first ideal is literalness . . . The very oddity and struggling dumbness of word for word version is what makes our own imagination jump. A man who has something really serious to say in a language of which he knows only a few words, manages to say it far more convincingly and effectively than any interpreter, and in translated poetry it is the first-hand contact—however fumbled and broken—with that man and his seriousness which we want. The minute we gloss his words, we have more or less what he said but

---

[8]  *CP* 1243.

[9]  See Silk in this volume.

[10]  The two editorials quoted here were printed in Nos 1 and 3 of *Modern Poetry in Translation* in the years 1965 and 1967 respectively. Though jointly written by Hughes and Weissbort, who were the co-editors of the journal, these unsigned pieces express the 'views and intentions' of Hughes (according to Weissbort's notes in *ST* 200).

[11]  Quoted from *ST* 200.

we have lost him. We are ringing changes—amusing though they may be—on our familiar abstractions, and are no longer reading through to what we have not experienced before, which is alive and real.[12]

These are some of the wider contexts for *The Storm* in Hughes's work of the 1960s. Once we explore the texture of the translation closely, we shall see how some more strongly characteristic preoccupations of Hughes as poet may be discerned in it.

The passage—111 lines in Homer (*Od.* 5.382–493), 94 lines in Hughes—comes from the point in Odysseus' story after which the hero has fallen foul of Poseidon's earthquake, which has demolished his boat. Athene, his divine patroness, checks the storm, but Zeus having already ordained the period it will take for Odysseus to reach the Phaeacians, the shipwrecked hero floats and flounders in the still heavy seas for two days and nights. Even when he spots a coastline he can see nowhere to get ashore safely, but with the help of Athene, the exhausted Odysseus eventually makes land. At the end of the episode, when darkness falls, he escapes the cold and his fatigue by finding a grove to sleep in. Here he creeps under a thicket of olive bushes and rakes together a pile of leaves, within which he nestles safely for the night.

In Homer this is a highly charged episode containing several distinct segments, each with something of its own mood. The moment of Odysseus' eventual emergence from the sea drew a memorable reaction from Keats when Charles Cowden Clarke introduced it to the poet in Chapman's translation (I quote from the latter's account):

One scene I could not fail to introduce to him—the shipwreck of Ulysses, in the fifth book of the *Odysseis*, and I had the reward of one of his delighted stares, upon reading the following lines:

> Then forth he came, his both knees falt'ring, both
> His strong hands hanging down, and all with froth
> His cheeks and nostrils flowing, voice and breath
> Spent to all use, and down he sank to death.
> The sea had soak'd his heart through . . . [13]

---

[12] Quoted from *ST* 201.
[13] Quoted from Colvin (1917: ch. 2). See further Bate (1963: 253).

The immediately following point in the tale, the image of Odysseus lying exhausted under the leaves which closes Book 5, involving a simile in which the safe preservation of the hero is compared to the careful guarding of a spark of fire by a man far from other men, has provoked a number of more recent writers to imitation or emulation. Perhaps most notably in recent years, Michael Longley, a poet who 'has remained Homer-haunted throughout his career', is responsible for a translation of this short excerpt (*Od.* 5.474–93) which is outstanding in its finely modulated simplicity:[14]

> A BED OF LEAVES
> He climbed to the copse, a conspicuous place near water,
> And crawled under two bushes sprouting from one stem (olive
> And wild olive), a thatch so close neither gale-force winds
> Nor sunlight nor cloudbursts could penetrate: it was here
> Odysseus snuggled and heaped on his mattress of leaves
> An eiderdown of leaves, enough to make a double-bed
> In winter, whatever the weather, and smiled to himself
> When he saw his bed and stretched out in the middle of it
> And let even more of the fallen leaves fall over him:
> As when a lonely man on a lonely farm smoors the fire
> And hides a turf-sod in the ashes to save an ember,
> So was his body in the bed of leaves its own kindling
> And sleep settled on him like ashes and closed his eyelids.[15]

As well as the copse, conspicuous here is Longley's obsolete or dialect word 'smoors' ('smothers', line 10), which corresponds to an ordinary enough Homeric verb but is not inappropriate within a passage which as a whole contains several words unique either to Homer or to Greek literature.[16] This moment of Odysseus' relaxing exhausted into the pile of leaves features also in several poems by Peter Reading. One illustration, from the start of Reading's collection *Final Demands* (1988), must suffice. Here Odysseus is crossed with a man 'clearing the family's papers for next crowd's vacant possession':

---

[14] Caitriona O'Reilly, reviewing Longley's *Collected Poems*, *TLS*, 16 March 2007, 11. On Longley's Homeric leanings, see further Hardwick (2006).

[15] Longley (1995: 33). Longley has also used Homer's lines 5.432–4, in the middle of Hughes's *Odyssey* passage, for an image of poetic tradition in the five-line poem 'Homer's Octopus' in the same collection (45).

[16] For examples, see Dawe (1993: 242).

Crapulous death-fright at 3 in the morning, grim fantasising...
Morphean, painless, idyllic expiry, easeful, Sabaean...
duvet and pillow-case metamorphose to sweet-smelling sered leaves,
thick-fallen under two olive boles grafted, canopied tightly,
such as the storm-wrecked Laertides, life-wracked, sunk in exhausted
snug at the end of Book V [ ... ]

dreamingly crawls and his hands have now raked a litter together,
spacious and deep, for the leafage is lying in plentiful downfall,
lays him to rest in the midst of the leaves and piles them around him,
just as a man might cover a brand with char-blacked ashes,
guarding the seed of the fire for his tribe to use in the future,
so does he deeply immerse in the fall of past generations,
litter of leaves, not from olives, but the sepia, brittle
leaves of the letters of lost correspondents, infinite, death-frail
(Croxley, papyrus and bond), sinks in the lines of the dead.[17]

There is no space to dwell on all these reactions to the *Odyssey* passage, but they clearly indicate that while the selection of lines for Hughes's translation exercise may have been externally imposed, it took him to a Homeric episode found highly suggestive and rewarding by other poets of his own time as well as other times.

Another twentieth-century translator remains to be mentioned. In assessing Hughes's work it may prove less productive to compare it with the Greek text than with the exactly contemporary translation of the *Odyssey* by Robert Fitzgerald, first published in 1961. (Hughes, like Logue, had no Greek, and presumably proceeded as Carne-Ross advised Logue, by 'reading translations by those who did'.) Fitzgerald's production, we should remind ourselves, was one of the most highly acclaimed translations of its era. It won the 1961 Bollingen Award for the best translation of a poem into English, was hailed in the *New Statesman* as 'the best poetic version of the *Odyssey* this century', and soon found its way onto innumerable 'great books' reading lists. It was the translation chosen as the basis of a full-scale commentary on the *Odyssey* and it is still in print today.[18]

Perhaps against the run of expectations, Hughes is in general restrained and respectful towards the Homeric material, refraining

---

[17] Untitled; quoted from Reading (1996: II, 119).

[18] Hexter (1993). The text is quoted below from *Homer: The Odyssey*, translated by Robert Fitzgerald (1961). For further critical reaction to Fitzgerald's Homeric translations see Carne-Ross (1974).

from stylistically heightening it. In this stretch, the point at which Odysseus finds himself unable to make land, Hughes's technique stops well short of 'defamiliarization', but leads to something of the quality of 'struggling dumbness' that he felt apposite to a good translation:

> Then the heart of Odysseus shrank and he groaned:
> 'Against hope, Zeus gives this glance of the land,
> And I have managed my body over the gulf
> Only to find no way from the water. Offshore, horns of rock,
> Surf bellowing and mauling around them,
> Behind them, empty cliff going up
> And the sea crowding in deeply. Nowhere foothold
> To step from disaster, but, in attempting,
> A surge would uproot me and shatter me on rock-edges,
> Sluicing my whole trouble to nothing. And if I swim on further,
> Seeking the sands of a bay where the sea goes in more peaceably
> Some squall will whirl down and drag me,
> For all my protesting, out into depths and the maws of ravenous fish,
> Or a god fetch something monstrous up from the pit to attack me—
> One of the horde that feed at the hand of Amphitrite;
> And I know too well how the Earth-shaker detests me.'
>
> (21–36)

There is a certain lack of smoothness and fluency, leaving the texture somewhere between the rough-hewn and sinewy, and the merely halting or awkward. It is, I would argue, much closer to the former than the latter end of that scale; but 'to maul' cannot be an intransitive verb (even supposing it is something surf is capable of doing), and the grammar of, for instance, the middle sentence ('Nowhere foothold . . . to nothing') would not pass muster as strictly correct English, though it could not be said to be particularly Greek either. Fitzgerald at least looks more natural here:

> No matter how I try it, the surf may throw me
> against the cliffside; no good fighting there.
>
> (415–16)

Overall, Fitzgerald's less coloured rendering, here as elsewhere, might be supposed on that account more faithful: is it Hughesian rather than Homeric violence and overstatement that leads to the 'ravenous fish' and the frighteningly overabundant progeny of nature (the 'horde that feed') in the last lines? In fact these elements are present in Homer—'some scholars', Dawe reports, 'have rightly complained that things are overdone here'.[19] The Loeb crib offers 'lest some god may even send forth upon me some great monster from out the sea— and many such does glorious Amphitrite breed'.[20] It is Fitzgerald who fights shy of presenting these features, offering only 'Or then again, some shark of Amphitritē's | may hunt me, sent by the genius of the deep'. True, Fitzgerald is committed to rendering the Greek in the same number of English lines, and economy is a basic principle; but there are more problems here than one. 'Genius' is surely a poor choice for δαίμων, and 'shark' for the non-specific κῆτος.[21]

This is a passage of interior monologue (there are four in this episode). Narrative passages require different handling, and Hughes achieves a tumultuous effect over long stretches here, partly by adopting a simple iterative mode throughout—'he felt', 'he groaned', 'it happened'. He can go further, too, into strongly paratactic writing:

> But within hail of the land, heard sea rending on rock,
> Eruption of the surge, whitening over the land-face,
> Bundling everything in spray. No harbour fit for a ship and no inlet,
> But thrust prows of crags and spines of reefs under hanging walls.
>
> (17–20)

In these ways Hughes manages something of much greater directness than Fitzgerald's more conventionally presented narrative, in which verbal markers like 'as', 'during', and 'when' are constantly organizing the material (this extends at one point to the lumbering interpolation '*During this meditation* a heavy surge | was taking him', 425–6, my italics). Compare with the above excerpt Fitzgerald's corresponding lines:

> But when he came in earshot
> he heard the trampling roar of sea on rock,
> where combers, rising shoreward, thudded down

---

[19] Dawe (1993: 243).

[20] Homer, trans. Murray (1919: 201), for *Od.* 5.421–2: ἠέ τί μοι καί κῆτος ἐπισσεύῃ μέγα δαίμων | ἐξ ἁλός, οἷά τε πολλά τρέφει κλυτὸς Ἀμφιτρίτη.

[21] A κῆτος could, according to Aelian (*NA* 9.45), be many types of sea monster. This is the *Odyssey*'s sole allusion to this danger (Heubeck *et al.* 1988–9: I, 285).

on the sucking ebb—all sheeted with salt foam.
Here were no coves or harbourage or shelter,
Only steep headlands, rockfallen reefs and crags.

(400–5)

Some of Fitzgerald's verbs are energetic enough, but the overall effect is constrained by his obvious determination to stick to fully grammatical sentences and introduce each new element with proper narrative clarity. Hughes aims rather for immediacy, in all departments.

Near the start of the episode Fitzgerald has a couple of typical narrative lines:

Two nights, two days, in the solid deep-sea swell
he drifted, many times awaiting death

(388–9)

These correspond to Hughes's

Two days and two nights he foundered in massive seas
With the darkness of death breaking over and hollowing under.

(6–7)

That second line of the Hughes strongly suggests the heavily swelling motion of the seas, and the movement of the body rolling helplessly in them. Which is to say that we are at least in the realms of poetry here, whereas with Fitzgerald this is scarcely so: we are *informed* that there was a 'sea swell', but there seems no attempt to summon one up. However, Hughes's adjective 'massive' is rather uncertain in its register, perhaps a little too informal for the surrounding material. It is notable that as he goes on Hughes actually eschews adjectives whereas Fitzgerald tends to insist on them. I do not mean epithets like (in Hughes's line 41) 'Owl-eyed Athene', which are something he may have seen as more or less obligatory in a Homer translation, but rather the way in which, within the cut and thrust of the violent action, the head-on quality is attained partly by throwing the onus onto nouns and verbs, making them carry the weight directly:

He plunged forward,
Both hands grasped rock, and he clung there groaning
As the mass ground over.

(41–3)

But, where Hughes does permit himself more adjectival writing, his expressions again partake of that quality he was to claim translations need to achieve in his *MPT* editorials, 'the very oddity and struggling dumbness of word for word version' which 'is what makes our own imagination jump'. The contrast with Fitzgerald could not be clearer in this respect; far from deploying the unexpectedly expressive word, the American translator tends towards stock phrases and even periphrasis. Keats might have admired Hughes's

> His flesh swollen and his heart swamped by the seas (64)

—but would surely have been non-plussed by Fitzgerald's

> all vital force now conquered by the sea (451)

Further examples show the same tendencies:

> A mounding wave heaved him (Hughes, 37)
> a heavy surge | was taking him (Fitzgerald, 425–6)

> calming the chop of its waves and smoothing a path (Hughes, 62)
> the river god made quiet water (Fitzgerald, 449)

Numerous other local felicities present themselves to the eye in Hughes's version. In line 40 he writes that the bones of Odysseus would have been 'pestled within him' had Athene not rescued him— a forgiveable example of stylistic heightening, since the *Odyssey* text contains nothing metaphorical at this point. But more than forgiveable; the verb, no verb in English hitherto, offers a small new possibility to the language. Towards the end of the passage Hughes drops in and out of an alliterative technique aptly suggestive, if that is the kind of Homer one wants, of Old English poems like *The Seafarer* and *The Wanderer*—the same sound being used in the second half of the line as the first, or in the second of two adjacent lines:

> He [ . . . ] climbed to a clump
> Of trees in a clearing, near the water.
> It was an olive and a wild olive knotting so densely one with the other
> Neither the stroke of the naked sun
> Nor wet sea-winds nor the needling rain could enter . . .
> Where dead leaves were littered abundant enough
> To warm two or three from the worst of winter.
>
> (80–4, 87–8)

Odysseus is here resolving a situation that has worried him in a way some of Homer's commentators have found distinctly valetudinarian: if he stays in the open, he fears, the frost, dew, and wind might 'overcome' him in his enfeebled state—or, as Fitzgerald renders this, 'how can I not succumb, being weak and sick, | to the night's damp and hoar-frost of the morning? | The air comes cold from rivers before dawn.' Hughes makes us hear a voice of bitter experience rather than of grandmotherly caution:

> Clamping frost and the saturating dews, sea-sodden as I am now,
> Could be my death. And I know how bleakly
> Wind before dawn comes off the water.

(73–5)

One could go on pointing out such successes, but it is time to suggest (as proposed earlier) how this translation contacts with the rest of Hughes's imaginative life of the time period in which it was composed.[22]

The commentary on *The Storm* in Weissbort's *Selected Translations* is based on occasions on which Hughes mentioned Homer in interviews. In these contexts he referred to Homer as one of the 'poets of violence', and to the story of Odysseus, like those of other epics, as a sort of shamanistic flight. 'The shaman's dream', Hughes is recorded as saying in the year of the translation 'is the skeleton of thousands of folktales and myths. And of many narrative poems, the *Odyssey*, the *Divine Comedy*, *Faust*, etc.'[23]

Hughes undoubtedly characterized the *Odyssey* in this way. But he only ever did so when speaking of it as one example among several of major poems that conform to some generalization he was making. These remarks seem to draw on his broader reading of the *Odyssey* more than his actual translating of this episode. And a broader reading of the *Odyssey* is something Hughes's work of these years reflects, as we have seen from the one use of the poem that most Hughes readers will recall, the short *Lupercal* composition 'Everyman's

---

[22] For a few further comments, including the intriguing suggestion that this is a rare instance in Hughes's verse in which the formal elements of classical prosody seem to exert an influence on his own, see Talbot (2006).

[23] *ST* 14–15.

Odyssey'. Hughes, that is, had taken an independent interest in the Homeric epic, and that interest was not confined to shamanism.

Hughes's first translation reflects several characteristic interests and emphases. Physical struggle is prominent. There is violence. A number of gods are invoked or otherwise mentioned. But none of these things is so central as a more fundamental subject still: the existential plight of man. The Homeric passage is one, after all, in which Odysseus is brought, by a bitter combination of divine wrath and divine assistance, to his lowest ebb; as a modern commentary observes of this moment at the end of Book 5, 'it is the poet's wish that the recovery of Odysseus' fortunes shall begin from the lowest possible point'.[24] The great English Homer translator Alexander Pope appears to have found in Odysseus' situation here one of the character's principal claims to distinction over Vergil's Aeneas, to judge by one of the notes on this passage in his translation:

The proposition of the Poem requires [Homer] to describe a man of sufferings in the person of *Ulysses*: he therefore no sooner introduces him but he throws him into the utmost calamities, and describes them largely, to shew at once the greatness of his distress, and his wisdom and patience under it. In what are the sufferings of *Æneas* in *Virgil* comparable to these of *Ulysses*? *Æneas* suffers little personally in comparison of *Ulysses*, his incidents have less variety, and consequently less beauty.[25]

One last comparison between Hughes and Fitzgerald should help bring out how superior is Hughes's response to this.

Halfway through the passage the exhausted Odysseus calls on the unknown god of the river in which he is attempting to swim to land. Fitzgerald and Hughes at this point offer respectively:

> O hear me, lord of the stream:
> how sorely I depend upon your mercy,
> derelict as I am by the sea's anger.
> Is he not sacred, even to the gods,
> the wandering man who comes, as I have come,
> in weariness before your knees, your waters?
> Here is your servant; lord, have mercy on me.
>                         (Fitzgerald, 442–8)
> Whoever you are, king, hear my prayers, for I come

---

[24] Heubeck *et al.* (1988–9: I, 288).
[25] Note on Pope's 5.550 in Mack (1967: 199).

Out of the sea's gape and Poseidon's anger.
The everlasting gods give ear to the prayer of a wanderer,
And a wanderer I come now, humbly to your waters,
After hard sufferings. Pity me, king, and take me into your care.

(Hughes, 56–60)

For Homer, Odysseus is of course a stranger and a supplicant,[26] and some of the phrasing of both translators reflects this: both present a 'wanderer' who asks to be 'heard'. Fitzgerald also suggests something of the special status of the stranger in the antique Greek world; his 'sacred' (445) equates to Homer's αἰδοῖος (447). But Fitzgerald has assimilated the episode overall to an obviously alien Christian ethos. Hughes envisages Odysseus offering 'prayers' to the unknown river-god; prayers, like the sacred, are something common to all religions. But the inescapably Christian, and indeed quasi-liturgical vocabulary used by Fitzgerald's Odysseus, most egregiously in the final line, places us at a far remove from anything Homeric. To speak of oneself as god's 'servant' is the most traditional of Christian tropes. It is quite a different thing from being an ἱκέτης (Homer's line 450)—a suppliant, a fugitive—who stands in need not of 'mercy' (another Christian import in Fitzgerald), but of a protector who will undertake to apply the laws of hospitality to a stranger in an alien environment. It seems unlikely that Fitzgerald was unable through lack of Greek to interpret what is happening at this point in Homer; his shortcoming is lack of control over his English vocabulary. In other words, Donald Carne-Ross was right: the primary qualification for a translator is to know his own language well.[27]

---

[26] This supplication scene, which has a special form because Odysseus' circumstances do not allow him to follow the normal ritual, can be considered 'an anticipatory doublet of the two major "supplication" scenes to follow' in Books 6 and 7 of the *Odyssey* (de Jong 2001: 146–7).

[27] I am grateful to Lorna Hardwick, Neil Roberts, Michael Silk, and Daniel Weissbort for discussion and further references towards this essay.

# 3

# Can (modern) poets do classical drama? The case of Ted Hughes

*Lorna Hardwick*

This is one of the most contentious questions that have been raised in recent discussion of modern adaptations of classical plays and it has been intensified in the critical reception of the work of poet/dramatists such as Seamus Heaney, Tony Harrison, and Ted Hughes. Analysis of this type of critical comment reveals some crucial issues about the basic requirements of translating and adapting ancient drama for and to the modern stage. These include the creation of a text that can not only be spoken aloud but also physically communicated in a modern acting space which is likely to be indoors, artificially lit, and accommodating anything from thirty to several hundred spectators. This differs greatly from the space for which the plays were first created. The ancient formal conventions make particular demands, especially the Chorus's combination of lyric, song, and movement. Greek drama was also poetry for the theatre and verse drama does not sit easily with the theatrical sensibilities and expectations of modern audiences. Furthermore there is debate about whether the Senecan tragedy that Hughes worked with was actually created with the intention of performance.

So far as the construction and communication of meaning is concerned, transplantation of classical drama to the modern stage has involved various poetic, dramatic, and theatrical ways of identifying and representing modern analogues and both the absence and the presence of these have provoked controversy. Many modern adaptations or 'translations' are written by authors who do not work directly from the ancient languages (Tony Harrison is an exception) and so there are further issues about the nature and use of 'mediating' translations and about the extent to which the modern version can or should acquire the status of a new work in its own right.

The crucial problem areas that provide the framework for this discussion focus on the extent to which translations and adaptations should or could primarily aim to convey a modern experience analogous to that of the ancient and the extent to which the writer's facility in the ancient languages is important for creating aesthetic quality for the modern stage.

Two clusters of issues are important for evaluation of Ted Hughes's classical work in this context. The first cluster involves the relationship between scholarship, knowledge of the source language, use of mediating or comparative translations, and the development of poetic and dramatic techniques that can accommodate these relationships and methods of working. The second focuses on the relationship between the classical adaptations and the rest of the modern writer's work. An underlying question relevant to both clusters concerns the characteristics of different kinds of drama and the media in which they are developed—within poems; audio/radio; for the stage. This last area is important for Hughes's classical work. It raises crucial questions about the roles of theatre directors, adaptors, and actors, especially in his collaborations with Peter Brook (in Seneca's *Oedipus*, 1968 and the experimental *Orghast*, 1971). There are important additional implications in the posthumous stage—direction of Hughes's work, notably *Tales from Ovid* (RSC, 1999), *Alcestis* (Northern Broadsides 2000), and the *Oresteia* (National, 1999), which interwove the director's reading of the Aeschylus visually and physically into Hughes's essentially aural poetic response. There are also questions about whether there are observable differences in Hughes's use of Latin sources (he had some knowledge of the language) and his use of Greek (of which, so far as is known, he had no knowledge), bearing in mind his approach in *Orghast* to the creation of a distinctive language drawn from a number of sources. Although 'translation' of various kinds and from several different language groups was a significant strand in Hughes's work, he was primarily a poet and dramatist and so his 'translations' have to be situated within his oeuvre as a creative writer as well as (and sometimes rather than) in the translation histories of the particular classical source texts.[1] This opens the way to comparison of Hughes's translational approaches to classical drama with the dramatic technique, including classical elements, that is displayed in his poetry as a whole (including *Prometheus on His Crag* and *Birthday Letters*).

Hughes's poetry and his translations of classical drama in many respects coalesce, not just because the ancient dramatists were writing theatre poetry but also because Hughes's approach to language actually embedded dramatic technique in all his poetry. Nevertheless, Hughes's primary impulse was always that of the poet—in a letter to Gerald Hughes written while he was working on Seneca's *Oedipus* (15 March 1968) he commented that 'my will to write poems is stronger than my will to write plays'.[2] Analysing the nature and directions of the linguistic traffic between the ancient drama and Hughes's writing suggests that Hughes's dramatic dialogue is with his own poetry and with the tradition he writes from rather than directly with the ancient source text and also that this 'intra-textual' characteristic has wider implications for the ways in which we can try to explain the relationship between ancient and modern in his work.

But first, why this particular topic 'Can poets do drama?' The issue has a long history and, to give just one example, had twentieth-century impact in debates about the theatre work of T. S. Eliot. I shall focus on the way in which it has recently resurfaced as a contemporary question in the study of the reception of canonical plays, raised specifically by recent discussions of modern translations, versions, and stagings of Greek plays. Particular attention has been paid to the adaptations of Sophocles by Seamus Heaney (*The Cure at Troy: after Sophocles' Philoctetes*, 1990, and the *Burial at Thebes: after Sophocles' Antigone*, 2004) and, most contentiously of all, to Tony Harrison's translation of Euripides' *Hecuba* (2005). This was prepared for the Royal Shakespeare Company and the production, starring Vanessa Redgrave and initially directed by Laurence Boswell and then by Harrison himself, was a source of intense debate and criticism. So not only does the question reveal an infrastructure of assumptions

---

[1] For an overview, see Weissbort and Eysteinsson (2006: 521–33).
[2] *LTH* 282.

and problems about ancient drama, it also directly refers to how a text is 'translated' to the stage.

What do modern poets have to tackle in order to translate or adapt drama? In simple terms it might be said poets have to move aside from the purely logocentric and produce a play-text that can be spoken aloud, staged, and acted, usually by a group and in a communal situation, physically communicating in an acting space. But the demands of doing this with *ancient* drama are even greater. A modern rewriter has to work with the ancient theatrical conventions, including the Greek Chorus' lyric, song, and movement. From this is derived a second problem. Verse drama does not sit easily with modern theatrical sensibilities and expectations, yet Greek drama was performance poetry, so ability to communicate theatre poetry is a defining criterion for translation and adaptation. This might suggest that poets are *more* suited to the task than are dramatists or scriptwriters, yet precisely because it puts a premium on the linguistic it raises questions about how facility in the ancient language relates to aesthetic quality in the modern language version. Debates about how aesthetic quality is created also raise questions about whether translations and adaptations should or could aim to convey a modern experience analogous to that of the ancient.

Translations of classical poetry have been a feature of twentieth-century literature in many different ways. Recently, however, engagement with Greek and Roman drama has been a defining feature of the work of most of the major English-language poets. Seamus Heaney, Tony Harrison, and Ted Hughes have all had major works staged in the last twenty-five years.[3] All have been criticized, sometimes heavily. I am interested both in the reasons for these criticisms and the criteria for judging the extent to which it is valid. These are aspects which provide a context for analysis of Hughes's work.

---

[3] I leave out Derek Walcott from the present discussion because his only stage play with a classical basis, *The Odyssey: A Stage Version* (1993), was derived from epic poetry, not from tragedy, see Hardwick (2000). I also omit from detailed discussion the work with classical drama by Timberlake Wertenbaker and Frank McGuinness, since both are primarily dramatists. It is worth noting, however, that Walcott's theatrical success in transplanting Homer across genres was preceded by a long career as a dramatist.

The reasons for criticism of Seamus Heaney's theatre poetry are of two kinds. The first arose from his *Cure at Troy* (1990) and is primarily concerned with his use of the Chorus. In this play he mainly followed Sophocles quite closely (especially through his use of Jebb's late nineteenth-century and Lloyd-Jones' twentieth-century scholarly translations) but he also made additions to the Choruses. In the non-Sophoclean lines, the Chorus not only challenged the moral and political validity of Philoctetes' self-pity and hatred but also used modern analogues to drive home the effects of intransigence within and between communities. The vocabulary and speech rhythms of Heaney's Irish/English located the play in the context of the Troubles in the north of Ireland and specifically referred to the sufferings of both communities. Heaney's interpolations became famous—the Chorus' line 'when hope and history rhyme' was used in politicians' speeches in the 1990s, culminating in press headlines at the time of the Good Friday Agreement in 1998.[4] However, references to the bereaved in the Troubles attracted criticism for their apparently even-handed approach to sufferings on both sides of the sectarian divide ('the hunger striker's father' and the 'police widow in veils . . . at the funeral home').[5] Heaney himself recognised the aesthetic difficulties involved in introducing contemporary allusions into the Choral lyrics but he also emphasized that the speeches of the Chorus (the odes were not sung in this play) were meant to 'contextualise the action and not just within a discourse that could apply to Northern Ireland politics. These two speeches (I see it even more clearly in retrospect) defend the right of poetry/poetic drama to be something other than protest'.[6]

There are two interrelated points here. One is the emphasis on the words, rather than the situation, as the bearers and creators of meaning in performance. The second is the issue of the modern resonances in Greek drama. *How* such allusions are created and then trigger recognition of transhistorical meaning is a key issue in translation of theatre poetry and has been discussed in detail by Heaney in relation to his version of Sophocles' *Antigone, The Burial*

---

[4] For discussion and examples, see Hardwick (2003: 103–7).
[5] Heaney (1990: 77).
[6] Heaney (2002*b*: 173).

*at Thebes* (2004). In this work Heaney used a variety of metres and diction to represent the Greek of the Chorus and of Antigone, Ismene, and Creon and to suggest how they resonated with Irish and English literary traditions and cultural politics.[7]

A second point in relation to criticism of Heaney's dramatic achievements is concerned with staging. The 2004 production of *The Burial at Thebes* at the Abbey Theatre, Dublin, was commissioned to mark the hundredth anniversary of the Abbey. In the published text (2004), it was clear that this time Heaney had composed the Choral odes without direct reference to the situation of Ireland. Yet there were in the language of the play, which again closely followed the Sophoclean model, richly textured allusions to various aspects of Irish culture and history, underpinned by development of idiom and metre appropriate to each character. However, the Abbey Theatre staging, directed by Lorraine Pintal was widely agreed to be disastrous. The point to be drawn out from this debacle is that the poet's text (whether we take the poet to be Sophocles or Heaney) is at the mercy of the director. The 'South-American dictatorship' setting for *Burial*, far from suggesting a 'universal' context merely disrupted the meaning and beauty of the text.[8]

In a slightly different way, these two points—that is, the extent to which the diction and registers of the text create meaning and interpretation by the spectators and the extent to which the director's production concept can make or mar the play, also underlay some of the criticisms of the Tony Harrison/RSC 2005 production of Euripides' *Hecuba*.[9] A review essay by the thoughtful (and classically erudite) critic Peter Stothard, published in the *Times Literary Supplement* in 2005, was almost alone among those who discussed Harrison's play in pointing out *both* that there were problems with the production *and* that Harrison followed Euripides' Greek closely (Harrison is classically trained so no Jebb equivalent was needed).[10]

---

[7] Heaney (2005), discussed further in Hardwick (2007*a*).

[8] For discussion, see Wilmer (2007). The 2005 production in Nottingham, directed by Lucy Pitman-Wallace and revived in 2007, restored the integrity both of Sophocles' and of Heaney's plays.

[9] I have written elsewhere about the extent to which some of the theatre critics misrepresented what actually happened on the stage, Hardwick (2007*b*).

[10] Stothard (2005).

Stothard made two important points. The first was that the problem with Harrison's translation was not that it used neologisms like 'coalition' (which actually describes the Greek force rather well) but that the translation was bulky and sometimes difficult to deliver in spoken performance—for example, 'hush-hush stash of gold', 'hair-splitter, shifty wits, molasses-mouth, mob schmoozer' (applied to Odysseus, of course). It was full of epithets and alliterations (a feature also of Harrison's 1981 *Oresteia*). Stothard's point was that the actors and especially the Chorus could not 'carry' all these words. According to Stothard, what Harrison offered was 'hard mouthfuls of text'. Interestingly, he did not take up comments made by other reviewers who had suggested that Harrison's characteristic use of rhyming couplets shaped and focused meaning to the extent of closure. Harrison's couplets and his alliteration domesticate Euripides to an English poetic tradition, but it is a tradition that is perceived as archaic, and certainly not well attuned to modern aural sensibilities nor to preconceptions about the language and rhythms of tragedy.[11]

The contrast drawn by Stothard was with a rival version of the *Hecuba*, by the dramatist Frank McGuinness, which had also been staged in London at the Donmar Theatre in the autumn of 2004, directed by Jonathan Kent. McGuinness did not work from the Greek but from a literal translation by Fionnuala Murphy. He then pared the text down, making it what Stothard called 'a skeleton around which a mystery is made', a skeleton that allowed the director and the actors space to develop and shape the performance and which actually resulted in a coherent relationship between the acting script and its translation to the stage.

So here we have a fascinating conundrum. The close-to-the-Greek translation by Harrison communicated Euripides' text and a lot of the density and subtlety (such as the parody of democracy in the dramatization of the decision-making processes of the Greeks) but it did this in an idiom that alienated at least some of the spectators (compounded perhaps by Vanessa Redgrave's portrayal of a Hecuba who was insufficiently manic for modern tastes). Perhaps the question should be: could Euripides do drama?

[11] See Silk (1999) which refers to the 'quaint and numbing (if sometimes brilliant) Anglo-Saxonism of Tony Harrison'.

The debate about the Heaney and Harrison texts and their staging raises problems that are important for classical reception research as well as providing a contrast with some aspects of Hughes's work and its critical reception. Academics are used to researching the history of productions, the lexical range and cultural politics of the translations and versions, their staging and their reception by audiences and critics. They engage enthusiastically with new primary sources but the emphasis is so often limited to how the new work relates to the ancient that they hold back from literary or aesthetic criticism. There are of course honourable exceptions. Oliver Taplin's 2002 essay 'Contemporary Poetry and Classics' did move towards making judgements and included a detailed comparison of the literary qualities of versions of the *Agamemnon* by Tony Harrison and Ted Hughes.[12] Taplin started by discussing the way in which Harrison works directly from the Greek. He conceded that 'of course there is nothing inherently superior about a translation which is made directly from the original language. Translations made through other translations have a distinguished pedigree going back to the Renaissance'.[13] However, Taplin also stated (questionably) that 'no one any longer regards it as even a consideration worth noticing, let alone as an invalidation', noting that the reason is probably that since the 1960s few people have learned Latin at school (let alone Greek). He went on to criticize Hughes by conjecturing that he had worked from Vellacott's Penguin translation, which in Taplin's view lacked scholarly rigour.[14] There is some evidence from other examples of Hughes's translation practice about how he liked to work. For example, for his translations of Pushkin he was provided with a literal version of the Russian and a guide to the sound and prosody and used these to dig beneath the sophistication for the primitive and visceral.[15]

Taplin was surely right to point to the indirect effect of the mediating translation on the final work. However, the question of the relationship between the ancient text and the eventual new work has a number of aspects. One of the most revealing discussions was that by Louis MacNeice who, almost uniquely, combined being a

---

[12] Taplin (2002) and also Silk in this volume.
[13] Taplin (2002: 2).    [14] Taplin (2002: 3).
[15] Weissbort and Eysteinsson (2006: 533).

professional classical scholar, a translator for the stage, a playwright, and a serious poet (Tony Harrison does not quite meet the first criterion although he probably could have done so). MacNeice also had a fifth string to his bow, that of a literary critic. His critique of Gilbert Murray's translation of Aeschylus' *The Seven Against Thebes* (an article published in the *Spectator* in 1935 when he himself was working on his *Agamemnon*) acknowledged the virtues of Murray's scholarship and enthusiasm but condemned him as 'neither a good translator nor a good poet'.[16] MacNeice went on to discuss how a poetic translation might be created—'a translation should start from the Greek, preferably line for line. Diction and rhythm will then differentiate'. Then the poetry can be infused (MacNeice recommended Gerard Manley Hopkins, presumably as an antidote to the pre-Raphaelite inflections that he deprecated in Murray)—'we improve both rhythm and diction and so make the whole more real. *This is perhaps where the non-scholar may translate better than the scholar* (italics added). His Greek original is so real to a scholar like Professor Murray that it is probably never out of his mind, and so he cannot see what the English looks like just as English'.[17] MacNeice's intervention introduces into the discussion two key questions about whether knowledge of and reverence for the Greek inhibits critical evaluation of the literary value of the translation and how and from where the poetic infusion comes.

Taplin's approach to literary comparisons between translations is helpful in this respect. In discussing choral lyric in lines 773–81 of the *Agamemnon* he pointed out that Hughes's diction and metrical composition are by comparison with Harrison's 'homogeneous throughout, whatever the dynamic of the original . . . The contrasts are extreme: the staccato phrases and heavy stopping against the unpunctuated Harrison, the vague moralising against the cascade of metaphors and images'. Taplin also added an ideological gloss— 'The iconoclastic, anti-monarchist Harrison makes the most of this anti-fanfare for the king: the royalist, male-sympathising Hughes plays down anything that might reflect badly on the sovereign' (cf. Rees in this volume). He also quoted another passage from the

---

[16] MacNeice (1935).
[17] MacNeice (1935), reprinted in Heuser (1987: 10).

Hughes in which Clytemnestra 'descants' (to use Taplin's term) on the purple dye of the cloth she has laid out for her husband. Taplin added tersely 'But all the polychrome physiology is pure Hughes. It would seem that in his last years he turned to translation because it unclogged the well of his Muse and gave him the material on which to embroider some of his leading pre-occupations'. This claim alludes to Hughes's Introduction to his *Tales from Ovid* (1997) in which he elides reception of Ovid ('saturating literature and art' with 'our unconscious imaginative life') and human passion *in extremis*. For Hughes, metamorphosis, whether Ovidian or more broadly transla-tional, 'operates as the symbolic guarantee that the passion has become mythic'. 'Mythic' is identified with 'unendurable inten-sity'—'a rough register of what it feels like to live in the psychological gulf that opens at the end of an era'.[18]

These debates highlight a number of issues: the scholarship of rewriters and translators, which may vary at points on the spectrum between knowledge of the ancient languages, ability to select and consult scholarly mediating translations, and use of popular transla-tions for information on content and form; the impact of this on the writer's poetic and dramatic technique; the relationship between the modern writer's translation or adaptation of classical texts and the rest of his or her work and life—the art and selectivity of the writing subject. The balance between all these factors reflects whether the modern author sees the new translation/version as situated more within the afterlife of the ancient text or more within the literary and dramatic tradition in which he or she aspires to 'star'. (A similar comment might be made about the perspectives of critics.) In either case the relationship with the rest of the modern author's work is a shaping factor, but its interaction with the classical text may be symbiotic or competitive, even confrontational. This of course raises the possibility that the new work may be excluded by classicists from the category of 'translation' or even 'version' if it is judged to be insufficiently 'classical', usually in the linguistic or formal sense, although considerations of content and value also come into the equation. J. Michael Walton has developed one typology for

---

[18] Hughes *TO*, xiii–xiv. See Tatham in this volume.

addressing this problem.[19] He uses seven categories ranging from literal cribs to 'Translocations to another culture' and has Hughes's classical work in his fifth—'Adapted from, or based on, the original but from playwrights/writers without a direct knowledge of Greek'. According to Walton, Hughes's companions in this category are Sartre, Anouilh, Kennelly, Heaney, McGuinness, and Morrison. Tony Harrison is in the fourth group—'Intended for, or deriving from, production, with occasional licence'. Also in this category is MacNeice. Walton's discussion recognizes the difficulties of any kind of categorization and draws attention to the importance of the theatre director's imagination, questioning why the text should be regarded as sacrosanct when the history of translation and performance of ancient plays is based on the fact that the source texts are so adaptable. However, not all classicists are as sensitive to the demands of performance as is Walton and even in his typology the relationship of the new work to the source and the new writer's 'direct' knowledge of Greek are major criteria for classification and therefore for judgement.

Clearly, therefore, there is a complex and shifting range of factors that affect why modern poets engage with classical drama, how they do it, and how their efforts are received in poetic, theatrical, critical, and cultural contexts that differ markedly from the ancient. The rest of this discussion focuses specifically on Hughes. His work offers insights that will help clarify these issues, especially concerning the types of intertext used by the writer who aims to produce a distinctive work. Two key aspects of Hughes's poetry/drama nexus are crucial—the physicality of his use of words and themes and the structural relationship between the 'poetry in the drama' and the 'drama in the poetry'. Taken together, they suggest that his contribution in the field is distinctive.

The first point to be made is that Hughes's work from the beginning included a large proportion of drama. Between 1960 and 1971 he wrote at least eighteen plays, although he later referred to them as 'mere bagatelles'.[20] In addressing this issue Jacobs commented that many critics had come to the view that what was interesting about

---

[19] Walton (2006: 182–3): 'When is a translation not a translation?'
[20] Jacobs (1983: 154).

the plays was 'the poems in them and the poems that came out of them'. This is not surprising, given that much of Hughes's early work was created for radio broadcasts in which the drama had to be created by the words and the audiences' response was aural rather than shaped in conjunction with the non-verbal semiotics of the stage. However, as Jacobs's essay also pointed out, the potential of Hughes's drama for live theatre was taken seriously, not least by directors. For example, Peter Brook's production of Seneca's *Oedipus* (1968 at the Old Vic in London) actually chose Hughes's work because it was more suitable for staging than the originally commissioned version by David Turner.[21] In a preface to Hughes's published text Turner comments on the difference that Hughes made: 'In a shivery rehearsal room Ted Hughes started to read, and with his vibrant Penine stabs of voice this book began . . . I was there because I had translated the play . . . [Peter Brook] was not satisfied with my script . . . So by telephone it was arranged that Ted Hughes be brought in to work on the text and improve it . . . it was obvious from the moment he spoke that improvement was too weak a word for what he had done. It was more like apotheosis. In place of good serviceable prose there was inspiration, elegance, fire, poetry. It was all magic. And all the magic was Ted's. At Peter Brook's insistence he went back to the Latin on his own and brought form to the present version'. Hughes himself gave the process a rather different gloss, commenting in his letter to Gerald Hughes that 'the further I've dragged it into my own territory (out of all conventional modern theatre even away from the avant garde) the more uniquely effective it is'.[22]

John Gielgud and Irene Worth, who as Oedipus and Jocasta respectively were the main actors in the *Oedipus* production, recall the effect that Hughes's script and his reading of it had on the rehearsal process.[23] Hughes is said to have written the script in a very short time (about four weeks) and to have composed the first Chorus parts in three days. He says in his introduction to the published text that he 'went back to the original Seneca, eking out

---

[21] For Turner's published translation, see Turner (1990).

[22] Turner (1969) and see Talbot in this volume. The extract from the letter is in *LTH* 282.

[23] Gielgud (1999) and Worth (1999).

my Latin with a Victorian crib'.[24] He also refers to the impact of Peter Brook, the co-director Geoffrey Reeves, and the composer Richard Peaslee who, according to Hughes, 'pieced the second chorus together, out of something four or five times as long, to fit a wild orchestration of voices'. Brook wanted a text that would release the inner power of the story in its bluntest and plainest form and would unearth, if possible, the ritual possibilities within it. He had, in fact, asked the actors to read the play in the translation by Frank Justus Miller, first published in 1917 in the Loeb Classical Library parallel text edition. Hughes described this as being 'extremely weighty and extremely literal'.[25] Hughes also wrote that Sophocles' *Oedipus* 'would not have been so suitable for this experiment as Seneca's because Sophocles' play was 'fully explored and, in spite of its blood roots, fully civilized' whereas in Seneca's *Oedipus* the figures were Greek only by convention—'by nature they are more primitive than aboriginals (sic) ... The radiant moral world of Sophocles is simply not present'. Moreover, Hughes considered that in spite of the rhetorical speeches and stoical epigrams in Seneca, the poetic mythical substance had not dated and it was this that he laid bare by stripping away the Senecan rhetoric and preserving some elements of Turner's language.[26] This emphasis on the primitive aspects of myth is also significant in Hughes's later theatre work.

The text of *Oedipus* was designed for Brook's production style—'the limited movement of the actors, the heightened and to some extent depersonalized manner of speaking, the interwriting and the overall headlong musical impetus'. Hughes also said that he developed a style suitable for the way the Chorus members were deployed all over the theatre. He added material for Jocasta. She was given a more reflective role than in Seneca, especially in the long speech at the end of her opening exchange with Oedipus. Critics have commented on the affinity between this speech and Hughes's *Crow* poems (1970), such as 'Crow and Mama', 'Song for a Phallus', and 'Snake Hymn'. Some years later Hughes commented in a letter to Nick Gammage (15 December 1992) that 'I translated Seneca's

---

[24] Preface to *O* 7.  [25] Weissbort and Eisteinsson (2006: 524).

[26] For an analysis, see Talbot (2006). Talbot also points out how 'Hughes's Seneca' was recycled in the *Crow* poems.

Oedipus in among writing the Crow pieces in the book. Main influence was—the stylistic release of finding a simple language and tone for a supercharged theme. The sheer day after day practice of striving for that. Affected the style of Crow. Though a good many of them I wrote before I touched Oedipus'.[27] The interpolated sequence in *Oedipus* is in contrast with the paring down of text in most of the rest of his version. The interest in interpolation sets a precedent for his later work with Greek drama. Otherwise, Hughes claimed, 'the text comes closely out of the original with much deletion, little addition'. The result has been described by Alison Sharrock as 'disjointed prose-verse [that] rises slowly and alliteratively, gaining momentum as Oedipus confronts what he has done'—

> birth birthbed blood take this open
> the earth bury it bottom of the darkness
> under everything I am not fit for the light.[28]

There are several points to be drawn out from Hughes's rewriting of *Oedipus* that raise significant points for comparison (and sometimes contrast) with his later work on drama. First, the text was created in partnership with the director and was liked by the actors. Secondly, there were elements of exchange with Hughes's poetry, partly in the interpolated Jocasta speech and partly in his overall conception of what Seneca was doing and the concepts of the primitive and the mythical that Hughes drew from this. Thirdly there was a disjointed presentation of the lines, both visually and orally, that meshed with the production style. This suggests that Hughes's engagement with classical material is a field (and perhaps also a catalyst) for formal and lexical disruption and disturbance. Clive Holes has described Hughes's animal poems as having a 'bleeding muscularity and sharpness of line'.[29] There is something of this in the *Oedipus* text. There are also some affinities with another rewriting by Hughes, of Racine's *Phèdre,* which Peter France described as—'unrhymed free translation, made for acting, sinewy and strong ... the rhythms are deliberately prosaic, only occasionally rising to Racine's grandeur'.[30]

   *Oedipus* showed not only that Hughes could work with director and cast; it also showed he could be inventive in the language of a

---

[27] *LTH* 618.     [28] *O* 47; Sharrock (2000: 532).
[29] Holes (2000: 147).     [30] France (2000) 266. See Gervais in this volume.

play script. Both these aspects were evident in *Orghast,* which he worked on with Brook in 1971 for an experiment at Persepolis, to mark the 2500th anniversary of the founding of the Achaemenid Persian dynasty. Irene Worth, who had played Jocasta, was again included. The experiment included a dramatic language invented by Hughes, and drew on ancient Persian ceremonial language, on Armenian drama, and on Seneca. The play also exploited Greek myth and historical drama, especially the tale of Prometheus and Aeschylus's *Persians.* This predictably caused resentment from the Persians who appreciated neither the reminder of defeat at Salamis nor association with the primitive, another theme in Hughes and, arguably, a travesty of the Aeschylus. Nevertheless, the connection with Prometheus is important, partly because it suggests that Hughes was interested in Aeschylus long before he came to work on the *Oresteia* and also because it signals the exchange between his poetry and his dramatic exploitation of classical myth. He was working on *Orghast* at the same point in his career that he was developing *Prometheus on his Crag.*[31] Peter Brook has recalled how Hughes approached the invention of the new language—'I listen to the patterns that arise in the deep level of the brain, when impulses become sounds and syllables'. Brook commented on Hughes's capacity to be in touch with a vast complex of movements that underlie human existence—'for this reason, logical language can never capsulate him'.[32] Brook describes this as 'powerful music'. Hughes's letter to Lucas Myers (thought to date from September 1971) describes the process more prosaically—

Very slowly and laboriously I made a play out of (a) story of Prometheus, (b) Calderon's life is a dream (c) Mannichean cosmology (d) Persian Creation mythology (e) sundry folk-lore and mythology . . . Very early I invented a language for it. After a while I moulded it all into one mythology so complicated and multi-dimensional that I've already completely lost my way in it—but it helped me produce the scenes. . . . Finally I had a play about 1 ½ hours, with odd passages of Greek(from Prometheus Bound) a passage of Latin (from Seneca's Hercules Furens) and much Avesta (sacred texts of

---

[31] See Talbot (2006), who suggests that there is a rare stylistic affinity with Aeschylus at this point and Zajko in this volume, who focuses on the anthropological aspects.

[32] Brook (1999: 154).

the Zoroastrians, as pronounced by a dotty inspired Kurdish woman . . . Her own readings of it are some of the most amazing beautiful sound I ever heard). The rest of the play was my invented language—more or less a method of frustrating the actor's inclination to speak merely verbal rattle of seeming meaning and forcing him to dig something up authentic from his midriff. It was a sort of musical notation really.[33]

This combination of physicality and aural quality in the use of words was a major feature in Hughes's *Tales from Ovid* (1997) which was the winner of the 1997 Whitbread Book of the Year award. David Hopkins has described this rewriting of twenty-four passages from the *Metamorphoses* as 'stabbing, short-breathed free verse' in contrast to Ovid's 'suavely flowing hexameters' and 'in their sheer energy, pace and liveliness . . . by far the most poetically compelling versions of *Metamorphoses* to have been written this century'.[34] I mention this to show the affinity in descriptions of Hughes's page poetry and theatre poetry. *Tales from Ovid* was not just poetically compelling; it also transplanted to the stage (Royal Shakespeare Company, 1999), adapted by Tim Supple and Simon Reade.[35] In their introduction to the published text they indicate how the stage directions were taken from the verse and how they largely retained the verse forms chosen by Hughes. Some Latin, always sung, was introduced into the performed version. Supple had been impressed with Hughes's *Oedipus* which he considered 'one of the finest theatrical texts I had come across'.[36] The particular hallmark was 'this almost unbearable clarity: the moment of thought seen in the moment of speech, glaring with an unavoidable definition'. He thought that Hughes was always most interested in 'the primitive flash—the sudden flare of rage or passion that takes us and makes us act or speak despite our rational will and that drives us to our death'—Myrrha, Tereus, Philomela, Semele, Pentheus, Midas. Supple considered that *Tales from Ovid* shared with *Birthday Letters* the personal, specific, and clear moments ('his words are nails, their meaning deep and fast'), embedded in 'life that is riddled with doom, gods, ghosts, Myth'. The violent vocabulary Supple used to characterize Hughes's diction and dramatic sense is striking. Critical reception of the production was favourable,

[33]  *LTH* 316–17.        [34]  Hopkins (2000: 522).
[35]  *TOa* (1999).        [36]  Supple (1999: 163).

especially of the precision and vigour of the language. However, there was some criticism of the literal translation of a poetic idea into a stage event in a way that sometimes involved illustration rather than drama, although the live music introduced another 'voice' that linked the words and the movement.[37]

Hughes was perhaps less well served by the other posthumous directions of his versions of the *Alcestis* (directed by Barrie Rutter for Northern Broadsides, 2000) and the *Oresteia* (directed for the National Theatre by Katie Mitchell, 1999).[38] The acting scripts did not grow through a process of interaction with director and actors as had been the case with his *Oedipus*. The text of the *Alcestis* in particular raises some crucial questions about Hughes's rewriting of Greek theatre poetry and about how he excavated the ancient theatre texts to lay bare the mythology in ways that allowed his own poetry to be an intertext. A feature of the *Alcestis* was Hughes's elaboration of the range of dramatic register in Euripides and his use of interpolation, both linguistically and theatrically. This attracted considerable criticism from classicists. Bernard Knox published an analysis which identified one hundred and fifty intrusive words that bore no relation to Euripides' text and pointed out that in the first eight pages of the Hughes only just over half of one page could be aligned with Euripides.[39] Hughes's text diverged in both tone and perspective from the narrative sequence in Euripides' text. Significantly, it was these variations that were in direct dialogue with other strands in his poetry, for example the staging of the Prometheus episode with its interpolation of the attacking vulture resonated with Hughes's poem exploring the figure of *Prometheus on His Crag*.[40] Comparison with the text of the translation *Alkestis* by the poet and classicist Anne Carson, who followed Euripides much more closely while nevertheless creating theatre poetry of her own, points up the areas in which

[37] For example, Michael Billington, *The Guardian*, 22 April 1999.

[38] For discussion of the staging of Hughes's *Oresteia* and especially the interventionist role of the director, see Walton (2005) and Hardwick (2005).

[39] He described the Hughes text as a 'desecration, the literary equivalent of spray-painting a moustache on the *Mona Lisa*', Knox (2000). For discussion, see Hardwick (2008: 354).

[40] The *Alcestis* performance I saw (2 October 2000, Lowry Centre, Salford) oscillated rather tantalizingly between the static, the burlesque, and the emotionally probing, rough at the edges in tone, style, and form.

Hughes in effect introduces new poems linked with the rest of his work into his version of the Euripides.[41] Paramount among these are the expansion in the opening sequence of Apollo's meditation on the events in the house, Prometheus' argument with God about man's freedom and pride, Heracles' repeated attempts to kill the Vulture that tortures Prometheus, and the underlying stress evident in Admetos' speech in which the physical environment of the house becomes not only a metaphor for his psychological suffering but its physical enactment.

Inevitably, critics and audiences related Hughes's choice of this play and his version of the text to his relationship with Sylvia Plath and to his collection of poems *Birthday Letters* (1998) and there were undoubtedly structural and allusive resonances.[42] Fiona Macintosh's Programme Notes approached the issue in a broader context and also situated Hughes's adaptation in literary and theatre traditions. These ranged from representations of women in Greek drama to Shakespeare's *A Winter's Tale* and the nineteenth-century Victorian burlesque version by Francis Talfourd as well as versions by James Thompson, Robert Browning, and T. S. Eliot.[43]

I have suggested that the traffic between drama and poetry in Hughes is not unidirectional. There is much that might be said about drama in his poetry, especially his variations on the dramatic monologue and dialogue, even hints at the *agon*-within-a poem.[44] The relationship between Hughes's drama and his poetry reflects the way in which he structures experience. It can be seen in action in the opening sequence of the poem '18 Rugby Street' in which he sets out an image of life as performance:

So there in Number Eighteen Rugby Street's
Victorian torpor and squalor I waited for you.
I think of that house as a stage-set—

---

[41]  Carson (2006).

[42]  See Brown in this volume on the relationship between Hughes's domestic history and that of Herakles.

[43]  For the history of Euripides' *Alcestis* on the British stage up to 1914, see Hall and Macintosh (2005).

[44]  Katherine Highman has written an extremely interesting MA thesis on this subject (University of Witwatersrand, as yet unpublished) and plans to explore it further. I benefited greatly from a conversation with her in 2005.

Four floors exposed to the auditorium.
On all four floors, in, out, the love-struggle
In all its acts and scenes. . . . .
A perpetual performance—names of the actors altered. But never the parts.
They told me:
'You should write a book about this house. It's possessed!
Whoever comes into it never gets properly out!
Whoever enters it enters a labyrinth—
A Knossos of coincidence! And now you're in it.'
The legends were amazing. I listened, amazed.[45]

Of course, this problematic sequence could be read from a number of perspectives—psychoanalysis, literary biography, formal, metaphorical. It also recalls Peter Sellars' image of classical culture as a house for reoccupation and alteration by subsequent writers and artists.[46]

In summary, analysis of the relationship between Hughes's poetry, his theatre poetry, and his versions of classical drama yields some points which are peculiar to Hughes's work and some with wider application. Taken together they suggest that models for mapping relationships between the ancient source texts and modern rewritings could be improved by some adjustments. In broad terms, it is clear that setting up polarities between poetry and drama is a misplaced activity; the two coalesce in two respects (at least). First, the ancient dramatists were writing theatre poetry and that makes formal, rhythmic, and poetic demands on translators and adaptors. However, the degree of intimacy that the modern writer has with the ancient text will focus these demands in different ways—for example, use of the formal convention of the choral ode may give the modern work a degree of closeness to the ante-text but does not necessarily result in the kind of lyric that differs in vocabulary and register from other parts of the work (as it does in the ancient text). Secondly, it is a matter of practice that poetry and drama interrelate in the work of all the writers I have discussed, not just because all the works were created as potential theatre pieces but because they constitute an integral part of the writers' works as a whole and are 'marked' as theirs.

[45] Hughes, *CP* 1055. The title of the poem possibly alludes to Robert Lowell's autobiographical poem '91 Revere Street'.
[46] Quoted in Lahr (1993).

Nevertheless, writers and rewriters depend on directors for success in staging. Where there is no symbiosis between the director's conceptual approach to the performance and the dynamics of the performance text, the polarity between poetry and drama tends to re-emerge. Hughes's work is a particularly interesting example of these processes of practice and of criticism. His theatrical dynamic is verbal and aural. In rhythm and idiom it is also sometimes startlingly physical. There are interesting tensions in his work between his tendency to pare down the verbal density and rhetoric of the Latin and his tendency to elaborate on or introduce interpolations into the Greek. There is, for instance, even less paring down in his later adaptations of Aeschylus and Euripides. Is this because it is later, less disciplined work? Was he less at home with Greek material than with Latin? Or did the late work have to bear the full impress of his poetic and personal history?[47] His work offers significant variations in types of linguistic inter-traffic (to borrow Weissbort's term for poetry translation).[48] I would suggest, however, that a better term for the relationship between his poetry and his theatre poetry and drama would be intra-traffic. This is not only because his aim in both was to produce new work; it is also because his knowledge of the source language was minimal in the case of Greek and basic in terms of Latin (O level to get into Cambridge University). So, to pick up the point made by MacNeice, Hughes's concern is always primarily with the English and how it sounds rather than with its philological relationship to the ancient language. He does not have the classicist's understanding and reverence for the ancient text that was present in Murray—and also perhaps in Harrison—and which determines what must be retained and explained in modern idiom. Hughes's sensibility is aural and his dialogue is with his own poetry rather than directly with the ancient source text. Nevertheless, engagement with the source text is important for the perspectives it offers on his reflections on his own poetry. This 'engagement-without-belonging' allows Hughes to contest, reject, and metamorphose what he finds in the ancient. His fascination with the classical material is

---

[47] Unfortunately an early variation on Euripides' *Bacchae* is lost, letter to Lucas Myers, possibly early 1958, *LTH* 116–19.

[48] Weissbort (2000: 89).

based on its stories and its mythologies rather than on its diction and the twists and turns in this intimacy (I might borrow the image from *Birthday Letters*' '18 Rugby Street' and call it a labyrinth) provide a kind of metanarrative on his own work.

This raises further questions about the extent to which comparisons between Hughes's writing and the source texts in themselves are still relevant. I suggest that they are useful in that they open the way to some different emphases in the study of contemporary translations of classical texts, especially those that are created by and for those who do not have a close (or indeed any) knowledge of the ancient languages. Much work remains to be done on the role of translation as *mediation*—that is, on the use of cribs, literal translations, and scholarly close translations by writers who are rewriting ancient drama and/or poetry, and on the effects these have on continuities and innovations in form, convention, diction, and register.[49] There are also potential modifications in approaches to the theory and practice of translation. For example, a useful conceptual tool has been Appiah's model of 'thick' translation.[50] This locates 'translation' (in the wide sense) in a rich cultural and linguistic context that 'aims to produce a new text that matters to one community the way the source text mattered to its community'. We can try to make judgements about how and why a text matters to a modern community and about how the ancient text mattered to its community. The difficult part comes in trying to judge the extent to which the modern 'mattering' corresponds with or is even infused with the ancient 'mattering'. In Hughes's case such comparisons are complicated by the fact that his versions of Greek drama are less 'public', less 'civic' in their implications than is the case with either Harrison's or Heaney's engagement with the ancient texts and contexts. Hughes digs beneath the civic and *polis* resonances of Greek tragedy to the underlying myths which the ancient dramatists themselves were reworking. It is significant that even in the staging of his version of Aeschylus' *Oresteia* the civic and political dimensions were largely grafted on by the director Katie Mitchell's performance concept.[51]

---

[49] A study of the indirect influence of Richard Jebb's translations on the poetry and staging of Greek tragedy would be a good starting point.

[50] Appiah (1993).

[51] For discussion, see Hardwick (2005) and Walton (2005).

Hughes rejected the aim of producing a 'parallel equivalent' of some original's unique verbal texture. That was perhaps why he liked to use close translations by scholars who were not poets.[52] This was not just a rejection of competition. It was part of Hughes's desire to engage with the primitive. This emphasis has sometimes been referred to as his 'anthropological classicism'. If the mediating translation does not have a distinctive poetic dimension to 'get in the way' then the modern poet can more easily engage with the bare bones of the myth.[53] So the 'equivalence' between ancient and modern is defined by taking possession of the myth. Such possession may turn out to be contested, even confrontational, rather than governed by recognition of the authority of the ancient or by a desire for emulation or imitation. Investigating this dimension of Hughes's work requires approaches and methods different from those which assume that a modern poet's relationship with classical material is necessarily shaped by acknowledgement of the authority and aesthetic value of the texts themselves. It also demands analysis of contemporary resonances that are personal rather than political.

Hughes's own reflections on translation are revealing. In an editorial in *Modern Poetry in Translation* (No. 3, Spring 1967) he suggested that there were only two justifications for anything other than the most literal translation. The first was where the impact of the original poetry was such that even a non-poet became poetic in translating it and the second was 'where the translator already is an interesting and original poet in his own right, and in his "versions" we are glad to get more of him, extensions and explorations of his possibilities, as in the extraordinary Heine and Rilke translations in Lowell's *Imitations*'.[54] Hughes's versions were made for himself as a poet.

These distinctive features of Hughes's relationship with the ancient drama texts could contribute to a multifaceted analytic model that might (for example) compare the texts produced by ancient author, classical translation scholar, modern poet/dramatist working from the source language, and modern poet/dramatist not working directly from the source language. This could not only enrich awareness

---

[52] Weissbort and Eysteinsson (2006: 522).

[53] For discussion of Hughes's 'anthropological classicism' see Talbot (2006) and Zajko in this volume.

[54] *ST* 200–1.

of what happens in the multiple activities that constitute translation, it would also open the way to exploring changes in cultural assumptions about the ancient world that are increasingly being shaped by types of contact with its literature and drama that are mediated rather than direct.[55]

[55] This discussion has grown from a work-in-progress paper first presented at the conference 'Ted Hughes and the Classics' held at the University of Edinburgh in 2005. I am extremely grateful to the organizer, Roger Rees, and to the participants for their discussion, criticism, and helpful suggestions.

# 4

## Eliot's Seneca, Ted Hughes's *Oedipus*

### *John Talbot*

Ted Hughes set about translating *Oedipus*, he claims, by returning 'to the original Seneca, eking out my Latin with a Victorian crib', but did he really lay eyes on the Latin?[1] He was no Latinist. 'I had set myself against Latin', he claimed of his schoolboy self, and had scraped by with just enough Latin to qualify for admission to Cambridge.[2] There is no evidence that Seneca's Latin played a direct role in shaping the English of his translation. The point of this chapter is to ask whether it makes sense to draw a line from Hughes's *Oedipus* to a more immediate model, T. S. Eliot, who had not only been writing about Seneca, but also writing poems in Senecan modes which Hughes himself had emulated.

It is difficult to see how any crib, Victorian or otherwise, of Seneca's Latin lies behind Hughes's *Oedipus*. Here is a passage from the original: a moment of high climax, when Oedipus discovers he is his own wife's son. Seneca's Latin packs a congested earful: gloomy accumulation of 'u's, pounding alliteration, hissing 's's:

> dehisce, tellus, tuque, tenebrarum potens,
> in Tartara ima, rector umbrarum, rape
> retro reversas generis ac stirpis vices![3]
>
> (868–70)

Split open, Earth! And you who govern the darkness ruler of the shades, carry off to the depths of Tartarus this inversion of the roles of stock and offspring.

---

[1] *O* 7.    [2] Hughes, *WP*, 6; see Sagar above.
[3] The text of Seneca's *Oedipus* quoted throughout this chapter is that of Fitch (2004).

For which Hughes gives:

>  birth   birthbed   blood   take this   open
>  the earth bury it   bottom of darkness
>  under everything   I am not fit for light[4]

One might think for a moment that Hughes had been listening to
the Latin: 'birth birthbed blood' seems to answer aurally (not seman-
tically) to *tellus, tuque, tenebrarum potens.* But that must have been
a fluke, because immediately thereafter any sense of formal or aural
correspondence to Seneca's Latin vanishes. In fact what one notices,
beyond the first three words, is how far Hughes's own, comparatively
unflamboyant, English has descended from the rhetorical pyrotech-
nics of the Latin. Hughes's translation corresponds less to any
Latin than to English, the English of David Anthony Turner, who
had prepared a prose translation of *Oedipus* for Peter Brook's 1968
National Theatre production.[5] Turner's version of the passage quoted
above, and the next few lines, runs like this:

Earth! Gape open! And you, emperor of darkness, snatch this monstrous soiler
of birth and bed down to the farthest part of Tartarus! Countrymen, together
now. Pile stones on my head—bury me! Take weapons—butcher me![6]

'Take weapons' is the English of no recognizable place or time: such
feeble prose would not do for Brook who, three weeks before re-
hearsals were set to start, announced his dissatisfaction with Turner's
translation and brought in Ted Hughes to create a new version of the
script. Hughes's phrase 'birth birthbed blood' owes more to the
English of his sacked predecessor ('soiler of birth and bed') than to
Seneca.

Therein lies a point of principle: effective criticism of Hughes's
classical translations depends as much on attention to his use of
mediating English sources as of the ostensible classical sources themselves.[7] Among the most conspicuous examples in Hughes's *Oedipus*

---

[4] *O* 47.
[5] See Sagar above. Brook (1998: 134–7) himself gives an account of the production.
[6] Quoted in Sharrock (2000: 532).
[7] For an elaboration on this principle see Talbot (2006). Gervais (2002) finds in
Hughes's translations of Aeschylus possible sources in Blake, Eliot, and Hughes
himself.

is Jocasta's long speech in Act I.[8] There Hughes is rendering not
the Latin—there is no Latin to render, for in Seneca's play Jocasta
makes no such speech—but rather the tone and substance of earlier
poems by himself. Hughes's interpolation finds Jocasta delivering an
account of the horror it was to give birth to her doomed son:

> blood from the roots of my hair blood from before
>     any time began
> it flowed into the knot of his bowels, into the knot of his
>     muscles
> the knot of his brain
> my womb tied everything together every corner of the
>     earth and heavens
> and every trickle of the dead past
> twisted it all into shape inside me[9]

The atmosphere of horror and gore feels Senecan, but takes its
language and imagery from poems like 'The Brother's Dream',
which Hughes had broadcast on the BBC Third Programme just
three years earlier. In that poem the speaker, fending off a bear attack
with a fatal knife, describes his escape in terms of a horrific and
bloody birth:

> But I rip upward till the heart-muscle
> Kicks at the dagger haft.
> And I have opened a river.
> And the bear slides from me like a robe
> I have cut the cords of.[10]

'Cut the cords' continues the imagery of parturition which culmin-
ates in 'I'm as bloody as a Caesarian babe—not my blood.' The
speaker in Hughes's poem rouses his ursine attacker from a cave;
Jocasta says of Oedipus, 'I knew the future was waiting for him like a
greedy | god a maneater in a cave'. And that thematic reference goes
along with specific verbal reminiscence: of the moment of giving
birth, Jocasta wonders: 'what a doorway was I what a cavemouth.'
This picks up 'But the bear is filling the cave-mouth' from the
earlier poem. It makes sense that in imagining Jocasta's travail—a
blood-soaked struggle to bring forth a monster—Hughes should

---

[8] *O* 16–18.      [9] *O* 17.      [10] *CP* 196.

have drawn on 'The Brother's Dream', a blood-soaked struggle with a maneater, described in terms of childbirth. The point is that Hughes was just as likely to turn to modern literature—including his own poems—as to Latin when he translated from the classics.[11]

That principle helps to explain the remarkable style Hughes developed for his *Oedipus,* with its strings of unpunctuated, uncapitalized phrases, neither exactly prose or verse, and utterly unlike any previous translation of Seneca into English.[12] (It is a style to which Hughes, later, would occasionally return, as in his 1970 'Crow's Vanity'.) The following portion of Oedipus' first speech is a characteristic sample:

> fear that came after me it followed me the
> fear the words of the oracle some day I would
> kill my father I would kill him and worse
> that other worse what could be worse the
> oracle pronounced it the words stick it is not
> possible but the god predicted the god
> threatened me with my father's bedchamber the god predicted
> it[13]

The style does not obviously seek to answer to the elaborate rhetorical and formal characteristics of Seneca's Latin, least of all the dazzling polymetrics of two of the choral odes, polymetrics which stand out all the more for occurring only in *Oedipus* and one other Senecan play, the *Agamemnon.* If you take from Seneca his rhetoric and his style, what do you leave him? Well, Hughes wrote, what's left is what most interested him: 'the basic, poetic, mythical substance of the fable . . . whatever may have happened to the rhetoric, this part has not dated at all'.[14] Hughes is prepared to let the elaborateness of Seneca's rhetoric and metre drop as dated, and as an obstacle to getting at the mythical core of the fable. All this by way of saying that if Hughes really did have the Latin before him as he worked, he

---

[11] See Hardwick in this volume for other examples.

[12] For a critical survey of English translations, 1591–1995, see Sharrock (2000: 531–2); for excerpts of translations, 1557–1995, with critical commentary, see Share (1998).

[13] *O* 13.       [14] *O* 8.

either could not perceive in it, or if he could, chose not to try to reproduce, its outstanding stylistic features. The style he found for his translation—a modern idiom far distant from Turner's conventional prose or the verse of any previous translation—is not the result of going back to the original Latin and eking it out with a Victorian crib.

Where would a poet like Hughes turn for models for a contemporary poetic idiom for Seneca? To an older poet, a great poet, who had helped to shape Hughes's English verse, and who had already engaged with Seneca more thoroughly than any major poet of the twentieth century.[15] T. S. Eliot's Senecan activities were double: first, in a pair of 1927 essays, 'Seneca in Elizabethan Translation' and 'Shakespeare and the Stoicism of Seneca', he had made a case for putting Seneca's plays back on the critical map, if only as a means of getting some better purchase on Elizabethan drama.[16] Second, Seneca had become an oblique but significant presence in some of Eliot's own poems, and in them he broke ground in finding a modern idiom for the dark complexities of the Roman dramatist, an idiom which, in turn, assisted Hughes in finding a style for his own *Oedipus*.

There is, for instance, Eliot's poem 'Marina', whose Senecan connection Eliot had explicitly signalled by assigning it an epigraph from *Hurcules Furens*. 'Marina' is an important poem to Hughes, who assimilated something of its style and substance into one of his own most famous poems. The opening lines of 'Marina':

> Those who sharpen the tooth of the dog, meaning
> Death
> Those who glitter with the glory of the humming-bird, meaning
> Death
> Those who sit in the sty of contentment, meaning
> Death
> Those who suffer ecstasy of the animals, meaning
> Death[17]

---

[15] For Hughes's own testimony of his admiration for, and emulation of, Eliot, whom he considered the greatest poet of his times, see *DG*.

[16] Eliot (1960: 51–88, 107–20). Relevant recent treatments include Braden (1985) and Miola (1992).

[17] Eliot (1963: 105).

Eliot's voice speaks unmistakably, if less loftily, through Hughes:

> Who owns these scrawny little feet? *Death.*
> Who owns this bristly scorched-looking face? *Death.*
> Who owns these still-working lungs? *Death.*[18]

and so on. 'Examination at the Womb-Door' was composed, like Hughes's *Oedipus*, in the late Sixties and saw print in 1970, a year after the publication of the play. Many of the poems from the same period demonstrate a move away from the tighter, more conventional formal structures of Hughes's first two books, *The Hawk in the Rain* and *Lupercal*, evolving a free-verse style whose characteristics include loose punctuation, incantory anaphora (as in 'Crow's Undersong'):[19] and, as in 'Examination at the Womb-Door,' antiphonal responsion. Given the connection of 'Marina' both to Seneca and to Hughes's poems of the late Sixties, it is significant that so many of the Crow poems are themselves connected to Seneca. Some Senecan parallels are diffuse, among them the atmosphere of hyperbolic grotesquerie and macabre. But there are more concrete instances, as when 'Crow-ego' invokes the Seneca of *Hercules Furens:* 'Grappling with Hercules' two puff-adders | He strangled in error Dejanira'.[20] Perhaps the most prominent point of connection between the Crow poems and Seneca is 'Song for a Phallus', a ribald re-imagining of the Oedipus myth in ballad metre and low, colloquial diction. It pointedly follows not Sophocles' play but Seneca's, in featuring an (appalling) appearance of the ghost of Laius. But a still stronger link to Seneca is that 'Song for a Phallus' was originally written as a comic coda—a nod in the direction of the traditional Greek satyr play—to the Peter Brook production of Seneca's *Oedipus*. In other words, Seneca, Eliot's 'Marina', Hughes's translation of *Oedipus* and the original poems he was composing around the same time are all bound together.

Given its Senecan associations, 'Marina' might have opened up a path in Hughes's mind as he considered how to translate *Oedipus*. 'Marina' is like *Oedipus* too, in that it dramatizes a recognition scene: the one between Shakespeare's Pericles and his long-lost daughter. The epigraph brings in a second recognition. It, again, is from

---

[18] 'Examination at the Womb-door', *CP* 218.
[19] *CP* 237.    [20] *CP* 240.

Seneca: the moment when Hercules awakens, bewildered, to discover he has slain his wife and children: *quis hic locus, quae regio, quae mundi plaga*, 'What place is this, what region, what shore of the world?' Through the epigraph Eliot arranges that his readers should feel the ghost of Seneca behind the Shakespeare—a 'criss-cross', he wrote in a 1930 letter to a friend, 'between Pericles' happy recognition scene, and the atrocious one of Hercules'.[21] The juxtaposition of Shakespeare and Seneca is all the more arresting because *Pericles*, like *Oedipus*, involves an incestuous parent, Antiochus, a fact which is recalled (a little disconcertingly) even in the words of Pericles to his daughter at their moment of reunion: 'O come thou hither | Thou that begett'st him that did beget thee' (5.1.183–4).[22] So there are three strands running through 'Marina' that all come together in *Oedipus*: (1) the epigraph from Seneca, (2) the recognition scene of parent and child, and (3) the connection between that recognition and incest. That is to say, trying to feel his way into a suitable style for a modern version of Seneca's *Oedipus*, in 1968 Hughes could hardly have done better than to take his cue from 'Marina', a modern poem in which so many of the key elements of the Seneca's tragedy had already been brought together.

The impact on Hughes's translation of these three strands in 'Marina' can be registered in part by the words Hughes puts into Jocasta's mouth when she is struck by the truth about Oedipus. Seneca has her express the recognition in terms of revulsion:

> quid te vocem?
> natumne? dubitas? natus es: natum pudet.
> invite loquere nate. quo avertis caput
> vacuosque vultus?
>
> (1009–12)

What shall I call you? Son? You object? You *are* my son: it is my son that feels shame. Speak, my reluctant son. Why turn away your head and empty eyes?

But Hughes's treatment of the scene is far closer to Eliot, and through Eliot Shakespeare, in that it brings in a note of tenderness:

---

[21] Quoted by Timmerman (1994: 141). Eliot repeated the idea in a letter attached to the draft of 'Marina' that he donated to the Bodleian Library: 'I intend it as a criss-cross between Pericles finding alive, and Hercules finding dead—the two extremes of the recognition scene—but I thought that if I labeled the quotation it might lead readers astray rather than direct them.' Quoted in Moody (1979: 363).

[22] The text is that of Gossett (2004).

> you are my son I lost you
> you're alive I've found you[23]

That sense of recovery—'I lost you', 'I've found you'—is hardly present in Seneca's Jocasta. It belongs instead to Eliot's 'Marina', by way of Shakespeare's Pericles, who, in his recognition scene, experiences not recognition only but also restoration:

> O Helicanus, strike me, honoured sir,
> Give me a gash, put me to present pain,
> Lest this great sea of joys rushing upon me
> O'er bear the shores of my mortality
> O Helicanus, strike me, honoured sir,
> And drown me with their sweetness.
> [*to Marina*]        O, come hither,
> Thou that begget'st him that thee did beget
> Thou that wast born at sea, buried at Tarsus,
> And found at sea again!—O Helicanus,
> Down on thy knees, thanks the holy gods as loud
> As thunder threatens us, this is Marina!
>
> (5.1.180–8)

Given these affinities of theme and tone, and given that Hughes at the same time was composing original poems that borrowed from its movement and cadences, is it possible to see 'Marina' as a model for the style in which he cast his *Oedipus?* There is the matter of punctuation. Most of 'Marina' is written in sentences of conventional punctuation. But the opening and closing 'stanzas' appear on the page as strings of unpunctuated phrases, as in these lines:

> What seas what shores what grey rocks and what island
> What water lapping the bow[24]

Both here and in Hughes's *Oedipus,* the ruminative phrases float ('glide' was Leavis's term), an effect which depends in part on being able to see the absence of punctuation, the indentations, the spacing, and, in the case of Hughes, the lower-case orthography.[25] How could an actor voice the orthographic eccentricities? *Readers* of Hughes's play, have access to a dimension of meaning unavailable to theatre audiences:

---

[23] *O* 53.    [24] Eliot (1963: 105).
[25] Quoted in Southam (1978: 225). For an account of the critical implications of the punctuation of 'Marina', see Ward (1973: 169–71). Donoghue (2000: 164–80) attends to punctuation obliquely but sensitively.

they can see on the page the orthographical similarities to a poem like 'Marina'. It mattered to man who put 'The Thought Fox' on paper how a writer might 'set neat prints' onto the blank page, what shape a reader might see in the words once 'the page is printed'.[26]

On the rhetorical level, the lines in 'Marina' embody a breathless asyndeton (indeed the lack of punctuation heightens the breathlessness). These very features are characteristic of Hughes's *Oedipus*, as becomes clear when Eliot's lines are set beside them, such as those of Creon from Act III:

> What seas what shores what grey rocks and what island
> What water lapping the bow

> I saw every disease I knew their faces I heard them
> and knew their voices[27]

Hughes's lines *look* like Eliot's on the page, and *move* like Eliot's rhetorically.

Even more tellingly, another feature of the style of 'Marina' can securely be linked to Seneca, precisely because Eliot himself had drawn the connection. His essay 'Shakespeare and Elizabethan Translation' succeeds in part because of his attention to the subtleties of Seneca's style. Among the Roman playwright's favourite rhetorical tricks, Eliot writes, was to get 'a kind of double pattern by breaking up lines into minimum antiphonal units', and by way of illustration cites this highly antiphonal exchange between an intransigent Medea and her pleading nurse:

> rex est timendus.
> > > > rex meus fuerat pater.
> > non metuis arma?
> > > > sint licet terra edita.
> > moriere.
> > > cupio.
> > > > profuge.
> > > > > praenituit fugae.
> > Medea,
> > > fiam.
> > > > mater es.
> > > > > cui sim vides.
> > > > > > (*Medea*, 168ff.)[28]

---

[26] *CP* 21.     [27] *O* 34.

[28] Eliot (1960: 73). Seneca's lines are given here as Eliot prints them; the translation is my own.

NURSE:   The king is to be feared.
MEDEA:   My father was a king.
NURSE:   Are you not afraid of his weapons?
MEDEA:   Not even if they had sprung up out of the earth.
NURSE:   Then you'll die.
MEDEA:   That's what I want.
NURSE:   Escape. MEDEA I regret escaping.
NURSE:   Medea . . .
MEDEA:   . . . is who I'll be.
NURSE:   But you're somebody's mother.
MEDEA:   You see by whom.

Whereupon Eliot exhibits a passage of Marlowe to demonstrate how English poets imitated such crisp effects:

A man like Marlowe, or even men with less scholarship and less genius for the use of words than he, could hardly have failed to learn something from this. At any rate, I believe that the study of Seneca had its part in the formation of verse like the following:

> —*Wrong not her birth, she is of royal blood.*
> —*To save her life, I'll say she is not so.*
> —*Her life is safest only in her birth.*
> —*And only in that safety died her brothers.*

It is only a step (and a few lines further) to the pun:

> *Cousins, indeed; and by their uncle cozen'd.*[29]

A man like Eliot could hardly have failed to learn something from this. For the antiphonal quality he finds so pronounced in Seneca and his English imitators is among the outstanding features of the style of 'Marina':

> What is this face, less clear and clearer
> The pulse in the arm, less strong and stronger—[30]

This is fitting, given the poem's links to Seneca directly (through the epigraph from *Hercules Furens*) and obliquely (through Shakespeare's *Pericles*). Against Eliot's lines set these of Tiresias in Act II of Hughes's *Oedipus*:

---

[29] Eliot (1960: 73).     [30] Eliot (1963: 105).

> voices are tearing me          voices but not words
> nothing is steady    whirling   impossible to hold
> this is something terrible    something hidden[31]

The antiphonal responsions, reaching out to each other over a strong caesura, lead back to Eliot, through the Elizabethan dramatists, and back finally to Seneca himself. Or, to put it in a way that may have pleased Hughes, who at Cambridge pointedly defected from English to Anthropology and Archaeology: Hughes's *Oedipus* is the topmost layer of an archaeological site whose lower strata include, in descending order, Eliot, Shakespeare, and Seneca.

There is another poem of Eliot's into which Senecan energies gather, and which might have offered Hughes some clues as to how to proceed with a translation of Seneca. The poem—(but does it belong where it finally resides, among the *Collected Poems*, or would it be more at home among the plays?)—the poem *or* play is 'Sweeney Agonistes'. Neither Eliot's own advertisement of the piece as 'Aristophanic melodrama', nor his epigraphs from Aeschylus and St John of the Cross, nor again even Eliot's sources in the music hall and jazz, should blind us to its Senecan connections. Ezra Pound was not blinded; in 1934 he insisted that 'the criticism of Seneca in Mr. Eliot's *Agon* is infinitely more alive, more vigorous than in his essay on Seneca'.[32]

Pound does not elaborate, but a number of Senecan qualities Eliot identified in 'Seneca in Elizabethan Translation' can be found vividly embodied in 'Sweeney Agonistes'. For instance: 'The characters of Seneca's plays have no subtlety', Eliot writes;[33] compare the deliberate crudity of his characterizations in 'Sweeney'. Seneca 'is not diffuse; he is capable of great concision; there is even a monotony of forcefulness';[34] one thinks of the relentless clipped compression of the dialogue in 'Sweeney'. A third observation of Eliot's needs to be treated delicately, given what we know or think we know about Eliot's prejudices. 'The characters in a play of Seneca behave . . . like members of a minstrel troupe sitting in a semicircle, rising in turn to do his "number", or varying their recitations by a song or a little back-chat.'[35] If that is his view of a Senecan play, then 'Sweeney Agonistes' is more Senecan than Seneca: the 'Fragment from an Agon' in

---

[31] *O* 27.    [32] Pound (1954: 75).    [33] Eliot (1960: 56).
[34] Eliot (1960: 59).    [35] Eliot (1960: 54).

particular presents pairs of characters taking turns at centre stage, often performing a song together; the link to a minstrel show is made explicit by a stage direction: 'Swarts as Tambo. Snow as Bones.' The piece is dominated by rapid-fire backchat banter. Most criticism of 'Sweeney' proceeds from the assumption that its language, rhythms, and tone are based in the twentieth-century music hall. A critic might then feel hard-pressed to draw a line between that type of popular culture and so remote a phenomenon as Senecan drama, had not Eliot himself, in the passage I have just quoted, bridged that gap himself.

Of the Senecan stylistic features identified by Eliot in his essay, two in particular stand out in 'Sweeney Agonistes'. The first is his idiosyncratic handling of stichomythia. Eliot calls it 'a trick of Seneca of repeating one word of a phrase in the next phrase, especially in stichomythia, where the sentence of one speaker is caught up and twisted by the next'. Whereupon Eliot produces an example from *Hurcules Furens* (the interlocutors are Lycus and Megara):

> sceptrone nostro famulus est potior tibi?
> quot iste famulus tradidit reges neci.
> cur ergo regi servit et patitur iugum?[36]

LYCUS:      Does a slave matter more to you than my royal sceptre?
MEGARA:   How many kings has that slave delivered to death!
LYCUS:      Then why does he serve a king and submit to the yoke?

The second line picks up *famulus* from the first, and the third line *rex* (varying the case) from the second. In the instance of this figure, as so often with others, the Elizabethan dramatists absorbed the Senecan manner. Shakespeare's masterful assimilation of the trope shines through this teasing exchange between the protagonists of *Anthony and Cleopatra*:

CLEOPATRA:   If it be love indeed, tell me how much.
ANTONY:       There's beggary in love that can be reckoned.
CLEOPATRA:   I'll set a bourn how far to be beloved.
ANTONY:       Then thou must needs find out new heaven, new earth.

---

[36] Seneca's lines are quoted here as Eliot (1960: 73) prints them.

*Enter a* Messenger.
MESSENGER:   News, my good lord, from Rome.[37]

(14–18)

The lovers' stichomythic rally that rings the changes on 'love', is outdone by Shakespeare's introduction of the messenger who picks up Antony's two instances of the word 'new' to twist it, without skipping a beat, into 'news'.

Eliot himself not only picks up this Senecan technique in 'Sweeney Agonistes', but accentuates it, exaggerates it:

DUSTY:     Yes I know you've a touch with the cards
           What comes next?
DORIS:                              What comes next. It's the six.[38]
                         * * * * *

SWEENEY:   Birth, copulation, and death.
           That's all, that's all, that's all, that's all.
           Birth, copulation and death.
DORIS:     I'd be bored.
SWEENEY:                    You'd be bored.
DORIS:     I'd be bored.
SWEENEY:                    You'd be bored.[39]
                         * * * * *

SWARTS:    What did he do?
           All that time, what did he do?
SWEENEY:   What did he do! What did he do?
           That don't apply.
           Talk to live men about what they do.
           He used to come and see me sometimes.
           I'd give him a drink and cheer him up.
DORIS:     Cheer him up?
DUSTY:     Cheer him up?[40]

And so on: even a casual reader will notice a half-dozen other instances of that Senecan form of stichomythia.

---

[37] The text is that of Wilders (1995).      [38] Eliot (1963: 114).
[39] Eliot (1963: 119).        [40] Eliot (1963: 122).

A similar rhetorical pattern occurs in Hughes's *Oedipus*. The natural explanation might be that this is to be expected, since Hughes is translating Seneca. But the Latin does not bear this expectation out. In translating stichomythic passages, Hughes regularly *interpolates* the rhetorical trick that Eliot noticed in Seneca: that is, he uses it even where Seneca does not. There is a rich illustration in the opening lines of Act III, where Oedipus is trying to squeeze the truth out of reluctant Creon:

OEDIPUS:    when Thebes is down this royal house your own house
            is down   **I command you to speak**
CREON:      **you command me to speak**   you will pray you were
            deaf
OEDIPUS:    ignorance cures nothing   this whole nation is sick
            Speak   you can **cure** it
CREON:      the **cure** can be so drastic   men prefer sickness
OEDIPUS:    when torture has crushed you   you will fear the
            anger of the **crown**   when will you speak
CREON:      **crowns** have been crushed by the words of the tortured[41]

In these three successive exchanges, Creon picks up a word or phrase of his interlocutor's and twists it to his own purpose. But a look at the corresponding passage from Seneca's text shows that only one of these instances is warranted by the Latin:

OEDIPUS:    si te ruentes non satis Thebae movent,
            at sceptra moveant lapsa cognatae domus.
CREON:      nescisse cupies nosse quae nimium expetes.
OEDIPUS:    iners malorum remedium ignorantia est.
            itane et salutis publicae indicium obrues?
CREON:      ubi turpis est medicina, sanari piget.
OEDIPUS:    audita fare, vel malo domitus gravi
            quid arma possint **regis** irati scies.
CREON:      odere **reges** dicta quae dici iubent.          (3.512–20)

OEDIPUS:    If the fall of Thebes is not enough to move you, at least
            be moved
            by the sinking sceptre of a kindred house.

[41] *O* 32.

CREON:    You'll wish you did not know what you too much seek to find out.

OEDIPUS:    Ignorance is a feeble remedy for dealing with calamities. Will you even conceal the disclosure of the deliverance of the public welfare?

CREON:    When the medicine is vile, it is painful to be healed.

OEDIPUS:    Tell me what you've heard, or you will discover what the power of an angered king can do, when you've been broken by the weight of punishment.

CREON:    Kings hate the words they force others to speak.

Seneca plays *regi* against *reges* in the last two lines, yes; but in the two previous exchanges, the trope does not occur at all. And yet it's there in all three exchanges of Hughes. The effect is of Hughes outdoing Seneca at his own game. That Senecan stylistic tic which Eliot singled out so pointedly in his essay, and which he himself used so prominently in 'Sweeney Agonistes' was precisely the feature that Hughes brought to his translation more often than it existed in the play he was translating. This offers grounds for thinking that Hughes had his eyes on Eliot—the essay or the play or both—at least as much as he had on the Latin.

There is another feature of Hughes's style that points in the direction of 'Sweeney Agonistes'. It may be best illustrated in the exuberant choral ode at the end of the second act. In Seneca, the ode (403–508) is an elaborate paean to Bacchus, replete with highly literary references, both straightforward and recondite. Hughes's repudiation of this ode is among his most striking points of divergence from the Latin. In its place there is something entirely different, and entirely unique to Hughes: a raucous apotropaic chant ('DANCE DEATH INTO ITS HOLE') to a vaguely defined, chthonic version of the god. What may be less obvious is the debt Hughes's ode owes to Eliot in the matter of style and tone. This comes clear when the styles of the three authors are contrasted.

Seneca's ode to Bacchus is a piece of metrical virtuosity, one of those rare (for him) polymetric odes, a compound of one elaborate metre after another:

> effusam redimite comam nutante corymbo,
> mollia Nysaeis armatus bracchia thyrsis,
> lucidum caeli decus, huc ades

votis, quae tibi nobiles
Thebae, Bacche, tuae
palmis supplicibus ferunt.
huc adverte favens virgineum caput,
vultu sidereo discute nubilia
    et tristes Erebi minas
    avidumque fatum.

(403–11)

You whose flowering hair is wreathed in nodding ivy,
and who bear the thyrsus of Nyssa as a weapon in your
    soft hands,
        shining glory of heaven, attend
            the prayers that your famous city
            of Thebes offers you, Bacchus,
        with palms lifted in supplication.
Turn your girlish face in favour;
with your star-bright countenance dispel the clouds,
    the grim threats of Erebus,
        and greedy fate.

(tr. Fitch)

There are half a dozen metrical shifts in these ten lines, and many
more to come in those that follow. It would take a Swinburne to
render the various metres in English and sustain them through their
hundred-plus lines. Hughes might have adopted a more modest
approach, suggesting the metrical veering by indenting and varying
the length of lines, in the manner of Wordsworth's 'Intimations Ode'
or Hopkins' 'Deutschland'. Instead he pointedly avoids the extreme
metrical refinement of the Latin in favour of all-out primitivism. The
opening of Hughes's 'Chorus to Bacchus':

OOO-AI-EE . . . KA
CHANT   3 times
REPLY   3 times
DANCE DEATH INTO ITS HOLE
DANCE DEATH INTO ITS HOLE
INTO ITS HOLE
ITS HOLE
ITS HOLE

ITS HOLE

HOLE
LET IT CLIMB
LET IT CLIMB UP
LET IT CLIMB UP
LET IT CLIMB
LET IT LIVE
OPEN THE GATE
OPEN THE GATE
LET IT LIVE
TEAR THE BLOOD
OPEN ITS MOUTH
LET IT CRY[42]

The chanting makes anthropological sense; Hughes writes in his introduction to the play that he had sought to 'release whatever inner poetry this story, in its plainest, bluntest form, still has, and to unearth . . . the ritual possibilities within it.'[43] But Eliot had already covered very similar stylistic ground in the choruses of 'Sweeney Agonistes'. The way that 'Dance death into its hole' gradually narrows to simply 'hole' has its antecedent in passages like this one from 'Sweeney', part of a song 'BY KLIPSTEIN AND KRUMPACKER SNOW AND SWARTS':

For it won't be minutes but hours
For it won't be hours but years
And the morning
And the evening
And noontime
And night
Morning
Evening
Noontime
Night[44]

In Eliot's final chorus, the tone swerves from music-hall drollery to something more primitively percussive:

And perhaps you're alive
And perhaps you're dead
Hoo ha ha

---

[42] *O* 30.        [43] *O* 7–8.        [44] Eliot (1963: 121).

Hoo ha ha
HOO
HOO
HOO
KNOCK KNOCK KNOCK
KNOCK KNOCK KNOCK
KNOCK
KNOCK
KNOCK[45]

That passage, though it would not see print until 1926, was in draft by 1923. That was the year Eliot published his essay 'The Beating of a Drum', in which he draws on the views of the Cambridge School of anthropology to lament the suppression of the elements of primitive ritual—above all of rhythm—in modern drama. 'The drama', he wrote,

was originally ritual; and ritual, consisting of a set of repeated movements, is essentially a dance. . . . It is. . . . possible to assert that primitive man acted in a certain way and then found reason for it. An unoccupied person, finding a drum, may be seized with a desire to beat it. . . . The next generation or the next civilization will find a more plausible reason for beating a drum. . . . We still have similar reasons, but we have lost the drum.[46]

Set this alongside the journal entry of the poet's friend Arnold Bennett, 10 September 1924, to whom Eliot had shown some drafts of 'Sweeney Agonistes': 'He had definitely given up that form of writing [lyric poetry?] and was now centered on dramatic writing. He wanted to write a drama of modern life . . . in a rhythmic prose perhaps with certain things in it accentuated by drum-beats.'[47] Later, in 1933, Eliot instructed Hallie Flanagan, about to perform the fragments at Vassar College, that he 'had intended the whole play to be accompanied by light drum taps to accentuate the beats (esp. the chorus)'.[48]

In Hughes, the elaborate choral odes of Seneca are replaced by pounding chants, meant, like Eliot's, to be anthropologically suggestive. The stylistic parallels, though, extend beyond the drumlike rhythms of the chorus to—once again—orthography. Eliot's use of capitals, the deployment of words on the page, show up again at the end of Hughes's ode:

[45] Eliot (1963: 124).    [46] Eliot (1923: 12).
[47] Flower (1933: 52).    [48] Flanagan (1943: 82).

YOU YOU YOU YOU
YOU YOU YOU YOU
UNDER BLOOD
UNDER THE EARTH
YOU[49]

Seneca's play is haunted by a ghost: Oedipus cannot solve the problem of the Theban plague without first summoning the ghost of his father Laius. Literature, sometimes, is a house that wants to be haunted, and it made sense for Ted Hughes, who had only a few weeks to solve the problem of Peter Brooks's foundering production of *Oedipus*, to summon the ghost of Eliot as he tried to find a suitable modern style. Eliot had done the groundbreaking work—critical in his essays, practical in 'Marina' and 'Sweeney Agonistes'—of bringing Senecan drama into relation with English literature (the Elizabethan dramatists in general, Shakespeare in particular) and with the twentieth century. It was for Hughes to perceive in Eliot's Senecan fragments the hints that could lead him to take the next step: a full Senecan play, a playable Seneca, with its own contemporary and handsomely answerable style.

<hr />

[49]  *O* 31.

# 5

## Living myths

*Janne Stigen Drangsholt*

One of the first things to strike a reader of Ted Hughes is that he is a mythic poet. This is particularly true of the poetic sequences he wrote in the late Sixties and Seventies, where myths such as Hercules, Oedipus, the Grail legend, and Genesis underpin the poetic discourse. Even though there are elements pointing in the same direction in *Hawk in the Rain* (1957) and *Lupercal* (1960), *Wodwo* (1967) marks a clear change in Hughes's oeuvre. *Wodwo* is moulded in a universe where 'Nothing lets up or develops', where the cycles of nature are perceived as purposeless, isolated re-enactments.[1] Like in Nietzsche's doctrine of the Eternal Return, the lack of a universal or transcendent goal deprives everything of meaning. Hence, there is no connection between self and other, whether this is envisioned as a relationship between various levels of being, or between the human being and God. The segregated subject is hopelessly and unfailingly 'ignorant of this other, this harebell', holding on to a falsified veil of sameness.[2]

In *Wodwo* this tragic condition could be seen to echo Hughes's belief that he had received a spiritual call while writing the sequence. In letters to Janos Csokits, Hughes claimed that he had experienced a 'demand from behind—from a subjective world', which he had failed to respond to.[3] In a letter to Ben Sonnenberg, Hughes describes the last part of *Wodwo* as 'belonging to a limbo between death and birth,

---

[1] *CP* 179.  [2] *CP* 147.
[3] Emory Mss 895, 1, 8.

seven years on hands and knees', which was the price he had to pay
for his deferral of the call.[4] This experience is poeticized as a series of
'crisis-poems', where the isolated subject experiences a numbing
terror or angst. The human being stares into the bulb-light, paralysed
with fear, but lacking the means to locate the cause of its pain and
horror ('Ghost Crabs').[5] With *Crow* (1970), however, we are presented with a will to locate and confront the horror. In this sequence,
the adventures of a trickster-hero are placed in the framework of an
intrinsically negative quest towards truth, which can only be transformed into something positive through the reconciliation with his
female counterpart. Even though Hughes in letters to Sonnenberg
declared that the Crow-project was left off in the early Seventies, the
mythic structures that bloomed in *Crow*, also pervade sequences such
as *Prometheus on his Crag* (1973), *Gaudete* (1977), *Cave Birds* (1978),
and *Adam and the Sacred Nine* (1979).[6] Rather than comprising a
break with the Crow-project, these sequences are placed in a dialogue
with it and basically seem to comprise the continuation of a dynamic
process of remythologization whereby the poetic idiom opens up to a
radical otherness.

In his article 'The Evolution of "Sheep in Fog"', Hughes illustrates
how a process of remythologization is frequently connected to a set
of recurring myths. According to Hughes, Phaeton and Icarus function to structure Sylvia Plath's *Ariel* without being explicitly referred
to.[7] In poems such as 'Sheep in Fog', overt incorporations of the
mythical narratives would bring up 'a whole world of meanings that
are too large and mythic (and raw) for this particular poem'.[8] What is
more, Plath's poetic incorporation of the two myths also signals the
extent to which they are transformed by her imagination. The Greek
narratives, it seems, have become mingled with the poet's inner
world to an extent where they are inextricably linked with it, forming
an 'all-inclusive system' from which the poetic work is generated.[9] It
follows from this that any process of remythologization is also one of
mythologization.

For Hughes, the myth of the quest constitutes a formative element
through which the poetic subject is forced to abandon a limiting

---

[4] Emory Mss 924, 1.      [5] *CP* 149–50.      [6] Emory Mss 924, 1.
[7] See *WP* 206.      [8] *WP* 201.      [9] *WP* 150–1.

form of perception and sets out on a journey to reconcile with a radical otherness. Interestingly, such an analysis finds a parallel in Harold Bloom's *The Ringers in the Tower,* where the Romantic paradigm is seen to be underpinned by a similar mythical substructure.[10] The Romantic bard is a Promethean quester whose aim is to ward off dualisms and rebuild the human being. According to Bloom, the rigidity of our 'spectral dualities' prevents us from truly interacting with each other. As a result, we die of loneliness.[11]

Something similar is found in Hughes, where dichotomies are perceived as battlefields. Every aspect of existence is pitted against its counterpart in a conflict where the other is finally subjugated into passivity or death, precluding any possibility of plurality. Consequently, the chaotic space of our 'inner world' is suppressed for the sake of the 'objective eye', whose single vision only registers provable, empirical facts.[12] This is the perception of the flawed subjectivity in 'Crow's Account of St George', for whom 'everything in the Universe | Is a track of numbers racing towards an answer'.[13] The result of such disconnectedness is an intelligence that turns into stupidity 'of the most rigid and suicidal kind', poetically presented as an extreme sense of isolation in the poetic subject.[14] In the poem cited above, the male persona ends up by killing his entire family. In other poems, such as 'Crow Wakes', the insulated consciousness experiences a sense of persecution from his own body parts: 'They came howling after me and I ran'.[15]

The human being cannot achieve an harmonious, peaceful existence under the strict register of dualities. To counteract such tendencies Hughes introduces a feminine trope characterized by heterogeneity. This metaphor is feminine for a number of different reasons. On the one hand, it is an attempt to name God without getting tangled up in the trappings and dogmatics of the kind of Christianity that Hughes opposed. In this, the metaphor's feminine appellation is a subversive strategy, opening up a set of associations different from those of a masculinized God. It is also a way of going back to the very beginning, namely the point when God's spirit

---

[10] Bloom (1971: 15).   [11] Bloom (1971: 336).
[12] See 'Myth and Education' in *WP.*
[13] *CP* 225.   [14] *WP* 146.   [15] *CP* 258.

hovers over the deep in Genesis 1: 2. In a mythical perspective, this moment marks the division of One into dualities. In the instant God is differentiated from the deep (*tehom*), the masculine is separated from the feminine, and order is distinguished from chaos.[16] In a Jobean manner, the poetic text scrutinizes the relationship between good and evil, unity and plurality, straining the dualities of existence and positing the 'goddess' as the ultimate point of departure. Truth, it appears, is not what poses for God, but that which lies in the deep, that which is hidden, but which must be revealed and made manifest in language if we are ever to be healed. This truth, resembling a pre-Socratic reconciliation of *muthos* and *logos* in its all-inclusive plurality, is found in the sleeping presence within the frail harebell of 'Pibroch' (*Wodwo*) and in the eagle-hunter's song in 'Something was Happening' (*Cave Birds*).[17]

This constituent element of the Hughesian metaphor is reminiscent of what Plato, in *Timaeus*, terms the third genus (or χώρα, '*khôra*').[18] Like the 'goddess' metaphor, χώρα is an ambiguous element that, according to Julia Kristeva, can only be referred to subversively or not at all. Signalling its liminality is Kristeva's definition of χώρα as 'matrix space, nourishing, unnameable, anterior to the One, to God and, consequently, defying metaphysics'.[19] χώρα is a space where the inherently temporal rhetorical code ceases to be operative, thus opening up to a central crux with Hughes's poetry: truth eludes rhetoric. In this, Hughes's quest might be seen to represent what Bloom refers to as 'demonic romance', which designates a quest where the goal is finally revealed to be false or impossible to

[16] The Hebrew *tehom* is considered to be a translation of *Tiamat*, the Babylonian female divinity who was destroyed by the male god Marduk, cf. Coupe (1997: 109).

[17] The metaphorical presentation of the 'goddess' is a composite entity which could be referred to as an 'absolute metaphor'. This is a term borrowed from the German philosopher Hans Blumenberg (2002: 23), and is applied to metaphors that cannot be paraphrased or reduced to purely logical concepts. Transposed onto the current reading of Hughes, one might say that the tenor of such a metaphor would be blank, while the vehicle would be denominations such as 'truth', 'time', 'death'. The 'goddess' in Hughes, then, is a metaphor for the wholly other, which means that although it is meant to evoke certain connotations, it is a 'term in progress' which evolves and develops as the quest progresses.

[18] Plato, *Timaeus* 50.

[19] Kristeva (1986: 191).

achieve.[20] Any attempt to verbalize χώρα poses a problem in relation to the question of reference, because its scope either goes beyond or falls short of the polarity of metaphorical sense versus proper sense. In a similar way, the goddess is always glimpsed rather than manifested. She appears to be situated in the lacunas and gaps following the poems, or balancing on a tenuous border in the 'faceless presence | By soft-hand absence' ('For weights of blood') or in 'The glare | of the falcon, behind its hood' ('Speech out of shadow').[21]

At the same time, the displacement of the goddess is also connected to the problematic single vision of the Western gaze. Even though the blindness of the Western subjectivity is frequently experienced as a disease, poems such as 'Criminal Ballad' (*Crow*) show that the masculine subject is unable to locate and enunciate his own guilt. As suggested above, this conflict results in a number of *crisis-poems*, such as 'Song of Woe'.[22] In these poems, the subject experiences his wholeness to be threatened, either by the presence of another ('Crow's Account of St George'), or by the heterogeneity of his own self ('Crow Wakes'). The subject attempts to resolve this crisis by transmuting the emptiness so that it appears as a state of transcendence. Even here, however, the subject is still confined within the hegemony of dialectics. Nothing is still opposed to something, female to male, and space to time.

In Hughes, the goddess metaphor comprises the one element through which dialectics are suspended. In *The Linguistic Moment*, Hillis Miller describes metaphor by pointing to the translation of the Greek metafora/ as 'transport', 'elevation', 'ecstasy', and being 'carried beyond or out of oneself'. For Hillis Miller, metaphor is based upon spatiality rather than temporality, rupture rather than continuation, and suspension rather than sustained movement. The metaphor, in fact, comprises a break with the linear accumulation of meaning in the text. What appears as a result of this rupture is the pure word, or 'representation in itself'.[23] Rather than *mimetic* reproduction, the metaphor is representation at work, rendering it self-sufficient or, at least, a process in which it communicates itself and nothing more. The lack of an ascertainable referent enables metaphor to inhabit a

---

[20] Bloom (1971: 3).  [21] *CP* 566, 570.
[22] *CP* 201.  [23] Hillis Miller (1985: 41).

liminal space between subject and object, referent and the unnameable, the real and the mythical. Metaphor does not refer to an empirically verifiable object, but comprises an attempt to name the unnameable, which means that it ultimately returns to itself as an enunciation of the eternal, or truth. Seen thus, metaphor is not founded on the basis of similarity, but constitutes a synthetic structure that appears to transcend, or, at least, move to the limits of the constituent dichotomies of discourse.

In this context, metaphor does not merely displace binaries, but is itself elsewhere, displaced from the centre of the discourse. As a consequence of this displacement, Hughes's metaphoric goddess is, as suggested above, only caught as a fleeting shadow or in the gaps of the symbolic registers of language. In 'Crow's Undersong', Hughes attempts to capture this unenunciability on a thematic level, rendering the goddess an entity that 'cannot come all the way'.[24] The verses that follow attest to her liminality: 'She comes as far as blood and to the tips of hair | She comes to the fringe of voice'. At the same time, the poem also asserts that she is never absent, on the contrary 'She stays | Even after life even among the bones'. The final verse, moreover, testifies that she is no mere pantheistic force of nature, because without the goddess '(There would have been no city)'. While this verse establishes her as the creator of all, the use of parenthesis simultaneously seems to signal her final unenunciability. Even though Crow takes the precaution of singing an undersong, the symbolic register of language proves inadequate to mediate the fullness of the goddess. This is also suggested in 'Crow Tries the Media', where the concrete presence of the world interferes with Crow's attempts to sing about the goddess. His inability to see the other unencumbered by the concrete realities of creation, results in her withdrawal: 'Raising a filthy haze, | her shape dimmed'.[25]

The displacement of the goddess in these poems echoes the etymological foundations of the noun 'transcendence', indicating the spatiality of such a sphere of being. *Trans* means 'across' or 'beyond', and *scandere* means 'climb', signalling that 'transcendence' concerns the establishment of a relationship with that which is separate. In *Crow,* there are only a few, isolated indications of such transcendence. One

[24] *CP* 237.        [25] *CP* 231.

example can be found in 'Crow on the Beach', where he manages to articulate the question 'What could be hurting so much?'.[26] Here, Crow manages to see beyond the surface of the sea and recognize its pain, placing him in a relationship with another and, consequently, beyond the disconnected enumeration of poems such as 'Crow Alights', where everything exists and nothing can escape.

In the isolated subjectivity, however, there are no signs of transcendence. The lack of a relationship between subject and other in poems like 'The Scream' and 'In These Fading Moments I Wanted To Say' (*Cave Birds*) exhibits the protagonist's guilt in failing to recognize the absolute worth of the other. The subject performs trivial tasks of nothingness and is in a state of complete ignorance towards the other's suffering:

> In the fifteen seconds
> I was scrubbing at my nails and glancing up through the window
> She began to burn
>
> ('Something was Happening').[27]

These *crisis-poems* not only problematize the subject's lack of perception of the other, but posit being itself is as an ethical problem. Although the masculine subject in 'The Scream' is clearly separate from the macrocosmic cataclysms of an uncaring universe, he is seen to identify with them in order to avoid a relationship with his other. This segregated mode of existence is cut short, however, by the imposition of a radical alterity. When his 'mate' is affected by the random 'weights of iron | That come suddenly crashing into people, out of nowhere', the energies of the universe no longer function to make him 'feel brave and creaturely'.[28] Although the subject fails to consciously recognize this realization of the other as an ethical subject, it is manifested physically in the silence usurping the poetic subject's intention to praise the efficiency of the universe: 'Then I, too, opened my mouth to praise— | But a silence wedged my gullet'.[29] This silence is the imposition of the other, depicted as a violence because it explodes the protective veil of narcissism. Although his

[26] *CP* 229.     [27] *CP* 427.
[28] *CP* 419.     [29] *CP* 419.

immediate interpretation of his mate's 'stone temple smile' is to see it as a reflection of his own automated praise, the encounter provokes a deeper response, which manifests itself as an incoherent scream. The meaningless violence that afflicts his mate also affects the subject, and forces him to open up to a sense of ethical mutuality.

The imbecile innocence characterizing these poems is connected to the way in which the masculine subject embraces the machinery of Western culture without questioning how such modalities operate, or why we believe in them. Throughout the Crow project, such 'innocence' is imbricated with the *leitmotif* of running.[30] In the unpublished 'Ballad of the Fall' (also entitled 'The Creation of Adam'), God moulds man from mud and tells him to rise and run. As soon as he starts moving, however, man is attacked by weapons such as howitzer shells, machine guns, and tanks. God is shown to be unable, or unwilling, to help him, so that with every hit, God merely raises Adam and tells him to keep running. In the course of time, Adam rises and runs on his own impetus. Pleased, God folds his hands and smiles.[31] The indication in this poem is that God is a construction that subjugates human existence to the restricting parameters of a sequential temporality. The act of running is presented as a meaningless exercise, something which is signalled through Hughes's ironic incorporation of Yeats's 'For we are running to paradise'.[32] What Hughes appears to suggest is that there is no paradise at the end, and that the act of running signals a human subjection to the paradigm of a numerical registration of existence. The strict adherence to a framework of consecutiveness prevents the human being's transcendence from the confining parameters of the isolated subjectivity.

For Hughes, a perception which lays out history as a consecutive process, or a progression of events that forms a path to a concrete goal, is misguided. In this context, the seeming meaninglessness of the cycles of eternal becoming in *Wodwo* appears to be connected

[30] Even though there are not many poems that incorporate running in the *Crow*-sequence as such, it is an important element in *Cave Birds*, and it is also a motif that Hughes returned to frequently in his notebooks (as found in the Emory Archives).

[31] Emory Mss 2.3, 85, 51; 2.3, 86, 48.

[32] Emory Mss 2.3, 85, 51.

with the perception of the flawed subjectivity. As was already suggested in 'You Drive in a Circle': 'Where are you heading? Everything is already here' (*Wodwo*).[33] In '?', Hughes asks

> Why should Time be a road?
> Why should tomorrow be a destination?
> Why should yesterday be another country?[34]

The inclusiveness embedded in these questions once again signals that the answer does not lie in replacing something with nothing, or running with stopping. In fact, as soon as the male subject stops running, he is devoured by dogs ('Existential Song').[35] What is more, the solution does not lie in replacing time with space, or being with non-being. The solution, it appears, lies in another mode of perception, which is figured in the inherent circularity of the quest, through which the wanderer inevitably ends up at the place of origin.

Seen thus, the answer seems to lie in metaphorical openness as a movement that displaces the linear structures of time. While an interpretation of metaphor as a trope based on inherent similarity would incorporate it within the paradigm of binaries, the Hughesian metaphor engenders an act of opening up. Metaphor is manifested as a series of displacements and condensations, resembling the uncertain relation between the subject and the other. This characteristic of metaphor renders it an open structure through which a relation can be established with the other as an alterity, transcending the unutterability of the name in its manifestation as a song, an invocation, a silence. In this respect, the metaphor engenders an act which appears to equal an amatory experience. The very dynamics of love allow the discourse to position itself on a border between self and other, exploring the liminal space in which a relation with an alterity can possibly be formed.

Thus, the metaphorical naming of the goddess becomes an amatory act, opening up a space between subject and object. Crucially, Hughes identified love poetry as a way of approaching the goddess in an unpublished, untitled manuscript. Here, Hughes says that a relationship with the goddess, albeit in its lowest and most secularized

---

[33] *CP* 177.    [34] *CP* 198.    [35] *CP* 202–3.

form, would have the form of love poetry.[36] Love is also a central theme in the mythological narrative underpinning the Crow project. In his readings, Hughes frequently posited the poems in this mythological framework and, even though none of the prose narratives were ever published, his manuscripts show that the Crow narrative is much more complex and developed than what emerges in the poems. The essential narrative in relation to the love poems is an episode where Crow arrives at a river and has to carry a hag over to the other side. Along the way, the hag asks Crow a number of questions, such as 'What does love think about life?' and 'What is there, besides love and magic?' When Crow answers correctly, she grows lighter, and when he answers wrongly, she grows heavier. Finally, they reach the other side of the shore, upon which she is transformed into a beautiful creature and becomes his bride.[37] This, presumably, is the end of the quest.

Hughes identified the love poems which spring out of this narrative as answers to the hag's questions. In the manuscript referred to above, the hag asks Crow seven questions. Hughes did not allude to seven poems to supply the answers, but pointed to poems about lovers in sequences such as *Crow* and *Cave Birds* and identified them as Crow poems. 'Lovesong' and 'Bride and Groom', moreover, have been concretely identified as answers.[38] Thus, these poems are to be seen as enunciations of various aspects of love, and vital to Crow's quest. Interestingly, however, *Crow* presents itself as an inversion of love, and is distinguished by lack, a blank, or negation. In *Crow,* this economy works in a circular manner. The moment of unity and wholeness is posited at the beginning, a temporality preceding the fall, which has been followed by what is experienced as an emptiness. Tragically, the origin longed for by the subject is also a nothing, which means that the individual's insatiable desire becomes circular.

This does not mean that Hughes prescribes to a Lacanian understanding of lack. While Lacan returns the human being to the *nihilo* and sees redemption only as an emptying of oneself onto nothingness, Hughes appears to regard such a conviction as a result of the

---

[36] Emory Mss 2.4, 115, 20.
[37] Emory Mss 2.2, 62, 13.
[38] Roberts (2006: 78).

rational ego's misguidedness. In the world of *Crow*, Lacanian lack has lead to a forgetfulness of the true God, the goddess. In the goddess' absence, the human being tries to fill its lack in ways that are ultimately damaging, but 'nothing religious is ever destroyed by logic; it is destroyed only by the god's withdrawal'.[39] One of the poems signalling the goddess's return is 'Crow's First Lesson', where she emerges through subversive manifestations of love. To paraphrase, the poem presents God trying to teach Crow language. Crow's attempts to speak repeatedly turn into mockeries of God's acts of creation, culminating in a near-asphyxiation of the first man by the female genitals, thus deriding the word that God has chosen as his point of departure, namely 'love'. While God, crying and cursing, attempts to clean up the mess, Crow flies 'guiltily off'.[40]

This sequence of events suggests that the so-called 'lesson' is provided not by God but by another entity. In the context of *Crow* as such, the God persona is presented as a human creation resembling Blake's Urizen. This positivist demiurge does not recognize the manifestations as love, and regards the entire 'lesson' as a failure. From a more inclusive perspective, however, Crow's retchings appear to be acts of *logos*, engendered by a force beyond him. This is signalled already in the first stanza, where Crow's efforts result in the emanation of a shark. In the short text 'Poetry and Violence', Hughes equals the image of the shark's fangs to the vehement energy characterizing the transformation of Saul to Paul. This kind of violence, he says, is a 'revelation', enabling the human being to experience truth, reality, redemption, and love.[41] Much like the metamorphical hare in 'Crow Goes Hunting', the shark is also evocative of the kind of mythical metamorphosis described in Hughes's introduction to *Tales from Ovid*, that is, a mythic image of the energies of the universe that seek out the subject and explode its defining framework, lifting 'the whole episode onto the supernatural or divine plane'.[42]

In this context, the shark is an act of kenosis, a manifestation of the transcendent divinity referred to as the 'goddess'. In his article 'God's Sex', Gerard Loughlin refers to the movements of the Trinity as the

---

[39] Heidegger (1993: 376).      [40] *CP* 211.
[41] *WP* 255.      [42] *CP* 236; *TO* x.

'spinning wheel of love', which continuously enacts an unceasing donation of self to another.[43] This description is reminiscent of the plurality and selflessness that also distinguishes the Hughesian goddess, and, more importantly, reveals the emanation of the shark as a singular, amorous event—an offering of love. The demiurge fails to recognize this. A representative of Reformed Christianity, which Hughes regarded as 'one of the ugliest and painful paragraphs' in the chapter of humankind's relationship with the goddess, the demiurge is caught up in his pre-expectations of what was to issue forth from Crow's mouth, and perceives the production of the shark as a failure.[44] Seen thus, the guilt lies with God, and not with Crow, because of the demiurge's unwillingness to recognize the shark and to embrace it as an offering. The presentation of the demiurge as a human construct once again signals the identification between this refusal and the unified subject's fear of otherness. The inherent violence of an amorous event such as the one offered by the shark, moreover, is reminiscent of Hughes's discussions of the poetry of Janòs Pilinszky, where the true God is represented as '[a] God of absences and negative attributes, quite comfortless. A God in whose creation the camps and modern physics are equally at home'.[45] Although the shark is love, Hughes's description reminds us that the goddess remains more dissimilar than similar to everything created. Thus, it seems pertinent to ask whether the human being can embrace or even survive an offering from such a divinity, or if it, like Semele, will be totally obliterated by the experience: 'Her eyes opened wide, saw him | And burst into flame'.[46] 'Crow's First Lesson' does not reach the limit where such a question needs to be debated, however, as the shark immediately turns towards itself, 'rolling downwards, discovering its own depth'. The liminal space denoting the relationship between subject and other is merely a lacuna, denied of an existence by of the parochial vision of the demiurge.

In the second stanza, God pedagogically meets Crow's failure by awarding him another chance. Again, Crow produces a physical result in the form of three insects. This second manifestation is

---

[43] Loughlin (1999: 145).        [44] Emory Mss 2.4, 115, 20.
[45] *WP* 233.        [46] *CP* 933.

concomitant with the recurrent theme of concupiscence in the sequence. The insect immediately zooms down to the receptacle of sustenance, signalling the status of hunger as the most fervent of instincts. This image is evocative of one of the earliest Crow pieces, the verse drama *Eat Crow* (written in 1964), which is underpinned by the ethical problem that all life subsists on the death of an other. Interestingly, however, the theologian Karl Barth also defines such a hunger as a form of *eros*. For Barth, *eros* is but a rapacious need, which is 'hungry, and demands the food that the other seems to hold out'.[47] This hunger is the only reason for the subject's interest in the other, and Barth compares the lover to the wolf who swallows and consumes both Red Riding Hood and her grandmother. While union with the beloved is the overarching goal, the result of such a union would be that the object of his love is 'taken to himself', so that 'even in the event he alone remains'.[48] In this, *eros* is solely an act of self-assertion, depending on the other only as an object that may be devoured and assimilated into the self.

At the same time, the endeavour to unite with the other also has a more positive mythical counterpart in Aristophanes' narration of the myth of the Golden Age, when humans were whole, round, vigorous, and strong.[49] The division imposed on the human beings by the gods was intended to make them weaker, insecure and incomplete. In this, sexual desire is based on the need to unite with one's former half. Even in the context of this myth, however, such a need for unity emanates as a lack of respect for the other's autonomy and alterity. What is more, it also makes the love-relationship an impossible endeavour. In *Crow,* such a ravenous desire also thematized in poems such as 'Lovesong', where the lovers feed on each other in order to survive psychologically and spiritually. In Hughes, any such attempt at self-assertion emerges as paradoxical in the sense that the individual tries to assert a selfhood that does not exist. Accordingly, *eros* emanates as a futile doubling of nothingness. The individual remains in a state of being-in-death, where the thought of the perishable body gnaws away at the conscious mind, as it tries to replace a spiritual sense of lack with the physical body of the other.

---

47 Barth (1958: 734).      48 Barth (1958: 734).
49 Plato, *Symposium* 190a–190b.

The brief moments of ecstatic unity between the two lovers only intensify this anguish, highlighting the fact there is no selfhood that might be asserted. As discussed above, however, the anguish produced seems to be so overwhelming that is inverted into something desirable. As such, the result is not a tendency towards suicide, but a nothingness that is more negative than negation and which, as a consequence, appears meaningful to the subjectivity pervaded by lack. Consequently, poems such as 'Song of Woe' portray the subject as achieving clarity and peace only after he has stripped himself of everything.

The third stanza of 'Crow's First Lesson' problematizes desire in the context of female sexuality, as the 'woman's vulva dropped over man's neck and tightened'.[50] In *Crow,* the female counterpart is frequently staged as the mythological scapegoat archetype, as a poetization of Hughes's perception of Reformed Christianity's demonization of women.[51] From the perspective of the goddess, Crow's retching of the first man's head is emblematic of the kind of love that God expects and encourages him to reproduce. Crow's gaping (a-gape) could be seen as a word-play, suggesting that the kind of love presented here is *agape*. In this register the difference between *eros* and *agape* might be regarded as one of direction: while *eros* rushes towards the desired object, *agape* descends on the subject as a disinterested gift. It is a love that is offered to the other in a totally selfless manner. Thus, the offerings presented to God by Crow's gapings are also manifestations of *agape*. The divinity engendering the emanations offers herself unreservedly, but is promptly rejected by the monocentric consciousness.

In a Christian context, the offering manifested as *agape* is achieved only at the expense of a sacrifice. The body of Christ opens up towards eternity, but only through destruction of the human body. In this, the poetic text once again emphasizes the duality of the human being, which, divided against itself, is stunted by the sinful, restrictive nature of the body. The only way for the soul to reach its full potential is by shedding its mortal coil. The implication of the poetic discourse, however, is that such a view of the human body is a

---

[50] *CP* 211.        [51] See Emory Mss 2.4, 115, 20.

misapprehension. Although *Crow* cannot be said to celebrate any aspects of human life, its stereotypical representation of sinful sexuality, and particularly the female libido, suggests a thematization of dogmatic Christianity's segregation of body from soul, and its reductive presentation of women.

Such a thematization is particularly poeticized in the figure of Eve. In the Midrash, Eve is preceded by Lilith who abandons Adam when he refuses to treat her as an equal: ' "Why must I lie beneath you?" she asked. "I also was made from dust, and am therefore your equal" '.[52] Unlike Eve, Lilith was not created from Adam's rib, but directly from the earth. With the creation of Eve, then, woman comes second and is restricted to a firmly established role. In an unpublished poem entitled 'Theology', Hughes asks the question:

> What was Eve for?
> To beget children [on], and what more?
> Adam, with his huge, vain head, was beguiled
> By her pure eyes, where his image smiled, doubled.[53]

From these verses, it seems clear that Adam perceives Eve as a doubling of himself rather than as an autonomous being. In this tableau of mirrors, Adam's love is based on Eve's pure, empty eyes as a *tabula rasa* on which he can double his own person. The description is reminiscent of the eyes of Phèdre at the moment of her death, when 'the sun's light at last | Can resume its purity unspoiled'.[54] Here, Phèdre is guilty and ashamed of her presence in the world, and regards it as an obstacle between the pure look and the object. In this prelapsarian context, however, Eve is not perceived as an obstacle, but is rather incorporated within the paradigm of sameness. In *Tales of Love*, Kristeva also demonstrates how *agape* is really formed on the basis of homology, assuming semblance between the self and the other.[55] This can also be seen in the relationship between God and the human being in 'Crow's First Lesson', where the rational demiurge transposes his own magnificence onto the other, failing to recognize the first man as an altogether different entity. While the boisterous claim of prodigiousness is ironically inverted through the

[52] Graves and Patai (1964: 65).   [53] Emory Mss 2.3, 84, 106.
[54] *P* 81.   [55] Kristeva (1987: 269).

undignified presentation of the first man as a blabbering idiot, *agape* as a homologous relation is also confirmed as God and the first man are revealed to be limited by the same kind of objective rationalism. The latter point is yet another ironic inversion in the sense that the demiurge of the poems is really a human invention, which means that every feeling or utterance attributed to God is a self-reflexive comment on the fallacy of Western rationality. Seen thus, the loving relationship between God and the first man is really a misnomer for the illusive veil of homology that is cast between the self and the other. Another implication, moreover, is that the disinterested offering of love presented by the goddess would explode the concept of *agape*. The divine goddess is underpinned by the manifold presence of an alterity that is totally foreign to the being in the world, or, if not totally foreign, it is at least all-embracing. The goddess is love in its absolute plurality and in the totality of its manifestations, such as in Crow's enunciations and in the poem as a saying of love.

The relationship between Adam and Eve, as presented here, appears to represent a love fallacy. If this is love, it is its negative manifestation where the subject subsists on the principle of narcissism, as Adam is both subject and object. Although Eve is physically present as an object, the real object is representation itself, the fantasy that Adam has conjured and projects unto Eve. Seen thus, Eve merely functions to anchor Adam's fantasy. Like Narcissus, Adam is deceived, mistaking 'That picture of himself on the meniscus | For the stranger who could make him happy'.[56] This tragic situation, where heterogeneousness is glossed over for the sake of homology, suggests a fear of alterity. Adam's gaze is characterized by the presence of a non-object. At the same time, it is also distinguished by the power of the imagination, as the eye imagines an object that takes the place of the woman, Eve. Once again like Narcissus, Adam's love is totally encapsulated within his gaze: 'Look away and what you love is nowhere'.[57] Adam's strategy of doubling is an attempt to maintain a sense of wholeness and sameness. He ensures the stability of the subject by blocking out the alterity of the physical other as well as that of his own unconscious. Seen thus, his tragic error is his perception of the other as a threat or a menace, which makes the other

[56] *CP* 919.        [57] *CP* 920.

into the archetypal shadow that Adam refuses to face. Adam's failure to recognise Eve's autonomy is an act of veiling—he veils the other with the imagination of the eye.

Ironically, it is Eve's sinful desire for the other, in the form of knowledge, that explodes the stability of self. In this context, 'Crow's First Lesson' also dramatizes another biblical cause for condemnation of the female as the one who brought sin, death, and punishment into the world. The unpublished 'Theology' explains this as the work of Lilith who

> [ ... ] held those mirrors steady
> Who was in Eden already
> Part of Lilith's deception
> Eve was a contraption.[58]

Here, the poetic discourse once again suggests the fallaciousness of Adam's reading of Eve. In the mythical schema of the goddess, Eve is always already Isis and Hecate, heaven and hell, 'the mother' and 'the whore, the baby-drinker, the sky'.[59] By suggesting the complexity of the other, the poem continues to challenge the hegemony of binaries, which are rendered as battlefields staging the struggle for supremacy. In his recurrent presentation of the female as victim and scapegoat, Hughes emphasizes the hierarchical negativity of the binary, in which the feminine element is denied a space.

In its musings on love, 'Crow's First Lesson' is reminiscent of a poem by the medieval poet Hadewijch, recently discussed by Warner.[60] In the poem 'The Strongest of All Things', Hadewijch has four wise masters argue about what is the most powerful of all things. The answers given by each are wine, a king, woman, and truth, which all represent love in different aspects.[61] A similar plurality can be found in the present poem in which the three manifestations, although none of them appear to represent love at first glance, nevertheless constitute singular, amorous events. The plurality embodied by these events is signalled mythologically in the androgynous character of Eros, and is also deliberated in Jean-Luc Nancy's article 'Shattered Love', where he postulates that to think love is to allow

---

[58] Emory Mss 2.3, 84, 106.  [59] Emory Mss 2.3, 84, 106.
[60] Warner (2000: 195).  [61] Warner (2000: 197–8).

for all its manifestations and possibilities. For Nancy, love is each singular event, neither of which should be privileged, hierarchized, or excluded. In fact, the thinking of love, which could be regarded as an act of love in itself, is to receive 'the collisions, and the contradictions of love, without submitting them to an order that they essentially defy'.[62] Seen thus, the ideal form of love is an immense generosity through which opposites are embraced and the other is recognized as an autonomous system.

As suggested above, the inability to see and recognize the other as a selfhood precludes any formation of love in *Crow*. *Crow* is a singular depiction of the *nigredo*, leaving the quester to fumble in a totality of darkness.[63] In poems such as 'That Moment', Crow's hunger leads him to shrug off the total destruction of the world.[64] This lack of compassion and empathy in the face of human suffering is, in effect, a denial of the other's humanity. Although Hughes envisioned Crow as eventually reaching fulfilment, there is no real sense of progress until *Gaudete*, where the subject is on an active quest to open up to the other. The songs of the epilogue are invocations and celebrations of the goddess, and the subject makes several attempts to offer himself: 'Me, too | Let me be one of your warriors' ('The grass blade is not without'). These efforts are pointless, however, as the singer proves unable to embrace the goddess' fullness: 'He almost lives | Who dare meet you' ('What steel was it the river poured').[65]

In *Cave Birds*, however, the process begun with *Wodwo* is once again taken up as the other offers itself and forces the subject to undergo a series of transformations. In his notes, Hughes wrote that he did not particularly care for these poems, but that they had proved efficacious.[66] This healing effect is reflected in poems such as 'His Legs Ran About' and 'Bride and Groom Lie Hidden for Three Days', where the relationship between the masculine and the feminine counterparts finally reaches some sort of fulfilment. As the two lovers enact a reciprocal act of recreation, love is presented as the supreme guarantee for renewal.

---

[62] Nancy (1991: 83).       [63] Jung (1967: 232).
[64] *CP* 209.       [65] *CP* 367, 372.
[66] Sagar letters, British Library, 10 June 1977(?) BL, Add. 78757, f. 3.

Importantly, the first act of refashioning happens as the female endows the male with a restored vision: 'She gives him his eyes, she found them | Among some rubble, among some beetles'.[67] This offering engenders a process of selfless giving, reminiscent of Corinthians I, where *agape* establishes a 'face-to-face' relationship between subject and object, leading up to true knowledge and recognition: 'but then shall I know even as also I am known'.[68] The supreme bliss experienced by these two lovers is the ideal that is attempted but not accomplished in sequences such as *Crow* and *Gaudete*. The relation is evocative of what Lévinas refers to as a 'face-to-face' encounter, where the subject, through a true meeting with the other as alterity, 'frees itself from being limited to itself'.[69] For Lévinas, the face of the other is God's way of signifying, rendering the other as *logos,* the manifestation of God's Word. In this, the relationship between the self and the other becomes a true source for a continued process of renewal.

The fundamental dynamicity of such a relationship is also signalled by the fact that 'Bride and Groom' is not the final poem of *Cave Birds.* The epigrammatical poem 'Finale' ends and effectively continues the sequence, by overthrowing everything that has been enunciated: 'At the end of a ritual | Up comes a goblin'.[70] Thus, the poem thematizes one of the problems that Hughes associated with the process of writing poetry: 'We go on writing poems because one poem never gets the whole account right'.[71] This, however, is also one of the victories of poetry. In this perspective, the processes of love become a metaphor for poetry as an open, dynamic system. Through the mythopoeic metaphor of the goddess, the poem stages itself in a pattern of continuous renewal and rebirth. Like the myth, the poem reminds us that there is always something other to be said or imagined. As a play of past events and future possibility, truth is always only enacted in the current encounter between self and other, sacred and profane. It is a discourse whose potential always evades the given order, and the verbalization of what Hughes referred to as 'the tension between [ ... ] extremes', ensuring transformation as a process of endless renewal.[72]

---

[67] *CP* 437.      [68] Cor. I 13: 12.      [69] Lévinas (1999: 56).
[70] *CP* 440.      [71] Faas (1980: 204).      [72] *TO* xi.

# 6

## 'Mutilated towards alignment?': *Prometheus On His Crag* and the 'Cambridge School' of anthropology

*Vanda Zajko*

The defiance of the chained Prometheus reverberates within literary history, articulating the tension between overwhelming despair and equally remorseless hope, between the existence, as Hughes articulates it in the second Prometheus poem, 'That cannot be otherwise | And could not have been otherwise | And never can be otherwise' and the promise of rehabilitation and rebirth.[1] The Titan who, in the remotest of pasts, gave fire to humankind in open rebellion against Zeus and was punished everlastingly for his action, has continued to be called upon in various moments when, in the words of Tony Harrison, 'history moves in directions where defiance and unfreedom cry for help.'[2] In this aspect he functions as the isolated champion of the voiceless oppressed and can be compared with other figures from Greek tragedy who act alone and insubordinately and have a similarly complex reception history, such as Antigone. But there is a more ambivalent tradition, beginning with the ancient sources, which emphasizes the danger of the gift of fire and the hubris and cost of Prometheus' role as benefactor of the human race. This kind of representation positions him as a 'trickster' figure, familiar above all to readers of anthropology as someone

---

[1] *CP* 285.    [2] Harrison (1998: vii).

whose excessive cleverness leads to his downfall, both rebel and creator, simultaneously ingenuous and accountable for his actions. It is Prometheus' double status as the immortal advocate of, and scapegoat for, the human race that seems primarily to have attracted Hughes.

This essay will investigate what is distinctive about Ted Hughes's representation of Prometheus in the 1973 series of twenty-one short poems entitled *Prometheus on His Crag* and consider, in particular, how it relates to the work of those classical scholars who collectively have come to be known as the 'Cambridge Ritualists', for whom the key to gaining an understanding of the origins of various ancient cultural phenomena lay in religious practice, and, in particular, in grappling with the less rational elements of human experience. In focusing thus on one set of influences it is inevitable that others will be neglected and in the case of Hughes, whose sense of tradition encompassed the linguistic, literary, and poetic traditions of many cultures, the partiality of such an analysis will be severe. Nonetheless, it is rare to find anyone responding to Hughes's work who does not comment on the centrality of myth to his engagement with the world and on the anthropological model of human consciousness that underpins it. Keith Sagar, for example, in the first monograph to deal exclusively with Hughes's work, speaks of how its territory spans 'the roots and sources of the myths and legends in the depths of the human psyche';[3] Dennis Walder discusses how Hughes imagines the troubled relationship between human beings and nature 'in terms of animal imagery and symbolism drawn from the vast storehouse of European mythology';[4] and Stuart Hirschberg, who devoted a whole book to the subject, describes 'Hughes'[s] continuing absorption with the psychological, moral, social and religious symbolism de-rived from ancient mythologies' as the attempt to 're-establish touch with the heritage of a long vanished past'.[5] For Hughes, then, myth represents not a consciously produced rationalized system of thought but a story of collective significance whose origins are lost in the archaic past but whose content expresses something vital about the relationship of human beings to their environment. Although his

---

[3] Sagar (1975: 2).     [4] Walder (1987: 23).
[5] Hirschberg (1981: 9).

sources of inspiration can clearly not be restricted to those associated with one particular place and time, there is substantial overlap between the nexus of ideas that emerged from the Cambridge School and those that manifest themselves in the frequent turns to Greek (and other) mythological figures in his poems.

Hughes's immersion in anthropological ideas is well attested, and is often attributed to his switch from studying English to Archaeology and Anthropology during the final year of his degree at Cambridge in 1953–4. The Section D paper of the Classical Tripos at Cambridge was, and is perhaps now again, most famously associated with the ideas of Jane Harrison, Gilbert Murray, Francis Cornford, and A. B. Cook, all of whom had been deeply influenced by the work of W. Robertson Smith and J. G. Frazer and all of whom, in various ways, contributed to the shift of focus away from myth and towards ritual that characterized the study of ancient religion in the early years of the twentieth century. From the perspective of intellectual history, there are dangers in homogenizing the work of a group of scholars in this way because significant differences can be elided and orthodoxies retrospectively created to suit the needs of the moment. But Mary Beard has pointed out that the obligation of such history can precisely be regarded as to 'identify structures, allegiances, and common ways of thinking that would never have been apparent at the time', even if 'to talk so consistently, as modern scholars do, of "membership" and "group" glibly concretizes and personalizes the fleeting, complicated, overlapping intellectual processes and relation-ships that (if anything) constitute the "movement", at Cambridge or elsewhere.'[6] Given that the time Hughes spent at Cambridge was roughly half a century after some of the seminal texts of 'the group' were published, his exposure to their ideas would already have been of the belated kind that Beard identifies and the mode of thinking about myth that he developed forms part of the reception of those texts. Along these lines, Miriam Leonard has recently discussed how the story of the textual reception of antiquity has tended to be kept separate from the story of institutions, of the intellectual, political, and personal ties which give rise to particular

---

[6] Beard (2000: 114–15).

investments in antiquity.[7] For the purposes of this essay, it is Hughes's investment in antiquity that is central, an investment that can be seen in part as a poetic response to the 'modern invention of Ritualism.'[8] The dynamics of the relationships between particular individuals and between different 'versions' of the ritualist project are less significant than the overall trajectory of the ideas associated with the movement.

There are two main features of this trajectory: first the insistence that the way to understand Greek religion is to understand the origins of its ritual practices; second, the broadening of the scope of the enquiry to allow the ancient rituals of other cultures to illuminate those of Greece; both have significant methodological implications for the study of 'Classics' as a discipline and in particular for its presumed status as the starting point of western civilization. They also have implications for the reading of individual texts and the standing of particular authors. In the introduction to *Prolegomena to the Study of Greek Religion* Jane Harrison spells out the consequences of her position as it relates to the canonical texts of Greek literature and especially to Homer: if Greek religion is regarded as an affair mainly of mythology, and of mythology seen through the medium of literature, then Homer represents a beginning, albeit a beginning that is already sophisticated in terms of its theology. But if Greek religion is approached via a minute examination of its ritual, then priorities change:

For literature Homer is the beginning, though every scholar is aware that he is nowise primitive; for theology, or—if we prefer so to call it—mythology, Homer presents, not a starting-point, but a culmination, a complete achievement, an almost mechanical accomplishment, with scarcely a hint of origins, an accomplishment moreover, which is essentially literary rather than religious, sceptical and moribund already in its very perfection. The Olympians of Homer are no more primitive than his hexameters. Beneath this splendid surface lies a stratum of religious conceptions, ideas of evil, of purification, of atonement, ignored or suppressed by Homer, but reappearing in later poets and notably in Aeschylus. It is this substratum of religious

[7]  Leonard (2006: 118).        [8]  Beard (2000: 114).

conceptions, at once more primitive and more permanent, that I am concerned to investigate. Had ritual received its due share of attention, it had not remained so long neglected.[9]

Harrison's investment in the 'ideas of evil, of purification, of atonement' that are given free reign by Aeschylus leads her to attach more importance to the texts of tragedy than to Homer and to reorganize the canon of Greek literature to give precedence to the works which, although not chronologically prior, in her view preserve traces of the earliest religious practices. From this perspective, literature becomes a site of preservation for religious conceptions that are, paradoxically, both primitive and permanent, and part of its potency comes from the capacity to 'continue myth's ancient and basic endeavour to create a meaningful place for man in a world oblivious to his presence'.[10] This figuration of literature entails a particular view of mythopoiesis that is at odds with contemporary emphases on the conditions for its production and transmission within particular cultures. But it is highly relevant both to Hughes's use of myth and to criticism of his poetry. The idea that the capacity to create myths is something that human beings have in common and that mythic symbols and structures underpin and organize literature as well as forming part of its content, coheres, as we shall see, with Hughes's own conception of myths as large-scale accounts of people's attempts to negotiate between their outer and inner worlds. It also resonates with the kind of analysis of Hughes's poems that sees his eclectic plundering of the cultures of the world as a tale of the search for liberation through understanding, as a struggle for illumination as to how human beings can be reconciled with the most elusive and brutal aspects of themselves and of nature.

In the case of Hughes, this kind of reading is not merely a form of biographical criticism that seeks to make meaning of the poems by reference to the events of a sensationalized life. Rather, it seems to arise directly from a sense of the poems themselves as expressing something 'archetypal', something over and above the surface

---

[9]  Harrison (1962: viii).
[10]  Vickery (1966: ix).

content and resistant to any easy, rationalizing interpretation. From the animal poems in the earliest collection *The Hawk in the Rain* to the later, complex, and perhaps overwritten *Gaudete*, it is rare that critics have not made some reference to Hughes's immersion in mythology as a way of articulating the distinctive qualities of his writing. In several instances they have also constructed a developmental narrative to fortify the argument that throughout the corpus there is a kind of 'working-through' of various anthropological roles and an increasing conciliation with the idea and experience of suffering.[11] On a smaller scale this pattern of movement from ignorant frustration to acceptance and understanding can be seen to structure the cycle of Prometheus poems which we shall consider in detail. But even if we do not consent to the idea that the broad configuration of Hughes's work follows the pattern of a kind of initiation ritual, with the poet himself cast in the role of scapegoat, there is a clear consensus that myth, not just ancient Greek myth, but myth derived from a whole variety of cultures, is the medium out of which his poetry emerges and which allows him to engage with a sense of the preoccupations of humanity beyond the temporally and psychologically immediate.[12]

Harrison's redefinition of the category of the primitive as something that is archaic but that can also be permanent is crucial to an

---

[11] Sagar (2005: 340), for example, contrasts the use of animals in the early poems and in the later. He argues that 'as he gradually struggled free from his fatalistic dualism, Hughes began to see the animal world as offering not primarily images of sickness and struggle, but rather images of harmony even between predators and their victims.' Hirschberg (1981: 211) gives the following developmental account: 'The flow of Hughes's poetry moves from a shamanistic identification with powerful, violent and destructive predators like the hawk, the bear, the jaguar and the pike expressed in a style at once self-controlled, self-possessed and vehement, through a series of changes to become the poetry of the suffering victim, the self offered to the self as sacrificed, crucified, motionless, in the grip of anguish and self-purgation. Between shaman and scapegoat, trickster plays a crucial role. He is the one figure in myth and legend who is alternately both predator and victim. In the cycle of Crow poems Hughes holds the balance for a few years and writes poetry that is objective, realistic, and grotesquely comic. The Crow poems are the turning point in Hughes's spiritual journey from his unspoken allegiance with the mythical life of devouring predators to the poetry of the scapegoat, a poetry of humilities that celebrates and embraces the symbolic death of his former self.'

[12] See the discussion of the different ways of formulating the relationship between myth and literature in Vickery (1966: ix).

understanding of the sense of myth that later came to inform Hughes's work. The cultural milieu within which she was working was influenced not only by Robertson Smith and Frazer but also by Durkheim and Freud and as such she shares her influences with some of the most prominent writers and artists of the period. The disaffection with the modern urbanized world led to a search for a simplicity and honesty deemed to be chiefly lacking and prompted the turn both outwards towards cultures not easily assimilable that offered an alternative vision of collective identity, and inwards towards the hidden depths of a multi-layered self that came to signify the radical alterity at the heart of the familiar. The pressing urge towards creativity was greater than any consideration of what we might today term 'cultural imperialism' and the sense of having access to the world as resource, in terms both of time and space, came to be typical of other icons of modernism such as Picasso, Stravinsky, Eliot, and Pound as well as those working within educational institutions.

Mary Beard, writing about the place of Jane Harrison's work in twentieth-century classical scholarship, stresses her legacy to succeeding generations in a passage that could equally apply to the other Cambridge scholars:

> ... the basic message of her work—that somewhere underneath the calm, shining, rational exterior of the classical world is a mass of weird, seething irrationality—is a tenet that almost everyone working in the history of Greek culture would now take for granted; so much for granted, in fact, that we have become more interested in how and why the pure 'rationalist' vision ever came to be invented in the first place, and in how our predecessors ever imagined that 'rationality' could be so easily distinguished from 'irrationality'.[13]

Hughes himself articulates a sense of despair at the limitedness and impoverishment of a purely rationalist outlook in his famous essay 'Myth and Education' in the prose collection *Winter Pollen*.[14] For Hughes, the modern world's idealization of the rational 'objective eye' evokes considerable despair, and he argues fervently that it is the simultaneous rising prestige of a particular kind of scientific

---

[13] Beard (2000: 7).          [14] *WP* 136–53.

epistemology and the lowering prestige of religious awareness that has persuaded human beings to identify themselves with what is a catastrophically narrow mode of perception. The corrective to such a Cyclopean perspective is, for Hughes, the strengthening and training of the imagination which alone can equip us for the inner and outer worlds that we have no choice but to occupy simultaneously. And certain traditional stories, stories in which, in Hughes's words, 'the full presence of the inner world combines with and is reconciled to the full presence of the outer world' are aids to the inevitable and continuous process of negotiating the demands of both. Sagar, in his most recent work, employs an Eliotic sense of tradition to situate Hughes at the end of a long line of authors, ancient and modern, for whom a central theme has been the attempt of human beings to redefine themselves in relation to Nature. He talks about the role of imagination, a key term for Hughes, in terms that position it in opposition to the mode of thinking about thinking that overvalues the processes of analytic reason:

The imagination is by no means the enemy of intelligence or civilization. Its function is to correct any imbalance, which has come about in the psyche, to reconcile and harmonize the warring, artificially polarized elements. What we call intelligence is often merely the analytical and manipulative aspects of intelligence developed to the exclusion of, at the cost of, all other aspects— intelligence cut off from its sustaining and validating connections with the rest of the psyche, with the body, and with everything outside itself . . . What is normally thought of as thinking, all those methods of 'thinking' which have been developed over the centuries in Western civilization, whose dualistic assumptions have been built into the very structure of our lan- guage, has specialized in separating things from each other, then separating the parts, analyzing, vivisecting, compartmentalizing, until it has drastically weakened our capacity for thinking in a way that puts things together, makes connections, perceives patterns and wholes. For most of the history of the human race the language of myth and folk-tale was to some extent generally understood, and understood to have a relevance not only to metaphysical truths, but to the health of the race and to the practical business of living.[15]

This idea that mythology or theology in its archaic sense (Harrison, in the passage cited above, uses the two terms interchangeably)

---

[15] Sagar (2005: 373–4).

promotes societal health is one that is shared by Hughes and by the Cambridge School. For Harrison *et al.*, generally speaking, mythology is a form of utterance that expresses in words what ritual expresses in deeds. Of the two, ritual is the comparatively permanent element, whereas the details of a myth shift and metamorphose over space and time. The potency of myth, however, derives from its association with the ritual that functions to open up everyday life to some transcendent being or force in order to tap into its transformative power. Although grounded in and operating at the level of the everyday, ritual is a religious negotiation which, as Hughes might put it, embraces and humanizes the archaic energies of instinct and feeling so that, again paraphrasing Hughes, the elemental and chaotic inner world becomes more manageable and our connectedness with it eases our sense of sterility, meaninglessness, and loneliness. Within their individual works and over time the views of the Cambridge scholars about the relative roles of myth and ritual shifted and evolved so that sometimes myth and ritual were conceived as occurring together simultaneously.[16] But what remained consistent was the idea that these early religious practices helped to identify and integrate the cultural communities who performed them and to deal with the 'uncharted region of human experience'.[17]

The promotion of societal health can be linked to Hughes's concept of the poet as shaman, which is perhaps the most well known example of his engagement with anthropological thought. The shaman is traditionally an individual who is valued for his immediate experience of other worlds, worlds of animality, death, and the unconscious, that are only accessible to the ordinary human being via ritual and myth. Joan Halifax has noted the following defining features of shamanism, all of which are relevant both to the self-perception of Hughes and to his use of myth in his poetry: an initiatory crisis; a vision quest, ordeals, or experience of dismemberment and regeneration; the sacred tree or axis *mundi*; spirit flight,

---

[16] Harrison herself, for example, moves from positing that 'ritual practice misunderstood explains the elaboration of myth' (1962: iii) to suggesting that there are times when ritual and myth arise *pari passu* (1912: 16). The status of the 'and' when considering myth and ritual continues to be a subject that preoccupies scholars of ancient religion. For an overview see Versnel (1990).

[17] Murray (1912*a*: 18).

mastery of the lower, middle, and upper worlds and the ability to enter an ecstatic trance; a healer and intermediary between the community and non-ordinary reality.[18] What this list suggests is that Hughes's identification with the shaman figure demonstrates his preoccupation with the public role of the poet, with his responsibility to share with his social group the special understanding he has gained from his trials. Terry Gifford and Neil Roberts describe his particular take on the shaman as follows:

A distinguishing feature of shamanic experience is the exceptionally vivid, coherent and shared forms taken by the unconscious life. The shaman can thus be seen as a man who, having experienced and overcome terrifying inward experience, is no longer at the mercy of death, of his animal self, of his unconscious in general and who, through a kind of artistic performance, shares this mastery with the community. It is clearly impossible for a modern English poet to *be* a shaman, but equally clearly Hughes'[s] preoccupations with the unconscious, with death, with the animal world and mythology show an affinity with the shaman's function. What a poet such as Hughes ultimately shares with the shaman is a concern for psychic equilibrium.[19]

In another essay from the *Winter Pollen* collection entitled 'Myths, Metres, Rhythms' Hughes expands upon precisely how he sees myth functioning to facilitate the psychic equilibrium of the group. He argues that mythologies are the picture languages we invent to embody, and make accessible to casual reference, the deeper, shared understandings which keep groups intact:

In an intact group the pool of shared understandings is like a shared bank account of the group wealth. Since it is spiritual or psychological wealth, it does not diminish by being spent. Rather, the more lavishly it is circulated, the greater the inner wealth and 'security' each single member feels to have. Intercommunication of those deeper shared understandings, through the tokens of mythology that represents them, strengthens the unified inner life of the group.[20]

---

[18] Halifax (1991).
[19] Gifford and Roberts (1981: 20–1).
[20] *WP* 310.

In a strategic mode reminiscent of the Cambridge Ritualists, Hughes projects the idea of an intact, psychologically coherent society backwards in time (to fifth-century Athens) and sideways to an exoticized location (contemporary Japan). But he does not rule out the viability of myth in the contemporary world. Indeed, he argues that every writer must work to resolve the dilemma of how to produce poetry or literature that has the potential to appeal, not only to those who share his particular cultural dialect, but also to a wider audience. He says: 'Each modern literary work has to take its place on a continuum between some sub-group's (the author's) system of shared understandings (and its mythology) and the most inclusive, ideally global wavelength of a multicultural lingua franca.'[21] Offering an example from his own work, he talks about the natural world as being one of the 'mythologies' he found he had to hand when he started writing that he assumed would provide a reliable, durable piece of mythological picture language that could be widely comprehensible. In fact, he discovered that it did not communicate effectively to, for example, a US urban poet who was not able to provide the missing 'reality context' for creatures from the natural world. He concludes that 'the atomization of shared "mythologies", which reflects the atomization of the deeper shared understandings, makes symbolic works less and less likely, and the old ones less and less comprehensible—except as scholarly reconstructions'.

It is clear, however, that, even as he acknowledged these difficulties, Hughes did not abandon the project of creating symbolic work nor, as we shall see, did he utilize mythological figures only in familiar, reconstructive, frameworks. Myth, in the broad terms in which he conceives it, is central both to his vocation as a poet, in that it provides a sort of alternative language in which he can mediate the emotion and experience of the inner world on behalf of the community, and to his choice of subject matter, in that if he draws on the wealth of myth, his poetry stands a better chance of becoming common currency amongst a wider group of readers. Poetry irrigated by myth is altogether more fertile.

The relation of myth to literature is something that as we have already seen is also considered by the ritual theorists. They interpret

---

[21]  *WP* 312.

works of literature, on the whole, as the 'outgrowth' or 'leftover' of myths that were once tied to rituals, either annual rituals that enact the death and rebirth of the vegetation god and/or, particularly in the case of Harrison, rituals of initiation into society. The most frequently discussed example of this phenomenon is tragedy which, in one way or another, is shown to hark back to myths which were originally the scripts of key ritual practices. Gilbert Murray, in his *Excursus on the Ritual Forms Preserved in Greek Tragedy*, originally published in Harrison's *Themis*, works through a list, not only of the extant plays, but also of the identifiable fragments, with the aim of showing how common formal features can be traced back to an origin in the myth of the death and rebirth of Dionysus. Tragic heroes, are all, for Murray, symbolic substitutes for this figure of Dionysus figured, in the mode of Frazer, as a vegetation god or 'Year-Daimon'. He is differentiated from other such divinities who emerge, obtain power, but are then slain by successors who are exactly identical to them. Dionysus, by contrast, did not die: he seemed to die but really it was his enemy, in his dress and likeness, it was Pentheus or Lycurgus who died, while Dionysus lived on in secret. As Murray puts it:

When the world seemed to be dead and deprived of him, he was there in the ivy and pine and other evergreens; he was the secret life or fire in wine, or other intoxicants. By this train of ideas Dionysus comes to be regarded not as a mere vegetation-spirit or Year-Daimon, but as representing some secret or mysterious life, persisting through death or after death.[22]

The word Dionysus in this passage could be regarded as an example of the kind of 'word that wields a story' mentioned in the 'Myth and Education' essay, a word, that is, that conjures up a story so well known that 'all its parts can be seen at a glance'. For those in the know, Dionysus is a name overburdened with symbolic meaning and its very mention has the power to summon up instantly 'the voltage and inner brightness' of the whole set of stories associated with him, just as, to paraphrase Hughes, you need only to touch a power line with the tip of your finger in order to obtain a spine-tingling electric

---

[22] Murray (1912*b*: 362).

shock. But in terms of Hughes's poetry who are we to assume constitute the category of those who are 'in the know'? If images from nature can lose their potency in a present-day urban setting, how do we expect figures from Greek mythology to continue to generate meaning in a modern multicultural world? These are questions provoked, of course, by any discussion of the processes by which the impact of texts transcends their particular cultural moment, of the complex possible relation between the time-bound and the timeless.

When Murray ponders the reasons for the enduring potency of Greek tragedy, he makes a clear distinction between content and form. He also recognizes that even when in thrall to progress, humanity still has need of, and recourse to, a sense of the elemental:

An outer shape dominated by tough and undying tradition, an inner life fiery with sincerity and spiritual freedom; the vessels of a very ancient religion overfilled and broken by the new wine of reasoning and rebellious humanity, and still, in their rejection, shedding abroad the old aroma, as of eternal and mysterious things: these are the fundamental paradoxes presented to us by Greek tragedy. The contrasts have their significance for other art also, perhaps for all great art.[23]

Perhaps, we might add, they might also provide an explanation for the saturation in Greek (and other) mythology of the poetry of Hughes. In 'Myth and Education' the latter develops a memorable image when he explicates the capacity of traditional stories to, as he puts it, 'think for themselves':

They not only attract and light up everything relevant in our own experience, they are also in continual private meditation, as it were, on their own implications. They are little factories of understanding. New revelations of meaning open out of their images and patterns continually, stirred into reach by our own growth and changing circumstances.[24]

The anthropomorphized stories here are seen to have a proverbial life of their own and are able both to illumine contemporary experience and to respond to it, ceaselessly giving birth to and nurturing fresh possibilities of interpretation. It seems a vigorous and life-enhancing,

[23]  Murray (1912b: 362–3).
[24]  WP 141.

if mysterious process of self-renewal and there is no sense here of the cultural sterility and resistance to or fear of change that have led some critics to censure the association of tragedy with cult, myth, and ritual on the grounds that it is a staple of profoundly conservative scholarship. In a typically combative piece, which parodies even as it articulates this position, Terry Eagleton draws out some of its political implications as follows:

Talk of blood sacrifice, dying gods and fertility cults smacks of a naturalization of history, an opposing of the mythic to the rational and the cyclical to the historical, along with a dubious belief that suffering is an energizing, revitalizing part of human existence. In this latter respect, the road from the plains of Argos to the playing fields of Eton is not as circuitous as one might suspect. It is the cultural ambience of the Cambridge School of anthropology and *The Waste Land*, an unholy *mélange* of Nietzscheanism and high Anglicanism which values the cultic above the commonplace, the premodern over the modern, natural vitality against urban decadence. It is a world of slain heroes and risen redeemers which shades easily into the Grail and Arthurian legends, and from there to the more fey dimensions of Oxford medievalism.[25]

Eagleton here brackets together the kind of myth-ritual scholarship and comparative method with which we have been concerned with Eliot's employment of myth and reference to *The Golden Bough* in *The Waste Land*. Whilst it is undoubtedly true that Eliot was very familiar, not only with the work of Frazer, but also with that of Harrison, Murray, and the other Ritualists, is it really the case that we want to argue that the former's hard-to-pin-down-but-almost-certainly-operative irony can be equated quite so easily with the projects of the latter grouping? And where, if anywhere, does Hughes's treatment of myth fit into the overall pattern? If we turn, at last, to the Prometheus poems we can begin to move towards some answers.

Hesiod explores the 'tricksiness' of the Titan in both *Works and Days* and the *Theogony*; Aeschylus, in *Prometheus Bound*, where the same epithets are repeatedly used of both Prometheus and Zeus, emphasizes the knowledge and insight of Zeus' rival, as well as his

---

[25] Eagleton (2003: 274).

unruliness, and draws attention to the doubleness of Prometheus'
theft, and gift, of fire. But the twenty-one short poems entitled
*Prometheus On His Crag* do not represent a linear narrative that
coincides with either the versions of the myth in Aeschylus or
Hesiod, although some details of the ancient authors' treatments
are alluded to fleetingly within them.[26] In poem 18, for example,
the stories of Io, Epimetheus, and Pandora appear in sound-bite
form in a curiously backhanded yet self-conscious way:

> The character neglected in this icon
> Is not moon-head Io, or the hornet
> That drove her through the limits.
> It is not the vulture
> With its solar digestion.
> Is not even Epimetheus the twin
> Who got away, in the end, with the heaven-sent girl.
> Is not even the girl
> With her gift pot, and its solitary hope.

But Hughes, having drawn attention in the first line to the iconic
status of the story, completes the priamel by introducing a completely new character to the tale:

> The figure overlooked in this fable
> Is the tiny trickle of lizard
> Listening near the ear of Prometheus,
> Whispering—at his each in-rip of breath,
> Even as the vulture buried its head—
> 'Lucky, you are so lucky to be human!

This small, mobile, reptilian figure articulates a sense of envy of
Prometheus which runs contrary to any rational reaction to the
sufferings of the shackled and tortured Titan. Its intervention, pre-
ferred by Hughes to those of the more familiar cast-list, is significant
both in terms of the novelty of the poet's mythopoiesis and in terms
of Prometheus' relation to the world of human beings, whom here he
seems to *represent* in spite of, or perhaps as a result of, the extremity
of his suffering.

---

[26] All references to the poems come from *CP.*

But it is not the case that it is impossible to trace any kind of developmental narrative throughout the series. It begins with Prometheus coming to after he has been pinned to the crag and not knowing what has happened, 'Returning,' he said, and 'Now I am | Feeling into my body,' and it ends (*Prometheus on his Crag* 21) with his release from torment in a dramatic representation of his messy symbolic rebirth:

> His mother covers her eyes.
> The mountain splits its sweetness.
> The blue fig splits its magma.
>
> And the cry bulges.
> And the veiny mire
> Bubbles scalded.
>
> The mountain is uttering
> Blood and again blood.
> Puddled, blotched newsprint.
>
> With crocus evangels.
> The mountain is flowering
> A gleaming man.
>
> And the cloudy bird
> Tearing the shell
> Midwifes the upfalling crib of flames.
>
> And Prometheus eases free.
> He sways to his stature.
> And balances. And treads
>
> On the dusty peacock film where the world floats.[27]

We could summarize the impact of the poems in-between by describing them as a record of Prometheus' struggles to make sense of and put into words the understanding he is able to gain only because of his torment. But this is not a straightforward process: there are times when he can not grasp who he is or what has happened (in poem 1 he asks 'Am I an eagle?'; in poem 5 he dreams that 'he had burst the sun's mass | And emerged mortal') so that the reader too is bewildered as to the geography and time-frame of the location of the story (in poem 6 when he bites off his 'prophetic tongue', frantic

---

[27] *CP* 296.

jumbles of pain-saturated words intersperse archetypal images of monumental landscapes with mundane descriptions of 'car-bumpers and shopping baskets'). In poem 20 he poses to himself a long series of questions, trying to work out the deeper significance of his plight: 'Was he an uninitiated infant | Mutilated towards alignment? | . . . Image after image. Image after image. As the vulture | Circled | Circled'.[28] But there are other times, such as poem 13, when moments of clarity allow him a firm grasp of what he has done and why he is punished:

> Prometheus On His Crag
>
> Heard the cry of the wombs.
> He had invented them.
> Then stolen the holy fire, and hidden it in them.
>
> It seemed to him
> The wombs drummed like furnaces
> And that men were being fed into the wombs.
>
> And it seemed
> Babies were being dragged crying pitifully
> Out of the wombs.
>
> And it seemed
> That the vulture was the revenge of the wombs.
> To show him what it was like.
>
> That his chains would last, and the vulture would awake him,
> As long as there were wombs
> Even if that were forever,
>
> And that he had already invented too much.[29]

Prometheus' potent and mysterious life-force persists in spite of the punitive world's denial and rejection, and is perceivable in the acceptance of the ruthless regeneration of nature and the circling reveries of an undying spirit that survives the torments of an earth-bound body. If we think back to the previous discussion, we might argue that in these poems Prometheus functions for Hughes as a complex amalgam of the shaman-poet, whose role is to mediate between inner and outer worlds on behalf of his community and who thus becomes the scapegoat who pays the price for communal

---

[28] *CP* 295–6.     [29] *CP* 291.

guilt, and the ubiquitous Year-Daimon or ritual initiand, whose participation in it lends an august weight to the story, and whose triumph over death and symbolic rebirth has the potential to transfigure even the bread-and-butter lives of twentieth-century mortals. In a later work, *Gaudete*, Hughes returns to the scapegoat figure, and in particular to Dionysus, and his work can thus be seen to mirror the trajectory of interest of a whole generation of classical scholars who were similarly fascinated with the arriviste god and who would concur with the idea of the scapegoat as 'The joker | That the confederate pack has to defer to', 'The champion of the swoon', and 'the lord of immortality . . . | A goat of testaments, a wine-skin of riddance.'[30]

Terry Gifford and Neil Roberts comment on Hughes's most conspicuously Dionysiac work thus, positioning it as central to his oeuvre in terms of its thematic concerns:

It seems to us to be connected with the necessity of establishing communications with the 'inner world' and creating some public, social embodiment of them, in a secularised world to which 'myth' has become synonymous with 'falsehood'. It must therefore be profoundly connected not only with the concerns of Hughes's other poetry but with his private and public identity as a poet. The reconciliation of the inner and outer worlds, and of the shamanic function with a fully, ordinarily human life, are essential parts of this preoccupation.[31]

This unusual work can be read as a modern-day 'version' of Euripides' *Bacchae* but with some significant differences. Hughes explains via the 'Argument' that functions as a preface that the main character, the Reverend Nicholas Lumb, is carried away into the other world by elemental spirits. During his absence an exact duplicate made out of a log but filled with 'elemental spirit life' takes his place and proceeds to organize the women in his parish into a coven and seduce them all, with the purpose of fathering a child who will become a 'messiah' figure. But at the point when the changeling is beginning to feel a nostalgia for 'independent, ordinary human life', the spirits who created him decide he must die, and the narrative of *Gaudete* recounts the last day of his life. When the men of the village discover what has been going on they kill him, but the original

---

[30] From 'The Scapegoat' in *Cave Birds*, CP 433–4.
[31] Gifford and Roberts (1981: 197).

Nicholas Lumb reappears, in the epilogue, in this world, in the west of Ireland, where he 'roams about composing hymns and psalms to a nameless female deity'.[32] The ordeal that he has undergone in 'the underworld, which is the spirit world and the animal world, the world under the world', leads to an experience of rebirth which mirrors that of the Prometheus/scapegoat figure in the shorter poems discussed above.[33]

It is clear from Hughes's 'plot summary' that the figure of Lumb encompasses both Pentheus and Dionysus because, in contradistinction to the *Bacchae,* there is no easy sense in which the champion of rationalistic discourse is vanquished by the embodiment of repressed elemental powers. However, such is the medley of cultural motifs used, combining the Christian liturgy suggested by the poem's title with the symbols of death and regeneration from a variety of 'pagan' cultures, that the experience of reading and making sense of the text involves a disorientating journey that can itself be figured as shamanic or transformative. Lumb's new mode of life with which the poem ends is not easy to evaluate, but it does seem to represent a vision of a harmony between inner and outer worlds that Hughes contrasts with the limited vision of the priest whose only way of making sense of the encounter with Lumb is to acknowledge to himself that 'something supernatural had happened'.[34] Hughes's religiosity in this piece is eclectic and hazily non-specific and it has led to the criticism that the attempt to portray a new public religion is 'tainted with a portentousness which, since it is not on any account possible to take it seriously, threatens to diminish the poem's genuine dealings with the "inner world"'.[35] However, at a time when there is a debate about the need for, and desirability of, a refined concept of universalism as a potential means of mediating between the old-fashioned transcendent universalism of 'cultural immobility' and an imminent universalism which centres on the idea of potential, there may be renewed appreciation for a sense of the religious which encompasses the imagery of more than one cultural tradition.[36] Jane

[32] In the introduction to the 1979 edition.
[33] Sagar (2000: 144).
[34] *G* 175.
[35] Gifford and Roberts (1981: 197).
[36] Cronin (2006: 30).

Harrison commented that 'it is when religion ceases to be a matter of feeling together, when it becomes individualized and intellectualized, that clouds gather on the horizon.'[37] Hughes knows too that there is a price to be paid for the true understanding which surpasses the merely intellectual. As Prometheus might have put it:

> Having first given away pleasure—
> Which is hard—
> What is there left to give?
> There is pain.
>
> Pain is hardest of all.
> It cannot really be given.
>
> It can only be paid down
> Equal, exactly,
> To what can be no part of falsehood.
>
> This payment is that purchase.[38]

---

[37] Harrison (1912: 487).     [38] *CP* 369.

# 7

## Hughes's Myth: the Classics in *Gaudete* and *Cave Birds*

### *Neil Roberts*

> I have often had the fancy that there is some one myth for every man, which, if we but knew it, would make us understand all he did and thought.
>
> W. B. Yeats, 'At Stratford-on-Avon: Ideas of Good and Evil', epigraph to *Shakespeare and the Goddess of Complete Being*

By this beguilingly capacious phrase 'Hughes's myth', I do not mean a coherent narrative that is detectable on the surface or even underlying his published works. I mean, rather, a way of thinking, an orientation to experience, especially subjective experience, that is fundamental to Hughes's identity as a poet. In this chapter I will say something about why myth is so important to Hughes, comment on two crucial personal texts in which Hughes is thinking mythologically about his own life, and finally discuss the classical contribution to two of his most mythological works, *Gaudete* and *Cave Birds*. I have chosen these two partly because in neither case is the classical element on the surface.[1]

Hughes as a man, or as a mind, presents his admirers with a paradox. He was an extremely intelligent man, a man of highly developed ratiocinative powers. His friend Peter Redgrove, when asked to identify the quality that most impressed him about

---

[1] See Sagar in this volume.

Hughes when he met him at Cambridge, came up with the word 'intellect'.[2] Hughes wrote a great deal of very persuasive prose, collected in *Shakespeare and the Goddess of Complete Being, Winter Pollen*, and elsewhere. Yet he hated discursive prose: 'all discursive prose vocabulary,' he said, is 'essentially false'.[3] He said about his own prose, 'My formal prose seems to exclude everything I want to say, as if some dalek had pushed me aside and taken my pen, and I loathe it.'[4] He is even said to have attributed his fatal illness to writing too much prose.[5]

Hughes's contribution to John Carey's collection of essays on William Golding, ostensibly a rereading of *The Inheritors*, is less a reading of Golding's novel than a meditation on the work of the early twentieth-century South African poet and naturalist Eugène Marais. From close observation of baboons, Marais convinced himself that the more intelligent these animals were, in the sense of being able to learn from experience, the less well adapted they were instinctively. Marais subsequently used experiments on hypnotized human subjects to prove to his own satisfaction that, in Hughes's words, 'the old animal brilliance of the senses emerged . . . performing nearly incredible feats of perception.' Hughes's meditation on Marais's work reveals his own profound engagement with the idea of

the subconscious as the lost, natural Paradise, where the lack of intellectual inquiry and adaptive ingenuity coincided with a perfect awareness of being alive in the moment, and in reality (an awareness approaching, maybe, a state of blessedness) and an inborn understanding of 'how to live'. He had explained, in a sense, man's perplexed feeling of being everywhere an exile, everywhere separated from his true being. And without saying that his smarter baboons had suffered something like The Fall, he had brought zoological evidence to the argument that the free intelligence is man's original enemy.[6]

The free intelligence is such a key value in our culture that that final sentence is, or ought to be, profoundly shocking, especially when

---

[2] Letter to Neil Roberts, 2 October 1979, Peter Redgrove Papers, University of Sheffield.
[3] Letter to Lucas Myers, Emory Mss 865, Box 1 ff4, April/May 1958.
[4] Letter to Ben Sonnenberg, Emory Mss 924, Box 1 ff4, 17 May 1992.
[5] Feinstein (2001: 237).
[6] Hughes (1986: 164). See Sagar in this volume.

cited in an academic essay. Without entering too thoroughly into the
polemical aspects of this world-view, which would consume the
whole of my chapter, it is Hughes's way of addressing the inherent
duality of human existence—the world as Will and Representation,
Dionysos and Apollo according to the two philosophers who most
deeply influenced him—the sense of being simultaneously separate
from nature and a part of it—which Hughes felt with exceptional
acuteness. And there is also, of course, the public aspect: the argument that the separation from nature that makes the free intelligence
possible is responsible for the destruction of the planet. The idea of
a Fall, explicitly stated in the Golding essay, constantly recurs
in Hughes's writing. It is also, in his view of human (or rather
Western) history, a constantly recurring event. At his most pessim-
istic, in the Golding essay, he sees it as a consequence of biological
evolution. More commonly he locates it in one or more of a series of
critical (in his view catastrophic) cultural moments: Greek rationalism, Judaeo-Christian patriarchal monotheism, the Reformation,
especially the downgrading of the feminine element in the Virgin
Mary, the scientific and industrial revolutions: all the events, in fact,
which have cumulatively shaped the world we live in.

The task Hughes set himself—or more accurately perhaps, that
was set for him by powers to which he owed allegiance—was to use
language in such a way as to circumvent the hegemony of the free
intelligence. At a personal level, he needed to capture for himself the
'perfect awareness of being alive in the moment' that he attributed to
the animals, and at a public level he was motivated to find language
in which to communicate this awareness.

Myth is central to this project. Hughes was the intellectual child of
Frazer but also of Freud and above all of Jung. The unconscious, and
above all dream, is where he primarily looks for his language. Dream
is the royal road to the unconscious; it is also, according to this view,
the royal road to the understanding of myth. In *Memories, Dreams,
Reflections* Jung describes his own search for his 'personal myth'.[7] He
asked himself the question, did he live in 'the Christian myth', and
answered no. Similarly, when Hughes writes of Ovid living in an age

---

[7] Jung (1963: 195).

when 'the mythic plane . . . had been defrocked', he is speaking of his own age too.[8] Jung embarked on a 'confrontation with the unconscious' in which he deliberately surrendered to the imagery of dreams and waking fantasies. He believed that if he had 'left those images hidden in the emotions' he would have been 'torn to pieces by them'.[9] In this dream world he met a guide called Philemon who 'said I treated thoughts as if I generated them myself, but in his view thoughts were like animals in the forest . . .'.[10] If, as is likely, he read *Memories, Dreams, Reflections* (published in English in 1963), the author of 'The Thought Fox' must have been profoundly struck by this passage.

The two personal documents that I am going to discuss are both based on dreams. The first is Hughes's account of the dream he had when reading English at Cambridge, which persuaded him to give up this pursuit and change to Archaeology and Anthropology. He published this as 'The Burnt Fox' in *Winter Pollen*. In the essay Hughes relates how, in his second year at Cambridge, he felt a strong resistance to writing the weekly critical essay that was then required of undergraduates. Having written poetry prolifically before going to Cambridge, he had either stopped writing it altogether or was dissatisfied with what he wrote. He came to blame academic study for this failure of his powers. One night he was struggling to write an essay, gave up and went to bed, where he dreamed that he was back at his desk, and a creature in the form of a fox, but larger and walking on its hind legs, entered the room. The fox was burnt: 'Every inch was roasted, smouldering, black-charred, split and bleeding.' Instead of paws it had human hands, one of which it laid on Hughes's essay and said, 'Stop this—you are destroying us.' When it lifted its hand it left a bloody print on the paper.[11]

I call this a myth, or an element in Hughes's myth, for two reasons. One, as already stated, the dream-work produces narratives that circumvent the rational intellect and, in Hughes's Jungian view, are a source of the myths that establish themselves in culture. But I also

---

[8] *TO* xi.    [9] Jung (1963: 201).
[10] Jung (1963: 107).    [11] *WP* 9.

mean that I do not take this as a reliable statement of autobiographical fact. It was by no means unusual for undergraduates to change from English to Anthropology, and F. R. Leavis, often prejudicially cited as epitomizing the anti-creative ethos Hughes struggled with, used specifically to encourage his students to do so. It did not need a crisis to provoke this move. But I do not mean that we should not take the story seriously. On the contrary, it is the most vivid and dramatic expression of Hughes's myth or creative consciousness.

The mythic element in Hughes's work is of course multifarious and does not reduce itself to a neat narrative. The story of Venus and Adonis is central to his interpretation of Shakespeare, and that of Orpheus was of such intimate relevance to his personal history that he wrote about it only in a children's play because it might seem too obvious an attempt to exploit his situation.[12] But in its central aspect, it consists of a limited number of key motifs: visitation, usurpation, and abduction. These were central motifs in Hughes's most celebrated early poems: the fox that 'entered the dark hole of the head' ('The Thought-Fox'); the pike that 'rose slowly towards me, watching' ('Pike'); the stoat that 'licked the stylist out of their skulls' and 'sucked that age like an egg' ('Strawberry Hill'); the crabs that 'press through our nothingness' ('Ghost Crabs'); the gnats whose dancing 'Rolls my staring skull slowly away into outer space' ('Gnat-Psalm').[13]

This myth is, or Hughes certainly thought it was, fundamentally shamanistic. His discovery of Mircea Eliade's *Shamanism* in 1964 was a critical moment in Hughes's conceptualization of his imaginative endeavour: above all his realization that the kind of poetry he most admired, and that he aspired to write, could be seen as a kind of shamanistic activity. The shaman is visited by helpers from the spirit world who usurp his everyday consciousness and/or abduct him into that world. As a consequence of this he acquires healing powers. How Hughes interpreted his dream immediately we cannot know, but we can be confident that after reading Eliade he would have identified his visitor as a shamanistic helping spirit, calling him to his true vocation, and away from false pursuits. He wrote in his review of

---

[12] Letter to Keith Sagar, BL Add. 78761, f27, 18 June 1998.
[13] *CP* 21, 84–6, 63, 149–50, 181–2.

Eliade, 'once you've been chosen by the spirits, and dreamed the dreams, there is no other life for you, you must shamanize or die'.[14] And much later, in the final year of his life, he described writing prose as 'burning the foxes' and interpreted the dream as a warning that prose was literally physically destroying him.[15] Another way of putting it, and a necessary counterbalance to the otherworldly implications of 'spirit world', is that Hughes's own biological self was speaking to him. In his important essay 'Myth and Education' he shows that he has a very distinctive understanding of subjectivity and the inner world: 'The outer world is only one of the worlds we live in. For better or worse we have another, and that is the inner world of our bodies and everything pertaining'.[16]

My second example of Hughes's personal myth is not nearly as dramatically vivid as his fox dream, but it is very important in that we can see him both explaining one of his most important volumes and interpreting a critical phase of his life in terms of the key motifs I have outlined. The collection *Wodwo* (1967) is puzzling in a number of ways. It is divided into three parts, the second of which consists of a radio play and five short stories. It was published seven years after its predecessor, *Lupercal*, and contains only forty poems. The intervening period of course includes the death of Sylvia Plath, and not surprisingly readers have tried to find in the book some reference to that tragedy. Perhaps the most puzzling thing about it is that it is prefaced by an Author's Note:

The stories and the play in this book are to be read as notes, appendix and unversified episodes of the events behind the poems, or as chapters of a single adventure to which the poems are commentary and amplification. Either way, the verse and the prose are intended to be read together, as parts of a single work.[17]

This instruction is even more confusing if we are aware that four of the five stories were written before 1960, during the period of *Lupercal*, the earliest of them in 1956, giving a total span of ten years for the composition of *Wodwo*. The intention of a single work is obviously retrospective. A very perceptive contemporary review by Daniel Hoffman saw the play 'The Wound' as central to this 'single adventure', and identified it as shamanistic in character, but by and large readers have ignored the instruction and treated *Wodwo* as a collection of discrete pieces.[18]

At the time of publication Hughes wrote to his friend the Hungarian poet János Csokits, explaining this 'adventure'. He described the book as 'a record—for me—of a rather baffled time' and went on:

> The order of the poems is not chronological, but arranged around the following theme: after an undisturbed relationship with the outside natural world, I receive a demand from behind—from a subjective world. The main event of the book—and of my life from 1961–2 onwards—is this invitation or importuning of a subjective world, which I refuse. I think I did refuse—or rather I deferred. And I paid for it quite heavily. The Rain-Horse [one of the stories in *Wodwo*] is the record of the importuning, & the refusal. The consequence of the refusal was a mental collapse into the condition of an animal. I refused the invitation, & so I was forcibly abducted. (All this is interpretation afterwards.) . . .
>
> All the poems in the first part are what I wanted to save, that were before the event, & yet seemed related to it. The stories are episodes of the event . . .
>
> The poems in the second part are poems after the event (though some were written quite a while before it. But prophetic poems don't come in order, in my experience.).[19]

This is not the place to speculate about the bearing of this on the actual events of Hughes's life in that period, including his affair with Assia Wevill, the breakdown of his marriage, and Sylvia Plath's suicide; or even on its equally obscure relationship to the poems of *Wodwo*. The important point for my theme is the centrality and urgency of the demand from the subjective world (the world of the inner body according to 'Myth and Education'), and the motifs of visitation (by the horse, a spirit-helper akin to the burnt fox) and abduction. The central text in *Wodwo*, and the one that may have precipitated the idea of the 'single adventure', is the radio play 'The

---

[18] Hoffman (1992).
[19] Letter to Janos Csokits, *LTH* 273–4.

Wound', which originated in a recurring dream. Apart from by Eliade's *Shamanism*, such ideas may also have been suggested by Jung's 'confrontation with the unconscious', if Hughes read *Memories, Dreams, Reflections* within a few years of its publication in 1963. He would have regarded Jung's account (as Jung himself probably regarded it) as the initiation of a modern shaman.

In the 1970s Hughes wrote what are perhaps his most ambitious and difficult works. This was the period in which, following on from *Crow*, his writing was most overtly mythological. The two longest and most ambitious of these texts are *Gaudete* (1977) and *Cave Birds* (1978).

The narrative of *Gaudete* is one of abduction and usurpation. The 'Argument' to the first edition actually states that Lumb is 'abducted by spirits into the other world.' If one were to choose a text by Hughes which exemplifies the 'single adventure', *Gaudete* would spring to mind much more readily than *Wodwo*. The 'invitation or importuning' takes the form of a visionary adventure (a dream in an earlier draft of the poem) in which Lumb is asked to heal a female figure who is described as 'half-animal . . . clear-dark back to the first creature'.[20] He refuses the summons, 'declares that he can do nothing', and consequently is assaulted, loses consciousness, and is usurped by the 'changeling', described in the later version of the Argument as an 'elemental nature spirit', made out of a log.[21] Especially in the light of the changeling's activities in the main narrative, having sex with as many of his female parishioners as possible, this might be glossed as 'mental collapse into the condition of an animal.'

Ever since I first read *Gaudete* in 1977 I have been fascinated by its resemblance to the *Bacchae*. It is like a distorted version of Euripides' tragedy, and it is of course the distortions that are most interesting. As Keith Sagar has told us, the *Bacchae* is 'the play which had meant more to [Hughes] than any other'.[22] It is also, perhaps, of all Greek tragedies, the most modern-seeming. Even more than *Oedipus Tyrannos*, it is an example of the post-modern trope of the text that is influenced by what was written after it, in this case most obviously

---

[20] *G* 14.    [21] *G* 15.
[22] See Sagar in this volume.

Nietzsche's *Birth of Tragedy*. For Hughes enthusiasts, one might add *Shakespeare and the Goddess of Complete Being*. Pentheus is a hero who perfectly fits Hughes's 'tragic equation', his synoptic key to Shakespeare's later works, based on the idea that the love-refusing Adonis of Shakespeare's first long poem switches over to the lust-maddened Tarquin of his second. Pentheus is a precursor of Angelo in *Measure for Measure*, of all Shakespeare's plays the one which is most illuminated by the 'tragic equation': the 'strict and exacting Puritan judge' who 'suddenly forgets his high office and duties, his reputation, his future, and lets lust overwhelm him'.[23] Not literally lust in Pentheus' case, of course, but the parallel is there. In *Tales from Ovid* 'Bacchus and Pentheus' is one of the poems which Hughes most elaborated beyond Ovid's text. The most striking of these elaborations are in Pentheus' invective against Bacchus, where Hughes writes with a relish and vigour that suggest a profound and not entirely unsympathetic engagement with the god's antagonist:

> How can you go capering
> After a monkey stuffed with mushrooms?
> How can you let yourselves be bitten
> By this hopping tarantula
> And by these glass-eyed slavering hydrophobes?[24]

Nicholas Lumb is another who is punished for his refusal by being 'switched over'. While we know little about the 'original' vicar, we can assume that he was a fairly conventional priest who, being unmarried, was probably celibate. His doppelganger is uncontrollably and destructively priapic.

Euripides' Dionysos, at different times in the play, refers to the god whose name he bears in both the first and the third person. It is all too tempting for Hughes scholars to see shamanism at every turn, but I think Hughes would have interpreted the controlling figure in Euripides' play as a shaman who had received and accepted the call, and is consequently a channel for the powers of the god. Lumb also, at least in the earlier stages of the work's development, was conceived by his author as a shaman: in one draft he is described beating a Siberian shaman's drum.[25]

---

[23] *SGCB* 167–9.
[24] *CP* 993.
[25] Emory Mss. 644, Box 68 ff2, pp. 39–45.

But Lumb is a failed shaman. As he confesses in one of the poems of the Epilogue, 'what I did only shifted the dust about'.[26] One of the most interesting ways in which *Gaudete* is a 'distortion' of the *Bacchae* is that Lumb combines the roles of Dionysos and Pentheus. He is the charismatic religious leader with female followers who engage in ecstatic religious ceremonies. He is also the man who refused the 'invitation or importuning', and is hunted down and killed by a mob at the end. But he is hunted down by men, not women—the second significant 'distortion'.

Keith Sagar asks in passing why Hughes did not choose to translate the *Bacchae* rather than *Alcestis*, since the former is not only a much greater play but also one that meant so much to him.[27] What he did with the *Bacchae* in *Gaudete* might help us to understand why he did not choose to translate this play. The motif of a man being hunted down and torn to pieces by frenzied women would have connected much more obviously with journalistic perceptions of Hughes's career than with his profounder themes. He was in the habit of referring to his feminist persecutors as 'Maenads'. In 1972 the American poet Robin Morgan published a poem, 'Arraignment', in which she accused Hughes of the murder of Sylvia Plath and exhorted her female readers to dismember him. Less sensationally, but more immediately, he was often barracked by feminists at readings of his poetry. His name attached to a version of this story is a provocation he is unlikely to have relished.

Even without this crude public risk, Hughes might have felt that, however much the *Bacchae* meant to him, it was not precisely the story that he wanted to tell. Dionysos invokes the great goddess, variously under the names Rhea and Cybele, but it is the male god who stands astride the world of the play. Dionysos may be very unlike Jehovah, the male god from whom Hughes was in flight, but the poet would not have wanted to give such a controlling and affirmative role to the charismatic and sexually alluring male. He was concurrently exorcising this version of masculinity in the *Cave Birds* poem, 'The Scapegoat':

> The beautiful thing beckoned, big-haunched he loped,
> Swagged with wealth, full-organed he tottered,

---

[26] G 187.     [27] See Sagar in this volume.

His sweetnesses dribbled,
His fever misted, he wanted to sob.[28]

In Hughes's myth the criminal is invariably male. Stereotypically, perhaps, he images the 'free intelligence' as masculine and the 'lost, natural Paradise' as feminine. He even described the hawk in 'Hawk Roosting', surely to most readers one of the most ferociously masculine-seeming of personae, as 'feminine' because it is 'Nature thinking'.[29] I suspect he would not have chosen to translate a play in which women are dramatized as frenzied murderers. It is true that they do not cut much of a figure in *Gaudete*, being mostly reduced to a state of numb imbecility by Lumb's ministrations, but it is important that the murder of Lumb is carried out by men. Moreover, it is also important that Lumb is not torn to pieces in a way that might be recuperated by analogy with Osiris, or shamanic dismemberment, but clinically shot, having been lined up in the viewfinder of a high-velocity rifle.

These considerations bring us to *Cave Birds*. Here the classical intertext is even more hidden, in the published text, than in *Gaudete*. *Cave Birds* is based on a series of drawings of grotesque birds by Leonard Baskin, out of which Hughes constructed a narrative, or as he puts it in the subtitle, 'drama'. The male protagonist is jolted out of his complacent consciousness by a series of symbolic visitants who accuse him of crimes against a female victim. He is brought to trial, found guilty, and executed. He is transformed in the underworld and reborn. In the course of the narrative his bird form changes from cockerel to crow and finally to falcon.

The motifs I have identified as central to Hughes's myth are all evident in this text. My reason for discussing it here is that, at least at some stage during the composition, Hughes identified his protagonist as Socrates. This may originate with Baskin, who titled one of his drawings 'A Tumbled Socratic Cock'. Hughes wrote the poem 'The Accused' in response to this drawing, and when he first published it he titled it 'Socrates' Cock'. At one stage the whole sequence was

---

[28] *CP* 433.
[29] Faas (1980: 199).

subtitled 'The Death of Socrates and his Resurrection in Egypt', and
Hughes explained this in a letter as

a critique of sorts of the Socratic abstraction and its consequences through
Christianity to us. His resurrection in Egypt, in that case, would imply his
correction, his re-absorption into the magical-religious archaic source of
intellectual life in the East Mediterranean, and his re-emergence as a
Horus—beloved child and spouse of the Goddess.[30]

Jolyon Pike pointed out that the response to the Socratic heritage in
Hughes's work as a whole is more complex than this implies. He cited
the favourable reference to Plato's ideas about myth in 'Myth and
Education', the uncollected poem 'River of Dialectics' in which water
is described as 'socratic', and above all the importance to Hughes of
Neoplatonism, in *Shakespeare and the Goddess of Complete Being*.[31]

I leave it to others who are more qualified to investigate the justice
of Hughes's conflation of Socrates and 'abstraction', and the implication that Socrates bears some originary guilt for the destruction of
the planet. (Incidentally, when reading his poem 'Tiger-Psalm',
Hughes used to say that the machine guns represented Socrates.)
Hughes may have been influenced by Robert Graves's attack on
Socrates' 'ideal homosexuality' as 'the male intellect trying to make
itself spiritually self-sufficient.'[32] I do however want to look a little
more closely at what the buried figure of Socrates actually means in
*Cave Birds*.

As we have seen, the reference to Socrates originates with Baskin. In
titling his image of a recumbent and indignant cockerel 'A Tumbled
Socratic Cock', Baskin may have had in mind the cock that Socrates
asked, with his dying words, to be sacrificed to Aesculapius. At this
stage, the reference to Socrates may be no more than a joke. Hughes,
however, took the connection seriously. If, as the notes to the Penguin
edition of the *Phaedo* (quite possibly used by Hughes) suggest,
Socrates's dying words are themselves a joke, implying that death is
the cure for life, and thanking the god of healing for putting an end to

---

[30] Letter to Neil Roberts and Terry Gifford, 29 October 1978, quoted in Gifford
and Roberts (1981: 260).
[31] At the 'Ted Hughes and the Classics' Conference, Edinburgh 2005.
[32] Graves (1948, rev. 1966: 12).

life, Hughes may have considered this a false transcendence that he wanted to resist.[33]

The word 'cock' may however have another connotation, one not usually associated with Socrates. Hughes's early poem 'The Perfect Forms' begins, 'Here is Socrates, born under Pisces, | Smiling, complacent as a phallus'.[34] Complacency, as I have said, is a prime characteristic of the protagonist of *Cave Birds*. When, in the first poem, he attempts to praise a world to whose suffering he is indifferent, his praise is usurped by a 'scream' that 'Vomited itself'—the retort coming, characteristically, from within his own body.[35]

In the same letter in which he described *Cave Birds* as a critique of Socratic abstraction, Hughes wrote that the guilt of the protagonist is 'the guilt of the extraverted, beady-eyed, predatory career of the organism making its way, clearing its space and setting up its fort and satisfying its needs.' These apparently contradictory meanings are combined in 'The Accused', where the cockerel-protagonist 'confesses' aspects of himself including

> his hard life-lust—the blind
> Swan of insemination.
>
> And his hard brain—the sacred assassin.[36]

There is a common term which I think makes sense of the yoking together of these heterogeneous ideas: masculinity. Hughes habitually thought of the rational intellect as masculine, and while the 'predatory career of the organism making its way' is not inherently gendered, Hughes's representation of it is invariably masculine as, here, in 'the blind | Swan of insemination', and in his interpretation of the Trickster hero as 'the immortal enterprise of the sperm'.[37] *Cave Birds* and *Gaudete* are Hughes's most intensely gendered texts, concerned centrally with masculine guilt, on both a personal and a cultural level.

I will end by making a more straightforward point about Socrates and *Cave Birds*, which will return us to our starting place. Plato's

---

[33] (1954: 168 n.60).
[34] *CP* 82.      [35] *CP* 419.
[36] *CP* 425.      [37] *WP* 240.

dialogues are arguably foundational texts not only of European philosophy but of discursive prose itself. Socrates, as the protagonist of Plato's prose discourse, starts a process that leads to the undergraduate Hughes struggling with his literary essays, and temporarily destroying his creative life in the process. His reading of Plato's dialogues and the *Bacchae* provided him with epitomes of the warring principles that shape his imaginative world.

# 8

## Between monarchy and democracy; neo-classicism and the laureate poetry of Ted Hughes

*Roger Rees*

In about 1954 Ted Hughes wrote for his sister-in-law Joan a charming dialogue between Elizabeth I and Elizabeth II—the apparition of an elderly Elizabeth I joins her young namesake at the fireside of Windsor Castle library, and they have an animated conversation about the influence a monarch could effect on the relationship between individuals and their society.[1] Characterization is strong, the writing efficient. At the age of 24, Hughes already had ambitions to spend his life writing, but his visions of his future no doubt fell short of what in fact was to happen—that twenty years later he would receive the Queen's Gold Medal for Poetry, ten years after that he would be appointed Poet Laureate, and that fourteen years later still he would be awarded the Order of Merit by Elizabeth II; and as Laureate he would get to know some of the royals quite well, notably the Queen Mother and the Prince of Wales.[2] But apart from an imaginative scope that allowed Hughes to leapfrog centuries of history to lay bare and refine his ideas, the dialogue he sent to his sister-in-law reveals his youthful interest in the British monarchy and its changing role in Britain. Many of the themes that appear in the

---

[1] Emory Mss 854, Box 1 FF38.
[2] On his youthful literary ambitions, Feinstein (2001: 5–49); on Hughes and the royals, Emory Mss 854 Box 1 to Gerald 18 May 1991; Middlebrook (2003: 267–8); *LTH* 551–2.

dialogue were to resurface in the more formal context of the laureate poetry Hughes wrote between his appointment in 1984 and his death in 1998.

The history of British laureate poetry from the institution of the office in 1668 is not one of many great literary moments. This is the case even though some (but not all) laureates have been the most distinguished poets of their day.[3] In the eighteenth century the laureate was faced with the restrictive obligations of composing poems for the monarch's birthday and for the New Year, leading to some particularly enervating literature. Typically a deliberately archaizing and classicizing genre, laureate poetry of the British Empire took as its model the panegyrical literature of the Roman Empire, where the Monarch-Emperor is the patron, their person and regime celebrated and praised in the venal creations of their client-poets. The correspondence between British and Roman Empires is particularly conspicuous when laureate poets have drawn explicitly on classical subjects for their praise of the British monarchy. Some lines from Nahum Tate's 'For the King's Birthday 1697' stand as a good example.[4] The poem for William III begins with an invocation to the Graces and Muses, and is dominated by celebration of the peace recently secured with France. The penultimate stanza apostrophizes William, and the closing one turns to the challenges left facing him:

> O favour'd both of earth and Heav'n!
> To thee, and only thee, 'tis giv'n
> Rome's first Caesars to out-do;
> Our Julius and Augustus too.

> War's dismal scene is chang'd to peace,
> Yet shall not his Herculean labours cease:
>     Nobler wars he now will wage,
>     Against infernal pow'rs engage,
>     And quell the hydra-vices of the age.

Such blandly classical references frequent many laureate works of the seventeenth and eighteenth centuries; and further direct debts to

---

[3] Broadus (1921); Hopkins (1954); Roberts (2006: 152); for a good sample of laureate verse from 1668 to 1981 with short critical biographies, see Russel (1981).

[4] Reprinted in full in Russel (1981: 35–6).

classical rhetoric, common in other laureate verse too, are the asser-
tions of divine support and of the subject's superiority to esteemed
predecessors.

Even after 1820 when the New Year and birthday obligations were
abandoned, the conventions of the office continued to exert a flatten-
ing, even deadening effect on the poets' literary imagination. For
example, an excerpt from John Betjeman's poem 'For a Royal Wedding
29 July 1981', the last laureate poem before Hughes's appointment:

> Blackbirds in City churchyards hail the dawn,
> Charles and Diana, on your wedding morn.
> Come College youths, release your twelve-voiced power
> Concealed within the graceful belfry tower
> Till loud as breakers plunging up the shore
> The land is drowned in one melodious roar.

There are no classical subjects here, but the ten syllable lines with
rhyme scheme is an archaizing form for the 1980s, and the implications of pathetic fallacies, the closing image of united national acclamation, and the fiction that the poem is a 'live' commentary on
the ceremony itself are rhetorical tropes of classical origins.[5] The
artificiality of certain clause structures and intermittently archaizing
diction reinforce the elitism of the poet's confident apostrophes; the
reader is excluded from the sentiment the poem purports to articulate, and is left a spectator not a participant. Nowhere evident is
Betjeman's much-loved sharp eye or independent stance, but all is
subordinated to an ingratiating tone.

But it is easy to sneer at laureate poetry. Pointed *animus* to the
many satirists who have ridiculed the laureates has been the political
ethic their official verse has tended to espouse: many laureates,
fulsome in their poeticized praise of the monarchy, have been the
butt of literary attack, seen to have sacrificed at once their artistic and
political integrity in return for the dubious benefits of office.[6] The

---

[5] For various similar examples, see also Thomas Shadwell, 'For Queen Mary's
Birthday 1691'; Nicholas Rowe, 'For the New Year 1716'; Laurence Eusden, 'For the
New Year 1720'; Colley Cibber, 'For the New Year 1731'; Alfred Lord Tennyson, 'A
Welcome to Alexandra, March 7, 1863'; Alfred Austin, '*Pax Britannica*'; John Mase-
field, 'A Prayer for a Beginning Reign'; Cecil Day-Lewis, 'For the Investiture'; and
Betjeman, 'November 1973' all reprinted in Russel (1981).

[6] Russel (1981: 1–5, 196).

tradition of satirizing the sitting laureate is almost as rich as the office itself, with Swift's *Tale of a Tub* and Pope's *Epistle to Dr Arbuthnot* and *Dunciad* eminent.[7] The emergence of democracy in the twentieth century (and with it the new respectability of the voice of republicanism) brought this issue into sharper prominence still, as it became increasingly embarrassing to articulate praise of the modern incumbents of the highest aristocratic elite of Britain.[8]

In the twentieth century there were further interesting decisions about candidates for the Laureateship—for various reasons, some established poets, such as Kipling, Hardy, and Housman never held the office; and in 1968 the ex-communist Cecil Day-Lewis was appointed. However, the appointment of Betjeman on Day-Lewis's death in 1972 can be regarded as 'safe'—a best-selling poet, in print and on TV a popularizer of Victorian architecture and Britain's landscape, a Christian, and since 1969, a knight—an institutional figure who was to write, as we have seen, some conventional laureate verse. The appointment of his successor was to be more problematic.

To commemorate the Queen's Silver Jubilee of 1977, Faber commissioned both Ted Hughes and Philip Larkin to submit a suitable quatrain to be inscribed at the publisher's offices in Queen Square, London. Both poems are essentially slight and conservative, as Neil Roberts has observed, but nevertheless, the Faber project is arresting—the juxtaposition of two poems of similar form and content would inevitably elicit comparisons, which might themselves inform (and oversimplify) opinion about the candidature for the Laureateship, when it was to become vacant.[9] When Betjeman died in May 1984, the Laureateship was offered to Larkin.[10] He declined. It was then offered to Hughes, who was cautiously interested.[11] His

---

[7] *A Pathetic Apology for all Laureates, past, present and to come* is an entertaining verse defence of the office by William Whitehead (1715–85), the seventh laureate, reprinted in Russel (1981: 85–8); Roberts (2006: 152–3).

[8] See *Laureate's Block* (2000) by the republican Tony Harrison. In a review, Reading (1992) cast Hughes's laureate poems as 'clumsily contrived, cringingly sycophantic, hack verse necessitated by the occupation of the anachronistic laureateship'; Roberts (1999).

[9] Roberts (2006: 156–8). Larkin had been thought a possible candidate in 1972.

[10] Cf. Hughes's conclusion 'Evidently Larkin hadn't been asked' in a letter of early 1985 to Leonard and Lisa Baskin, *LTH* 496.

[11] Letter to Leonard and Lisa Baskin, early 1985, *LTH* 494–6; Craig Raine in *The Daily Telegraph*, 2 April 2005.

hesitation was understandable—perhaps he feared his literary imagination would be dulled by the conventional duties of office; more
likely, as a man who had valued his privacy for many years, perhaps
he was turned off by the levels of publicity the office would be bound
to bring; yet perhaps too, the enthusiasm for the monarchy that his
1954 dialogue records made competing claims in the heart of the
now famous and controversial poet.[12] Hughes accepted, and was
appointed Laureate in December 1984.

In 1992 Hughes published *Rain-Charm for the Duchy and other
Laureate Poems*, a collection of nine poems, all but one of which had
originally appeared in national broadsheets.[13] One later poem can be
considered of a piece—entitled simply '6 September 1997', published
in *The Guardian* on the day of the funeral of Diana, Princess of
Wales.[14] The *Rain-Charm* collection is prefaced with a revised version of Hughes's 1977 Silver Jubilee quatrain; its inclusion confirms
the sense that Faber's 1977 exercise had been to some extent and to
some eyes an early audition for the Laureateship. By coincidence,
1992 also saw the posthumous publication of an alternative jubilee
quatrain that Larkin had written fifteen years earlier, but not for
publication.[15] The partisan politics and virulent racism of this alternative poem prompt Neil Roberts to wonder what would have
happened to the Laureateship had Larkin accepted the office.[16]
Clearly, the mid 1980s was a period of great import for the institution, and the Laureateship of Hughes, already a controversial and
scrutinized figure, was going to be of keen critical interest.[17] In this
chapter, I argue that *Rain-Charm for the Duchy and other Laureate
Poems* is an important body of work, which within the generic and
social restrictions of the form, offered new directions and energy to

---

[12] Hughes admits his 'boyhood fanatic patriotism' in his notes to *The Dream of the
Lion*, published in the *Rain-Charm* collection and reprinted in the *Collected Poems*.

[13] The exception is 'For the Christening of Her Royal Highness Princess Beatrice of
York'. Not included in the collection or *CP* is 'The Zodiac in the Shape of a Crown',
commissioned by the *Sunday Times* in 1982 when Betjeman was still alive, but
ultimately published in Brown (1987); *LTH* 497.

[14] Reprinted in *CP* 861.

[15] Roberts (2006: 156–8).

[16] *Ibid.*

[17] Russel (1981: 8), wrote 'If there is real competition next time around, interest in
the outcome should be enormous'.

the Laureateship.[18] Ironically, Hughes achieved much of this by redeploying some conventions of the panegyrical literature of the classical world.

In a letter in 1988 Hughes insisted 'The Office of Laureate carries no writing duties'.[19] He was right, of course—the British laureate can now choose whether, when and what to write. But where some other modern British laureates have in their official publications opened up to a wider agenda, such as in Day-Lewis's poems on the deaths of JFK and T. S. Eliot, or Andrew Motion's on the success of the 2003 England rugby team, with all the freedom of choice available to Hughes, the occasions of original publication of individual poems in the *Rain-Charm* collection signal a marked royalist dedication.[20] Royal christenings, royal birthdays, a royal wedding, an anniversary of accession to the throne, (and Diana's funeral); akin to the neo-classicizing tendency of earlier British laureate verse, Hughes's choices promote the image of a latter-day imperial cult, where the familial occasions of the reigning aristocracy provide the inspiration, structure, and focus for state ceremonial. What Hughes chose to commemorate in laureate verse suggests a return to this imperialist ideology. Despite this, the poems prove curiously resistant to simple categorization as works of profound conservatism, as Hughes's un-usual powers of absorption enabled him, across much of his laureate work, to attune the traditional rhetoric of classical panegyric to the contemporary ear. Some poems are more successful than others, of course, but across the ten there are distinctive, unifying features which mark the oeuvre as a genuine collection where the whole is greater than the aggregate of the parts; the cohesiveness of the poems is itself a vindication of Hughes's decision to publish the 1992 laureate collection, an unprecedented step in the history of the office.

The poem reprised from 1977 appears under a new title, 'Solo-mon's Dream'.[21]

---

[18] For other responses to Hughes's laureate verse, see Roberts (1985, 2006: 152–66); Reading (1992).

[19] Emory Mss box 78.1 to Mr Campion, 12 October 1988.

[20] NB Hughes's 1987 ecological-political poem 'Lobby from Under the Carpet' is not in the laureate collection, *CP* 837–8.

[21] The revision transposes the first two lines.

A Soul is a wheel.
A Nation's a Soul
With a Crown at the hub
To keep it whole.

The poem is dominated by monosyllables, but metaphor is fundamental to its economy—the ordinary and the elevated in tension.[22] A
religious dimension is manifestly there, in the new title (in keeping
with the British monarch's role as the head of the Church of England[23]), but its function is hard to pin down. With its conspicuous
symbolism and elusiveness, 'Solomon's Dream' seems at once both to
crystallize meaning and to resist exegesis, an ambivalence that can be
seen in many of the poems it prefaces. In Hughes's 1954 dialogue,
Elizabeth II's development of the image of the monarchy as a circus is
cut off by Queen Elizabeth I's outburst 'Stop this metaphorical talk.
I had enough with my court poets. Clearly now.' As the court poet
himself thirty years later, Hughes was to turn repeatedly to symbolic
registers.[24] The crown, rivers, animals, stars, and numbers occur and
recur to generate internal connections and resonances, a unifying
dynamic. Several laureate poems, notably 'Rain-Charm' itself, 'A
Birthday Masque', 'A Masque for Three Voices', and 'The Unicorn'
are artistically ambitious, narrated in different voices (or in the case
of 'Rain-Charm', a single voice in different settings), dense with
iconography, allusions, learning and lore, but Hughes was well
aware of the obscurity of some of the shorter works too, and the
1992 publication included the fullest set of dedicated notes he wrote
for any of his collections.[25] The notes vary in style and length, from
the anecdotal and personal to the more pointed detail of the traditional commentary form, their inclusion (as with Eliot's 'Waste-

---

[22] For the Jungian origins of the metaphors, see Roberts (1999).

[23] See Hughes's opening remarks in his note to 'An Almost Thornless Crown', the
second section in 'A Birthday Masque' in the *Rain-Charm* collection, reprinted in *CP*
1217.

[24] The rhyming imagery of crown/clown from the 1954 dialogue reappears in the
opening stanza of 'A Masque for Three Voices'.

[25] E.g. 'Little Salmon Hymn'; without Hughes's helpful note that the Queen
Mother was the Patron of the Salmon and Trout Association, the status of this as a
laureate poem would mystify most readers, *RC* Notes 53, reprinted in *CP* 1216; *LTH*
509–10.

land') a testament to Hughes's wish to bring difficult poetry within the grasp of wider comprehension.

The full title to the collection's eponymous poem is 'Rain-Charm for the Duchy. A Blessed, Devout Drench for the Christening of His Royal Highness Prince Harry'.[26] The poem is about a rainstorm in Exeter, and the rivers of the Duchy of Cornwall, loosely understood.[27] Neil Roberts said the poem 'would not be out of place in *River*... There is little internal evidence that it was written for the occasion, but the decision to use it was an inspired one'.[28] External evidence for the poem's evolution confirms this, since the various manuscript and typescript drafts are headed by different titles, including 'After the five-month drought', 'Rain-charm', and 'Rain-charm for bringing back the Salmon'—and the final version's royalist leverage is gained solely by its title, as there is no mention of royalty anywhere else in the text.[29] Hughes's final note on the poem identifies the drought as that of 1984, a spell of dry weather that he mentioned, for example, in three separate letters to his brother in Australia.[30] And yet, in what seems to have been a disingenuous claim, Hughes said in his note to the storm's break, 'A memorable moment. I recorded it then, in verses, as a fitting splash for the christening of HRH Prince Harry, the Duke of Cornwall's second son.' Truth be told, when the storm broke over Exeter, both the royal christening and Hughes's appointment as Poet Laureate were still some months in the future.[31]

A rain-charm is an example of control of the elements by proxy, or climatic obedience, an argument central to classical panegyric—many subjects of flattering addresses heard from their poets and orators that the weather had changed in their honour or that the connection between climate and natural fertility was dependent on

[26] Roberts (2006: 157).
[27] See Hughes's notes to the poem.
[28] Roberts (1985: 4, 2006: 155). Hughes's *River* was published in 1983.
[29] Emory Mss 78.5–6. Similarly, only the stark title '6 September 1997' identifies that poem as a laureate work. The objection of Reading (1992) 'there is not a member of the royal household in sight' misses the point.
[30] Emory Mss 854, dated 12 June 1984, 6 August 1984, and 4 September 1984. Notes to *RC* 52, reprinted in *CP* 1216.
[31] The christening was on 21 December 1984; Hughes became laureate the same month.

them.[32] In *Rain-Charm* Hughes casts an Angel of Water and another of Earth bringing their gifts ('A Birthday Masque'); a bee sings its song for a royal wedding ('The Song of the Honey Bee'); the totemic lion of British insignia is animated ('The Dream of the Lion'[33]); a catalogue of flowers wreath a crown ('An Almost Thornless Crown' in 'A Birthday Masque'[34]); in the same poem, the wings of thirty birds, again in catalogue, represent sixty candles. The consistent dynamic here is the traditional one that the forces and riches of nature marshal their support for the monarchy—historicism and *Realpolitik* are nullified as royalty is identified as a component of cosmic order. Of Hughes as Poet Laureate, Tom Paulin said the 'Nature poet reports back to society from the wild. He does not address us as citizens or preach the civic virtues, nor does he express opinions about public events or political issues'.[35] Instead, by redirecting his lifetime's interests in animals and flora, the 'nature poet' could write fundamentally celebratory poetry, which like much else of his oeuvre would reach into a timeless shared memory to a primitive truth.[36]

The formulae of celebratory poetry have to be refreshed and repositioned to reflect new light, and most British laureates have lacked the literary imagination to carry this off—Betjeman's City blackbirds are a case in point, where the link between the birds and the royal wedding is heavy-handed, even ostentatious.[37] Hughes's

---

[32] E.g. Homer, *Od.* 19.108–14; Hesiod, *Works and Days* 171–3, 225ff.; Vergil, *Eclogue* 4; Horace, *Odes* 4.5; Calpurnius Siculus, *Eclogues*; Tacitus, *Annals* 16.1.1; Pliny, *Panegyricus* 30, *Panegyrici Latini* X(2)11; Menander Rhetor, *Basilikos Logos* 377.

[33] Hughes explained his attempt to use the lion as a totem of British unity to Keith Sagar.

[34] This second section of 'A Birthday Masque' was revised from the original appearance in *Flowers and Insects* (1986)—a clear-cut example of Hughes working existing material to fulfil a laureate brief. On Hughes's regular revising and reprinting, see Keegan, *CP* viii.

[35] Paulin (1992: 252).

[36] Roberts (2006: 153).

[37] Another example is a stanza in Tate's 'For the King's Birthday 1697', mentioned above, which runs

> Let winter smile, the fields be gay,
> Woods and vales in consort sing,
> Flowing tides their tribute bring,
> To welcome peace and Caesar's day.

version of a similar conceit, a stanza in 'Candles for the Cake' within 'A Birthday Masque', shows an engagingly lighter touch:

> Thrush and Blackbird, ringing alarms
> For worms who lie too late in the dew, while dawn
> Snorts and tramples in the dark stable—
>     Fourteen candles.

Unlike Betjeman's, the language is contemporary, the form freer with notable enjambement (until the third line), but the text is allusive.[38] As the stanza progresses, the focus remains squarely animal, moving from the birds to the worms to the arresting equine metaphor—the celebratory, laureate content is understated, trimmed and squashed into a hyphen and a prosaic, clipped closing phrase. The ideology remains entirely conservative, but the style and balance of the writing give it a radical charge to make the poem more acceptable to modern taste.[39]

    Even when it has invoked the forces of nature, panegyric has been a civic genre. *Panegyris* was the Greek word for the assembly of state, and panegyric was the speech or poem that celebrated in praise in front of the gathered crowds, literally a showpiece genre for show-casing its subjects, in ancient times in front of senators, ambassadors, courtiers, usually in grand and public settings such as palaces, senate houses and basilicas.[40] Ostensibly then, from his farm in Devon, Hughes would find laureate verse difficult to write, and as the poet of the cruel realities of farming life, in, for example, 'Ravens' and 'February 17th', he would recoil from civic poetry embellished by the cloying sentimentality of the genre of pastoral.[41]

---

[38] Hughes's 'dawn | Snorts and tramples' recalls Eliot's 'Out at sea the dawn wind | Wrinkles and slides' ('East Coker' in *Four Quartets*); see in this volume Talbot and Silk.

[39] Hughes's least imaginative laureate poem, 'The Song of the Honey Bee', employs conceits much like Betjeman's, such as in the opening stanza

> When all the birds of Roxburghshire
> Danced on the lawns, and all
> The Salmon of the Tweed cavorted
> Over the Garden Wall.

[40] E.g. Burgess (1902, reprinted 1987); MacCormack (1981); Walker (2000).

[41] Gifford (1994, 1995: 114–39).

In fact, 'Rain-Charm for the Duchy' explores a tension between the civic and natural. The poem is set in Exeter city centre. This is part of its narrative authenticity, a reminiscence of the occasion of the downpour, but there is no attempt to make the city the majestic focus, the grand architectural backdrop to mirror the high ceremonial of an imperial or royal occasion (as Betjeman had St Paul's). Rather, in 'Rain-Charm' the classical way of presenting civic space is undercut by the elemental forces of the weather—'Thunder gripped and picked up the city', 'The cathedral jumped in and out | Of a heaven that had obviously caught fire | And couldn't be contained'— and ironized by the transfer to the elements themselves of the conventions of British urban celebration, 'Thunder was a brass band accompaniment | To some festive, civic event', 'And the heaped-up sky | Moved in mayoral pomp'. Through the metaphors, natural workings replace civic order and the city centre is diminished and subordinate in the grander scheme—heaven is on fire, there is an image of shipwreck, buildings are under attack, even cartography is overridden ('Uprooted chunks of map'). The style of this first half of the poem consists of conversational parataxis ('almost . . . almost . . . really . . . '), even including unresolved sentences ('Squeals and hurry', 'With tourist bunting'). In this abrupt and colloquial syntax, verse form and sentence structure frequently collide in a chaotic rush that mirrors the downpour.

This paratactic style is not untypical of Hughes, but it is particularly effective in contrast with the composed hypotaxis cataloguing West-Country rivers in the second half of the poem.[42] Throughout this catalogue, 'And' segues to a present participle ('clearing . . . deepening . . . beginning', etc.), and the different rivers' names provide further rhetorical structure.[43] This movement from the chaos and inconcinnity of the civic setting, reinforcing the images of violent disruption of man-made order, to the elaborate but controlled catalogue of the response of the natural world to the same storm is a dynamic which might argue for the inferiority of social

---

[42] The change occurs at 'You remembered earlier harvests'. Cf. the claim of Reading (1992) 'There is no formal structure'.

[43] Cf. the structured 'Here . . . And here . . . And here . . . ' etc. in 'The Ring' in 'A Birthday Masque'.

order to nature, a hierarchy visible in much of Hughes's output generally, but here geared towards his laureate agenda.

For classical poets from Homer through to late antiquity, rivers were peculiarly rich subjects for ideological and representative expression. Most grandly, Homer's Scamander and Vergil's Tiber are personified agents in their epics. This capacity of rivers to represent the nation state was pressed into the service of British laureate poetry as an attractive means of urging a sense of identity through geography.[44] Hughes's 1983 collection *River* is a series of intimate, sometimes autobiographical reflections on river ecologies and experiences, some specific in time and place, others less so.[45] In turning again to rivers in many of his laureate poems but maintaining the intimacy of voice and perspective that characterizes *River*, Hughes was able to resuscitate a traditional form without becoming stuffily archaic. In 'Rain-Charm' the representative burden is carried not by Britain's biggest rivers (such as the Thames, the Severn, or the Avon) but a river system of England's south-west, well known to Hughes of course, but not generally familiar. There is a more expansive canvas in 'A Birthday Masque', when the Angel of Water brings purity to 'All the kingdom's hurt rivers', where the contemporary edge of the environmental intimations counterbalances the elevated imagery. In 'A Masque for Three Voices' the second voice has a distinctive setting—the rural north of Scotland with details of its landscape and wildlife, far removed in place and tone from the historical narratives of the poem's first voice.[46] Here again, Hughes uses the detail and atmosphere of Britain's waterways, this time unnamed 'gravelly burns' and 'lit lochs', to effect a counterpoint. A metaphorical vein continues in the opening lines of '6 September 1997', when the unifying effect of Diana's death on the public is cast 'Mankind is many rivers | That only want to run'. The river, as natural reality and national icon, was a fertile subject for the nature Poet Laureate, one which allowed him variously to invest the ordinary with the symbolic without sacrificing accessibility. For Hughes, a river could be more

---

[44] E.g. N. Rowe, 'For the King's Birthday 1718', T. Warton, 'For the King's Birthday 1790', (both reprinted in Russel 1981: 53–4, 98–100).

[45] Roberts (2006: 140–51).

[46] The voice moves from the North Esk (Angus) to Scapa Flow (Orkney) to Ben Nevis.

than a river provided it kept its wetness; his most successful laureate treatments preserve both the realism and the iconicity.

Rivers in the 'Rain-Charm' catalogue are symbols of British history, metaphors for the passage of time. In this poem and 'A Masque for Three Voices', the incarnation of rivers as national history is an inspired solution to the problems panegyrical writers have faced in situating their specific subject in the endless context of time.[47] The vicissitudes of time have always enjoyed the potential to mock panegyric, as the typically extravagant claims and flattering predictions have been proved wrong over the course of years. Hughes himself fell foul in 'The Song of the Honey Bee', when the pathetic fallacies and elevating similes were to be cruelly exposed by the subsequent history of the marriage of Prince Andrew and Sarah Ferguson.[48] In a different strategy, in two short poems for Beatrice of York, Hughes followed squarely in the footsteps of panegyric from classical antiquity for which the attractions of time's coincidences had been irresistible, with natural prodigies and astronomical phenomena eagerly exploited as signs of a cosmic welcome offered to their subjects.[49] Both poems focus on the curious cluster of eights in the precise time and date of the Princess's birth (8.18, 8/8/88). Hughes's interest in the zodiac is well documented, and the two poems deny that the timing of Beatrice's birth was a mere coincidence but rather a Fate intentionally brought about by the workings of the cosmos.[50] 'For Her Royal Highness Princess Beatrice of York' begins

> Time sieved every
> Hour and date
> For Leo's every
> Lucky Eight—
> Linked and locked them
> Into a necklace
> For so fortunate
> A Fate

[47] For Hughes's lack of interest in history, or the conventions of historiography, see Brandes (1994); O' Brien, (1998: ch. 2, 'Ted Hughes: Time not History').

[48] O' Brien (1998: 40).

[49] Menander Rhetor, *Basilikos Logos* 371.

[50] On Hughes and astrology, Middlebrook (2003: 51–6); NB Hughes's comment 'Almost as if there were something in Astrology', regarding a horoscope poem for Prince William, excluded from *RC* and *CP*; *LTH* 497.

The diction is unassuming, the collocations more elaborate—the alliteration and assonance of 'Leo—Lucky—Linked and locked', and with less insistence in 'fortunate | A Fate' reinforce the classical argument that a person's happiness, (in Latin, *felicitas*) is their due reward, and not something randomly given.[51] But contemporary scepticism is too widespread for such lines to be other than an amusing but contrived distraction for most readers, themselves excluded from what seems Hughes's personal indulgence. More coherent is the contribution of time and history to the panegyrical argumentation of the two laureate poems set for long sections in riverscapes.

'Rain-Charm' recalls the downpour as experienced by two people, 'I' and 'You'. The various surviving drafts record that the stanzas of the river catalogue in the second half of the poem underwent particularly heavy revision and one notable feature is the ultimate suppression of many first-person references.[52] Another rejection was the line 'You knew the water was a god'. The effect of this editing is to pare down the personal elements of the poem and to make the rain and its effects a stronger focus. At the same time, the rejected line recalls the opening to T. S. Eliot's 'Dry Salvages' from the *Four Quartets*:

> I do not know much about gods; but I think that the river
> Is a strong brown god—sullen, untamed and intractable.

Despite the ultimate rejection of the line, the intertext prompts interpretation of Hughes's river catalogue as a realization or enactment of the reflections that follow Eliot's opening:

>                     the brown god is almost forgotten
> By the dwellers in cities—ever, however, implacable.
> Keeping his seasons, and rages, destroyer, reminder
> Of what men choose to forget. Unhonoured, unpropitiated
> By worshippers of the machine, but waiting, watching and waiting.

In Hughes's poem, the rivers of the Duchy are precisely these ageless *numina*, observing human affairs and ready to awaken at an appro-

---

[51] Cf. 'The props . . . | Stopped at felicity' in 'The Song of the Honey-Bee'.
[52] Emory Mss 78.5–6.

priate time. Rivers are an elemental force, but not arbitrary—that the appropriate time for them to stir is Prince Harry's christening is the decisive, laureate twist.

When, in catalogue, the rivers respond to the rainfall, they reanimate and bring up to their surfaces the distant histories they have witnessed and shared. The gorges of the river Lyn 'rehearse forgotten riffles'—forgotten, presumably, by others, such as men in cities such as Exeter. The Scamander of Homer and the Tiber of Vergil were spokesmen for their epics' great cities, Troy and Rome, but Hughes evokes rivers in rural settings, not immune from the effects of urbanization, as we shall see, but not civic agents either. The narrator thinks of the river Mole

> Rousing the stagnant camps of the Little Silver, the Crooked
>     Oak and the Yeo
> To a commotion of shouts, muddied oxen
> A rumbling of wagons.

The images call to mind mobilization for any conflict up until the First World War, just as the 'Flak and shrapnel | Of thundercracks' in the city centre recall the bomb damage Exeter suffered in the Second World War. The river Tamar revives the mediaeval era ('her rusty knights tumbling out of their | clay vaults, her cantrevs assembling from shillets'[53]) and the river Dart, 'her shaggy horde coming down | Astride bareback ponies' the pre-Roman period. The history Hughes chooses here is legendary and military—that is, the staples of traditional, panegyrical conceptions of national identity and culture[54]— but the narrative method's play with time is indebted to the manner and matter of Eliot's 'eternal present'. Through these snapshot stills and the interstices of imagery, Hughes co-opts British history to generate a temporal dimension against which Harry's christening could have significance. History is not in the past but in the rivers,

---

[53] A 'cantrev' (or 'cantref') is an Old Welsh term for an administrative district, but can be used, such as in the *Mabinognion* collection of Celtic myth and legend, as the military strength such a unit can muster. 'Shillet' is a soil type from south-west England. Hughes's language here draws on ancient, indigenous dialect, just as the soldiers are figured as emerging from the earth.

[54] NB the importance of the two World Wars in shaping Hughes's vision of British identity, as explained in his notes to 'A Masque for Three Voices'.

waiting to be replayed in the present.[55] The numinous ageless rivers represent British history's consent to the christening. The grand gestures of the granting of consent by nature and time are the engines of the panegyric and render it unnecessary, irrelevant even, to detail the date of the birth or the christening, or the name of the child.

In his notes to 'A Birthday Masque' Hughes elaborates on notions of temporal scales when he identifies the Crown of Flowers as a symbol of 'natural time', to be differentiated from 'historical time'— 'the flower of five million years ago is still absolutely up-to-date'— and the Crown is, of course, the monarchy's best-known icon. The argument that the monarchy is part of the order of natural time, above the 'tabloid scrimmage of ideologies' is reprised by association with the riverscape in 'A Masque for Three Voices'.[56] The poem was written for the Queen Mother's ninetieth birthday in August 1990; it is an elaborate work whose first voice in a neat and inviting conceit consciously maps the events of the twentieth century onto the life-span of the Queen Mother. This voice romps through its stanzas, a quickfire narrative of political and cultural 'historical actuality' in ballad metre.[57] In more contemplative mood, in rhyming triplets the third voice reflects on these historical changes and their impact on a sense of Britishness. Distinguished by its freer verse form, the second voice is a bold contrast, a witness to the changelessness of the Scottish wildernesses it observes.

> But here, a drama
> None has revised
> Since it rehearsed
> The first scene first.

At this point, 'historical time' is simply irrelevant to the voice, every process instead part of the endless iteration of nature's rhythms. From a white stone in the River North Esk, a fish is seen pausing to rest:

> A weightlessness
> Nudging the future

---

[55] A similar conceit is used of the eponymous plants in 'Thistles', the opening poem of *Wodwo* (*CP* 147).
[56] *CP* 1217.
[57] Roberts (1999: 10). For the phrase 'historical actuality', see *CP* 1221.

That presses and freshens,
Resting,
With a shiver,
There, where, wordless,
The eyes of the bear
Watched that same sleeked
Silhouette stroked
By the flow, on the same
White stone where,
A moment ago,
It slid into place

Nature's changelessness, seen in a crown of flowers, or here in the shared experience that unites the speaker with the bear of prehistory, is a continuity that overrides the detail of civic and political contingency. The fabric of the second voice's repetitions and the insistence and excitement of its breathless punctuation as it sets the particular against the general, again recalls the 'eternal present' of the *Four Quartets*.[58] But with the voice's further reflections and its resonances with Hughes's earlier laureate poetry, the riverscape illustrates not history's futility but its potential for congruence with natural time. The river's 'salmon beneath | A breathing shawl | Of bubbles', cradled by the (unidentified) 'mother of heather' recalls the images of weaving and birthing in 'Little Salmon Hymn', where, as Hughes explained in his note to the poem, the Queen Mother was 'godmother of the salmon'.[59] The association between the Queen Mother and nature is pressed further in 'A Masque for Three Voices' by the image of a deer 'crowned with the peaks | Of her own home' giving birth to a fawn—the 'Queen's daughter'. The maternal theme then combines with the riverine when Hughes intersects historical and

---

[58] E.g. 'A Masque for Three Voices', 'Before you can say | I am here, now, | This day, this moment, | Watching that fish, Stilled'; cf. 'Burnt Norton' and 'Little Gidding', 'Quick, now, here, now always—'; 'East Coker', 'I am here | Or there or elsewhere'. A tempting parallel for engagement with the *Four Quartets* from his laureate years is Hughes's 1994 poem 'Snapshot', 'O salmon, arc up, shatter the goggling lens—| Fall back into the cradle of beginning | And ending'; cf. 'East Coker'.

[59] See above, n.25. Note too the salmon in the first stanza of 'The Ring' in 'A Birthday Masque' and the restrained final stanza of 'Rain-Charm' and Hughes's notes to that poem. For a classical precedent for river fish as a nation's jewels, see Ausonius's *Moselle*; and cf. Hughes's 'The River in March' and 'Mackerel Song' from *Season Songs* (*CP* 308–9, 316–17).

natural time: the Queen Mother's well-known ministrations to the victims of London's Second World War blitz are figured as the water of the Cairngorms' streams:

> It was there
> That the snowmelt speechless water spilling
> Off the island's
> Highest, holiest hill—the sudden hill
> Unveiled only at the last moment,
> Flowed through a Queen's arms
> Poured from the palms of her hands
> Into the powdered shape on the stretcher,
> Into the burnt thirst, the bomb-wounds.

This elaborate imagery and conspicuous attention to sound effect provide the culmination of the poem's argument, according to which the healing powers of the monarchy and the land are one, and in the person of the Queen Mother there are numinous and chthonic essences that transcend historical time of which, at once, she is part; and just as in 'Rain-charm', where Exeter city-centre's vulnerability to the thunder-storm's warlike 'flak and shrapnel' contrasts with the rural rivers' resilient response to the elements, so too here, it is the pure water of Scotland's countryside that helps the war-afflicted city.[60] Panegyric has always sought to locate its subjects in the grand dimensions of place and time, immediately exposing itself to ridicule; ambitiously configured, 'A Masque for Three Voices' constitutes a serious attempt to combine the spatial and the temporal in a definition of national identity, based not so much on the character of the Queen Mother as on what she could represent—in this case, the cleansing strength of water.

Hughes's laureate collection avoids the classical practice of characterizing subjects by reference to an ethical canon (such as justice, courage, wisdom, etc.) and prefers to sustain, through a range of figures, an elevated representative register.[61] A clear example of this is

---

[60] For sound effect, note the instances of alliteration ('speechless...spilling', 'highest, holiest hill', 'poured...palms...powdered', 'burnt...bomb'), repetition ('hill...hill', 'Into the...Into the') and assonance ('arms...palms', 'burnt thirst').

[61] O' Brien (1998: 40).

the final lines of 'Envoi', the last section of 'The Unicorn', itself the last poem in *Rain-Charm*, written for the Queen:

> Looking at her
> All see the Crown.
> Some, their mother.
> One, his wife.
> Some, their life.

But while untrammelled praise of a royal individual's virtues may jar in modern Britain and Hughes perhaps did well to avoid it, there would be dangers too with a heavy reliance on iconicity and representation. For a British laureate in the late twentieth century, a problem with royal iconography such as crowns or lions, was that it was too easily associated with a purely sentimental or nostalgic vision of nationality, removed from the grit of reality. The second voice in 'A Masque for Three Voices', couched in soft focus, courts this very danger and perhaps fails to bear the weight of its own ambitions with conviction. The very iconicity of the Scottish landscape and its metaphorical application are too little tempered by touches of realism to appeal to contemporary taste.

More successful in this respect is 'Rain-Charm' itself. 'Rain-Charm' is narrated in an inconspicuous voice, its occasionally clichéd and prosaic speech-patterns amounting to an engaging sense of vulnerability beside the scaffolding of the poem's massive panegyrical project; by contrast, the apostrophes of the four concluding stanzas in 'A Masque for Three Voices' ('You have worn', 'You thread', 'You made', etc.), and the absurdly grandiose claims to be a spokesperson for 'us' ('Much like our heartbeat, like our verb "to be"') signal a switch to the explicitly panegyrical and elitist voice of traditional laureate poetry. The 'you' of 'Rain-Charm' is a friend or partner, not Prince Harry, and for all its careful reworkings, this intimate monologue comes over as an unstudied recollection.

Similarly, where 'A Masque for Three Voices' distils a picture-postcard view of Scottish riverscapes, ('I watch a hind | Lightly climb | Crowned with the peaks | Of her own home'), 'Rain-Charm' has more candour:

> And the Okemont, nudging her detergent bottles, tugging at her
> Nylon stockings, starting to trundle her Pepsi-Cola cans

Hughes's own environmental interests can be seen here, as also in a completed stanza he suppressed entirely.[62] The honesty of the image of the Okemont claims an integrity for the poem that engages modern taste. In combination, the tricolon of participles and the everyday language for everyday pollutants poeticize the ordinary, keeping traditional style and contemporary diction in tension, granting easy access to a broad spectrum of readers. Hughes achieved a similar effect in this and certain other laureate works by his diction, when he turned boldly to the lexis of Anglo-Saxon to sit alongside classical derivatives, or to colloquialism to accompany elevation: words such as 'blobby', 'sploshing', 'quartzy', 'odd bits of dead stick', 'shaggy' ('Rain-Charm'), 'spermy', 'can-can music', '*TV Times*' ('A Birthday Masque') do not so much deny the formality of the royal occasions the poems celebrate as insist with unashamed delight that space be made for a demotic character in a genre conventionally the preserve of the elite.[63] Where the generally assured grandeur or ingratiating tone of earlier laureate poetry had alienated the ordinary society it purported to represent, and thus reinforced the social hierarchy whose summits it celebrated, at its most successful, Hughes's choreographed informality represented the ordinary without claiming to.

The irony that Hughes's best-loved laureate poem, 'Rain-Charm', was in a sense the only one that could be labelled 'accidental' (in that

---

[62] 'Surprising what effect the Poet Laureate label has', Hughes wrote to Keith Sagar, 21 January 1985, British Library MS ADD 78757, p.150, quoted by Gifford (2006: 42–3). 'The line about the pollution (quite mild and domestic) of the Oakment caused great agitation in Oakhampton (responsible for the refuse)—might even affect the Council's laissez faire. These are the perks. Pity I didn't leave in the lines about the Torridge—they were

> And the Torridge, that hospital sluice of all the doctored and
> scabby farms from Welcombe to Hatherlea to Torrington
> Poor, bleached leper in her pit, stirring her rags, praying that this
> at last is the kiss of the miracle,
> That soon she'll be plunging under her sprays, splitting her lazar
> crust, new-born,
> A washed cherub etc.'

[63] On Hughes's diction, Heaney (1983), Talbot (2006: 137–8); Roberts (2006: 14); see also *WP* 40–1; Ingelbien (1999).

it had originally been drafted for *River*) exposes the difficulties of writing royal panegyric in a modern democracy.[64] The ideals of egalitarianism and freedom of speech must militate against praise of the aristocracy.[65] Concluding his reaction to the *Rain-Charm* collection, Peter Reading suggested that Hughes had turned from laureate poet to court jester.[66] In the context of the excoriating review, the remark seems intended cruelly to ridicule Hughes rather than to characterize him as the paradoxical figure of the wise clown who offers advice to the powerful. Certainly, Hughes appears to have enjoyed being laureate;[67] and at no point does he appear to have sought to influence the British monarchy in the way some critics have understood certain classical panegyrists to have attempted to influence their subjects.[68] He channelled much energy into the wider opportunities the laureateship gave him to extend his interests in areas such as education and the environment, but the coherence of his official verse attests too how seriously he took his literary duties.[69] Undeniably, *Rain-Charm* offers no challenge to the monarchy, politically or ethically, but celebrates the institution by articulating a sense of its symbolic role in society.[70] This had exercised Hughes as a

[64]  Hughes characterized the poem as an ordinary poem of a type 'incidentally dedicated to some royal person or occasion', *LTH* 620.

[65]  O'Brien (1998: 38). Hughes wrote to Keith Sagar 'Who can write in an amiable way to any member of the royal family without it looking like flattery? Can't be done', *LTH* 510.

[66]  Reading (1992); Roberts (2006: 161).

[67]  Emory Mss box 53 to 'Simon' 9 February 1992 (the day of publication of the laureate poem 'The Unicorn') 'I get a lot of fun out of writing these laureate pieces.' There are dashes of humour in the poems too—Roberts (2006: 153), for example, says some lines from 'The Song of the Honey Bee' are 'obviously meant to be funny'. See also the letter to Terence McCaughey, 7 March 1985, *LTH* 497–8.

[68]  See the controversial paper of Ahl (1984).

[69]  Emory Mss 854 to Gerald 23 July 1986, 'On Friday our Minister of Education is coming for lunch. So you see what distortions and transformations this Laureateship has effected. Many a revelation it provides, many a temptation. A lot of it is fun. At least I now feel I've tasted the whole gamut, top to bottom. Big lessons'; Middlebrook (2003: 267).

[70]  Taplin (2002: 5) sees grounds for relevant characterization of contemporary poets in their choices in translating Aeschylus's *Oresteia*: Hughes as a 'royalist, male-sympathizing' contrasts with the 'iconoclastic, anti-monarchist [Tony] Harrison'. For some of Hughes's thoughts on the British monarchy and the Laureateship, *LTH* 529–30, 619–20.

young man, but his laureateship gave him the opportunity to elaborate his own poetic vision of the relationships between time, landscape, monarchy, and society. In creating and reworking this representative register, Hughes stayed true to his ideological and literary self, as his borrowings from and resonances with his wider oeuvre attest—in that sense, *Rain-Charm for the Duchy and other Laureate Poems* is unembarrassed.

Despite the conservatism inherent in the choice of occasion of Hughes's original laureate poems and their subsequent collection for republication, Hughes found a radical new voice for the office; and although like laureates before him, Hughes used classical precedents for his poems for the monarchy, he found this voice by reworking the traditional panegyrical forms of classical antiquity to produce laureate poetry, at its best, well suited to the sensibilities of a modern democracy. The ten laureate poems generally avoid the tropes that most earlier laureates had borrowed from classical antiquity and then exhausted, and they eschew the ephemera of politics and sociology; instead, they revert to a more fundamental conception of the interrelationship between natural order and human culture. They constitute a distinctive set, an intelligent poetic vision of monarchy and nationhood, identifying Hughes as an important court poet, one who knew how and when to apply the weight of tradition without sacrificing his own integrity.[71]

[71] I gave versions of this paper at Emory, Edinburgh and Newcastle. With thanks to audiences there for their prompts and comments, in particular to Terry Gifford, Jennifer Ingleheart, Diane Middlebrook, Neil Roberts and Colin Wilcockson.

# 9

## 'A holiday in a rest home': Ted Hughes as v*ates* in *Tales from Ovid*

*Garrett A. Jacobsen*

In 1996 Ted Hughes remarked in a letter to Ann Skea that 'I also did 25 tales from Ovid's *Metamorphoses*—enjoyed that. A holiday in a rest home!'[1] The appeal of Ovid's *Metamorphoses* to Ted Hughes on one level was no doubt the exercise of the mythic imagination, the focus of so much of Hughes's own oeuvre. Even at Cambridge, Hughes had changed from English to reading Archaeology and Anthropology in his third year, confessing that he had found in himself an increasing resistance to the weekly critical essay in English literature, a resistance symbolized one night by the dream of a fox-like creature admonishing him for his pursuit of the pro-saic.[2] Hughes mythologizes this crisis of conscience in 'The Thought-Fox', whose opening lines invoke the mystery of the creative process and its transformation of the mundane and solitary act of writing into a communion with the unseen and, but for poetry, the incomprehensible:

> I imagine this midnight moment's forest:
> Something else is alive
> Besides the clock's loneliness
> And this blank page where my fingers move.[3]

---

[1] Sagar (2000; xxxii).    [2] *WP* 8–9.
[3] From *HR*; *CP* 21.

The poet of 'The Thought-Fox' could only be fascinated by Ovid's wholly animate and mutable Nature, enmeshed with humanity, where anything is possible, and where the coin of the realm is metaphor. So artfully crafted by a 'sylleptic imagination', the tales told by Ovid illuminate the dynamic nature of existence and the need to understand that there is always 'something else alive', a sensibility consistently iterated in the Roman poet's frequent marriage of the literal and figurative.[4]

At a deeper level it may have been the vatic force of 'Ovid's poetics of presence through absence', best exemplified in the *Metamorphoses*, that also intrigued Hughes.[5] Ovid's facility with language and clear interest in the power of words to interpret and create reality enabled him to assume easily the role of the Roman *vates*, the poet as priest or prophet of divine signs and inspiration.[6] But the *Metamorphoses*, an epic played out on the stage of human experience and divine intervention, was the perfect vehicle for the poet as *vates* to bring to life both the gods and their creations. Hughes himself, too, had associated the transcendent and procreative quality of words with classical mythology in his cycle of poems to the Titan Prometheus, a figure who 'created men, stole fire from heaven for them, and arranged sacrifice to their advantage'.[7]

> For words are the birds of everything—
> So soon
> Everything is on the wing and gone
>
> So speech starts hopefully to hold
> Pieces of the wordy earth together
> But pops to space-silence and space-cold
>
> Emptied by words
> Scattered and gone.
>
> (*Prometheus On His Crag* 19)[8]

The symbolic nature of words and speech, here 'the birds of everything', at once would bind the universe, but at the same time these winged words evoke the transitory nature of the external world. Like

---

4 Tissol (1997: 18–26).
5 Fowler (2000: 157).
6 Dumezil (1996: vol. I, 127).
7 Burkert (1985: 171).
8 *CP* 294–5.

Prometheus, the visionary and the creator, poets may act both as bards and as seers, especially in the sense of interpreting signs, and their texts become 'a repository of great (and even sacred) hidden truths'.[9] With godlike power the words of the poet can create a momentary presence in the face of an existential emptiness. Yet even more importantly these words also embody the poetic imagination and its language of metaphor to reveal the potential meaning of the world around us, what Seamus Heaney in *The Diviner* explores as the poet's capacity as *vates* for 'making contact with what lies hidden'.[10]

Hughes's role as translator also resonates with the function of the *vates* in the *Metamorphoses*. Richard Bentley's much-quoted comment, as reported in Johnson's *Life of Pope*, 'It is a very pretty poem Mr. Pope but you must not call it Homer', concisely discloses the choice confronting every translator and the ultimate source of almost every attendant criticism, especially in the translation of literature from classical antiquity. But as Sir Moses Finley argued in reference to the intelligibility of a 'desperately foreign' Greek drama, we should remember that 'all art is dialogue' and 'in the end, it can only be a dialogue in the present, about the present'.[11] With this guiding principle, Bentley's barb changes into a simple statement of fact, and Pope's 'very pretty poem' becomes a successful dialogue between two poets separated by great discontinuities of time and culture. Harold Bloom's statement that 'critics, in their secret hearts, love continuities' would support this needed dialectical nature in translation.[12] Indeed, it may be that this sense of dialogue 'in the present and about the present' between ancient and modern poet is the best measure of success for a translation. Whether or not a reader perceives the absent presence of that 'desperately foreign' ancient poet should be the determining questions for critical reviews. Has the translator, like the poet-*vates*, interpreted the signs, the words of a poem, successfully and thus communicated their import in a meaningful and authentic manner? To give at least some answer to this question for Hughes and his *Tales from Ovid*, let us consider his

---

[9] Struck (2004: 38).   [10] Heaney (2002a: 22).
[11] Finley (1968: 3–6).   [12] Bloom (1973: 78).

appropriation of the role of poet-*vates*, focusing primarily on the opening 'Creation' cycle of stories, but noting also the vatic narrative in the central triptych of Orphic tales, as well as in the final myth of 'Pyramus and Thisbe'.

In the Introduction to *Tales from Ovid*, a title to be read as denoting both the source material for translation and the voice of the poet himself, Ted Hughes immediately gives presence to the absent Ovid. That Hughes intends to become in a sense the Roman *vates*, a mediator between myth and reality, and to blend his voice with Ovid's in the translation of text and poetic persona, is perfectly clear from the Introduction to *Tales from Ovid*:

> As a guide to the historic, original forms of the myths, Ovid is of little use. His attitude to his material is like that of the many later poets who have adapted what he presents. He, too, is an adaptor. He takes up only those tales which catch his fancy, and engages with each one no further than it liberates his own creative zest.

If one substitutes the name of Hughes for Ovid, the reader has a summary description of what Hughes does in his translation of the *Metamorphoses*; and the Introduction becomes a kind of invocation to the translated *Tales*. Choosing only twenty-four episodes from an epic tapestry of nearly 250 major and minor Greco-Roman myths, Hughes adapts the material to his own creative agenda, assuming the same vatic and innovative role identified with Ovid himself. Although selecting only a small number of tales from Ovid's epic and even abandoning Ovid's ordering of the tales, Hughes does follow Ovid's opening series of myths, beginning with the programmatic invocation to the *Metamorphoses*, and then proceeding to the first episodes of Creation. The quite literal and prosaic translation of the invocation by Frank Justus Miller, from the same Loeb version of Ovid used by Hughes, is instructive in apprehending both how Hughes translates Ovid's Latin and how Ovid's poetics stimulated the mythic imagination of Hughes:[13]

> in nova fert animus mutatas dicere formas
> corpora; di, coeptis (nam vos mutastis et illa)

---

[13] Sagar (2000: ch. 1).

adspirate meis primaque ab origine mundi
ad mea perpetuum deducite tempora carmen.

(*Metamorphoses* 1.1–4)

My mind is bent to tell of bodies changed into new forms. Ye gods, for you yourselves have wrought the changes, breathe on these my undertakings, and bring down my song in unbroken strains from the world's very beginning even unto the present time.[14]

To underscore just what may be lost in a literal translation, the informed reader of the Latin original may note how Ovid's striking juxtaposition of *perpetuum* and *deducite* (line 4) echoes the promise of *in nova fert animus* (line 1), lines framing what seems to be at first glance a conventional epic invocation to the gods. Miller's typical rendering of the invocation, while preserving the traditional aspect of the poet as *vates* calling upon divine inspiration and knowledge, misleads the reader on two points: first, he delays and thus de-emphasizes the concept of 'new forms' until the end of the first sentence; and second, he translates *deducite* with a lexical primary definition of 'bring down', losing the connotation of other possibilities. In this translation Miller loses both the initial Ovidian signature of innovation (*in nova fert animus*) and the allusion to a literary term (*deductum* or 'fine-spun') more closely associated with Callimachean brevity than Homeric epic.[15] Moreover, *deducite*, in the sense of spinning thread, is most certainly a proleptic nod to another icono-clastic weaver of divine myths in the *Metamorphoses*, Arachne, whose own storied fate is one of the tales chosen for inclusion by Hughes. Ovid's subtle implication of a new and different kind of epic, from the imagination of a poet who consistently challenged artistic and societal conventions, can easily be lost in an ordinary or literal translation. But *Tales from Ovid* is neither ordinary nor literal, and Hughes remarkably intuits Ovid's best intentions, despite his own limitations in Latin and the workmanlike efforts of Miller. Ovid's *Metamorphoses* encourages the creative impulse in Hughes, if only perhaps to restore the power of the original words by what Hardwick has termed the 'creative blurring of the distinction between different

---

[14] All translations in this essay are quoted from Miller's version.
[15] Wheeler (1999: 26).

kinds of translations, versions, adaptations and more distant relatives', a perfect approach for an epic of shifting and blurred identities (*mutatas formas*).[16]

In the Introduction to *Tales from Ovid*, Hughes also establishes the parallels between his own poetic inspiration and that of Ovid:

> Above all, Ovid was interested in passion. Or rather, in what passion feels like to the one possessed by it. Not just ordinary passion either, but human passion *in extremis*—passion where it combusts, or levitates, or mutates into an experience of the supernatural.[17]

Hughes perceives in the 'mythic arena' of the *Metamorphoses* and its spectacle of human passions *in extremis* the same seductive and mythopoeic voice that Yeats possessed and whose 'The Wanderings of Oisin' had so impressed Hughes with the powerful spell of 'Irish folklore and myth and the occult'.[18]

> But the tale, though words be lighter than air,
> Must live to be old like the wandering moon.
>
> (Yeats, 'The Wanderings of Oisin')

It is in the telling and re-telling of tales where true poetic power rests, and the oldest tales are usually the ones reflecting genuine human experience—tales of human passions so powerful as to be divine or supernatural forces, embedded in the human psyche. Ovid's own ability to adapt timeless myths into a Roman milieu and 'to realise the illusion of presence, whether motivated by erotic desire, the desire for fame, or a more ludic delight in illusionism' becomes the template for Hughes to approach translating the *Metamorphoses*.[19] It is the supernatural element in passion and in poetry that defines 'the poetic Self' for Hughes, as he proposed in tribute to T. S. Eliot.[20] In the opening myth (actually a quartet of stories—'Creation; Four Ages; Lycaon; Flood') of *Tales from Ovid* Hughes places himself in

---

[16] Hardwick (2000: 12).        [17] *TO* ix.

[18] Heinz (1995: 63).        [19] Hardie (2002*a*: ch. 3).

[20] *WP* 268, 'The qualifications of the poetic Self (apart from its inspiration) were: that it lived its own life separate from and for the most part hidden from the poet's ordinary personality; and that it was not under his control, either in when it came and went or in what it said; and that it was supernatural. The most significant of these peculiarities was that it was supernatural.'

the company of Yeats and Eliot as a poet-*vates*, embodied by the visionary Prometheus, 'the body of humanity'.[21] Between a 'Creation' emerging from 'a bolus of everything' and the tragic climax to the 'Flood' of a 'drowned mankind', passion is the transformative agent for the gods and humanity, to be recorded by the poet-*vates* and translator in language that 'imports new and alternative options of being'.[22]

Hughes begins his translation proper, as does Ovid his epic, with a simple, yet suggestive declaration of purpose and identity in a universe defined by change:

> Now I am ready to tell how bodies are changed
> Into different bodies.
>
> ('Creation' 1–2)[23]

With 'Now I am ready' Hughes returns the force of the poem back to its first words (*in nova fert animus*), and the emphasized first person and present tense call attention to the identity of the poet and the nature of his work. This introductory couplet, metrically more suitable for elegy than epic, invites the reader to consider closely the question: Who is ready now? Is it Ovid, who would turn from erotic elegy to epic, but without abandoning his favourite theme—passion? Or is it Hughes, who having read Ovid's poetry is ready now to translate those tales of passion and metamorphosis into new being? The *corpora* in Ovid's text (both physical bodies and bodies of artistic work) perfectly translates into the doublet of 'bodies' in Hughes, as he alludes to a metamorphosis of both the poetry and the poet—the elegiac epic of Ovid becomes the episodic lyrics of Hughes, the ancient bard becomes the modern poet.

This motif of mutability is the heart of Ovid's *Metamorphoses*, and Hughes grasps its protean character like Peleus does the shape-shifting Thetis in a later tale:

> He shut his eyes and hung on, ignoring
> Her frenzy of transformations
> Till they shuddered to stillness. She knew she was

---

[21] Sagar (1975: 151).     [22] Steiner (1998: 371).     [23] *CP* 865.

beaten
By that relentless grip, 'Heaven has helped you,'
She panted, 'only heaven
Could have given me to you, and made me yours.'

('Peleus and Thetis')[24]

Just as the mortal Peleus needed to sacrifice and call upon the gods
for their help in his impassioned pursuit of the immortal Thetis,
Hughes needs supernatural power, that peculiar characteristic of the
poetic Self, to revive Ovid and pursue his own passion for poetic
expression:

I summon the supernatural beings
Who first contrived
The transmogrifications
In the stuff of life.
You did it for your own amusement.
Descend again, be pleased to reanimate
This revival of those marvels.
Reveal, now, exactly
How they were performed
From the beginning
Up to this moment.

('Creation')[25]

Here Hughes, again with a purposefully ambiguous first person,
carefully translates the language of the absent poet to conjure up
the illusion of divine and poetic presence in Ovidian style. Philip
Hardie has proposed that the 'equivocation between absence and
presence haunts the Ovidian *corpus* to a degree that makes of it a
recognisably Ovidian response to language and literature', and
Hughes appears to understand this.[26] This séance-like invocation,
certainly more Hughes than Ovid, summons the absent poet in two
ways: first, the direct address in the second person, the emphatic
'You', referring to the supernatural beings, may encompass both gods
and poet; second, the allusions to elements of humour—the implicit

---

[24] *CP* 936.        [25] *CP* 865.
[26] Hardie (2002*a*: 3).

hyperbole of 'transmogrifications', the explicit verdict of 'for your own amusement'—are equally suitable to either the manipulative Olympian gods or to the notably playful Ovid. The final plea for revelation may then also be understood as questions addressed at once both to the gods and to the poet by the present poet and translator, Hughes. How did you perform these metamorphoses? How did you compose these marvels? The answers are in the voice of *Tales from Ovid*.

When Hughes transforms the metre and the structure of the *Metamorphoses*, he is endowing his own poetry, if not himself, with the 'godlike novelty' he later attributes to mankind in the 'Creation' tale. Like one of the gods invoked in Ovid's proem, or at the very least like a Roman patron, Hughes grants Ovid's suppliant request for a new style, a more fine-spun substance (*deducite . . . carmen*), while in turn Ovid provides Hughes with endless source material (*perpetuum . . . carmen*). It is as if each poet-*vates*, in their religious or supernatural function, is able to communicate across time and space, each fulfilling the contractual obligations inherent in the Roman formula of prayer: *do ut des* ('I give so that you may give'). Like his depiction of Pygmalion, whose art 'took possession of his fingers,' or Arachne, for whom 'A grace like Minerva's, unearthly, | Moved her hands', Hughes, too, becomes an instrument for an unseen supernatural force. The voices of Hughes and Ovid then harmonize in the incantation 'Descend again, be pleased to reanimate | This revival of those marvels.' For Ovid, the gods (*di*) are the Muses; for Hughes, Ovid is the Muse. For both poets there is an expressed need for a divine and unseen power to give body to a world beyond normal mortal ken, and to legitimate the sacred nature of their texts.

The opening lines in *Tales from Ovid* also form a vatic response to the closing lines of the *Metamorphoses*. At the closure of his epic, Ovid again resumes the first person in his narrative, claiming immortality specific to his function as poet-*vates*:

> ore legar populi, perque omnia saecula fama,
> si quid habent veri vatum praesagia, vivam

> (15.878–9)

I shall have mention on men's lips, and, if the prophecies of bards have any truth, through all the ages shall I live in fame.

The final body changed of the epic is Ovid himself, as he transmutes his poetic Self into the text of his poem. Ovid's final word, the oracular *vivam* ('I shall live'), then becomes true each time his work is read, even in translation. The 'revival' of Ovid's marvels, his *Metamorphoses*, by Hughes thus reanimates Ovid himself and fulfils Ovid's vatic prophecy. Translating Ovid's 'stuff of life' is the creation of life, and thus Hughes affirms his artistic dictum that 'the poem is a new species of creature, a new specimen of life outside your own'.[27] Hughes midwifes Ovid from the terrible Chaos preceding Creation, aptly rendered into modern idiom by Hughes with the intimated image of a threatened and aborted fetus:

> A bolus of everything—but
> As if aborted,
> And the total arsenal of entropy
> Already at war within it.
>
> ('Creation')[28]

Divine intervention, however, eventually permits the existence of the universe and the birth of life:

> God, or some such artist as resourceful,
> Began to sort it out.
>
> ('Creation')

Chaos then will be 'sorted out' (both 'put in order' and 'put to rights') by a God or artist with divine resources—the poet-*vates*. With words and speech, like *Prometheus on His Crag*, the poet does hold together 'pieces of the wordy earth' and translates Ovid out of 'space-silence and space-cold'. In his restoration of Ovid's voice, Hughes validates George Steiner's concept that 'translation can be pictured as a negation of entropy'.[29]

Reviving the *mutatas formas* of Ovid's powerful voice and the dominant motifs of passion and mutability does not mean, however,

---

[27]  *WP* 12.        [28]  *CP* 865.
[29]  Steiner (1998: 319).

ignoring or glossing over the present. Indeed the opposite is true. In his Introduction to *Tales from Ovid,* Hughes clarifies his intent to recast the *mythos* of the Augustan Age with elements from the post-modern world, an equally 'defrocked' culture, paralleling each era as an apparent nexus of conflicting ideals and identities. Writing as the new millennium loomed, Hughes found the 'crucifix' a telling symbol, at least for himself and a modern western culture which dates itself by the birth of Christ. Representing the chiastic tensions between the satiation of 'bottomless appetites' and the quest for 'spiritual transcendence' in those Romans at the beginning of the so-called original millennium, this Christian imagery most strongly materializes in the climactic couplet at the abrupt end of the 'Creation' quartet of tales:

> Drowned mankind, imploring limbs outspread,
> Floats like a plague of dead frogs.
>
> ('Flood' 601–2)[30]

The corpses, as if in cruciform prayer, allude to the biblical stories of the plagues on Egypt, and for a moment the angry Jove unites with the vengeful Yahweh of the Old Testament. Like Ovid's own frequent anachronistic references to Roman cultural touchstones in the ancient Greek myths of the *Metamorphoses,* as when he compares the divine palaces on Olympus with the aristocratic homes on the Palatine Hill (1.175–6), the use of Judeo-Christian imagery in *Tales from Ovid* enables Hughes also to remind his audience in subtle fashion that the voice of the narrator is located in both the present and the past.

At times Hughes himself seems more Roman than Ovid. The absolute justice exercised in Jove's earlier condemnation of all mankind for Lycaon's sins possesses a Judeo-Christian sense of the scapegoat to be sacrificed, but the Roman sensibility is equally inescapable:

> In this universal new religion
> All are fanatics—suckled
> Not by the sweet wisdom of heaven
> But by a wolf. All adore, all worship
> Greed, cruelty, the Lycaon

[30] *CP* 880.

In themselves. All are guilty.
Therefore all must be punished. I have spoken.

('Lycaon' 471–7)[31]

In his translation Hughes expands the meaning of Ovid's single line *qua terra patet, fera regnat Erinys* ('Wherever the plains of earth extend, wild fury reigns supreme', 241). The ancient Furies, so frightening on the stage of Aeschylean tragedy, are transformed into the modern world's bane, the fanatical and immoral religious terrorists. Even more striking in this particular adaptation and expansion of Ovid's image is how Hughes here appears to have in mind the ancient Roman audience. Jove's judgement comes after he gives a lengthy account of mankind's failings to the other gods. Preceding his speech to the gods, Ovid and Hughes both compare Jove to Augustus:

> O Augustus, just as you see now
> The solicitude of all your people
> So did the Father of Heaven
> Survey that of the gods.

('Lycaon' 374–7)[32]

From this comparison, anachronistic in both Ovid and Hughes, those 'suckled | Not by the sweet wisdom of heaven | But by a wolf' may easily be read as descendants of another famous child suckled by a wolf—Romulus, not only the eponymous founder of Rome and the distant legendary ancestor of Augustus, but also its fratricidal first king. The Romans have too much of Lycaon in them, too much greed and cruelty. In Ovid's portrait of Lycaon's metamorphosis, rooted in that wolfish king's *solitaeque cupidine caedis* ('his accustomed greed for blood', 234), there may be a subtle allusion to a constant theme of social criticism among contemporary Roman poets and historians. It is Hughes, however, at the end of the second millennium, who actually makes the stinging point about the inherent nature of Roman guilt, as if he were a Roman poet himself, his audience Roman citizens. Moreover, remembering Hughes's remarks on the parallels between past and present in the Introduction, the modern

---

[31]  *CP* 876–7.          [32]  *CP* 874.

audience cannot help but for that moment recognize a certain kinship with those Romans. The ancient and modern worlds coalesce into one being through the power of words summoned by the poet-*vates*.

The worlds of Ovid and Hughes intersect at an apocalyptic moment, in recognition of a coming annihilation, but also in anticipation of a promised renewal. Each poet-*vates* collaborates with the gods to reproduce humanity in the face of death and destruction:

> God comforted the gods.
> If everything was left to him, he promised,
> He could produce a new humanity—
> Different from the first model and far
> More prudently fashioned.
>
> ('Flood' 493–7)[33]

Slipping back on Hughes's Judaeo-Christian mask of the capitalized God, Jove comforts the other deities with the birth of a 'new humanity ... more prudently fashioned.' The epic Flood, pagan or Christian, may bring a dismal end to mankind, but in both traditions there is the prophetic promise of the repopulation of the earth with a chosen people. With this image, Hughes is hinting to the reader that the poet's world, the poem's 'new humanity' will continue in the tales to follow. At this point Hughes begins restructuring the *Metamorphoses* into his own Creation; Ovid's own post-diluvian story of Deucalion and Pyrrha repopulating the earth disappears into Hughes's selection of 'more prudently fashioned' myths, stories that mostly have an instructive Aeschylean sense of human beings suffering into wisdom. After the 'Flood' (*Metamorphoses* 1.253–312), Hughes jumps ahead several stories to 'Phaethon' (2.1–366), a tale of youthful hubris at the dawn of this new age, linked to the 'Flood' perhaps as a 'second ecological disaster'.[34] The omission of more than half of Ovid's first book of the *Metamorphoses* signifies that it is Hughes, not Ovid, who is now the poet-*vates*. Hughes, however, offsets this by some very Ovidian humour and word-play on 'sun' and 'son' at the beginning of the tale:

---

[33] *CP* 877.
[34] Ziolkowski (2005: 202).

> How could the sun be anybody's father?
> You are his child. You are the son
> Of that great star which lights up the whole world.

('Phaethon')[35]

At the end of the tale, too, it is Ovid's Roman cultural language that restores the prophetic voice of the ancient poet-*vates*, promising a comforting resolution to Phaethon's tragic demise:

> But then, through that bark,
> There oozed lymph like tears, that in the sun's light
> Solidified as amber.
> These dropped from the boughs
> Into the hurrying river
> Which carried them off
> To adorn, some day far in the future,
> Roman brides.

('Phaethon')[36]

This image of renewal in the flow of time, 'the hurrying river', signifies how Ovid's presence is a constant in one form or another, even as Hughes departs further from a literal translation of the *Metamorphoses* and imposes his own interpretation of the world and its poets.[37] In *Tales from Ovid* the words and reality of both ancient and modern poet-*vates* is present; even with a change in form, the particular voice of the seer remains intact. In his structuring of the *Tales from Ovid*, with its frequent remediation of death by resurrection, Hughes envisions for his audience the wisdom to be gained from myth and poetry. The utter annihilations in 'Erysichthon' and 'The Death of Cygnus' are followed respectively by tales of renewal in the face of destruction ('Semele' and 'Arachne'), and Ovid's tale of Pyramus and Thisbe, a story of the immortality of love from the first pentad of Ovid's *Metamorphoses*, becomes the quiet coda for the whole of *Tales from Ovid*, rehearsing the cycle of birth and death from Hughes's tales of 'Creation' and accentuating

---

[35]  *CP* 880–1.       [36]  *CP* 896.
[37]  Sagar (2000: 82–3). Sagar interestingly notes that Hughes had found the story of Phaethon to be a 'subliminal myth' as the key to Sylvia Plath's *Ariel*.

the vatic promise of life again, even if changed in form, 'some day far in the future'. The poet-*vates* transcends the moment and uncovers the true state of Nature.

To Ovid and the Augustans, Orpheus is the 'exemplar for the *civilizing vates* ("poet-seer")'.[38] While Hughes may have rejected the actual Orpheus-Eurydice tale as 'too obvious an attempt to exploit my situation', nevertheless Orpheus must have had a symbolic resonance, if not vatic force for him.[39] *Nunc opus est leviore lyra* ('but now I need the gentler touch', *Metamorphoses* 10.152) is the Orphic proem in the *Metamorphoses* for stories not traditionally epic in scope or subject, echoing both Ovid's own proem to the *Metamorphoses* and Hughes's more lyrical approach to the translation of the epic. In the central triptych of *Tales from Ovid*, Hughes translates three of the most powerful songs of Orpheus from Book 10 of the *Metamorphoses*—'Myrrha', 'Venus and Adonis (and Atalanta)', 'Pygmalion'—tales of dark perverse passion rooted in the mythic poet's grief for his dead wife, Eurydice.[40] With an Orphic gaze, Hughes discerns his own absent presence in Ovid's poetry, and in these tales the identity of the poet-*vates* in *Tales from Ovid* is at once Ovid, Orpheus, and Ted Hughes himself.[41]

Hughes reorders Ovid's original Orphic cycle, as he begins with the tale of incestuous libido ('Myrrha'), follows with a story of insuperable passion of 'Venus and Adonis, and Atalanta', and ends with the myth of the artist possessed ('Pygmalion'). These linked tales in Ovid's *Metamorphoses* actually begin with Pygmalion's story, necessitated by Pygmalion being the grandfather of Cinyras whose daughter Myrrha gives birth to Adonis. But Hughes has placed 'Pygmalion' at the end of this series, and he purposefully signals this surprising inversion by ending 'Pygmalion' with 'Pygmalion's bride | Bore the child, Paphos' who appears at the beginning of 'Myrrha' in 'Cinyras,

---

[38]  Barchiesi (2001: 57).

[39]  Sagar (2000: 84). 'The Orpheus story was the first that occurred to Hughes after Sylvia Plath's death. He rejected it as "too obvious an attempt to exploit my situation"' (Letter to Keith Sagar, BL Add. 78761, f 27, 18 June 1998).

[40]  Anderson (1972: 449) notes, in reference to the tale of incest of Byblis, 'we start a new sequence on unnatural love, which will continue into Book 10 in the series of stories narrated by Orpheus.'

[41]  Solodow (1988) remarks that 'it suggests that the boundaries between the poem's narrators are blurry.'

the son of Paphos'. Such an overt change, obvious even to the reader less familiar with Ovid's poem, makes it unlikely that Hughes does this 'for no apparent reason'.[42] At the very least, the rearrangement credits Hughes's own voice as the controlling poet-*vates* in this Orphic cycle, and its unusual ring-composition invites the reader to return from 'Pygmalion' to 'Myrrha' and then to ponder the import of the series as a whole, in much the same way as the linked tales of 'Creation' require a holistic approach. Translating these three tales as if a cathartic *Birthday Letters* for the grieving Orpheus in the *Metamorphoses*, Hughes alludes to the tragically impassioned relationship between himself and Sylvia Plath and how such passion may create an artistic vision.[43]

Some brief examples are suggestive of how Hughes may have read these tales, at least as a poet-*vates*. Introducing Myrrha's tragic tale of incest, the poet addresses and admonishes the reader directly:

> The story I am going to tell you
> Is so horrible
> That fathers with daughters, wherever you are,
> Had better not listen to it—
> I beg you to stay clear.
> Or if you find my song irresistible
> Let your ear
> Now become incredulous.
> May you convince yourselves this never happened.
>
>                         ('Myrrha')[44]

Like the poet-*vates* in the invocation from the 'Creation' tales, this 'I' engages in dialogue with an absent presence, here the reader, as opposed to Ovid and the gods. But the effect is similar. There is a supernatural tone in the narrator's prophetic expectation that the 'horror' of the song will be 'irresistible', as well as in the enhanced perception of the relationship formed between the narrator and his hopefully 'incredulous' audience of tales that 'never happened', or as Hughes translated in Ovid's invocation proper, 'this revival of those marvels'. An incestuous relationship between fathers and daughters

---

[42] Ziolkowski (2005: 203).
[43] Sagar (2000: ch. 2 'From Prospero to Orpheus').
[44] *CP* 942.

remains an object of horror even to a modern audience, as Hughes recognized in the tragic conflation of himself and Plath's dead father:

> Till your real target
> Hid behind me. Your Daddy,
> The god with the smoking gun.
>
> ('The Shot')[45]

With an Orphic sensibility toward love and death, Hughes perceives that the destructive and transcendent natures of passion both dwell in its metamorphic capacity. The mythic imagination may realize one's deepest fantasies, but there are dire consequences: Myrrha's godlike licentiousness ends in a 'nerveless limbo', Plath's mythic passions have deadly consequences. Stepping away from the father figure, Hughes also imagined himself to Plath as 'the male lead in your drama' ('Visit'[46]). Adonis embodies this role in a tragic affair with the besotted Venus:

> 'These,' she cried,
> 'O my beloved, are your malefic planets.
> Never hesitate to crush a coward
> But, challenged by the brave, conceal your courage.'
>
> ('Venus and Adonis')[47]

Venus with divine foreknowledge would have scripted a different life for her beloved Adonis, but her efforts are doomed by his essentially unchangeable and thus tragic character. Yet death and suffering may be alleviated by divine power, reflected in the climactic transfiguration of Adonis by Venus:

> The circling year itself shall be your mourner.
> Your blood shall bloom immortal in a flower.
>
> ('Venus and Adonis')[48]

The goddess and the agent of divine power, the poet-*vates*, perpetuate the existence of the ephemeral Adonis in a flower symbolic of his

---

[45] *CP* 1052–3.  [46] *CP* 1047–9.
[47] *CP* 955.  [48] *CP* 963.

bloody death, but also of Nature's endless vegetation cycle and Ovid's *perpetuum carmen.* Hughes performs a similar transformation for Plath in the final poem of *Birthday Letters,* as she, too, becomes appropriately the flowers from which her name originated in blood-soaked imagery:

> And outside the window
> Poppies thin and wrinkle-frail
> As the skin on blood,
> Salvias, that your father named you after,
> Like blood lobbing from a gash,
> And roses, the heart's last gouts,
> Catastrophic, arterial, doomed.
>
> ('Red')[49]

In poetry, then, anything is possible, even the manifestation of the disembodied. The creative force of art and poetry, of passion, within the lives of Hughes and Plath is the central theme of 'Pygmalion'. The final tale of the Orphic cycle legitimates the vatic identity of Hughes declared in 'we | Only did what poetry told us to do'.[50] In Pygmalion and his creation, artists from Ovid to Shaw to Hughes have examined the relationship between the dreams of imagination and reality of life. Hughes at first summons the tone of Orpheus to shape his translation:

> Though this dream
> Was not so much the dream of a perfect woman
> As a spectre, sick of unbeing,
> That had taken possession of his body
> To find herself a life.
>
> ('Pygmalion')[51]

The 'dream of a perfect woman', so Ovidian, is now a Eurydice attempting escape from Hades. These supernatural forces and the voice of Eros, associated with the poetic process by Hughes, are the dominant images in the tale:

---

[49]  CP 1170.        [50]  CP 1085.        [51]  CP 965.

> She moved into his hands,
> She took possession of his fingers
> And began to sculpt a perfect woman.
>
> ('Pygmalion')[52]

Pygmalion, like the poet-*vates*, is possessed by some unseen force, is consumed by the spirit of passion, and 'his love . . . Became his life'.[53] When Pygmalion's sculpture is brought to life by Venus, the artist is 'incredulous | At the softness, the warmth | Under his fingers.'[54] In 'The Rabbit Catcher' Hughes also attributed such powers to the poetry of Plath:

> Those terrible hypersensitive
> Fingers of your verse closed round it and
> Felt it alive. The poems, like smoking entrails,
> Came soft into your hands.[55]

In the end it is the poet-*vates* who delivers life, even from the darkest corners or most tragic experiences of the human psyche.

Ovid's loosely temporal structure of the *Metamorphoses* undergoes its own metamorphosis, therefore, to underscore the eternal symbiotic relationship between poet and experience. By adapting and adopting Ovid's role as poet-*vates*, Hughes addresses the problems inherent in any mythology dependent on shared cultural understandings.[56] Understanding that Ovid's epic most essentially is a discourse on and of change, an idea best mirrored in Nature, Hughes through the voices of Ovid and Orpheus emphasizes the truths unbound by human ideologies. Orpheus sang to Hades in the *Metamorphoses* that the transcendent potential of mortality is in the imperative of Love ('*vera loqui . . . vicit Amor,*' 10.20–6, 'to tell the simple truth . . . Love has overcome'), and his powerful songs moved even the natural world ('*dis genitus vates et fila sonantia movit,* | *umbra loco venit,*' 10.89–90, 'when here the heaven-descended bard sat down and smote his sounding lyre, shade came to the place').

---

[52] *CP* 965.    [53] *CP* 966.    [54] *CP* 968.    [55] *CP* 1138.

[56] *WP* 310 'Mythologies are dodgy things. By "mythologies" I mean nothing more than the picture languages that we invent to embody and make accessible to casual reference the deeper shared understandings which keep us intact as a group—so far as we are intact as a group.'

Such poetics are readily adopted by a modern poet notable for his embrace of myth and nature.

Ted Hughes quite successfully assumed the persona of the ancient oracular poet-*vates*, whether through conscious craft or 'influenced by the spirit of Ovid'.[57] We return to Seamus Heaney's 'The Diviner' and its final strophe with its suggestive imagery of dowsing:

> The bystanders would ask to have a try.
> He handed them the rod without a word.
> It lay dead in their grasp till nonchalantly
> He gripped expectant wrists. The hazel stirred.

Heaney's own comments on his poem underscore its meaning: 'When I look at the thing now I am pleased that it ends with a verb, "stirred", the heart of the mystery; and I am glad that "stirred" chimes with "word", bringing the two functions of *vates* into the one sound.' Upon reflection, Heaney's verses have become a kind of mystery even to the poet himself, as if they were imbued with a divine force or even possess their own life. In this way, perhaps, we must acknowledge that the conscious craft or technique of the poet, like the rituals performed by any priest or shaman, may have unexpected and thus uncanny results. Like Pygmalion, the poet-*vates* may discover that 'His own art amazed him, she was so real.'

The final image of the funerary urn for Pyramus and Thisbe is a fitting closure to *Tales from Ovid*:

> The gods were listening and were touched.
> And the gods touched their parents. Ever after
> Mulberries, as they ripen, darken purple.
>
> And the two lovers in their love-knot,
> One pile of inseparable ashes,
> Were closed in a single urn.
>
> ('Pyramus and Thisbe')[58]

The absence of Pyramus and Thisbe in death is negated both by the ripening each season of the purple fruit, now the signifier of the eternally inseparable lovers, and by each re-telling of their famous tale by the poet-*vates*. The mythic 'love-knot' imagery of Pyramus

---

[57] Brown (1999: 219).     [58] *CP* 1042.

and Thisbe conjures up the shamanistic voice of Hughes from the
Crow cycle of poems:

> He showed her how to make a love-knot . . .
> In their entwined sleep they exchanged arms and legs
> In their dreams their brains took each other hostage
> In the morning they wore each other's face
>
> ('Lovesong')[59]

The merging of identities in poetry occurs in every metaphor, expressing the power of the poet and language to make reality. In
Hughes's artful arrangement of Ovid's *Metamorphoses*, death can
never be a true ending, no more than it was in Ovid's epic. But it is
only through the language of the poet-*vates*, or 'some such artist as
resourceful' that the creation of order is possible. Language is reality,
and 'language has its true being only in dialogue', as Gadamer has
proposed.[60] The dialogue between Ovid and Hughes reveals that it is
human passion, whether in the guise of gods or poetry, which
underpins the world and its existence. The final myth in *Tales from
Ovid* revisits the theme of love and death from the central Orphic
triptych, balances the cycle of regeneration from the opening quartet
of 'Creation', and underscores the vivifying power of the divinely
inspired poet-*vates*. For Hughes, poetry was always about human
passion and Nature, and the successful poet was one who 'captured a
spirit, a creature'.[61] Ted Hughes proves himself as poet-*vates*, giving
voice to Ovid and to the hidden meanings in poetry, human passion,
mutability, and Nature.

---

[59] *CP* 255–6.          [60] Gadamer (1989: 446).          [61] *WP* 13.

# 10

## Passion *in extremis* in Ted Hughes's *Tales from Ovid*

*Anne-Marie Tatham*

In his introduction to *Tales from Ovid* (1997), Ted Hughes places passion at the centre of Ovid's work:

> Above all, Ovid was interested in passion. Or rather, in what a passion feels like to the one possessed by it. Not just ordinary passion either, but human passion *in extremis*—passion where it combusts, or levitates, or mutates into an experience of the supernatural.[1]

In the above passage, Hughes's description of Ovid's (and his own) handling of passion highlights two aspects of the concept: passion is extreme and it is a form of possession. Both ideas need to be examined. The extremeness of a feeling might be easy to conceptualize. It is simply a greater or more intense variant. Possession, however, is more complex. It is a form of power over someone (or something) by someone or something else (like a demon, for example). It can also be a form of obsession (with an emotion). In both of these cases, it is an encounter with an 'other', something alien to what one considers one's self, and traditionally has been viewed as a form of contact with the supernatural. Shamans and oracles, for example, are said to experience such a contact in trances. To be possessed is therefore to experience a loss, the loss of one's power over one's thoughts, feelings, emotions, and actions, of one's self. This loss is not replenished by 'passion'—quite the contrary. In fact,

[1] *TO* ix.

Hughes's definition of passion exalts this loss in the last part of the quotation above. Passion burns (reducing things to cinders or less), it 'levitates' (leaving the ground), it transforms into something altogether different. So, contrary to most traditional definitions of passion where the feeling heightens something that was already there (strong sexual desire, love of someone or of an activity), passion in Hughes's vision is a purging alteration.

Furthermore, 'passion' in Hughes's vision is based on metamorphosis, a key element of Ovid's work:

The act of metamorphosis...operates as the symbolic guarantee that the passion...has achieved the unendurable intensity that lifts the whole episode onto the supernatural or divine plane...

In every case, to a greater or lesser degree, Ovid locates and captures the peculiar frisson of that event, where the all-too-human victim stumbles out into the mythic arena and is transformed.[2]

Metamorphosis is conventionally defined as a 'change of shape' (from the Greek μεταμόρφωσις). Hughes alters this basic definition in the above quotation to redefine it in terms of passion and, bizarrely, in terms of geographical location. 'The act of metamorphosis' is what links two opposite places (planes or arenas) set in Hughes's mythopoetic mindscape: the human and the mythic. The middle, the in-between space, is characterized by movement and incompleteness: it is a shambolic forward lurch, a 'stumble', or even a 'frisson'. This allows the entire process to take place: 'where the all-too-human victim stumbles out into the mythic arena and is transformed' (the focus of the definition apparently being on the 'where' rather than on the 'how' or 'when').

However, a close analysis of Hughes's poems seems to counter the poet's own definition of passion. Contrary to what the poet writes, one could contend that Hughes's writing of passion and metamorphosis does not only raise the victim onto another plane, that of the supernatural and the divine, but also roots them firmly into the 'all-too-human', thus rendering the transformation all the more potent in that it retains some of its former state. How can we solve this apparent conundrum? What *is* the meaning of passion for

[2]  *TO* x.

Hughes? Could it be read as the sign of a paradox in his poetry, between transformation and stasis, a paradoxical state of change within a stasis, a liminal stage, a 'stumble', or a 'frisson'?

In order to explore the paradox of 'passion *in extremis*' in Hughes's work, we will first briefly explore Hughes's writing in *Tales from Ovid* to ascertain how much of it is a rewriting which can thus be analysed in terms of Hughes's *oeuvre*. This will enable us to examine passion according to the definition Hughes gave in his introduction and then underline the changes he brought to Ovid and, seemingly, his own definition. This will lead us finally to an exploration of the concept of passion through the idea of metamorphosis, which will in turn lead on to a possible solution to our conundrum in shamanism (a 'technique' central to Hughes's writing).[3]

## OVID RE-WRITTEN

First of all, we need to ascertain the extent to which Hughes rewrote *Tales from Ovid*. Hughes was, of course, an experienced translator.[4] Contrary to the great linguist Jakobson (who declared poetry 'by definition . . . untranslatable'), Hughes believed that the translation of poetry was not only possible, but necessary.[5] As for what is lost in the process, he wrote that:

Poetry inevitably loses hugely in translation, but those purists who claim that it is precisely 'the poetry' which is lost are speaking as though 'the poetry' were some separable ingredient, some additive like the whitening

---

[3] Since Hughes's definition of passion is circumscribed to 'where the all-too-human victim stumbles out into the mythic', our analysis of the concept will mainly focus on those tales which depict the stumbling woes of humans.

All the excerpts given in this chapter are taken from Hughes's *TO* and *CP*, and all the Latin translations are taken from Hill's 1985 and 1992 editions of Ovid's *Metamorphoses*.

[4] See *ST*.

[5] In 'On Linguistic Aspects of Translation' Jakobson argues that 'all cognitive experience and its classification is conveyable in any existing language'; however, the 'pun, or to use a more erudite, and perhaps more precise term—paronomasia, reigns over poetic art, and whether its rule is absolute or limited, poetry by definition is untranslatable' (1959: 238).

agent in a detergent. We feel that enough of the whole is preservable in some, though by no means in all, poetry.[6]

The kind of translation he sought to achieve is very specific. He describes it best in his *Modern Poetry in Translation* editorials:

The type of translation we are seeking can be described as literal, though not literal in a strict or pedantic sense.[7]

The only justification, it would seem to us, for anything but the most literal of translations, is [i] in those rare cases where the original poetry somehow makes an original and interesting poet of the translator..., [ii] where the translator already is an interesting and original poet in his own right.[8]

The one element which comes up, time and again, is how Hughes tried to achieve, or at least aimed to achieve, a 'literal' translation.

Surprisingly, however, in the case of *Tales from Ovid*, Hughes seems unsure as to how literal his own translation might be. The manuscripts held at the University of Emory, Atlanta, record how Hughes sought to clarify what he had achieved exactly. Page after page, he wrote and re-worded his introduction to *Tales from Ovid*. In some of the earlier versions of his draft introduction, Hughes toys with how literal his translations might be: 'These translations are not literal in the sense that they could be used as a crib' (in a translation exam for example).[9] A few pages later, he tries again, adding more distance to the original:

While not being exactly literal on the whole, my versions run reasonably close to the original. Even where I introduce a flourish of my own, usually nothing more than a metaphor, I take my cue from Ovid.[10]

This observation linking translation and metaphor is not to be taken lightly, and we will come back to it later, for these 'flourishes' were at

---

[6] Taken from *Modern Poetry in Translation* 1 (1965), quoted in *ST* 200. Could Hughes be referring to Robert Frost? The idea that poetry is what gets lost in translation is usually attributed to the American poet. See Barry (1973), especially 159.

[7] *Modern Poetry in Translation* 1 (1965), quoted in *ST* 200.

[8] *Modern Poetry in Translation* 1 (1965), quoted in *ST* 201.

[9] Emory Mss 644, Box 135, ff.10.

[10] Emory Mss 644, Box 135, ff.11.

times much more than a mere 'metaphor', as we shall see, and as Hughes himself underlined:

As a guide to the historic, original forms of the myths, Ovid is of little use. His attitude to his material is like that of the many later poets who have adapted what he presents. He too is an adaptor. He takes up only those tales which catch his fancy and engages with each one no further than it liberates his own creative zest.[11]

Hughes followed in his footsteps. So in a paradoxical sense, Hughes, by being faithful to the spirit of the text, becomes 'an adaptor', a 'translator'. By rewriting Ovid's *Metamorphoses*, Hughes is in fact following him closely. And indeed a close study of the poems reveals how much Hughes liberated his 'own creative zest' in terms of structure, theme, and style, and how, in fact, he chose to centre the tales on the idea of passion.

The most obvious 'adaptation' and departure from Ovid's *Metamorphoses* is Hughes's choice of structure and pattern. Of the 250 stories of transformation, Hughes has only retained about a third woven into twenty-four tales, which do not follow Ovid's structured fifteen books, but are shuffled, thereby producing new juxtapositions and trajectories. The *Tales* contain many of the well-known stories with a few notable exceptions. No passionate and inspired Orpheus laments his Eurydice. Missing are the devotedly married couples such as Deucalion and Pyrrha, Cadmus and Harmonia, Baucis and Philemon, Ceyx and Alcyone. Gone are Cyparissus, Ganymede, and Hyacinth and their homosexual passion, as well as Jason and Medea, Cephalus and Procris. As for the contents of Books XIII to XV, they are absent altogether.

What is left is a compelling weave of interlocking themes of love, lust and passionate desire, fate, transgression, and violence. According to the editors of *After Ovid: New Metamorphoses* in which Hughes first published four of his tales, this speaks directly to the concerns of the modern reader thanks to its

direct, obvious and powerful affinities with contemporary reality. They offer a mythical key to most of the more extreme forms of human behaviour and suffering, especially ones we think of as especially modern: holocaust,

---

[11] *TO* viii; my underlining.

plague, sexual harassment, rape, incest, seduction, pollution, sex-change, suicide, hetero-and homosexual love, torture, war, child-battering, depression and intoxication.[12]

Hughes's *Tales* encompass the whole range of human and supernatural extremes, starting with the birth of all births in 'Creation' and ending with death and posterity in the tragic tales of ill-fated passion, whether it be lustful desire in 'Tereus', or contrasting youthful pure love in 'Pyramus and Thisbe'.

The internal composition of *Tales from Ovid* seems to be based on a thematic structure. It starts with 'Creation' and ends with death in the concluding tale of 'Pyramus and Thisbe'.[13] The *Tales* seem to be structured around an internal set of dichotomies: after the four tales of creation ('Creation; Four Ages; Flood; Lycaon') come tales linked with the skies above ('Phaethon', 'Callisto and Arcas') and the netherworld below ('The Rape of Proserpina', 'Arethusa'). This then leads to the exploration of an in-between; be it that of characters of divided self ('Tiresias', 'Echo and Narcissus') to those constantly shifting shapes—or shape-changers—('Erisychthon', 'Semele'). The overall storyline of the tales creates a spiralling, cyclical, yet dichotomous, pattern, going from creation to dissolution, from above to below, from the divided to the multiple, from the gods to the humans, etc. This overall pattern was fashioned by Hughes entirely, for apart from the first three tales, all the others have been rearranged in a different order from the original so as to create this greater, general, multifaceted metamorphosis.

This effect is further heightened by Hughes through his removal of the transitional parts. There are many examples of this. One of the most amusing passages is, ironically, to be found after 'Pyramus and Thisbe'. In the very last stanza of *Tales from Ovid*, the young and naïve secret lovers, having committed suicide to be together at last, are knotted into 'One pile of inseparable ashes', united in a Keats-like 'single urn'.[14] The tale ends with their love and lives being

---

[12] Hofmann and Lasdun (1995: xi).
[13] One could of course see a hint of a possible rebirth in the tinted ripening of subsequent generations of mulberries.
[14] *CP* 1042.

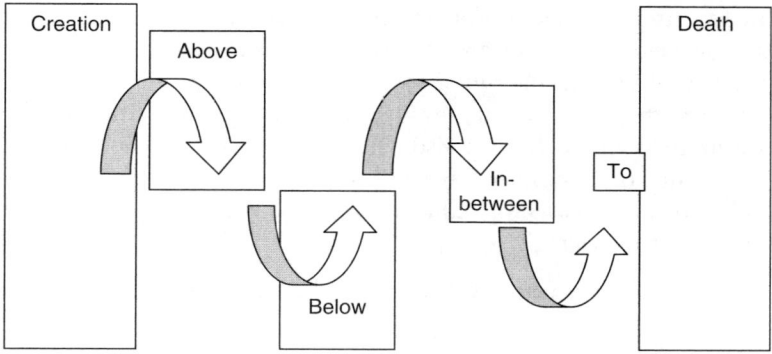

**Figure 1:** The interweaving stories in *Tales from Ovid,* from creation to death, via the above, the below, and the in-between.

commemorated, not by the immortal urn, but by the metamorphic change of colour of the mulberry tree, which, as it ripens, 'darkens purple'. This focus on the earnestness of the characters' plight is all the more heightened by the removal of the linking passage. Indeed, in Ovid's *Metamorphoses,* the tale does not end with the 'single urn' containing the lovers' ashes, and the pathos of the scene is completely reversed as the tale continues after 'a brief interval' (*breve tempus,* 4.167) with Leuconoe's story. The sun, she explains, was the first to see Venus's adultery with Mars. He informed Vulcan, the cuckolded husband who, incensed, forged chains which he put around the marital bed in such a way as to trap the lovers in the middle of their embrace. As soon as they were ensnared, the gods trooped in to have a look:

> illi iacuere ligati
> turpiter, atque aliquis de dis non tristibus optat
> sic fieri turpis; superi risere, diuque
> haec fuit in toto notissima fabula caelo.
>
> (*Met.* 4.186–9)

they were lying there bound shamefully, and one of the unabashed gods was saying he would like to be put to shame like that: the gods laughed and for a long time this was the best-known tale in the whole of heaven.

In fact, the removal of the transitional parts could be seen as an alteration of the very core structure of Ovid's work. Indeed, the transitions in *Metamorphosis* are far from being anecdotal. Not only are they often as interesting, amusing, and intriguing as the stories themselves, they are also a means to ensure the continuity of the poem. For continuity is what Ovid prays for in the very first lines of his *Metamorphoses* where he asks the gods to inspire him and lead his 'continuous song':

> ad mea perpetuum deducite tempora carmen
>
> (*Met.* 1.4)
>
> lead my continuous song down to my own times.

Since Ovid was about to launch into hundreds of stories, taken from both Roman and Greek cultures and loosely structured into fifteen books of poems, this was a plea which was not to be taken lightly. But the gods, it seems, complied. Some critics have expressed their regrets that these pivotal elements have disappeared from Hughes's version. However, Hughes's opening poem reveals that his rewriting does not include Ovid's prayer. The very first lines of *Tales from Ovid* are:

> Now I am ready to tell how bodies are changed
> Into different bodies.
>
> I summon the supernatural beings
> Who first contrived
> The transmogrifications
> In the stuff of life.
> You did it for your own amusement.
> Descend again, be pleased to reanimate
> This revival of those marvels.
> Reveal, now, exactly
> How they were performed
> From the beginning
> Up to this moment.[15]

Not only is there no prayer for inspiration, no appeal to the gods (just a summons) and no plea for one continuous song, but the core of the *Tales from Ovid* itself has been changed.[16] The act of meta-morphosis, around which most tales revolve as a core element, has

---

[15] *CP* 865.        [16] See Jacobsen in this volume.

been transformed. Indeed, many readers and critics have interpreted Ovid's subject as 'bodies changed to different forms', and the actual word chosen by Ovid to denote what is to be transformed has variously been translated by 'forms' or 'shapes' (*in nova . . . mutatas formas corpora,* 'shapes changed into new bodies', *Met.* 1.1–2). However, the word 'forms' implies a certain malleability of contours, and includes a range of formal changes which, reducing the word to 'body' as Hughes does, precludes. As for the metamorphosis itself, it has morphed into an act of grotesque and often humorous portent, a 'transmogrification'.

Clearly, *Tales from Ovid* is a rewriting of Ovid's *Metamorphoses.* Its stories and its storyline are redrawn, its aim is subtly, but fundamentally, different, and its central theme of 'metamorphosis' is transformed into a 'transmogrification'. The tales are 'from Ovid', but their writing and their exploration of passion are 'by Hughes', and can thus be analysed in terms of the poet's *oeuvre*.

## WHAT IS 'PASSION *IN EXTREMIS*'?

To answer this question we will first explore Hughes's use of the word itself in the tales and then trace his depiction of the notion. The first noticeable element is that the word 'passion' rarely occurs in the *Tales*—which is very strange for a theme Hughes deemed so central to his work and Ovid's. It appears about ten times in the entire twenty-four tales and 254 pages. When it is used, it hardly tallies with the definition given in the 'Introduction' at all. Our first encounter with the word is deceptive. In Arcas' tale, we are told the young man has a 'passion' for hunting.[17] His enthusiasm for this activity is hardly mythically uplifting—unless of course, one takes the meaning literally. In that case, it makes for rather dark humour. For after all, it *is* through his hunting that Arcas meets his mother transformed into a bear. Mistaking her for a real bear, he tries to spear her, and is changed into a star by an onlooking god and sent to the heavens, where he became the Little Bear.

---

[17] 'Hunting was his passion', *CP* 900.

The word 'passion' is next uttered in 'The Rape of Proserpina' by Cyane, a Sicilian nymph, as she attempts to stop the 'Lord of Hell', Pluto, from abducting the young woman. The nymph contrasts her tale of love to the acts of the god. Interestingly, her use of the word is in the negative, her story counterpointing that of Proserpina. Anapis, she explains, 'did *not* carry me off in a violent passion'.[18] As in the first example, the significance of the word 'passion' is limited and decreased by its accompanying words. The apposition of 'violent' and 'passion', indicates that passion was not all that violent in the first place (there is apparently 'passion' and 'violent passion,' the second being stronger—and therefore the first must be weaker). The adjective weakens its accompanying noun.[19] Here again, the word 'passion' is reduced to 'a strong emotion', rather than the uplifting, transmogrifying mythic experience Hughes's 'Introduction' to the tales had led us to expect.

The word 'passion' then appears in the tale of 'Myrrha'. The young girl seduces her father and bears him a son, Adonis. Passion here seems to mean 'incestuous lust', and, again, it is used with negative connotations, undertones and moral overtones:

> She was both aghast at her own passion
> and reckless to satisfy it.[20]

In 'Tereus' this later use of the word 'passion' as 'lust' is heightened. Here again it signifies a concupiscent desire and is associated in a negative way with the word 'greed':

> [Tereus] pressed Pandion again with Procne's request—
> The glove of his own greed. Passion
> Made him persuasive. . . . [21]

---

[18]  *CP* 904. My italics.

[19]  Can passion be that all encompassing mythical experience if it needs an adjective like 'violent' to increase its potency?

[19]  *CP* 946. It is a negative form of possession:

> As if mere words could have a hope
> Of altering such a passion . . .
> But her passion was deaf (CP 949).

[21]  *CP* 1026.

The concluding tale of 'Pyramus and Thisbe' contains the only mention of 'passion' as that of a possibly passive heightened feeling of something akin to love and that could lead to another plane of human experience (even if it is through death). The two lovers meet at the wall separating their two houses. They 'kneeled, confessing their passion' through a crack in the masonry.[22] Again though, the potency of the word 'passion' is somewhat diminished in a darkly humorous way, for within the same sentence we are informed that along with their vows of undying love, 'cooking smells' also wafted through the same fissure in the wall dividing the lovers from each other. So the word 'passion' can apparently be defined in terms of desire in *Tales from Ovid*: a desire to hunt, to be intimate (lust, incest), and to love, or at least to meet. It is a strong desire, but certainly not a 'stumble' into any kind of mythic arena. This use of the word is all the more perplexing as none of these occurrences of the word 'passion' comes from Ovid's text—for obvious reasons. They have, without exception, been added by Hughes. Why give one definition of such a central term and then go to lengths to use the word differently?

In fact, if one looks closely at *Tales from Ovid*, two uses of the term 'passion' seem to emerge. The first is the faintly humorous use of the word we have just examined and the second is the concept as it is explored in the tales. The depiction of passion—the feeling, not the word—is primarily a physical process in *Tales from Ovid*. In his definition of the word, Hughes repeatedly described passion in vivid physiological terms:

'one possessed by it' ( *TO* ix)

'passion where it combusts, or levitates, or mutates into an experience' (ix)

'the all-too-human victim stumbles . . . and is transformed' (x)

Passion, combustion, levitation, transformation—and of course stumbling—refer to a physical process as well as a possible mental or spiritual one. And in the tales themselves, passionate feelings do indeed concern the body first and foremost. The various embodiments, when analysed together, form a strange picture though. They

---

[22] *CP* 1037.

seem to be governed by one main broad idea: the idea of flow. Passion in Hughes's *Tales from Ovid* is a form of flow, as we shall see.

Flow is movement. Passion, in the most fundamental way, moves its 'all-too-human' victims. Myrrha seized by desire is 'like a wide-eyed sleepwalker | Hypnotised by a dream of wild lust'.[23] Tereus, when he first sees Philomela and his desire is awakened, is 'the puppet | Of instant obsession'.[24] Tereus is moved from the outside (as a puppet) and from the inside by his fiery blood:

> [he] ... felt his blood alter thickly.
>    Suddenly he himself was like a forest
>    When a drought wind explodes it into a firestorm.[25]

This translation incidentally is an example of Hughes's many 'flourishes', distancing his text from the Latin. Ovid mentions no blood flow and no forest, although he does mention fire. Though the reference to blood might be Hughes's way subtly to underline that Tereus, the Thracian, cannot be trusted because of his origins, it occurs too often to be ignored. Indeed, there are over forty occurrences of the word 'blood' in *Tales from Ovid*. This highlights the importance of circulation and flow. The very last story ends with a bloody death-wish

> Let our blood mingle
>    As never in love, in this veil torn by a Lion

and the sight of the gory Mulberry tree whose fruit, as we saw, are 'the colour of ... blood'.[26] The idea of flow here takes a bigger physical dimension than that of just one body. Indeed flow can be the movement of anything fluid such as blood, sap, water, and more.

Passionate flow in *Tales from Ovid* mainly concerns blood, as well as sap and water (as the victims try to escape 'passion' by turning into plants, trees, and rivers).[27] More generally though, it comprises

---

[23] *CP* 950.
[24] *CP* 1026; cf. Ovid, *Met.* 6. 465–74. Note that Ovid's Tereus retains some form of (relative) freedom of action.
[25] *CP* 1026.
[26] *CP* 1040–2.
[27] For example Arethusa, Myrrha, or Hermaphroditus who tried to escape Salmacis's passion but ended 'Melted into a single body | Seamless as the water', *CP* 1024.

anything related to flow—strangely including magnetic current (for instance in 'Arethusa')[28] and electric current. In the tale of Callisto for example, Jove's lust 'bristled up his thighs | and poured into the roots of his teeth' when he saw the 'Arcadian beauty'. When the girl was later 'grabbed with electric hands', she 'bolted' (with a pun intended?).[29] Even the ubiquitous heat associated with passion in Ovid is transformed into a flow, a melting, molten flow. In Narcissus, the young boy's body melts away

> Like wax near a flame, . . .
> He melted—consumed
> By his love.[30]

Myrrha's cool tears 'brimmed as if they melted' when seeing her beloved father.[31] Words themselves flow and as they do, they take on a literal physical dimension. They are linked to water, air, and even body parts in the tales of Arethusa, Echo and Narcissus, and Pyramus and Thisbe. In Tereus, this goes one step further. The flow of Philomela's words is made incarnate in her tongue. As it is cut off with her protests it seems to take on a life (and death) of its own as it twists on the floor like a snake, literally incarnating her death wish and her struggle:[32]

> . . . the tongue squirmed in the dust, babbling on—
> Shaping words that were now soundless.
> It writhed like a snake's tail freshly cut off
> Striving to reach her feet in its death-struggle.[33]

The flow of passion is all-encompassing and, as such, it is a form of ultimate possession. Whilst some characters are, as we have seen, transformed into sleep-walkers and puppets, others writhe in failed escapes from the throes of passion. Erisychthon, possessed by 'insatiable Hunger', 'writhes awake in twisting, knotted | Cramps of hunger'.[34] Myrrha tosses and turns in her sheets as she resists her

---

[28] *CP* 912.     [29] *CP* 896–8.     [30] *CP* 922.     [31] *CP* 945.

[32] Though the elements of the story might be those of Ovid, the details are Hughes's. He added details to the description of the cut (the 'bronze' pincers, the tongue dragged out to 'its full length' before being cut) and slightly altered the process itself (muting the tongue to make it soundless rather than 'muttering', transforming the dying tongue into a struggling one), *CP* 1030.

[33] *CP* 1030.

[34] *CP* 926–8.

passionate desire for her father, and Philomela's resisting tongue struggles on the ground.

In fact, in 'Tereus', Hughes is so intent on emphasizing this loss of initiative and its growing possession of the body, that he transforms the story more profoundly. Not only does he add anachronistic details of his own invention, such as Tereus transformed into an 'automaton', but he also omits much of Ovid's political, racial description of Tereus.[35] Again, not only does Hughes modernize many geographical references, but he also leaves out the entire war prologue, and most of the geopolitical as well as racial references.[36] Gone is the frequent thematic repetition of the idea of the barbarian—possibly so as to avoid any xenophobic undertone, but also thereby focusing on the man. Hughes added lines to Philomela's direct speech to underline Tereus's different nature in another way: 'You sadistic monster!', then three lines later 'You are inhuman' and again, seven lines later, the comment on his inhumanity 'Your bestial pit'. Hughes has altered the description of the bodily impact of passion in a radical way, and has thereby changed its core definition.[37]

Passion depicted by Hughes is characterized by its physical aspects. It moves its victims, it possesses every inch of them and their surroundings, be it in the flow of blood, sap, water, magnetic resonance, or electric current. It even transforms the flow of the story line with a new focus on passion instead of geopolitical elements of the tales that Ovid had expanded and that Hughes omits. We now turn to this idea of alteration, and especially metamorphosis, in our exploration of passion in *Tales from Ovid*—for it is central to Hughes's definition of passion.

## A METAMORPHOSED DEFINITION OF PASSION?

Hughes's definition of passion includes metamorphosis—a metamorphosed metamorphosis. We will therefore first examine more

---

[35] *CP* 1030.
[36] See also Monluçon (2006: 290).
[37] *CP* 1028.

closely how Hughes changed the concept of metamorphosis in his tales and then explore how this conjunction of changing metamorphosis and passion might be better understood through an idea Hughes explored throughout his *oeuvre*—the idea of shamanism.

We saw how Hughes's introduction to his work suggested a different idea of metamorphosis from the traditional change of shape. This transformation of the very concept of metamorphosis is continued in the tales themselves. The first few hundred lines of Ovid's tale of creation are often portrayed as the very first metamorphosis, the original transformation of shapeless matter into the various bodies comprising the visible world. Ovid focuses on the development of form, on how an indefinite deity brings chaos to an end by separating out the basic elements of earth, water, and air.

*Tales from Ovid* begins by following the Latin poet closely:

> Land, sea, air, were all there
> . . .
> God, or some such artist as resourceful,
> Began to sort it out.
> Land here, sky there,
> And sea there.
> Up there, the heavenly stratosphere.
> Down here, the cloudy, the windy.
> He gave to each its place,
> Independent, gazing about freshly.
> Also resonating—
> Each one a harmonic of the others,
> Just like the strings
> That would resound, one day, in the dome of the tortoise.[38]

If the first lines are true to Ovid's idea, the last four lines are nowhere to be found in the original. They are Hughes's re-writing of the text and they give us an insight into his understanding of metamorphosis. In Hughes's version, the chaos-repairing god does not metamorphose his surroundings. Indeed this God or 'some such artist as resourceful' is not in fact a creator *ex nihilo* or a worker of the living matter, but rather a separator, a classifier, or even a taxonomist.[39]

---

[38] *CP* 865–6.

[39] It is interesting to note that Hughes translates Ovid's nature into yet another anthropomorphic figure, thus maybe helping the reader focus on the changes being made rather than who made them.

There are no poetics of the living matter, or consubstantiation. Rather, the demiurge disposes of the various elements by giving them limits, by defining them in terms of space, place, and name. This might explain the addition of the four new lines. This 'creation' is not about something new coming into the world, about a seminal, original source or power, but about linking the old forms to the new through 'resonating . . . harmonic[s]'. It is about the power of words, of sounds (underlined by the semantic field of music), of poetry. In Hughes's version of creation, the demiurge is both a taxonomist and a poet, organizing his world in terms of words and sounds which were already there.

Indeed, philosophically the notion of metamorphosis presupposes an 'already there'. There cannot be an understanding of such transformation without, equally, a belief—be it magical or other—in an essence, a soul, something which will remain and be the same—thereby distinguishing the metamorphosed as a transformed shape, and not as a new being. This might explain why so many of the changed protagonists of *Tales from Ovid* keep part of their human attributes after their metamorphosis: the wolf Lycaon retains the savagery of the man; Actaeon his pain;[40] and, ironically, his love of hunting, even though he is a hunted stag;[41] Callisto the bear keeps her motherly love;[42] and even Myrrha whose 'feelings had gone into wood, with her body', still has the ability to shed tears.[43]

In his introduction, Hughes claimed that passion and metamorphosis raised the victims onto another plane, that of the supernatural and divine. It would seem, however, that a study of the poems proves that the opposite is happening. The key elements of passion and metamorphosis in Hughes's poetry (as in Ovid's) firmly root their victims in the 'all-too-human' plane. The result is a paradoxical state of change within a continuum as the victim has both undergone a

---

[40] 'Human tears shone on his stag's face | From the grief of a mind that was still human' *CP* 939.

[41] 'He heard his name | And wished he were as far off as they thought him. | He wished he was among them | Not suffering this death but observing | The terrible method | Of his murderers, as they knotted | Muscles and ferocity to dismember | Their own master' *CP* 941.

[42] 'Out of the long grass his mother | Reared upright to face him, | Standing tall to see him better, fearless, | As if she recognised him. She recognised him.' *CP* 900.

[43] 'Now all her feeling had gone into wood, with her body. | Yet she weeps', *CP* 953.

metamorphosis and yet retained attributes of their former self. It is a transformation within a stasis, which we could call—using Hughes's vocabulary—a 'stumble', or an *in extremis* in-between.

This paradoxical state of change within a continuum and the conundrum of Hughes's definition might be solved when placed in the larger context of Hughes's writing. Indeed, drawing a parallel between passion and metamorphosis as explored by Hughes and the idea of the shamanic flight helps explain the poet's paradoxical stance towards 'passion' at the end of a full career.[44] Hughes wrote a great deal about shamanism and what it entailed because, as he explained, he saw shamanism as 'the fundamental poetic event'.[45] He repeated that sentiment often, both in writing and orally. In a 1970 interview with Egbert Faas for instance, Hughes linked his libretto translation of the Bardo Thödol (1960) with shamanic flight for, as he explains,

the shaman's dream is the basis for the hero story. . . . it is the skeleton of thousands of folk tales and myths. And of many narrative poems, the *Odyssey*, the *Divine Comedy*, *Faust*, etc.[46]

In 'Regenerations', Hughes reiterates how he views shamanic flight as the 'basic experience of the poetic temperament', for it lies behind

many of the best fairy tales, behind myths such as those of Orpheus and Herakles . . . It is the outline, in fact, of the Heroic Quest . . . one of the main regenerating dramas of the human psyche: the fundamental poetic event.[47]

Most of Hughes's definitions of shamanism are based on Mircea Eliade's work, for Hughes appreciated how the academic carefully reviewed 'all that is known about Shamanism in a scholarly, fascinating manner'.[48] Hughes's definition is especially close to those found in Eliade's *Shamanism: Archaic Techniques of Ecstasy.*

---

[44] *Tales from Ovid* was published one year before Hughes's death in 1998.

[45] *WP* 58.

[46] Hughes viewed the work as 'basically a shamanistic flight and return.' He thought that 'Tibetan Buddhism was enormously influenced by Tibetan primitive shamanism'; Faas (1980: 208).

[47] *WP* 58. Other examples of Hughes linking poetical work to shamanism would include his famous analysis of Shakespeare as a shaman in *Shakespeare and the Goddess of Complete Being.*

[48] *WP* 58.

In *Winter Pollen*, Hughes describes shamanism in a way that is interesting for our analysis of passion and metamorphosis in the tales. Hughes first distinguishes shamanism from religion: 'shamanism is...a technique for moving in a state of ecstasy among the various spiritual realms, and for generally dealing with souls and spirits, in a practical way, in some practical crisis.'[49] He then describes how the shaman is 'chosen', usually by 'spirits' who 'approach the man in a dream'. Many types of dreams can be found. Some dreams are simple. They are 'no more than a vision' of an animal (an eagle, for example) or a person (like a beautiful woman). Some dreams are 'long and complicated, and dramatise in full the whole psychological transformation that any shaman, no matter how he has been initially chosen, must undergo.'[50] Finally, the dream itself is described. Although the dream itself might vary, many aspects are similar all around the world. The central episode of the dream includes a fundamental transformation of the dreamer, who undergoes

magical death, then dismemberment, by a demon or equivalent powers, with all possible variants of boiling, devouring, burning, stripping to the bones. From this nadir, the shaman is resurrected, with new insides, a new body created for him by the spirits.[51]

This central initiation dream, 'the general schema of the shamanic flight', is for Hughes

the basic experience of the poetic temperament we call 'romantic'. In a shamanizing society, *Venus and Adonis*, some of Keats's longer poems, *The Wandering of Oisin*, *Ash Wednesday*, would qualify their authors for the magic drum; while the actual flight lies perceptibly behind many of the best fairy tales, behind myths such as those of Orpheus and Herakles, and behind the epics of Gilgamesh and Odysseus.[52]

In Hughes's vision of literature, some of the best work is shamanic.

This definition of shamanism becomes all the more fascinating when compared to the tales Hughes chose to work on in *Tales from Ovid*. The person is 'chosen' (does not actively choose), usually by spirits (the supernatural) to undergo the shamanic flight (a form of bodily and mental possession). That is very much the case in the

---

[49] *WP* 56.        [50] *WP* 57.        [51] *WP* 57.        [52] *WP* 58.

*Tales* where the characters do not actively choose to live their passion but, usually through some form of contact with the supernatural (be it before or during the tale), undergo a form of bodily or mental possession (and most often both). Furthermore, both the shamanic flight and Hughes's definition and description of passion centre on what happens to the body. In the first it undergoes a magical trans-formation ('magical death . . . From this the shaman is resurrected, with . . . a new body'), in the latter, metamorphosis. Finally, the metamorphosis itself, or 'magical' transformation is uncannily similar: it is violent, it undermines the physical integrity of the body and leads to a renewal (but not a radical change: the former self is retained through the transformation). In fact, Hughes's definition of passion and his earlier exploration of shamanism are so similar that one has to wonder whether Hughes did not in fact still have the concept of the shamanic flight in mind when writing *Tales from Ovid*. He had, after all, published *Shakespeare and the Goddess of Complete Being* just six years earlier.

In the very first chapter of *Shakespeare and the Goddess of Complete Being*, Hughes analyses Shakespeare's adaptation of Ovid's *Venus and Adonis* (which Hughes also rewrote) and concludes that the poem depicts a typical shamanic initiation dream:

It would be interesting to . . . narrate the plot and details of *Venus and Adonis* to various primitive groups, or at least to groups that still hang on to their old ways of dealing with the supernatural. Or to narrate it without names to any anthropologist who specializes in such things. They would all recognize this poem as a classic example of the dream of spontaneous shamanic initiation . . . [53]

According to Hughes, this 'classic example' of a shaman dream can thus be summarized:

The dreamer, Adonis, is the uncomprehending, resisting ego, who simply wants to get on with his ordinary life. . . . When he reject[s] [the Goddess], she appears in animal form, tears his ego-body to pieces, then reassembles it afresh as her obedient servant—the servant of the spirit world. [54]

---

[53] *SGCB* 87.          [54] *SGCB* 87.

In his footnote to his own analysis of Shakespeare's adaptation of 'Venus and Adonis', Hughes insists:

In the light of this heavily documented shamanic tradition, it is not easy to see Shakespeare's reshaping of his Ovid . . . as anything but a preoccupying inner event of this kind.[55]

Hughes's rendition of 'Venus and Adonis (and Atalanta)' is obviously closer to Ovid's version than to Shakespeare's. So the core elements of the initiation dream described by Hughes are all the more apparent, in that they are the only parts that are similar in both Ovid's and Shakespeare's versions: the young 'uncomprehending . . . ego' (Adonis), 'who simply wants to get on with his ordinary life' (hunting), is torn to pieces by an animal form (the boar), and reassembled into a new (ego-)body (as a flower, the 'windflower').

Thus Hughes's vision of passion in *Tales from Ovid* might be seen as a definition of shamanic experience. It seems his understanding of the concept and its depiction fit the core definition of the phenomenon. Hughes's version of 'passion *in extremis*' explores a certain intense, dream-like possession of the body (a trance?), involving a central episode where a transformation is forcibly effected and results in a magical death of self, a change of form but not of content (metamorphosis), with some form of dismemberment (some bodies burn, other are torn apart, etc.) and displacement (internal and external circulation, flux, journeying) and some form of rebirth (into a new body).

In that case, Hughes's definition of passion in his introduction to *Tales from Ovid* seems far less paradoxical. Hughes writes about Ovid in his introduction, but his words could apply to himself:

Above all, Ovid was interested in passion. Or rather, in what a passion feels like to the one possessed by it. Not just ordinary passion either, but human passion *in extremis*—passion where it combusts, or levitates, or mutates into an experience of the supernatural.

The act of metamorphosis . . . operates as the symbolic guarantee that the passion . . . has achieved the unendurable intensity that lifts the whole episode onto the supernatural or divine plane . . .

---

[55] *SGCB* 88.

In every case, to a greater or lesser degree, Ovid locates and captures the peculiar frisson of that event, where the all-too-human victim stumbles out into the mythic arena and is transformed.[56]

'Passion *in extremis*' as described in Hughes's *Tales from Ovid* with its emphasis on possession, transformation, dismemberment, and an encounter of the mythic plane, magical death and physical renewal, can be considered as a form of shamanic flight.

So, in fact, Hughes's paradoxical definition of 'passion *in extremis*' has to be understood, not in terms of leaving one plane to achieve another, from the human to the divine, but in terms of the movement in itself, the shamanic *flight*. 'Passion *in extremis*' is movement. It is altogether an event, a stumble and a frisson (taken in its etymological meaning of shivering, from the French, *frissonner*). This might explain why 'passion' in Hughes's text is such a physical rather than an emotional or intellectual concept, why it focuses on movement such as flow and flux (of the blood, sap or even current), rather than on what type of desire passion inflames (incest, true love, or lust). It might explain why the word itself seems so empty of any meaning one might have traditionally wanted to associate with it.

Furthermore, this makes sense of why the core definition of metamorphosis was itself changed and why Hughes based his concept of passion on metamorphosis, that is to say a change of shape rather than a change of feeling (such as a heightened love, or desire). Finally, this definition of 'passion *in extremis*' helps to explain one last quirk in Hughes's explanation of what passion is. If you look at Hughes's various attempts at outlining the concept in the 'Introduction' to the *Tales,* the emphasis is not so much on 'who', 'how', 'why', or 'when' things happen, but on 'where' they do:

passion *in extremis*—passion <u>where</u> it combusts, or levitates, or mutates <u>where</u> the all-too-human victim stumbles.[57]

Indeed, it does not matter 'when' the events take place, so much as 'where', if one thinks in terms of shamanism. In the shamanic flight, the elements of the journey, and the various multifaceted tales of the moment of physical change it entails, are more important than the

---

[56] *TO* ix–x.          [57] My emphases.

contents of the passion—which might be lustful, innocent, or incestuous just as the bearer of the dreams and the supernatural elements
encountered might be. (Hence the focus in certain tales on the
exploration of location through details—such as the cooking smells
wafting through a crack in the wall—rather than of the psychology of
passion itself.) 'Passion *in extremis*' is a form of shamanism for
Hughes and as such it is central to his *Tales from Ovid*. This 'passion'
is indeed the locus 'where' the 'all-too-human' 'stumbles' in contact
with the supernatural—and makes the *Tales from Ovid* fascinating
as a milestone in Ovidian reception and as a thread in Hughes's
*oeuvre*.[58]

[58] The author wishes to thank the AHRC for its support and the University of
Emory and Robert W. Woodruff Library for access to the Hughes archive.

# 11

## The transformations of the Actaeon myth: Ovid, *Metamorphoses* 3 and Ted Hughes's *Tales from Ovid*

*Jennifer Ingleheart*

'He . . . is an adaptor. He takes up only those tales which catch his fancy, and engages with each one no further than it liberates his own creative zest.'[1] So Ted Hughes, in the introduction to *Tales from Ovid*, on Ovid's handling of mythological subject matter in his epic *Metamorphoses*. This description of Ovid's engagement with his material looks very much like a self-referential comment upon Hughes's own approach to the many myths contained within the *Metamorphoses*, only twenty-four of which feature in *Tales from Ovid*[2]—and the

---

[1] *TO* viii. My thanks are due to audience members at the Classical Association Annual Conference in Reading, 2005, and the Edinburgh conference, for their helpful comments on earlier versions. I also owe an important debt of thanks to Josephine Balmer, Barbara Graziosi, Keith Sagar, and, above all, Justine Wolfenden for criticizing and encouraging fledgling versions. The translations here provided, unless otherwise acknowledged, represent my attempts to render Ovid as simply as possible. All errors are my own.

[2] Cf. too Hughes's comment on Ovid and the *Metamorphoses* ('The right man had met the right material at the right moment', vii), and his rendition of the opening lines of the *Met.* ('Now I am ready to tell how bodies are changed | Into new bodies', 3). It is hard not to read these as referring to Hughes's perception of the place of *TO* in his own career: having treated mythological themes in his earlier works, as well as previously producing versions of shorter classical works, Hughes could now as Poet Laureate aspire to the greater challenge of adapting the famous, lengthy, and frequently translated *Metamorphoses*. Cf. Hardie (2002*b*: 1–3), and Kennedy (2002: 321). Sagar notes that although Hughes had been familiar with the *Metamorphoses* throughout his working life, an invitation to contribute to Hofmann and Lasdun (1994) led Hughes to compose *TO*: cf. Sagar above.

collection has indeed garnered high praise for its perceived similarities to Ovid's *Metamorphoses*.[3] However, it is not so much the similarities that can be detected in Hughes's adaptation that are most interesting, but rather the differences; that is, the ways in which Hughes takes control of Ovid's material and reshapes it as his own. Nowhere do these differences appear more marked than in Hughes's treatment of the Actaeon myth. In this paper, I examine in detail an aspect of Hughes's version of this episode which might be seen dramatically to alter its focus: his strong emphasis on the sexual elements within the myth. I argue that Hughes's treatment of Actaeon results from a polemical engagement with Ovid's version, and that the motivation behind Hughes's interpretation can be recovered from his introduction, which provides a programme for his adaptation of the *Metamorphoses*. I examine whether Hughes, by playing up the sexual elements, has transformed the Ovidian Actaeon beyond all recognition, and attempt to assess the value of Hughes's Actaeon as a response to the version of the myth found in Ovid. Finally, I investigate to what extent Hughes followed Ovid in exploring autobiographical resonances in the Actaeon myth.

But first to Hughes's source. At *Metamorphoses* 3.138–255, Ovid had related how the young hunter Actaeon accidentally stumbled across Diana, goddess of hunting and virginity, bathing naked. The goddess was angered, and transformed Actaeon into a stag, and in that form he was subsequently torn to pieces by his own hounds. Ovid presents this as a tale of tragic, unwitting error:

at bene si quaeras, Fortunae crimen in illo,
non scelus inuenies; quod enim scelus error habebat?

'But if you seek/ask well, you will find the fault of Fortune in that case/man, not a crime; for what crime did a mistake/wandering have?'

(*Met.* 3.141–2)

This direct address to Ovid's reader, found before the narration of Actaeon's downfall, pre-emptively colours our reading of the entire episode, demonstrating that Ovid is following an earlier version of

---

[3] Cf. e.g. Hofmann (1997): 'Hughes is as broad as Ovid and as subtle, as violent and as erotic, as elegant and as folksy—and often all at the same time. It is simply a beautiful match'.

the myth by the Hellenistic poet Callimachus (*Hymn* 5.107 ff.), and putting to the fore Ovid's view as narrator that Actaeon was guiltless, in marked contrast with most other accounts of the myth, which portray Actaeon's punishment as deserved, for a variety of offences.[4] In the earliest example we have of the reception of the *Metamorphoses* version of the myth, Ovid in his exile poetry appropriated his earlier narrative as a parallel for his own situation, equating his exilic downfall (for seeing something that he shouldn't have seen) at the hands of the divine emperor Augustus with Diana's destruction of the innocent Actaeon:[5]

> cur aliquid uidi? cur noxia lumina feci?
> cur imprudenti cognita culpa mihi?
> inscius Actaeon uidit sine ueste Dianam:
> praeda fuit canibus non minus ille suis.
> scilicet in superis etiam fortuna luenda est,
> nec ueniam laeso numine casus habet.
> illa nempe die, qua me malus abstulit error,
> parua quidem periit, sed sine labe domus.

> 'Why did I see something? Why did I make my eyes guilty?
> Why was a crime discerned by me, all unawares?
> Unintentionally Actaeon saw Diana divested of her clothes:
> no less was he the prey for his own dogs.
> It is clear that among the gods even misfortune must be atoned for,
> and when a divinity is injured an accident receives no pardon.
> To be sure, on that day on which a bad mistake carried me away,
> a house small but without a stain perished.'

> (*Tristia* 2.103–10)[6]

[4] For Actaeon's varying offences, we have the pre-Ovidian evidence of e.g. Stesichorus fr. 236 Page (Actaeon punished by Artemis—henceforth Diana—at the request of Zeus/Jupiter for lusting after Semele), Euripides *Bacchae* 337–40 (Artemis boasting about his skill at hunting), Apollodorus 3.4.4 (*Zeus*'s revenge for Actaeon's sex with Semele, although Apollodorus records that it is more commonly thought that Actaeon saw Diana naked). After Ovid, Nonnus, *Dionys.* 5.287 ff. attributes lustful motives to Actaeon's viewing of Diana, following Statius, *Thebaid* 3.203 ff. and Apuleius, *Metamorphoses* 2.4. See also Forbes Irving (1990: 80–90 and 197–201) and Heath (1992).

[5] Ovid's exile poetry frequently mythologizes his exilic experiences, often drawing on myths from the *Metamorphoses*: see Broege (1972). Ovid claims that he was banished from Rome for *carmen et error* (= 'a poem and a mistake', *Tristia* 2.207); for more on Ovid's *error* (the mysterious thing he saw), see Ingleheart (2006*a*, *b*).

[6] For specific verbal parallels between Ovid and Actaeon in these lines, see Ingleheart (2006*a*: 72–5). If we do not confine parallels to this passage, where the

The relationship between these two passages is complex and disputed; scholars speculate whether the exiled Ovid revisited his *Metamorphoses*, a work which Ovid claims was unfinished when he went into exile, revising it to stress Actaeon's lack of guilt and thereby play up similarities between Actaeon and his own situation.[7] The knotty issue of the dating of the composition of the *Metamorphoses* 3 version is ultimately insoluble, as are so many of the problems surrounding Ovid's exile. Yet whenever the version of the myth recorded in *Metamorphoses* 3 was produced, it can be seen that Ovid had a strong investment—whether primarily literary or more personal and political—in portraying Actaeon as an innocent who suffers an unjust, brutal punishment.

It is easy to see why this episode from the *Metamorphoses* fired Hughes's imagination, given that the Ovidian tale encapsulates themes important in Hughes's verse: hunting, man's connection with the natural world, and the violence inherent in that world. For example, Hughes's gory finale of the myth—where the transformed Actaeon, unable to communicate his 'true' human identity, is dismembered by his hounds in view of his comrades[8]—is anticipated by Hughes's 1967 short story 'The Harvesting', which had explored the ironic role reversal of hunter and hunted, hinting at a hunter's

---

equation is explicit, further correspondences might be posited: e.g., Ovid's comment that he kept his life despite his crime (*Tristia* 2.127) recalls Diana being satisfied by Actaeon's loss of life (*Met.* 3.251–2); *me mea **fata** trahebant* (= 'my fates were dragging me onwards', *Tristia* 2.341, on Ovid's unwilling composition of the erotic verse that destroyed him) parallels *Met.* 3.176, where Actaeon is led into Diana's path by Fate (*sic illum **fata** ferebant* = 'so the fates were carrying him'); the final line of Ovid's exile corpus (*Pont.* 4.16.52: *non habet in nobis iam noua plaga locum* = 'There is no space in me now for new wounds') may evoke Actaeon's mangling at *Met.* 3.237 (*iam **loca** uulneribus desunt* = 'now places are lacking for wounds').

[7] *Tristia* 1.7, 2.63, 555–6, 3.14.19 ff., and (perhaps) 4.10.63; Bömer (1969–86) on *Met.* 3.141–2 believes the couplet Ovid's exilic interpolation. I prefer the case presented by Galinsky (1975: 66–7): that these lines are integral to Ovid's presentation of the episode in *Met.* 3, since they emphasize his adherence to Callimachus' version of the myth.

[8] Hughes finds an appropriate modern verse parallel for Actaeon's fatal inability to communicate in this allusion to Stevie Smith's 'Not Waving, But Drowning': 'His head and antlers reared from the heaving pile. | And swayed—like the signalling arm of somebody drowning in surf' *CP* 941.

metamorphosis into a hare and subsequent dismemberment by dogs.[9] Hughes had previously explored the reversal of hunter and hunted in the poem for children 'A Moon Man-Hunt':[10] and also in the 1978 short story 'The Head'.[11] The myth also allowed Hughes to revisit *Gaudete* (1977), where male voyeurism is frequent, Major Hagen is, to his astonishment, attacked by his own dog, and Lumb is hunted down and killed for sexual offences. Moreover, Hughes had already translated a poem by Ferenc Juhasz from the Czech about a boy transformed into a stag, which clearly owes much to Ovid's Actaeon myth.[12] It is no surprise, then, that Hughes chose to treat the story of Actaeon, the foundational myth of rural hunting leading to violent dismemberment by dogs. Yet Hughes's version of the myth appears to diverge sharply from that found in Book 3 of the *Metamorphoses*: for he presents Actaeon as a voyeur, a Peeping Tom who is keen to see the goddess naked, and consistently stresses sexual elements within the myth. Although other differences can be detected, this seems the most significant, as it could be argued to change the very focus of the myth.

Hughes's interpretation of the myth as a story of voyeurism starts early on; I give his opening stanzas below:

> Destiny, not guilt, was enough
> For Actaeon. It is no crime
> To lose your way in a dark wood.
>
> It happened on a mountain where hunters
> Had slaughtered so many animals
> The slopes were patched red with the butchering places.[13]

---

[9] The epigraph to the story ('And I shall go into a hare | with sorrow and sighs and mickle care', from a medieval shifting song) signals its theme of metamorphosis: cf. O'Brien (1997). 'The Harvesting', like the other short stories from *Wodwo* (1967), was omitted from *CP*.

[10] From *E-O*. Hughes's description of the hounds seizing Actaeon (Melanchaetes seizes Actaeon's 'ankle'; contrast *Met.* 3.232, where this dog wounds Actaeon's *back*) can usefully be compared with the final stanza of this earlier poem: 'Five catch his *heels*, and one on his nose, and ten on each arm, he goes down with a yell. | It is terrible, it is terrible, O it is terrible!'.

[11] First published in *Bananas* 11 (1978), reprinted in *DB* (1995); the narrator decides not to kill again, after hunting in the wilderness: 'My whole being was saturated with animal wounds and animal pain and animal death' (146).

[12] 'The Boy Changed into a Stag Cries Out at the Gate of Secrets' in *ST* 24–37; space does not allow a further consideration of its relation to the Actaeon of *TO* here.

[13] *CP* 937.

Hughes's 'It happened on a mountain' creates suspense here in a more overt way than Ovid's simple scene-setting *mons erat infectus uariarum caede ferarum* ('There was a mountain dyed with the slaughter of various wild beasts', *Met.* 3.143), making voyeurs out of his readers: we want to read on, to discover what exactly it was that happened on this mountain.

Erotic imagery lurks in Actaeon's address to his men as he calls off the hunt:

> 'Our nets are stiff with blood,
> Our spears are caked, and our knives
> Are clogged in their sheaths with the blood of a glorious hunt.'

The words 'stiff' and 'sheaths' have no direct counterparts in the comparable line of Actaeon's speech in Ovid, and seem open to a sexual reading which figures Actaeon and his companions in hunting as both male and potential sexual predators, since the men are about to trespass upon the woods that are the haunt of the virgin goddess.[14] Sexual possibilities intensify in the gendered description of the location of the transgression:[15]

> And the hunt was over for the day.
> A deep cleft at the bottom of the mountain
> Dark with matted pine and spiky cypress
>
> Was known as Gargaphie, sacred to Diana,
> Goddess of the hunt.

Potentially there is a sexual thrust to 'cleft', which the *OED* defines as 'The parting of the thighs, the "clearing" or the "fork"'.[16] Hughes's 'dark wood' of the opening stanza might also be read as female by post-Freudian audiences, given that Hughes paints the Actaeon myth as an example of male sexual intrusion upon female territory. Such intrusion becomes clearer as the tale progresses: Hughes has Diana come to her grotto 'aching and burning from her hunting . . . to cool

---

[14]  *lina madent, comites, ferrumque cruore ferarum* ('The nets and the iron are dripping with the blood of wild beasts, comrades', *Met.* 3.148). Cf. Shakespeare's *Venus and Adonis* for erotic hunting.

[15]  The valley in which Actaeon sees the naked Diana is already presented as female and virginal in Ovid (cf. e.g. the way in which it is stained with blood when the men hunt on it at *Met.* 3.143 and 148), and Hughes arguably plays up such Ovidian hints; see further n.28.

[16]  Gargaphie is later a 'goyle'; the Devonian dialect renders the poem Hughesian.

the naked beauty she hid from the world': Hughes would have been aware of 'aching' and 'burning' as metaphors for sexual desire from the ancient world onwards, and his concentration on Diana *hiding* her naked beauty sets us up for a story of voyeurism;[17] from Ovid, we learn merely:

> hic dea siluarum uenatu fessa solebat
> uirgineos artus liquido perfundere rore.

> 'Here the goddess of the woods, tired from hunting, was accustomed to drench her maiden's limbs with moist dew.'

> (*Met.* 3.163–4)

This reference to the goddess' *uirgineos artus* may already suggest that Diana's virginity will be violated by what follows, but Hughes's wording produces this effect more strongly.

Both Ovid and Hughes then describe at length how Diana prepares for her bath by taking off her clothes item by item, and handing them to her attendant nymphs, in this safe female space (*Met.* 3.165–72 ∼ *TO* stanzas 11–14; I discuss these lines below). Hughes emphasizes the sequestered nature of the bathing scene that Actaeon comes across, with the result that the intrusion that follows seems more marked than in Ovid: compare the following:

> The goddess was there, in her secret pool,
> Naked and bowed
> Under those cascades from the mouths of jars

> In the fastness of Gargaphie, when Actaeon,
> Making a beeline home from the hunt
> Stumbled on this gorge.

> dumque ibi perluitur solita Titania lympha,
> ecce nepos Cadmi dilata parte laborum
> per nemus ignotum non certis passibus errans
> peruenit in lucum. sic illum fata ferebant.

> 'And while the goddess born of a Titan bathes there with her usual water, behold! The grandson of Cadmus with part of his toils deferred wandering through the unfamiliar wood with uncertain footsteps came into the grove. So the fates were leading him.'

> (*Met.* 3.173–6)

---

[17] The notion of Diana hiding may be mediated through Spenser's *Faerie Queene* 7.6.42.

Hughes spells out what is understated in Ovid, reminding us that Diana is 'naked' as she bathes;[18] Ovid, having already related Diana's disrobing, focuses rather on the mundane, quotidian nature of the scene for Diana, which renders the shock of male intrusion all the greater. In what follows immediately afterwards, Hughes persistently presents Actaeon in sexual terms and as a voyeur:

> . . . Surprised to find it,
>
> He pushed into it, apprehensive, but
> Steered by a pitiless fate—whose nudgings he felt
> Only as surges of curiosity.

Where Hughes's vocabulary is suggestive, Ovid's is flat and unemotional: 'He pushed into it' appears an aggressive male, sexual action, violating this female haven, whereas Ovid tells us simply that Actaeon entered the grove. 'Steered by a pitiless fate' works well as a translation of Ovid's *sic illum fata ferebant* (= 'so the fates were carrying him', *Met.* 3.176), although 'pitiless' is the narrator's subjective, pathos-evoking assessment of a situation presented in the original's detached Latin. Furthermore, nothing in Ovid corresponds to Hughes's 'nudgings' of fate, experienced by Actaeon as 'surges of curiosity'; a phrase capable of an erotic, physiological interpretation.[19]

In Hughes we then read:

> . . . He peered
> Into the gloom to see the waterfall—
> But what he saw were nymphs, their wild faces
>
> Screaming at him in a commotion of water.
> And as his eyes adjusted, he saw they were naked,
> Beating their breasts as they screamed at him.
>
> And he saw they were crowding together
> To hide something from him. He stared harder.
> Those nymphs could not conceal Diana's whiteness,

---

[18]  Cf. Lyne (2002: 261–2).

[19]  This looks more like a description of Lucius, the narrator of Apuleius's second-century CE novel *Metamorphoses*; Lucius suffers from excessive curiosity. Indeed, he even sees a statue which depicts Actaeon's encounter with Diana as a story of voyeurism (*Met.* 2.4–5), anticipating Lucius' transformation into an ass as the result of his own curiosity.

> The tallest barely reached her navel. Actaeon
> Stared at the goddess, who stared at him.
> She twisted her breasts away, showing him her back.

Ovid's Actaeon, unlike Hughes's, does not have the intention of seeing *anything*; the vision that he gets is entirely accidental, as he lacks both curiosity and volition. Furthermore, at this point in the Latin, the focus is not on what Actaeon sees, as in Hughes, but instead upon the horrified nymphs as *they* see *Actaeon*:

> qui simul intrauit rorantia fontibus antra,
> sicut erant, nudae *uiso* sua pectora nymphae
> percussere *uiro* subitisque ululatibus omne
> impleuere nemus circumfusaeque Dianam
> corporibus texere suis . . .
>
> 'As soon as he entered the cave bedewed with spray,
> just as they were, the naked nymphs *at the sight of a man*
> beat their breasts and with sudden howls
> filled the entire grove and having poured around Diana
> covered her body with their own . . .'

(Met. 3.177–81)

Hughes effectively communicates the male violation of the space occupied by the nymphs and Diana, by concentrating on what Actaeon sees, and through the gradual revelation of the nymphs' nudity. Hughes's reference to Diana's breasts thereby emphasizes what Actaeon sees and Diana's consequent discomfort; the Latin that Hughes responds to is more neutral: *in latus obliquum tamen adstitit oraque retro | flexit* ('However, she stood with her side turned aside and bent her face backwards', *Met.* 3.187–8). Hughes's interpretation of the myth as one of voyeurism is then clear in his description of Diana's blush: 'She blushed like a dawn cloud | In that twilit grotto of winking reflections'. Ovid talks about Diana blushing at *Met.* 3.183–5, but 'that twilit grotto of winking reflections' is entirely Hughes's addition, and, coming at the end of the narrative of Actaeon's sighting of the goddess, retrospectively confirms that, for Hughes, the episode is a peep show.[20]

---

[20] 'Reflections' here may allude to parallels between the virgin goddess of hunting and the adolescent hunter Actaeon: cf. e.g. Brown (2005: 70). The wording also sets up a nice link with the story of Narcissus (which Hughes places *before* the Actaeon

How did Hughes get from Ovid's version of the myth, which emphatically states Actaeon's innocence, to such an erotic interpretation?[21] The answer must partly lie in his introduction, which propounds Hughes's views on Ovid's methods and achievements in the *Metamorphoses*, and offers an insight into Hughes's adaptation of this episode and, in particular, the erotic focus of his version.

First, Hughes's attribution of the enduring popularity of Ovid's *Metamorphoses* to Ovid's interest in passion must have played a large part in determining the voyeuristic nature of Hughes's Actaeon:

> What has gone deepest into his long succession of readers, and brought him so intimately into the life of art, is what he shared with Shakespeare. Above all, Ovid was interested in passion. Or rather, in what a passion felt like to the one possessed by it. Not just ordinary passion either, but human passion *in extremis*—passion where it combusts, or levitates, or mutates into an experience of the supernatural . . . This is the current he divines and follows in each of his tales—the current of human passion. He adapts each myth to this theme. Where details or complexities of the traditional story encumber or diffuse his theme, he simply omits them.[22]

episode), who falls in love with his own reflection. Hughes may also allude to Titian's *Actaeon Discovers Diana Bathing* (1559), where the grotto that is the setting for the encounter between goddess and mortal contains several mirrors.

[21] Hughes's separation of the Actaeon episode from other myths adapted from *Metamorphoses* 3, such as those of Semele and Pentheus (like Actaeon, victims of divine anger), and Tiresias and Narcissus (whose downfalls are also strongly connected with sight), and placing it between the stories of Peleus and Thetis (*Met.* 11) and Myrrha (*Met.* 10), appears relevant. Henderson (1999: 312), comments unfavourably upon Hughes's (and the other contributors' to *After Ovid*) lack of interest in the 'architectonics' of the *Metamorphoses*, noting that the excerpting of the poem means that narrative connections between myths are 'blurred, downplayed or lost entirely'. Nevertheless, Hughes's placing of the myth in a new context creates its own effects. The frames (Peleus's rape of Thetis; Myrrha's incestuous love for her father) fit with Hughes's focus upon the transgressive nature of Actaeon's vision: by placing it with other myths of unnatural sex, he suggests a similar trajectory here too. Hughes also makes innovative connections between Actaeon and surrounding myths: for example, Myrrha is 'netted | In a mesh of family conundrums'; such hunting imagery is absent in the Latin. This adds pathos: Hughes's readers have just seen a human hunted to death. Hughes's portrayal of Actaeon as a voyeur also gains force from the fact that his readers have *already* seen the desiring male gaze operating in the Narcissus myth, which precedes Actaeon's episode in Hughes. I am currently preparing a paper on the architectonics of *TO*.

[22] *TO* ix.

This is a partial assessment of Ovid's focus in the *Metamorphoses*; it fits with myths such as Myrrha's incestuous love for her father (*Met.* 10.298–502) or Echo and Narcissus (*Met.* 3.339–510), and it is no surprise that Hughes adapts these episodes. However, Hughes's view of Ovid proves hard to reconcile with, for example, the Roman and historical myths of the later books of the *Metamorphoses*, a part of the poem with which Hughes does not engage.[23] But this view of Ovid helps to explain why Hughes's Actaeon is a voyeur; an innocent accidentally stumbling across a goddess hardly shows Ovid following the 'current of human passion'. In Hughes's version, however, the 'surges of curiosity' that drive Actaeon on, and the moment where goddess and man stare at each other, clearly demonstrate 'the current of human passion' and the way in which such passion can transmute 'into an experience of the supernatural'.

Hughes's comment on the influence that the *Metamorphoses* has had upon the Western visual arts ('Different aspects of the poem continued to fascinate Western culture, saturating literature and art') explains another aspect to Hughes's portrayal of Actaeon as voyeur.[24] Hughes may allude to the setting of paintings of the myth when he describes how the dogs pursuing Actaeon 'flowed across the landscape'. This corresponds to nothing in the Latin, and may nod towards the popularity of the myth with landscape artists, who locate it firmly in a rural setting. The complexity of the role of the viewer which is inherent and problematic in visual depictions of the myth— do we inevitably become voyeurs because of the very medium?—is perhaps echoed in Hughes's description of the encounter of man and divinity: 'Actaeon | Stared at the goddess, who stared at him'.[25] Hughes expands the role of viewer and viewed by making Diana look in turn at Actaeon; this has no counterpart in the Latin, although Ovid does focus on the *nymphs'* vision of Actaeon. Another way of looking at the mutual vision of man and goddess in Hughes, however, would be to see Hughes narrowing down the roles of viewer and viewed to the myth's protagonists, whereas Ovid's version leaves the role of viewer open to the *reader* as well. To turn from the general to

---

[23] Cf. Lyne (2002: 262) and Henderson (1999: 315).
[24] *TO* viii.
[25] *CP* 938.

specific representations of the myth, it seems likely that Titian's
*Actaeon Discovers Diana Bathing* (1559) influenced one aspect of
Hughes's version: his description of Diana twisting her breasts
away. The naked female in Titian's foreground, who must be Diana,
given the iconography, twists her breasts away, showing the viewer
her back, just as in Hughes's description of Diana's evasive action.

However, Hughes's comments on different versions of myths provide the fullest explanation of his choice of focus:

> As a guide to the historic, original forms of the myths, Ovid is of little use.
> His attitude to his material is like that of the many later poets who have
> adapted what he presents . . .
>
> (*TO* viii–ix)

Such talk of 'the historic, original forms of the myths' betrays a
significant misunderstanding of the nature of classical mythology:
its fluidity; the way in which it is itself in a constant process of
metamorphosis; the near impossibility of identifying the 'historic,
original' version of any myth. However, it also casts light on Hughes's
treatment of Actaeon. Indeed, a structuralist approach would support Hughes here: it is clear that in the majority of the versions of the
myth, Actaeon is punished by Diana, goddess of virginity. In every
single version, his offence involves *women* in one way or another;
usually—but not always—Actaeon's offence is *sexual*.[26] Hughes's
eroticization of the myth can thus be read as an attempt to return
the myth to what Hughes believes to be its 'historic, original' form,
and there is surely some validity to such sexual interpretations of
the myth.

The focus of Hughes's adaptation of the Actaeon myth is thus
explicable as a polemical response to the Ovidian version. But what
of the validity of Hughes's programmatic engagement with Ovid? We
have already seen that Hughes is flawed in his ideas about the nature
of classical myth and in his (perhaps) self-reflexive view of Ovid as a
poet of passion. Are there any grounds on which Hughes's polemical
rendering of the Actaeon myth can be defended as a 'Tale from
Ovid'? I would suggest that the greatest value of Hughes's Actaeon
as a version of the Ovidian Actaeon may be that it forces us to turn

[26] Cf. Forbes Irving (1990: 81).

back to the Ovid in detail in order to see if we can detect any elements that support this reading.

Despite the explicit disclaimer at the start of the tale in which the narrator of the *Metamorphoses* stresses Actaeon's innocence (*Met.* 3.141–2), there are several hints in the episode of sexual, voyeuristic elements.[27] Such nods and winks would be very much in tune with what I perceive to be Ovid's narrative method in the *Metamorphoses*: far from omitting complicating or contrasting details from other versions of myths, he frequently alludes to them, showing his awareness of different traditions.[28] Ovid's hints at erotic elements in the Actaeon episode are far from obvious, but lurk in the undergrowth. For example, the description of the cave and pool which are the setting of the encounter (155 ff.) is a standard depiction of a *locus amoenus*. In the *Metamorphoses*, the deserted, woodland *locus amoenus* is frequently the setting for rape or attempted rape, particularly if its description also involves such elements as water, which Ovid often explicitly associates with purity; hunting, frequently associated with the pursuit of love; divinities and nymphs.[29] Given the narrative expectations associated with the *locus amoenus* in this work, on coming across a description of a young hunter encountering the goddess of hunting and virginity bathing nude in a secluded pool, Ovid's audience probably anticipate *sexual* violence.[30] Other whiffs of sex as Ovid sets the scene may be scented in the way in which Ovid before Hughes seems to present Diana's surroundings at the start of the episode in terms reminiscent of the female body, about to be violated by the entrance of the male

---

[27] Alternatively, Ovid invites readers to take sides by asking questions (*quaeras*, 141) about crime and responsibility from the start. Cf. Brown (2005: 69).

[28] For reasons of space, a single example must suffice. In *Met.* 2, Phaethon dies because he fails to handle the chariot of the Sun, yet Ovid hints at a version of the myth, found e.g. in Euripides, *Phaethon*, in which Phaethon is transformed into a constellation, via a simile which provides a 'concealed' metamorphosis of Phaethon into a star (*Met.* 2.319–22).

[29] Cf. e.g. the myths of Daphne (1.474 ff.), Io (1.568 ff.), Syrinx (1.689 ff.), Callisto (2.401 ff.), Narcissus and Echo (3.407 ff.), Salmacis and Hermaphroditus (4.296 ff.), Proserpina (5.385 ff.) and Arethusa (5.572 ff.), where many of the themes mentioned above coalesce. See too e.g. Parry (1964), Krier (1990: 41–65), and Heath (1992: 53 ff.).

[30] Cf. Brown (2005: 70).

Actaeon;[31] the protracted, teasing scene of Diana stripping for her bath;[32] and Ovid's emphasis on the fact that Diana's bathing was utterly ordinary, which might remind us that voyeurs usually spy on women engaged in their everyday lives rather than overtly sexual activities.[33]

I also detect traces of sexual elements within the encounter itself. First, at line 174, where Ovid talks of Actaeon entering the glade as Diana bathes, *ecce* (= 'look'/ 'behold') alerts us to the importance of sight in what follows. The presence of this word appears problematic; by instructing his readers to look at this point, Ovid may thereby implicate them in Actaeon's crime and figure them as voyeurs, with implications for Actaeon himself. Secondly, Ovid's description of how Diana in the cave towers above her nymphs, and is therefore seen by Actaeon:

> ... tamen altior illis
> ipsa dea est colloque tenus **supereminet omnis**.

> However, the goddess herself is much taller than them,
> and overtowers them; they only reach as far as her neck.

(*Met.* 3.181–2)

This closely recalls some lines from the *Aeneid*:[34]

> qualis in Eurotae ripis aut per iuga Cynthi
> exercet Diana choros, quam mille secutae
> hinc atque hinc glomerantur Oreades; illa pharetram

---

[31] Cf. Salzman-Mitchell (2005: 47); I would add to her comment on the description of the pool in which Diana bathes as *hiatus* ('... significant in the construction of space as a great female opening') that this word is found for the opening of the vagina; cf. Adams (1982: 95–6), who however notes that it is specifically used of *laxus cunnus*, usually a topic of obscene invective suggesting female sexual promiscuity. Might Ovid thereby hint that Diana is not quite the virgin she presents herself as?—cf. Brown (2005: 73 ff.).

[32] See Ingleheart (2006*a*). That Diana's hair is bound up (*Met.* 3.168–70) means that she will not be able to cover her nudity; and the description of Diana as *Titania* (173), a daughter of the Titans—an ancient outsized mythological race often associated with the Giants—stresses that Diana is taller than her companions (181 ff.), which is why she cannot avoid Actaeon's vision.

[33] Cf. *solebat* (163) and *solita ... lympha* (173).

[34] Cf. Morgan (2003: 68–9); however, Morgan does not take the correspondences far enough, seeing Ovid's exploitation of Vergil as an example of Ovid's 'low and physical' humour.

fert umero gradiensque deas **supereminet omnis**
(Latonae tacitum pertemptant gaudia pectus):
talis erat Dido . . .

She was like Diana leading the dance on the banks of the Eurotas or along the ridges of Mount Cynthus with a thousand mountain nymphs thronging behind her on either side. She carries her quiver on her shoulder, and as she walks, she is the tallest of all the goddesses. Dido was like Diana. . . .

(Vergil, *Aen* 498–503; translation: D. West)

Ovid's line ending at 182 repeats the line ending at *Aeneid* 1.501, and he then follows these lines with his own simile, as if to remind us that we previously encountered these words about Diana overtopping her nymphs in a Vergilian simile which itself adapts a simile from *Odyssey* 6.102–9. The context of Vergil's simile is significant for Ovid's allusion to it here: these lines describe Dido as she first appears to Aeneas, who is shortly going to become her lover (in a cave, after they have gone hunting together, no less!). The undeniably erotic force of the Vergilian passage—which expands erotic hints in its Homeric model—surely affects how we read this Ovidian passage.

Hughes's Actaeon can thus be seen as an interpretation of the myth which plays up elements present—one might say integral—in many other classical versions. In terms of its value as an adaptation of the version found in *Metamorphoses* 3, it also underlines some interesting possibilities for Ovid's readers. Hughes's interpretation of the myth as one of voyeurism opens up a reading of the myth which is present but muted in the *Metamorphoses* and which Ovid in his exile poetry attempts—with limited success—to shut down.[35] Hughes's re-reading of the episode forces us to confront the complexities and mixed messages found within Ovid's *Metamorphoses*, sending us back to Ovid for a version of the myth in which, despite Ovid's explicit narrative statements to the contrary, Actaeon is poised delicately between innocence and guilt. Hughes also gives us an Actaeon for our own times: for how can a contemporary audience read a story of a young man coming across naked, beautiful women as anything but compromised?

---

[35] There is a major problem here: what are we to make of Ovid's exilic pleas of innocence when they are linked with Actaeon's supposed lack of culpability, given the sexual and ambiguous elements in the episode in *Metamorphoses* 3?

Finally, I want to return to the way in which Ovid appropriated the Actaeon myth in exile, investing it with a political and personal significance. Modern adaptors of Ovid—Hughes included—have been reprimanded by classical scholars for not engaging with those myths in the *Metamorphoses* which have a political dimension.[36] This issue could be seen to crystallize around the Actaeon episode, which, in the light of the exile poetry, is open to a very political reading. Yet Hughes's treatment of the myth apparently bypasses this aspect. Hughes knew of Ovid's exile: he refers to it in his introduction's opening sentence, but seems unaware of the role that sight played in Ovid's downfall:

Ovid was born the year after the death of Julius Caesar and flourished in the Rome of Augustus. He completed the *Metamorphoses* around the time of the birth of Christ, was later banished for some unknown offence against the Emperor, and spent the last ten years of his life in exile at Tomis on the Black Sea.[37]

This lack of acknowledgement of the use to which Ovid later put the story could be seen as a serious flaw in Hughes's adaptation of Ovid's Actaeon myth, since it means that Hughes misses out on an important facet of the reception of this myth: that is, Ovid's role as the first adaptor of this episode. Hughes's interest in the reception of the *Metamorphoses* is evident both from his introduction—where he talks about reception of the *Metamorphoses* in Shakespeare and the visual arts—and the episode itself, yet he seems to leave the autobiographical aspect of the Actaeon myth unexplored.[38]

I am reluctant however to believe that Hughes was blind to the autobiographical possibilities of using myths from the *Metamorphoses*, and both Lyne and Hardie have discerned an Ovidian, autobiographical pattern in Hughes's choice of the myth of Pyramus and Thisbe to close his collection, looking forward to his next and final

---

[36] Cf. Henderson (1999: 315).     [37] *TO* vii.

[38] A few more examples from the text: Hughes's Diana 'raged' for a weapon, perhaps drawing on Spenser's Diana who 'woxe half-wrothe' (*Faerie Queene* 3.6.19) against her nymphs for allowing her to be seen; Hughes's 'rack of antlers' is already found in Slavitt (1994: 48), who picks up on the phrase by describing Actaeon as 'meat' (50), whereas Hughes stresses associations of *torture* in Actaeon's death: cf. e.g. stanzas 51 ff.

collection, *Birthday Letters*, on his relationship with his dead wife, Sylvia Plath.[39] Furthermore, Actaeon and his fate had already been explored as a personal parallel by other artists following in Ovid's footsteps.[40] In fact, if we turn back to Hughes's Actaeon, the opening stanza's 'It is no crime | To lose your way in a dark wood' raises the spectre of poetic autobiography in connection with this myth by evoking the opening of Dante's 'autobiographical' *Inferno*.[41] This makes it the more surprising, then, that Hughes does not further pick up on Ovid's personal use of the myth. In fact, I wish to speculate that Hughes may have had reasons poetic, personal, and political for not doing so. In 1976, Hughes had published in the *Atlantic Monthly* a poem entitled 'Actaeon', which updates the myth to a contemporary, domestic context, seemingly revealing the secrets of a destructive marriage.[42] It is hard not to read this poem in the light of Hughes's own life and marriage to Sylvia Plath. This earlier treatment of Actaeon's myth may explain why Hughes, other than hinting at the autobiographical via an allusion to Dante, chose not to (re-)emphasize personal elements in the myth of Actaeon. Following Plath's suicide, women in particular harried him over his treatment of Plath, believing him to be the cause of her death. Actaeon's myth told of a blameless man destroyed by pursuing, violent women closing ranks and claiming female solidarity in the face of his imagined offence against their gender. There was no need for Hughes to follow Ovid in overtly connecting the myth with his own life.

[39] Lyne (2002: 263); Hardie (2002*b*: 1–3); in this volume, see Liveley; cf. also Sagar, Brown, and Gervais for autobiographical readings of Hughes's use of the Alcestis myth.

[40] Cf. stanza 31 of Shelley's *Adonais* (a self-description of the poet who 'Had gaz'd on Nature's naked loveliness, | Actaeon-like, and now he fled astray | With feeble steps o'er the world's wilderness, | And his own thoughts, along that rugged way, | Pursu'd, like raging hounds, their father and their prey'). Self-descriptions as Actaeon in Fritz Bultman's papers about his paintings represent his own homosexuality: cf. Firestone (2001).

[41] '*Nel mezzo del cammin di nostra vita | mi ritrovai per un selva oscura | che la via diritta era smarrita*' ('In the middle of the path of my life. | I found myself in a dark wood; | for the straight way was lost', *Inferno* 1.1–3). An attendee at the Edinburgh conference suggested that allusion to Dante is maintained through the formal aspect of the episode, laid out as if in terza rima.

[42] Reprinted in *CP* 558–9.

# 12

## Birthday Letters from Pontus: Ted Hughes and the white noise of classical elegy

*Genevieve Liveley*

> . . . More to reach you
> Than to reproach you, more to spark
> A contact through the see-saw bustling
> Atmospherics of higher learning
> And lower socializing, than to correct you
> With our archaic principles, we concocted
> An attack, a dismemberment, laughing.
> We had our own broadsheet to publish it.
> Our Welshman composed it—still deaf
> To the white noise of the elegy
> That would fill his mouth and his ear
> Worlds later, on Cader Idris,
> In the wind and snow of your final climb.
>
> Caryatids (2)[1]

Hughes ends his *Tales from Ovid* not with Ovid's envoi or any one of the tales from Book 15 of the *Metamorphoses* but with the story of Pyramus and Thisbe, the ill-fated lovers—prototypes for Shakespeare's Romeo and Juliet—who, separated in life, come together only in death. Reordering Ovid's own selection of tales, Hughes closes his translation—or, better, transformation— of Ovid's epic poem with the elegiac image of two lovers united in death:

---

[1] *CP* 1047.

And the two lovers in their love-knot,
One pile of inseparable ashes,
Were closed in a single urn.[2]

The selection of this final tale as a conclusion to the work is significant. And, as Raphael Lyne has suggested, 'Hindsight enhances this impression, since *Tales from Ovid* was published so close to the end of the poet's life and the reassessment of his career and in particular his relationship with Sylvia Plath'.[3] This ending to *Tales from Ovid* seems to offer a particularly poignant conclusion then, inviting us to identify the two mythological lovers, 'inseparable ashes', as Hughes and Plath—indeed, Hughes invokes a similar image of himself and Plath as 'knotted lovers | Lifted from Pompeii's ashes' in 'The Difference', a poem collected in *Howls and Whispers* and published the year after *Tales from Ovid* in 1998.[4] The end of *Tales from Ovid*, then, seems to invite us to read the elegiac *topos* that here unites lovers in and after death as something more than a classical or literary commonplace. It invites us too, towards a reading of Hughes's *Birthday Letters* as a work that picks up this elegiac thread to weave another story of love and death, of mythological lovers in their love-knot, contained in the well-wrought urn of Hughes's poetry—the story of Sylvia Plath and Ted Hughes.

Published in 1998, in the last year of Hughes's life, *Birthday Letters* collects together eighty-eight poems written over a twenty-five year period, all either addressed to Plath or concerning her relationship with Hughes, and seems to tell at first-hand the story of that famous relationship: from the first encounter of two Cambridge undergraduates, through Plath's suicide, to Hughes's life with their children after her death. An 'autobibliography', *Birthday Letters* tells its story through the prism of poetry, constructing an allusive literary web which interweaves Chaucer, Shakespeare, Donne, Eliot, Coleridge, and, above all, the poetry of Plath and Hughes themselves—expecting, even demanding, 'to be read as a set of public conversations about memories of the creative partnership' these two poet-lovers shared.[5] Indeed, in a letter to the judges of the Forward Poetry Prize, written in 1998, Hughes described his *Birthday Letters* as:

---

[2] *CP* 1042.     [3] Lyne (2002: 263).     [4] *CP* 1177.
[5] Middlebrook (2006*b*: 54). On the use Hughes makes of Plath's poetry in *Birthday Letters* see also Silk in this volume.

a gathering of the occasions—written with no plan over about 25 years—on which I tried to open a direct, private, inner contact with my first wife—not thinking to make a poem, thinking mainly to evoke her presence to myself, and to feel her there listening.[6]

Like her poetry, Plath's ghost and the spectre of her suicide haunt the lines of each poem in the collection, and each poem can be read as an attempt by Hughes to use the power of his poetry to effect a kind of reunion with his dead wife. The collection draws some of its coherence from this attempt, no less than from its apparently autobiographical or autobibliographical narrative frame, but if—as Hughes claims—the *Birthday Letters* were not originally conceived as 'poems' or written in accordance with any planned sequence, then their thematic unity is striking. Remarkably, as Keith Sagar observes of the imagery of *Birthday Letters*:

> Given that the poems were written over a long period, with no thought of publishing them as a collection, let alone as a sequence, there is amazing richness and coherence of imagery. All the interwoven strands of imagery—dreaming, sleepwalking, the labyrinth, acting parts in an already written play . . ., drowning, burning, blood—lead to the same inexorable finale, the same triumph of death (in the person of the dead father) over everything that can be set against it.[7]

The same richness and coherence can be traced through the collection's dense and complex layering of classical references and mythological allusions—from its opening poems, 'Caryatids (1)' and 'Caryatids (2)', referring to the first poem by Plath that Hughes ever read and 'disliked through the eyes of a stranger' to its closing sequence, where their children are metamorphosed into orphaned babes like Romulus and Remus ('Life After Death'), and where their daughter's fingers, in their similarity to Plath's, come to represent 'The Lares and Penates of our house' ('Fingers').[8] Indeed, at the time of its publication in January 1998, the extensive and elaborate classical allusivity of the *Birthday Letters* prompted many readers to draw explicit parallels between this new work and Hughes's *Tales from*

---

[6] Quoted in Churchwell (2001: 138–9).
[7] Sagar (2000: 70).
[8] *CP* 1045–7, 1160–1, 1167–8.

*Ovid*. Reviewers of the collection presented a persuasive case for reading *Birthday Letters* as part of a continuum with Hughes's earlier and more explicitly classically influenced poetry—particularly his *Tales from Ovid*—prompted not least of all by Hughes's use of stories from classical mythology as a backdrop to the story of his relationship with Plath.

In her reading of the metaphors in one of the collection's early poems, 'Trophies', Diane Middlebrook unequivocally links *Birthday Letters* and *Tales from Ovid*. In Hughes's account of his immediate 'animal' attraction for Plath, the poet figures himself and Plath in the roles of panther and game hunter, and—suggests Middlebrook—as 'he succumbs to her transformation of him—his sense of smell grows keen, his hair turns to fur—as if he were a character in one of Ovid's tales'.[9] Moreover, she notices that:

Hughes'[s] 'Trophies' specifies that forty years have passed since he felt the impact of that fateful look in 1956. If so, 'Trophies' was written in 1996, the year Ted Hughes was working on *Tales from Ovid*, his translation of selections from *Metamorphoses*. In his introduction he summarizes Ovid's achievement in a way that applies to 'Trophies': 'Ovid locates and captures the peculiar frisson of that event, where the all-too-human victim stumbles out into the mythic arena and is transformed.' *Birthday Letters* is building exactly that case: that Ted and Sylvia each stumbled into the other's power to transform mere human beings into characters in a myth.[10]

In the *Birthday Letters*, Plath is 'transformed' into various characters from classical myth—most often into Eurydice or Ariadne—while Hughes himself is most frequently metamorphosed into an Orpheus or Theseus.[11] Indeed, the myth of Orpheus and Eurydice, of the poet who tries—and fails—to rescue his wife from the land of the dead,

---

[9] Middlebrook (2003: 280).    [10] *Ibid.*

[11] In her own poetry Plath variously figures herself as a series of tragic heroines from classical mythology, among them Dido, Phaedra, and Medea. Hughes, however, saw Plath writing in *Ariel* as a Phaeton. Thus, in *WP* (200–1), he writes: 'Phaeton, son of a mortal woman and Apollo (the god of the Sun and of Poetry), took his father's Sun-chariot for a run, and the solar horses, under his half-mortal hands, ran out of control through the heavens. The chariot, it might be supposed, was wrecked and he was killed. As an image of her Ariel flight in the chariot of the God of Poetry, which was also her attempt to soar (plunge) into the inspirational form of her inaccessible father, to convert her former physical suicide into a psychic rebirth, that myth is the parable of the book *Ariel* and of her life and death.'

has been seen by several critics as the central myth underlying
*Birthday Letters*.[12] In 1970, Hughes produced a version of the myth
for children, transforming the myth's classical ending of loss into a
happier rendering in which Orpheus convinces Pluto, the god of the
dead, to restore to him the soul of his beloved wife—in return for
using the power of his poetry to transform Pluto's own wife, Persephone, into a beautiful flower.[13] An echo of this version of the myth
can be heard in *Birthday Letters* in the poem 'The Literary Life', where
the poet Marianne Moore is placed by Hughes 'into the second or
third circle | Of my Inferno' after wounding Plath with a careless
critique of some of her poems. Meeting Moore ten years later, after
Plath's suicide, Hughes sees her as a Persephone, 'holding court . . .
Under her great hat-brim's floppy petal' like the flower-faced queen
of the underworld in his own *Orpheus* poem.[14]

In 'A Picture of Otto', Hughes again transforms the traditional
ending of the Orpheus myth. The poem's speaker addresses (a picture
of) Plath's father Otto, figured here as Pluto:

> I understand—you never could have released her.
> I was a whole myth too late to replace you.
> This underworld, my friend, is her heart's home.
> Inseparable, here we must remain.[15]

While the image of Plath and Hughes as 'inseparable' shades may
recall the 'inseparable ashes' of Pyramus and Thisbe in *Tales from
Ovid*, it is significant that the myth of Orpheus is conspicuously
absent from this collection: the story is, perhaps, 'too obvious' a
parallel to his own situation.[16] Although it is one of the primary
myths of Ovid's *Metamorphoses*, Hughes does not include it at all in
his own translation of the poem.[17] In *Birthday Letters*, however,
Hughes ingeniously links the myth of Orpheus and Eurydice with
that of Theseus and the Minotaur—taking his cue from overlapping

---

[12] For Sagar (2000: 83), this myth lies behind all of Hughes poems written after
1963. See also McClatchy (1998), Whitehead (1999), and Bundtzen (2000).
[13] See Sagar (2000: 84ff.) and in this volume.
[14] *CP* 1090–1.
[15] *CP* 1167.
[16] Hughes's own assessment of the parallel, cited in Sagar (2000: 84).
[17] Further allusions to the Orpheus and Eurydice myth can be seen in 'The Rag
Rug', 'Portraits', '9 Willow Street', and 'The Badlands'.

elements in the classical versions of these myths. For, in classical literature, King Minos is identifiable not only as the keeper of the Minotaur in his Cretan labyrinth, and as father of Theseus's Ariadne, but as one of the three judges who sit in the Stygian court of the underworld, passing sentence upon all the souls who enter there. Theseus too, is associated not only with the Minotaur, the labyrinth, and Ariadne—but with another of Minos's daughters Phaedra, and another unsuccessful Orpheus-like descent into the underworld to 'rescue' Persephone.[18] As Hughes is transformed into Orpheus in *Birthday Letters*, then, so is Orpheus in turn transformed into Theseus—while Plath is seen to metamorphose into and between the characters of Eurydice, Ariadne, and Persephone. And more.

So, in '18 Rugby Street', which introduces the labyrinthine imagery that will recur throughout the collection, Hughes's home is described as 'a labyrinth—| A Knossos of coincidence' and waiting for Plath (an Ariadne) to join him there, Hughes himself is an 'amazed' Theseus.[19] The Minotaur of this myth frequently stands as a metaphor for Plath's dead father Otto. So, for Plath, Paris 'Was a labyrinth . . . Was a dream where you could not | Wake or find the exit or | The Minotaur' ('Your Paris').[20] But in other poems in the collection Plath herself is figured as the monstrous half-man, half-bull creature. 'The Minotaur' narrates how Plath's violent rage once caused her to smash an heirloom sideboard when Hughes arrived late one day for babysitting duty. This violent act:

> Left your children echoing
> Like tunnels in a labyrinth,
> Left your mother a dead-end,
> Brought you to the horned, bellowing
> Grave of your risen father—
> And your own corpse in it.[21]

[18] For a comparison of the 'Minotaur complex' in Hughes's 1998 translation of Racine's Euripidean *Phédre* and *Birthday Letters*, see Berry (2002). According to Berry (2002: 542), 'Hughes'[s] attraction to the Minotaur myth and its taurine associations can be traced back and linked to an early poem in *Lupercal* where, in 'The Bull Moses', the image of a huge bull confined in a dark habitat becomes a symbol for the depth and mystery of mental space.'

[19] *CP* 1055. In 'Error', the 'brambly burrow lanes' of Devon, Plath and Hughes's new home, is another 'labyrinth', *CP* 1121–3; see Hardwick in this volume.

[20] *CP* 1067.    [21] *CP* 1120.

In 'Setebos' we see Hughes and Plath subjected to a protean series of such metamorphoses, as the poem's initial characterization of Hughes and Plath as a Shakespearean couple—the *Tempest*'s Ferdinand and Miranda—is itself transformed with Plath becoming first the savage Caliban and then the Minotaur—her Ovidian-style metamorphosis marked by 'The bellow in your voice'. Unaware as yet of this transition from the world of Shakespeare to the world of classical myth, Hughes describes how he lay, asinine, as in a midsummer night's dream:

> I lay
> In the labyrinth of a cowslip
> Without a clue. I heard the Minotaur
> Coming down its tunnel-groove
> Of old faults deep and bitter. King Minos,
> Alias Otto—his bellow
> Winding into murderous music. Which play
> Were we in? Too late to find you
> And get to my ship.[22]

Here Hughes is metamorphosed into Theseus, Otto into both Minos *and* his monstrous bull-man-monster—who is also Plath, and who here, no longer Ariadne, offers Hughes's Theseus no help through the tortuous maze that has come to symbolize their failing marriage.

As in his *Tales from Ovid* then, we can see in Hughes's *Birthday Letters* a rich and creative engagement with the classical tradition. But *Birthday Letters* can be seen as a work that makes use not only of 'tales from Ovid' and from the canon of classical mythology, but one that also employs 'tropes' from Ovid and from the canon of Roman love elegy. For as he transforms 'personal tragedy into metaphor and mythology', metamorphosing the tragedy of Orpheus and Eurydice, Theseus and Ariadne, into that of Sylvia and Ted, Hughes turns to elegy.[23]

Thomas Hardy's *Poems of 1912–13*, written after the death of his estranged wife Emma Gifford in 1912, and Douglas Dunn's *Elegies*, similarly written and published after his wife's death, offer us a modern elegiac tradition in which to locate Hughes's *Birthday*

---

[22] *CP* 1129.          [23] Wagner (2000: 2).

*Letters.*[24] Yet, as Erica Wagner suggests, Hughes's poems in this collection can be seen as 'one link in a chain of elegy and lament that stretches back to the very beginnings of poetry'.[25] From Antimachus of Colophon's *Lyde*—literary history's earliest extant collection of elegiac love poetry, inspired by and addressed to the Greek poet's dead mistress—through the *corpus* of Roman love elegy and the poetry of Propertius, Tibullus, and Ovid, classical elegy had proved a powerful vehicle for poetic expressions of love and loss, autobiography, and confession. And it is with each of these aspects of classical elegy that Hughes can be seen to engage in his elegiac *Birthday Letters.*

The elegiac tradition traces its roots back to ancient Greece where, among its earliest forms, it was used for funerary inscription—hence its traditional etymology of ἒ λέγειν (*e legein*) 'to cry woe', or 'to lament'. Elegy was an obvious choice of metre then for the first known elegiac poet Antimachus in his poetic memorial to his dead mistress Lyde. But this early example of love elegy, an assorted collection of narratives from Greek myth chosen to parallel the 'love story' of Antimachus and Lyde, was very different in character and style to the love elegy that would later emerge in Rome. This Roman form of elegy, while similarly dedicated to a beloved mistress and set upon a stage peopled by mythological exempla, established a new elegiac tradition in which a first-person poet-lover offered an 'autobiographical' narrative, confessing his slave-like devotion (*servitium amoris*) to a single girl—typically a hard-hearted, ultimately unattainable, and unfaithful mistress (*dura puella*)—who inspired his poetry, who gained fame and immortality through that poetry,

---

[24] On the parallels between Hughes, Hardy, and Dunn, see Wagner (2000: 22–7). Parallels might also be drawn between *Birthday Letters* and Hughes's contemporary poet Robert Lowell who, in his quasi-autobiographical *Life Studies* (1959) used the lyric love poetry of Catullus as a foil for reflections upon his own difficult relationship with his wife. Lowell also translated Propertius' Elegy 4.7 in which the poet addresses the ghost of his dead mistress returning from the grave to criticize him for his neglect. For a view that sees Lowell's classicism as a contrast rather than a parallel to Hughes's, see Talbot (2006: 140).

[25] Wagner (2000: 22). While Ovid directly connects himself to Antimachus and the origins of elegy in the opening lines of *Tristia* 1.6.1–4 ('Not so great was the love of the Clarian poet for Lyde . . . as is the love that clings in my heart for you, my wife'), Hughes does not explicitly acknowledge his ties to this chain.

and with whom he might hope to be united (if not in life) after death.[26]

Indeed, despite its transformation in the hands of the Roman love elegists, the traditional association of elegy and death continued to dominate the genre in its new form. Typically, the elegiac poet fears that his beloved will be taken from him by death—so, he fears that any illness she may suffer will prove fatal, or that any journey she takes will end in shipwreck and disaster. He also imagines that after his own death his beloved will come to realize the depth of her true feelings for him, that she will weep at his funeral and over his grave. But he also fears that she will be unfaithful to his memory, that she will neglect his ashes, and move quickly on to another lover. He claims too that his own devotion will stay true after the death of his beloved, and even looks forward to their reunion in the afterlife, where—it is imagined—the husbands, rivals, and guardians, together with the social and legal constraints that have kept the lovers apart in life will no longer force their separation, and where they can be together in eternity.[27]

We can clearly see the potential attraction in this elegiac topos for Hughes and his *Birthday Letters*, and close reading of these poems reveals numerous elegiac figures and tropes in and across the collection. Among them, we can see Hughes represented as an *exclusus amator*, the lover shut out of his beloved's inner life throughout the course of their relationship, and finally locked out by her suicide. In one of the collection's early poems, the 'Visit', Hughes is cast unambiguously in the elegiac role of *exclusus amator* as he writes—in the style of an elegiac *paraclausithyron*—how:

> With my friend,
> After midnight, I stood in a garden
> Lobbing soil-clods up at a dark window.
>
> Drunk, he was certain it was yours.
> Half as drunk, I did not know he was wrong.[28]

---

[26] On the character of Latin love elegy, see Luck (1968), Lyne (1980), Veyne (1988), and Kennedy (1993).

[27] For this elegiac theme see Tibullus 1.1, 1.3, 1.5, 2.4; Propertius 1.19, 2.15, 4.7, 4.11; and Ovid *Amores* 2.5, 2.13–14.

[28] *CP* 1047–9.

The same trope appears again in '18 Rugby Street' where a 'High-explosive, black, insane Alsatian | That challenged through the chained crack of the door | Every entrance and exit' guards the girl in the ground-floor flat (an archetype for Plath) from all potential seducers, including Hughes, but 'Not, seven years in the future, from her gas-oven'.[29]

In turn, we can see Plath herself figured in the *Birthday Letters* as an elegiac *dura puella*, beautiful, seductive, violent, jealous, unpredictable, elusive, and—in the sense that she is seen to leave Hughes to be with another man, her dead 'Daddy'—ultimately unfaithful. In 'St Botolph's', the 'swelling ring-moat of tooth-marks' that she leaves on Hughes's cheek at their first meeting (branding his face for a month, his soul 'for good') marks Plath herself as a stereotypical elegiac mistress—the eroticized violence that accompanies this first physical encounter between the two soon-to-be lovers, yet another elegiac commonplace.[30] What is more, like the Roman love elegists who write of Venus and Cupid interfering with their love-lives and their literary lives, in this poem Hughes too sees 'Opposed Venus' overseeing a life-changing event for himself and Plath.[31]

With Plath as his new girlfriend, Hughes figures himself in the early stages of their relationship as her faithful dog—subserving his *domina* like the elegists in their (pose of) eroticized slavery or *servitium amoris*—following her around on their honeymoon 'happy to protect you | From your agitation and your stone hours, | Like a guide dog, loyal . . . ' (in 'Your Paris'), or like ' . . . a strange dog, | The silent shadow of a dog | That had befriended you' ('Moonwalk').[32] After his marriage, we can see Hughes as an elegiac poet-lover, like Tibullus, attempting to live, to love, and to write poetry in a rural idyll, cultivating his garden, living a simple country life with his beloved—who is less persuaded by the charms of the

---

[29] *CP* 1055–8. For classical examples of the drunken *exclusus amator* trying to get in to his girlfriend's house, see in particular Tibullus 1.2, Propertius 1.16, and Ovid *Amores* 1.6. And for the guard dog set to protect the girl from would-be lovers, see Tibullus 2.4 and Propertius 4.5.

[30] *CP* 1051–2. On the eroticized violence of elegy see in particular Ovid *Amores* 1.5, 1.7; Propertius 2.5, 2.15; and Tibullus 1.6, 1.10. See also Fredrick (1997) and Cahoon (1988).

[31] See in particular Ovid *Amores* 1.1, 1.2, and 3.1.

[32] *CP* 1069–70.

countryside.[33] We might even see Plath's father Otto as Hughes's elegiac rival, the elegiac *vir* whose claim upon Plath is stronger than her lover's. And in the 'witch's daughter', the 'Lilith of abortions . . . With tiger-painted nails . . . soot-wet mascara, | in flame-orange silks, in gold bracelets' who seduces Hughes and mesmerizes Plath in 'Dreamers', we might see the archetypal elegiac witch—the manipulative *lena*, fond of expensive clothes and cosmetics, who asserts her baleful influence over both elegiac lovers.[34]

Less obviously perhaps than in some of these explicitly elegiac characters and commonplaces, Hughes can also be seen to evoke the elegiac trope of *militia amoris*, or love as warfare in *Birthday Letters*. In his 1977 'Unknown Warrior', a poem uncollected before Keegan, Hughes offered a deliberate and self-consciously Ovidian reworking of the elegiac conceit that '*militat omnis amans*'—'every lover is a soldier'—playing in particular upon Ovid's own ludic elaboration of this topos in *Amores* 1.9.[35] Composed in quasi-elegiac couplets, 'Unknown Warrior' opens with a further allusion to the first line of Propertius' *Monobiblos*—'At curious eyes | He was conscripted'— suggesting a familiarity not only with Ovid's use of the *militia amoris* conceit, but with its role in Roman love elegy more broadly.[36] In *Birthday Letters*, the *militia amoris* trope appears in 'The Shot', in which Hughes evokes the devastating impact of his first meeting with Plath.[37] Like Propertius in the opening poem of his elegiac *Monobiblos* 'captured' by Cynthia, or Ovid in the opening poem of his *Amores* pierced by Cupid's arrow, Hughes employs hunting and quasi-militaristic imagery to describe Plath herself as a bullet: 'gold-jacketed, solid silver. | Nickel-tipped. Trajectory perfect'. The

---

[33] See Tibullus 1.1, 1.2, 1.5, and 1.10 for the poet's dream of living with Delia in a rural idyll, and 2.1 and 2.3 where he projects the same countryside fantasy onto his relationship with Delia's 'replacement', Nemesis. For Hughes's parallel evocation of an elegiac rural idyll see 'Error' (*CP* 1121–3), 'The Lodger' (*CP* 1123–5), 'Daffodils' (*CP* 1125–6), and 'The Rabbit Catcher' (*CP* 1136–8).

[34] *CP* 1145–6. In 'Dreamers', the witch character is identified as Assia Wevill, Hughes's lover. For the *lena* in Roman elegy see in particular Propertius 4.5 and Ovid's *Amores* 1.8.

[35] *CP* 380. See Talbot (2006: 148).

[36] Propertius famously opens his work with the line: *Cynthia prima suis miserum me cepit ocellis*, 'Cynthia first captured my sorry self with her eyes'.

[37] *CP* 1052–3.

same elegiac topos appears again in 'A Pink Wool Knitted Dress', where the image of Hughes in his funereal black cord jacket and RAF black tie as 'a post-war, utility son-in-law' ('No ceremony could conscript me | Out of my uniform') makes a soldier out of this lover even at his own wedding.[38]

For Hughes—as for the Roman elegists before him—it is his relationship with Plath that provides the narrative framework within and around which he arranges his *Birthday Letters*. The work begins (like Ovid's *Amores*) before the poet has actually met or fallen in love with his *puella*—when she is no more to him than (possibly) one of the 'Fulbright Scholars' pictured in a public display of photographs.[39] The poet then records their first meeting, their first fight, their first sexual encounter, their mutual infatuation, mutual feelings and displays of jealousy and desire, his infidelity, the breakdown and eventual break-up of their relationship. The collection effectively draws to a close with Plath's suicide—but Hughes includes several poems staged after her death. 'Freedom of Speech' sees Plath at her sixtieth birthday, at a 'reunion' attended by authors, scholars and literary critics, while 'The Dogs Are Eating Your Mother' imagines Plath's remains—her literary *corpus*—defiled by those who misread and misrepresent her, those who 'Bite the face off her gravestone', 'Jerk their tail-stumps, bristle and vomit | Over their symposia'.[40]

These poems evoking Plath's ghost similarly evoke the grotesque apparitions of the beloved dead *puella* in Roman elegy. 'The Dogs Are Eating Your Mother' (one of the few poems in the collection not addressed directly to Plath), is evocative in particular of Propertius' image of Cynthia returning from the dead, her dress charred by the funeral pyre, to complain that she has been misrepresented in his poetry (4.7). Indeed, the ghostly Cynthia's complaint of misrepresentation, her charge against Propertius that he has been unfaithful to her and her memory, her attempt to set the record straight about the nature of their relationship, and the promise (or threat) that the two of them will soon be together again (4.7.94f *mox sola tenebo:* | *mecum eris, et mixtis ossibus ossa teram*, 'Soon I alone will hold you: You will be with me, and I will grind bones mixed with bones')— elegiac lovers reunited in death, their bones 'entwined' together ('one

---

[38] *CP* 1064–5.    [39] *CP* 1045.    [40] *CP* 1168–9.

pile of inseparable ashes'?)—can be heard echoed and answered in
the *Birthday Letters*.

Hughes declared in his letter to the judges of the Forward Poetry
Prize that, 'Except for a handful, I never thought of publishing these
pieces . . .'.[41] He emphasized rather the 'private, inner' dialogue with
his dead wife that he hoped to open up through these poems. And yet
readers of *Birthday Letters* have consistently noticed the extent to
which many of the 'letters' in the collection seem to 'function as
replies'—answering, justifying, illustrating, responding, rather than
corresponding.[42] Indeed, the collection as a whole seems to effect at
the same time both a confessional and a corrective tone. Thus, it is
worth noting that, in Hughes's account of his first meeting with Plath
in the poem 'St Botolph's', the headscarf he takes as a trophy from her
hair is blue. In Plath's description of the same incident in her journal,
the headscarf is red.[43] But Plath's 'autobiographical confessions' are
apparently no more reliable than Hughes's. As Hughes himself wrote
of Plath's poetry in 1966:

> Her poetry has been called 'confessional and personal', and connected with
> the school of Robert Lowell and Anne Sexton . . . Their work is truly auto-
> biographical and personal, and their final world is a torture cell walled with
> family portraits, with the daily newspaper coming under the door. The
> autobiographical details in Sylvia Plath's poetry work differently. She sets
> them out like masks, which are then lifted up by dramatis personae of nearly
> supernatural qualities. The world of her poetry is one of emblematic vision-
> ary events, mathematical symmetries, clairvoyance, metamorphoses . . . [44]

But so too is the world of Hughes's poetry. And we are rightly
hesitant in accepting his personal confessions about the details of
his relationship with Plath at face value. In her introduction to *Ariel's
Gift*, Erica Wagner adds *Birthday Letters* to a long literary history of
poetry as confession, stretching back through Byron's *Childe Harold*,
Wordsworth's *Prelude*, to Augustine's *Confessions*.[45] But 'the history

---

[41]  Quoted in Churchwell (2001: 138–9).

[42]  Cf. Whitehead (1999: 227).

[43]  For a detailed survey of such discrepancies between Hughes's and Plath's
'personal disclosures' see Feinstein (2001) and Middlebrook (2003). On the insincer-
ity of the Roman elegists see Veyne (1988).

[44]  Faas (1980: 180).

[45]  Wagner (2000: 1).

of personal disclosure' stretches back much farther than Augustine. Confession—or rather, 'confession'—is a signature feature of classical elegy, yet in this context the sincerity and authenticity of such disclosure is constantly brought into question. Nothing that an elegist confesses can be taken at face value—including Propertius' paradoxical confession that elegy itself is a *fallax opus* (a deceitful genre).[46] Read in this light, the reliability and accuracy of Hughes's personal disclosure in *Birthday Letters* is open to challenge and suspicion, his elegiac 'autobiography' revealed as a self-consciously unreliable text.

A significant parallel to this aspect of Hughes's *Birthday Letters* appears in Ovid's quasi-autobiographical elegies from exile—including his own 'birthday letters'[47]—in which he writes elegiac epistles to his wife, now separated from him by the 'living death' that he sees as his exile.[48] Thus, in the *Tristia*, he represents his departure from Rome and into exile as a funeral (1.3.21–4), describing himself as a ghost, and imagining that his body has already been cremated and buried (3.11.25f.). He even casts himself in the role of an elegiac *exclusus amator*, now a love poet locked out and knocking futilely on death's door (3.2.21–4).[49] Transforming his personal tragedy into myth in both the *Tristia* and *Epistulae ex Ponto*, Ovid identifies himself as an Orpheus figure who writes elegy because he has lost his beloved wife (*Tristia* 4.17f.), and through which he seeks to evoke her image and presence.[50] Indeed, the poetic form of the elegiac epistle provides Ovid with an ideal vehicle through which to open up a 'private' dialogue with his wife, to speak (with a sincerity that is radically different from the playful tone of his *Amores*) of his love for

---

[46] As elegy is described by Propertius 4.1.135.

[47] That is, the poems written to mark Ovid's own birthday in exile (*Tristia* 3.13) and that of his wife (*Tristia* 5.5).

[48] *Tristia* 1.6, 3.3, 3.13, 4.3, 5.5, 5.11, and *Ex Ponto* 3.1.

[49] On Ovid's self-representation as one of 'the living dead', see Dufallo (2007).

[50] Ovid's self-identification with Ulysses is the most prominent (*Tristia* 1.5.57, 1.6.22, 3.11.61, 5.5.51f., 5.14.35f., and *Ex Ponto* 1.3.33, 3.1.53, 107, 3.6.19, and 4.14.35). But he is Orpheus at *Tristia* 4.1.17 and *Ex Ponto* 3.3.41; Phaethon at *Tristia* 1.1.79 and 3.4.30; Icarus at *Tristia* 1.1.90 (and Daedalus) at 3.4.21–4; Actaeon at *Tristia* 2.105; Admetus at 5.5.55f., 5.14.37 and *Ex Ponto* 3.1.106). He particularly identifies with Jason, whose own (mis)adventures once brought him to Tomis (*Ex Ponto* 1.3.75, 1.4.23–46, and 3.1.1). He also observes in one letter to a friend that 'anyone who likes can be a Theseus' (*Ex Ponto* 4.10.78).

her, of his regret for having been the cause of her unhappiness, of his pain and grief at their separation. In these letters to his wife Ovid can be seen 'to open a direct, private, inner contact with [her] ... to evoke her presence ..., and to feel her there listening'. But at the same time, the elegiac letter provides Ovid with an ideal vehicle through which to correspond publicly with his critics (Augustus among them), to bid them mind the gap between reality and representation in his poetry, and to argue that his life and work (especially the *Ars Amatoria*) have been misread and misrepresented.

To this end Ovid provides his readers with a wealth of 'autobiographical' detail as supporting 'evidence' in his poetic defence against the charges of immorality and obscenity that had led to his banishment from Rome. In particular, he stresses that readers have confused his books with his life, claiming that they have failed to appreciate the difference between his 'autobibliography'—his life as narrated in his elegiac poetry—and his real life ( *Tristia* 2.353–7):

> Believe me, my character is different from my verse;
>     My life is virtuous, my muse is playful.
> The greater part of my work is fiction and made up,
>     And allows itself more freedom than its own author.
> A book is not proof of character, but honest pleasure.

Moreover, in both the *Tristia* and *Epistulae ex Ponto*, Ovid uses familiar themes and tropes from erotic elegy to correspond with not only his wife but also his critics and detractors. So, in *Ex Ponto* 2.2 Ovid again evokes the language of the elegiac locked-out lover to represent himself as an *exclusus amator* barred not from his mistress's bedroom but from Augustus's Rome. In another letter, the poet begs his friend Messalinus to plead his case to Augustus's hard-hearted successor, Tiberius—just as an elegiac lover might beg a doorkeeper or slave to plead his case to a hard-hearted mistress (2.2.39f.). Thus, public and private discourse, mythology and personal history, seem to merge in the 'white noise' of Ovid's exilic elegy.[51]

In 'Dog Days on the Black Sea', a poem written between 1967 and 1970 but uncollected before Keegan, Hughes evoked Ovid's exilic poetry and persona to express the frustrations of literary life,

---

[51]  See Miller (2004: 210–36).

identifying himself unequivocally with the exiled poet.[52] While Hughes's sultry evocation of an exile where 'The world hangs like a bead of perspiration | In the writer's eyebrow' sits in contrast to Ovid's own exaggerated portrait of the frozen world of Tomis, this self-identification with the exiled love poet is significant. For, in the same way that 'Dog Days on the Black Sea' can be seen to transform and translate Ovid's experience of exile into a new poetic shape, Hughes's *Birthday Letters* can be seen similarly to metamorphose Ovid's elegiac letters from exile.

For, just as Ovid's letters from Pontus interweave public and private discourse, Hughes's 'private' dialogue with his first wife in *Birthday Letters* is also characterized by its 'public' character. Ian Sansom, in an early review of *Birthday Letters*, claimed that Hughes had strategically used the collection as an opportunity to defend publicly and finally the reputation of his relationship with Plath, to revise the story of their private life together. Sansom asserted that: 'The book has a clear and practical purpose—correcting distortions, setting the record straight, putting right the gossips and the speculators, the detractors and the critics'.[53] This is a view shared by many critics—of both Hughes and the *Birthday Letters*—who draw our attention to poems such as the 'Visit' in which Hughes writes, a decade after his wife's suicide: 'You are ten years dead. It is only a story. | Your story. My story.'[54] The grammatical isolation of 'your story' from 'my story' in the final line of this poem seems to give Hughes the last word, making his version of the history of their

---

[52] *CP* 197–8. Talbot (2006: 148), suggests that 'because this instance of self-identification with Ovid lay uncollected until Keegan, it has until now not been taken account of.'

[53] Sansom (1998: 8). see also McClatchy (1998: 159): 'It seems that now in *Birthday Letters* ... [Hughes] wants the last word—a word to his critics as well, a word to the unwise'.

[54] *CP* 1047–9. This poem also introduces one of the key tropes of the *Birthday Letters*—the identification of both Hughes and Plath as 'players', 'puppets', and 'actors' performing their relationship upon a public stage—see Hardwick in this volume. Here, Hughes writes of 'being auditioned | For the male lead in your drama, | Miming through the first easy movements | As if with eyes closed, feeling for the role. | As if a puppet were being tried on its strings ...'. Again in '18 Rugby Street', he locates their first sexual encounter upon a 'stage-set', exposed to an 'auditorium'. Their love-making consists of a series of 'acts and scenes', 'perpetual performance— names of the actors altered, | But never the parts.'

relationship final. Yet, as Sarah Churchwell points out, the line also brings the two stories, the two poets, and the two former lovers together. In fact:

> The last lines of 'Visit' . . . try to have it both ways: it is both his story and her story; they are implicitly the same and yet separated by a 'full-stop'. The poems in *Birthday Letters* consistently entangle Hughes'[s] words and Plath's, as if to bring the stories back together again, to erase the 'full-stop' between them.[55]

If, indeed, Hughes sought in his elegiac *Birthday Letters* to 'open a direct, private, inner contact with [his] first wife', then that intimacy seems compromised by the public audience that his poetry evokes, the viewers and voyeurs who have apparently 'intercepted' this private correspondence. And, if *Birthday Letters* represents instead an attempt to defend Hughes, to revise the received story of his relationship with Plath, and to 'set the record straight', then that aim appears compromised too. There is little to suggest that Hughes, Plath, or any of the other characters in this story are transformed in their new elegiac roles—or that 'his' story rewrites 'hers'. For *Birthday Letters* tells us very little about this relationship that we did not already know—particularly from Plath's own writing (including her own posthumously published *Letters Home*). The (private) role that Hughes plays in *Birthday Letters* is essentially the same (public) role that he played in Plath's poetry, journals, and letters.

Yet, if we look again at *Birthday Letters* through the lens of classical elegy, we can see that Hughes effectively achieves both of these ends. The *fallax opus* of elegy allows Hughes the opportunity to correspond with his wife and his detractors in the same poems. It allows him to open up a 'private' dialogue with his first wife, to speak (sincerely) to her of love, of regret, of pain, and grief—and at the same time publicly to address his critics, to bid them mind the gap between reality and representation, to remember that whether told by Sylvia or Ted, the story of their life together 'is only a story'—to merge public and private discourse, mythology and personal history, in the white noise of elegy.

---

[55] Churchwell (2001: 123).

# 13

## Ted Hughes: Allusion and Poetic Language

### Michael Silk

Ted Hughes's late collection, *Birthday Letters*, contains, among many notable poems, one called 'The Rabbit Catcher'. This looks back to a poem of the same title by Hughes's first wife, Sylvia Plath, written in the remarkable period of creative activity near the end of her life, in May 1962. Plath's poem:[1]

> It was a place of force—
> The wind gagging my mouth with my own blown hair,
> Tearing off my voice, and the sea
> Blinding me with its lights, the lives of the dead
> Unreeling in it, spreading like oil.
>
> I tasted the malignity of the gorse,                                    5
> Its black spikes,
> The extreme unction of its yellow candle-flowers.
> They had an efficiency, a great beauty,
> And were extravagant, like torture.
>
> There was only one place to get to.                                    10
> Simmering, perfumed,
> The paths narrowed into the hollow.
> And the snares almost effaced themselves—
> Zeros, shutting on nothing,
>
> Set close, like birth pangs.                                           15
> The absence of shrieks

[1] *SPCP* 193–4.

Made a hole in the hot day, a vacancy.
The glassy light was a clear wall,
The thickets quiet.                                        20

I felt a still busyness, an intent.
I felt hands round a tea mug, dull, blunt,
Ringing the white china.
How they awaited him, those little deaths!
They waited like sweethearts. They excited him.          25

And we, too, had a relationship—
Tight wires between us,
Pegs too deep to uproot, and a mind like a ring
Sliding shut on some quick thing,
The constriction killing me also.                        30

And Hughes's:[2]

It was May. How had it started? What
Had bared our edges? What quirky twist
Of the moon's blade had set us, so early in the day,
Bleeding each other? What had I done? I had
Somehow misunderstood. Inaccessible                      5
In your dybbuk fury, babies
Hurled into the car, you drove. We surely
Had been intending a day's outing,
Somewhere on the coast, an exploration—
So you started driving.
                    What I remember                       10
Is thinking: She'll do something crazy. And I ripped
The door open and jumped in beside you.
So we drove West. West. Cornish lanes
I remember, a simmering truce                             15
As you stared, with iron in your face,
Into some remote thunderscape
Of some unworldly war. I simply
Trod accompaniment, carried babies,
Waited for you to come back to nature.                    20
We tried to find the coast. You
Raged against our English private greed
Of fencing off all coastal approaches,
Hiding the sea from roads, from all inland.

---

[2] *CP* 1136–8.

You despised England's grubby edges when you got there.
That day belonged to the furies. I searched the map     25
To penetrate the farms and private kingdoms.
Finally a gateway. It was a fresh day,
Full May. Somewhere I'd bought food.
We crossed a field and came to the open
Blue push of sea-wind. A gorse cliff,     30
Brambly, oak-packed combes. We found
An eyrie hollow, just under the cliff-top.
It seemed perfect to me. Feeding babies,
Your Germanic scowl, edged like a helmet,
Would not translate itself. I sat baffled.     35
I was a fly outside on the window-pane
Of my own domestic drama. You refused to lie there
Being indolent, you hated it.
That flat, draughty plate was not an ocean.
You had to be away and you went. And I     40
Trailed after like a dog, along the cliff-top field-edge,
Over a wind-matted oak-wood—
And I found a snare.
Copper-wire gleam, brown cord, human contrivance,
Sitting new-set. Without a word     45
You tore it up and threw it into the trees.

I was aghast. Faithful
To my country gods—I saw
The sanctity of a trapline desecrated.     50
You saw blunt fingers, blood in the cuticles,
Clamped round a blue mug. I saw
Country poverty raising a penny,
Filling a Sunday stewpot. You saw baby-eyed
Strangled innocents, I saw sacred     55
Ancient custom. You saw snare after snare
And went ahead, riving them from their roots
And flinging them down the wood. I saw you
Ripping up precarious, precious saplings
Of my heritage, hard-won concessions     60
From the hangings and the transportations
To live off the land. You cried: 'Murderers!'
You were weeping with a rage
That cared nothing for rabbits. You were locked
Into some chamber gasping for oxygen     65

Where I could not find you, or really hear you,
Let alone understand you.
                              In those snares
You'd caught something.
Had you caught something in me,
Nocturnal and unknown to me? Or was it                              70
Your doomed self, your tortured, crying,
Suffocating self? Whichever,
Those terrible, hypersensitive
Fingers of your verse closed round it and
Felt it alive. The poems, like smoking entrails,                    75
Came soft into your hands.

The two narratives have a common reference, but a quite different basis. Plath's 'Rabbit Catcher' presupposes a personal story, which is gestured towards, as much as presented; but otherwise it seems self-sufficient. Like Sappho's *phainetai moi* or Hardy's 'After a Journey', her poem is focused on a notional personal event, almost to the total exclusion of any other point of reference.[3] The poem is technically brilliant. One notes the astonishing series of similes (mostly at the ends of stanzas): the 'lives of the dead . . . spreading like oil' (4–5); 'extravagant, like torture' (10); the snares, 'Set close, like birth pangs' (16); those 'little deaths' that 'waited like sweethearts' (25); and 'the mind like a ring' (28). One notes the dazzling theatricality of some of the phrasing—the 'malignity of the gorse', the 'extreme unction of its yellow candle-flowers' (8), the 'glassy light' as a 'clear wall' (19)—and the way that in those phrases sensuousness is not reflective of any feeling of independent nature, but only of its asserted subjective meaning. And one notes also the disconcerting sense of one passing evocation, which does, perhaps, constitute a momentary second point of reference, the sub-Shakespearean 'vacancy'(18):

---

[3]  On the Lawrentian 'reference' in Plath's poem, see n.5 below; its several hostilities very obviously include hostility to Lawrentian blood-consciousness (see, succinctly, Middlebrook in Gill (2006: 166–8)); nevertheless, this informing, positive and negative, leaves the sense of single focus unaffected. In an acute essay, Seamus Heaney distinguishes those of Plath's late poems that triumph as 'events rather than the records of events' from those limited by being 'entangled in biographical circumstances' (Heaney (1988: 151, 165)). One may well find it hard to decide precisely where her 'Rabbit Catcher' belongs on this spectrum.

> The absence of shrieks
> Made a hole in the hot day, a vacancy.

Compare, from *Antony and Cleopatra* (II, ii, 220–5), Enobarbus' account of Cleopatra on her barge, on another hot day:[4]

> The city cast
> Her people out upon her; and Antony,
> Enthroned i'th' market-place, did sit alone,
> Whistling to th' air; which, *but for vacancy,*
> Had gone to gaze on Cleopatra too,
> And *made a gap in* nature.

The irony in this passing evocation of the great tragic lovers—doomed to die, separately, by their own hands: him in effective ignorance, herself in full knowledge—serves to make Plath's dying fall ('killing me also', 30) apt beyond due measure.[5]

Once we know Plath's poem, Hughes's reads irresistibly like a commentary on it, if only because of the shared title—though, on the face of it, his 'Rabbit Catcher' is, rather, an independent version of the assumed event behind her 'Rabbit Catcher', complete with the assumed motivational consequences of that event, in the shape of (as his closing reference indicates) unspecified, but plural, 'poems' (75).

I wish to draw attention to three features of Hughes's poem in relation to, and by comparison with, Plath's. First, there is, precisely, the discreet way that his poem alludes to hers, without at first, indeed, evoking its detail. With its shared title, his goes out of its

---

[4] Cleopatra's slaves were fanning her: II, ii, 206–8.

[5] As various commentators have noted, the subject matter of Plath's 'Rabbit Catcher' recalls D. H. Lawrence's poem, 'Rabbit Snared in the Night'. More pertinently, its imagery of 'Tight wires . . . | . . . and a mind like a ring' (27–8) has a direct source in another Lawrence poem, 'Love on the Farm', where the husband brings a dead rabbit home to his wife, as preface to an act of love: 'With his hand he turns my face to him | And caresses me with his fingers that still smell grim | Of the rabbit's fur! God, I am caught in a snare! | I know not what fine wire is round my throat; | I only know I let him finger there | My pulse of life'. A source and a decisive private connection (Plath, in an earlier phase, had been preoccupied with Lawrence, including, no doubt, *this* Lawrence: Middlebrook in Gill (2006: 166–7) and Middlebrook (2003: 169)—but not an allusion the way the Shakespeare is. This, not only because the Lawrentian source, by comparison, is esoteric, but because for Plath the Lawrentian Other is, in effect, identified with Hughes/'him' and is not a point of 'external' reference at all. See, further, n.56 below.

way to summon up hers as a kind of parallel presence, but without doing with Plath what Plath herself does with Shakespeare—calling up a particular poetic passage, along with its context and its other relevant associations.

In the second place, there is an utter contrast of tone between the two poems, which centres on Plath's almost overpowering sense of certainty. She is the classic omniscient narrator: she sees what matters and knows what she sees. She knows precisely what she felt, and the narrative follows the contours of her feelings: 'I felt a still busyness' (21), 'I felt hands' (22). (She knows what *he* felt, too: 'They excited him', 25.) Nature, as we observe, is shaped by her feelings (the 'malignity' of the gorse, the glassy light as a 'wall': 8, 19), and on closer inspection the whole natural (or anti-natural) setting is seen to be determined by her unqualified reading of it: it was 'a place of force' (1), and there was 'only one place to get to' (11). And then that awesomely depersonalized 'him', 'him', is (so to speak) personified by an unnervingly specific simile: 'How they awaited him, those little deaths. | They waited like sweethearts' (24). That 'him' is the passive object of her narrative and its meaning—and not only because 'we, too, *had* a relationship' (26), which is now, simply, past tense and over. From first to last, her reading is the only reading. 'It was a place of force' (1), 'killing me also' (30): her understanding is closed to any alternative, and the poem itself closes shut on this understanding, as tight as the ring that, for her, is 'sliding shut' (29).

By contrast, Hughes, thirty-plus years later, is acutely and pervasively aware—but only of his own bafflement, his uncertainty, his *not* understanding: such, undeniably, is the presentation.[6] His is a tale of trying to catch up and never succeeding, not then and not now; of half-recalled unspecifics, of helpless confusion, of rhetorical questions that no one is there to answer (here, in a different sense, things have slid shut, for him): 'How had it started?' (1); 'What had I done?' (4); 'I had | Somehow misunderstood' (4–5); 'We surely ... | Somewhere ...' (7–9); 'What I remember | Is ...' (10–11); 'Somewhere I'd

---

[6] For convenience, I date Hughes's poem to, or soon before, its publication date, irrespective of the possibility that it, like at least some of the poems in *BL*, it was composed, or substantially composed, earlier. The earliest datable instance from *BL* is 'You Hated Spain' (*CP* 1068), which was first published in 1979 (see the editorial note in *CP* 1301).

bought food' (28). Things may have 'seemed' to be working (33), but of course they weren't. 'I sat baffled' (35); 'I | Trailed after like a dog' (40–1): the actor in the tale is doing his best, like a family pet, uncomprehending.

When things do start clearing, within Hughes's narrative, it is only into hypnotic frustration—'I saw' (49), 'You saw' (51), 'I saw' (52), 'You saw' (54)—and all the disquieting certainties of (indeed) a see-saw leave his deeper ignorance unaffected. In that narrated past, as still in the narrator's present, bafflement is, and remains, determinative:

> You were locked
> Into some chamber...
> Where I could not find you, or really hear you,
> Let alone understand you.
> In those snares
> You'd caught something.
> Had you caught something in me,
> ...unknown to me? Or was it
> Your...
> ...                    Whichever,
> Those terrible, hypersensitive
> Fingers of your verse closed round it and
> Felt it alive...
>
> (64–75)

'Felt it alive': compare Plath's 'killing me also'. With that echo (of rhythm, as well as sense) we do eventually, at the end of Hughes's poem, have a kind of hurtful convergence with hers: something *is* 'alive' (or not).[7] And meanwhile, and finally (73–6):

---

[7] There is also an (undiscussed?) allusion in the poem to Plath's Lawrentian source (see nn.5 above and 56 below) and, more simply and directly, the lightest of allusions to Plath's poem in Hughes's opening words: both poems begin, 'It was'. For the record, though, this is a characteristically Hughesian opening in *BL* (cf. 'Sam', 'Fidelity', 'A Short Film': *CP* 1049, 1060, 1129), whereas the only other 'It was' Plath poem in her whole *Collected Poems* (including juvenilia) is 'Night Shift' (*SPCP* 76). By contrast, dactylic cadences, including dactylic hexameter cadences (like 'killing me also'), turn up in both: e.g. Hughes's 'Dream Life', from *BL*, ends 'Preparing his Feast of Atonement' (*CP* 1136), and Plath's 'The Moon and the Yew Tree' ends 'blackness and silence' (*SPCP* 173).

> Those terrible, hypersensitive
> Fingers of your verse closed round it and
> Felt it alive. The poems, like smoking entrails,
> Came soft into your hands.

'Hypersensitive fingers' and 'soft into your hands'. How unlike the 'hands' *she* 'felt', in her poem, then (22–3):

> I felt hands round a tea mug, dull, blunt,
> Ringing the white china.

That detail in her version, however, Hughes has, uniquely, evoked earlier on: 'You saw blunt fingers . . . | Clamped round a blue mug' (51–2). The evocation comes with a curious change of colour (*blue* mug in his version, *white* in hers), as if by way of briefly protesting the independent authority of his memory. In the event, the correction, once noted, adds an odd sense of awkwardness, which (when we get to the 'Fingers of your verse') seems to play into that disquieting convergence at the end.

The third contrast consists of a stark difference in language, including the rhythms and the aural shapes that the words of the two poems work by. Plath's language is taut and all-encompassing (there is the tea-mug, as well as a Cleopatra), but by contemporary standards predominantly 'poetic'. All this is epitomized by the tight rhyme and the diction near the end—'a mind like a ring | Sliding shut on some quick thing'—and by the heightening pun on 'quick' (in ordinary idiom *swift*, in traditional idiom *alive*), with the final, more prosaic, phrase, 'The constriction killing me also', left to gasp for momentary life outside the stability of the couplet. By comparison, Hughes's verses have a few, but only a few, striking flashes of heightened language—'the moon's blade . . . | Bleeding each other' (3–4), 'the open | Blue push of sea-wind' (29–30), 'Your Germanic scowl, edged like a helmet' (34), 'The poems, like smoking entrails' (75)—albeit the particular, almost Plath-like, abrasiveness of that simile at the end means that there is, after all, something of a procedural convergence between the two poems too.

Despite these heightenings, Hughes's poem seems to exist primarily in a conversational realm, where the idiom is speech idiom and the voice, at times, bare and uncoloured, if scrupulously toned—'It was May' (1), 'Without a word | You tore it up' (45–6), 'I could not find you, or really hear you, | Let alone understand you' (66–7), 'Whichever' (72)—so that the closing lines, less conversational, feel like an upward charge, of emotion but especially of stylistic level, from the conversational low.

The allusive relationship between Hughes's poem and Plath's, and between Hughes's poem and Plath's person and persona, is characteristic of *Birthday Letters* and well understood. No less characteristic, but seemingly not understood, is the allusive relationship of the whole collection with a wider network that connects Hughes's poems in *Birthday Letters* (including this one) and Plath's poems (including this one) with Hughes's contemporary recreation of Aeschylus' *Oresteia*.[8] 'Contemporary' here I mean in two senses: Hughes's *Oresteia* is a work produced in the same period as *Birthday Letters* (*Birthday Letters* was published in 1998, the *Oresteia* in 1999), while, like Hughes's translations in general, his *Oresteia* (to borrow a set of distinctions from Dryden) is not a work in the range of metaphrase/paraphrase, but one that operates in the range between paraphrase and imitation:[9] a range that leaves open how far, or whether, the idiom of the new version will seek to convey the idiom of its original—which, in the present case, it both does and does not.

In general terms, Hughes's *Oresteia* is set, no doubt, still in Aeschylus' Greece, but by a kind of bifocalism it looks also to Hughes's and my and your contemporary present. On the linguistic level, Hughes's star-gazing watchman, on his roof, at the beginning of *Agamemnon*, is duly waiting, in duly timeless language, for the return of 'the rightful King', and invoking 'You gods in heaven', and straining to see 'A beacon-flare . . . from Troy'[10]—but, then again, he can also see the moon as a 'tide | In its prison yard', and can tell us 'I'm sick of the heavens', halfway between an ancient functionary and a modern technologico-Benthamite, disdaining any interest in the apparatus of

---

[8] I welcome in this connection a more general demonstration by Talbot (2006) of a 'pervasive, and as yet largely ignored, interrelation between Hughes's classical translations and his own original English poems' (131).

[9] 'Preface to Ovid's *Epistles*' (1680): Watson (1962: 288).

[10] *O* 3–4, corresponding to (or expanded from) Aesch. *Agam.* 35, 1, 9–10.

poetic-mythological tradition.[11] The result is that we do not feel any clear gap between *us* here and the Greek *them* there: from the very first, the Greek traditional-poetic Other is fused with, or mediated by, a more familiar tone. And this bifocalism is actually at its most protracted, and its sharpest, in respect of an unannounced and unsuspected allusiveness to Hughes and Plath. The outcome is a new poetic relationship which (I suggest) brings into sharp focus the issue of poetic language that is surely central to the appreciation of Hughes's work as a whole.

I think of the issue as one of poetic language, understanding that phrase in a wide sense. More widely still, the issue might also be thought of as one of personality and impersonality.[12] Hughes has long been associated with the impersonal, and on various grounds— praised by Derek Walcott for reducing the 'I', criticized by Terry Eagleton for a lack of self-reflectivity.[13] Hughes is widely felt to be impersonal in his ubiquitous uses of, and identifications with, natural life, animals and birds, as also in the peculiar directness of his commitment to myth and folklore. Then there is his inclin- ation—especially marked in the latter part of his career—to express himself through translation (rather like Dryden), with the *Oresteia* itself one main product of this inclination. And then, most relevantly, there is the habit of allusion itself, which is a fairly constant factor throughout Hughes's whole career.

In Hughes's work, allusion often takes place, or often concentrates itself, with respect to ends of poems: ends of his own poems, or ends of the poems alluded to, or both. This is what we have in Hughes's 'Rabbit Catcher', where a phraseological evoking of Plath's poem only takes decisive shape at the end of his, and partly involves the end of hers: for Hughes, there is something decisive and final about allusion itself, perhaps. Compare, almost at random, Orestes' last words in Hughes's *Choephori* (the second play of the *Oresteia* trilogy), right at the end of the play, 'You cannot see them but I see them', where

---

[11]  *O* 3: cf. Aesch. *Agam.* 7, 20.
[12]  Compare and contrast Bishop (1994: 1–10).
[13]  Walcott in Scigaj (1992: 41–2): 'His poetry is lonely and remote . . . The "I", when it is there, is not taller than its surroundings'; Eagleton (1987: 78–9): 'Hughes's language . . . is positioned laconically outside [what it speaks of]'.

'them' is the Furies, and where the phrasing adjusts itself to the conversational urgency that Eliot invested the words with in his epigraph to 'Sweeney Agonistes': 'You don't see them, you don't— but *I* see them.'[14]

Or, from *Birthday Letters*, take the poem 'The Dogs Are Eating Your Mother' (where 'you' is Hughes's and Plath's two children, and Plath herself the 'mother'). The poem ends,

> Imagine
> These bone-crushing mouths the mouths
> That labour for the beetle
> Who will roll her back into the sun.[15]

with graceful allusion to the opening (this time) of Wilfred Owen's 'Futility': 'Move him into the sun.' There is no concealment of such relationships. The presence of Owen, for instance, is flagged a couple of pages before, in *Birthday Letters*, in 'A Picture of Otto', which has— near *its* end—

> like Owen, after his dark poem,
> Under the battle, in the catacomb.[16]

Hughes had this allusive habit from the first. For instance, 'Shells' (first published in 1959), ends,

> From that gigantic bed of the sea
>     . . .
> Only shells come
> To chatter of emptiness, or lie
> Lovely as dumb.[17]

recalling, unmistakably, lines from Gerard Manley Hopkins's early poem, 'The Habit of Perfection',

> Shape nothing, lips; be lovely-dumb
>     . . .
> Be shellèd, eyes—

---

[14] *O* 142: Aesch. *Cho.* 1061. Cf. e.g., from Hughes's *Agamemnon*, 'What monstrous reality | Is pushing to be born | Through that tormented mouth?' (*O* 57), evoking the last words of Yeats's 'The Second Coming': 'And what rough beast . . . | Slouches towards Bethlehem to be born?'

[15] *CP* 1169.     [16] *CP* 1167.     [17] *CP* 55.

with one early poem recalling another, then.

In a poem of the mid-1970s, 'Caprichos', Hughes writes: 'If only the words coming from this throat | Were my words.'[18] We talk, vulgarly, about a poet 'having' or 'finding' his or her own 'voice'. Such talk, of 'the poet's voice', properly assumes the situation of the poet in the modern world, in and after the Romantic revolution, which, on various grounds, one may identify as a uniquely momentous turning-point in Western consciousness and art. It makes no sense to use the expression of communal poetry like Homer's, or even like Pindar's. It makes superficial, or partial, sense to use it of a great idiosyncratic, like Euripides or Milton. It makes reasonable sense, only with the problematization of poetry, and the language of poetry, epitomized by Wordsworth's spokesmanship of 'a selection of language really used by men'—in contradistinction to the apparatus of tropes, conceits, and elevated diction of traditional poetry.[19] It makes reasonable sense, no doubt, to use the phrase in discussion of Hughes.

In his first impact on English poetry, Hughes has, certainly, a distinctive 'voice'—represented, for instance, in his first collection, *The Hawk in the Rain* (1957). Yet this 'voice', distinctive as it is, both is and is not an independent 'voice'. In part, it impinges as a pre-existing 'voice', half-recognizable as a modern poetic 'voice', pitched somewhere between (most recognizably) Hopkins and Auden—an impersonatory 'voice', almost—so that often we hear something like the one, but not quite, or something like the other, but not quite. 'The Horses', for instance, begins with Hopkins,

> I climbed through woods in the hour-before-dawn dark[20]

while the next poem, 'Famous Poet', begins, quite differently, with Auden:

> Stare at the monster: remark
> How difficult it is to define just what

---

[18] *CP* 353.
[19] Wordsworth, Preface to *Lyrical Ballads* (1802 edition): Brett and Jones (1963: 244).
[20] *CP* 22. Cf. the opening line of Hopkins's 'Moonrise': 'I awoke in the Midsummer not-to-call night'.

> Amounts to monstrosity in that
> Very ordinary appearance—

Auden via early Eliot, perhaps ('remark').[21] But then, in 'Famous Poet', there is also this,

> ... his dreg-boozed inner demon
> Still tankarding from tissue and follicle
> The vital fire[22]

and then, in 'The Horses', there is also this,

> ... my breath left tortuous statues in the iron light[23]—

in both of which we seem to feel Hughes reaching towards an idiom truly independent, as well as distinctive: sensuous, expressionist, capacious in diction and tone, as also in terms of recognizably 'poetic' formal structures.

In general, in this and the other early collections, it is sensuousness that predominates in Hughes's work. And it is a distinctive sensuousness, which correlates with, and helps to embody, a distinctive set of related allegiances: to the animal and the realm of the animal, as in 'The Horses' (and *passim*);[24] to the raw, physical, primal nature of Being, summed up, almost to the point of self-parody, in lines like

> That cry for milk
> From the breast
> Of the mother

---

[21] *CP* 23. Cf. e.g. the opening of Auden's 'Watch any day ... ': 'Watch any day his nonchalant pauses, see | His dextrous handling of a wrap as he | Steps after into cars ... ' (early Auden, too (1929), in which one notes the characteristic mannerism of the counter-natural line break after 'he', echoed by Hughes's breaks after 'what' and 'that'); and e.g., in Eliot, 'Remark the cat which flattens itself in the gutter' and 'Particularly I remark | An English countess goes upon the stage ... ' (both early Eliot: 'Rhapsody on a Windy Night' and 'Portrait of a Lady').

[22] *CP* 23.

[23] *CP* 22.

[24] In awe of animal powers and realities, Hughes could even write: 'I think of poems as a sort of animal. They have a life of their own ... And they have a certain wisdom' (Hughes, *WP* 10).

Of the God
Of the world
Made of Blood

from 'Karma' (first published in 1966);[25] and not least to the holistic, vividly represented in a poem from that first 1957 collection, *The Hawk in the Rain*, the quaintly titled 'The Man Seeking Experience Enquires His Way of a Drop of Water'—an early-Yeats-like title, but making way for a not-very-Yeats-like acclamation that we are all 'Droplet-kin, sisters and brothers of lymph and blood'.[26]

In a 1976 essay on 'Myth and Education', Hughes, like many in the world of modern letters before him—Goethe and Schiller, Nietzsche and Freud, Lawrence and Eliot—critiques human dissociation, but, distinctively, in terms of two worlds, inner and outer:

> The inner world, separated from the outer world, is a place of demons. The outer world, separated from the inner world, is a place of meaningless objects and machines.[27]

Hughesian man needs to 'keep faith' with both—with 'the world of things and the world of spirits equally': a distinctive holism, this, which can only complicate the personalizing of any poetic 'voice', and seems likely to require for it some distinctive linguistic articulation.[28]

Hughes's output was, and remained, extensive; and within the range there are many experiments, large and small, which serve to modify, or even challenge, the now established Hughesian linguistic norms, not least by an experimental replacing of the range with a narrower, sharper idiom. The first big experiment comes with the 'Crow' poems (1967–73).[29] This set of poems recentres itself on an abrasively ritualized conversational wit—all rhetoric, yet somehow

---

[25]  *CP* 167–8.

[26]  *CP* 34–5. 'Hughes's perception of his poetic world was one of connection, not separation. As the poet . . . could feel himself "droplet-kin", so the work of the true poet was holistic': Wagner (2000: 15).

[27]  Reprinted in *WP* 151.

[28]  Reprinted in *WP* 150 (invoking Goethe specifically). Up to this point in his career, Hughes's allusive habit might seem to recall the well-documented practices of Roman poets (see e.g. Hinds 1998). The counter-issue of 'distinctive linguistic articulation', along with the yet more distinctive uses to which, in *BL*, Hughes puts his habit, are hard to parallel in Latin poetry or elsewhere.

[29]  Subsuming, but not restricted to, the 1970 collection *Crow* itself.

denying rhetoric—which seems designed to problematize, but also deflate, Hughes's own earlier characteristic sensuous mode. 'Crow and the Birds' (1970) is a text-book example. The poem begins in one mode,

> When the eagle soared clear through a dawn distilling of emerald

and ends in an almost satirical version of it:

> Crow spraddled head-down in the beach-garbage, guzzling a dropped ice-cream.[30]

With new idioms and new configurations of language, new preoccupations become apparent—and, not least, a preoccupation with language itself, its capacity for elemental simplicity and its perceived limitations.[31] In the following years, anxieties about language seem to sharpen. Note this, for example, from the *Gaudete* Epilogue (1977), where language is unexpectedly brought into relationship with medicine:

> And I hear speech, the bossed Neanderthal brow-ridge
> Gone into beetling talk
> The Java Man's bone grinders sublimed into chat.
>
> Words buckle the voice in tighter, closer
> Under the midriff
> Till the cry rots, and speech
>
> Is a fistula
>
> Eking and deferring
> Like a stupid or a crafty doctor
> With his year after year
> Of sanguinary nostrums

---

[30]  *CP* 210.

[31]  'Crow's language sheds anything we can recognise as poetry, as style. He tries to get back to what seems to him the irreducible starting point: "I eat, therefore I am" ': Sagar (2000: 123). (Eliot's 'Sweeney Agonistes' suggests itself as a precedent, with both its 'Birth, and copulation, and death. | That's all the facts when you come to brass tacks' and its 'I've gotta use words when I talk to you.') Hughes himself subsequently theorized his poetic project as a quest for 'words that cannot be out-flanked by experience' (Hughes, *WP* 68), while, of the Crow poems themselves, he wrote: 'my idea was to reduce my style to the simplest clear cell—then regrow a wholeness and richness organically from that point. I didn't get that far' (letter to Keith Sagar, quoted by Sagar (2000: 127) ).

Of almosts and their tomorrows
Through a lifetime of fees.[32]

With *River* (1983), there is impressive evidence of a new achieved poise, both in language and about language. The earlier sensuousness, now, is not so much challenged as purified, and put in the service of a new kind of intellectual compression. In 'Go Fishing', a masterpiece from that collection, the relationship between language and medicine has matured into an exquisite enactment of Hughes's holism:

Join water, wade in underbeing
Let brain mist into moist earth
Ghost loosen away downstream
Gulp river and gravity

Lose words
Cease
Be assumed into glistenings of lymph
As if creation were a wound
As if this flow were all plasm healing

Be supplanted by mud and leaves and pebbles
By sudden rainbow monster-structures
That materialize in suspension gulping
And dematerialize under pressure of the eye

Be cleft by the sliding prow
Displaced by the hull of light and shadow

Dissolved in earth-wave, the soft sun-shock,
Dismembered in sun-melt

Become translucent—one untangling drift
Of water-mesh, and a weight of earth-taste light
Mangled by wing-shadows
Everything circling and flowing and hover still

Crawl out over roots, new and nameless
Search for face, harden into limbs

Let the world come back, like a white hospital
Busy with urgency words

Try to speak and nearly succeed
Heal into time and other people.[33]

---

[32]  *CP* 357.
[33]  *CP* 652.

This 'healing' poem I take to be the most adequate acknowledgement in the English language, since Eliot's *Four Quartets*,[34] of the modern consciousness of the inadequacy of language itself (articulated variously by Nietzsche, by Eliot himself, by Adorno, by Derrida) and equally of the modern problematic of traditional poetic idiom in an anti-traditional world, famously articulated in that Wordsworthian demand for 'the language really spoken' by men, and reformulated by (for instance) Hopkins, with his insistence that poetic language should aspire to be 'the current language heightened'.[35] One way of summing up the distinction of 'Go Fishing' is in fact to say that here Hughes has found a composite mode and idiom that can encompass *both* the sensuous aural linkages and charged compound neologisms of a Hopkins ('mist into moist earth', 'earth-wave', 'sun-shock', 'sun-melt') *and* a maturely achieved version of his own youthful expressionism ('Let the world come back, like a white hospital') *and* a new range of harshly defamiliar pared-down abstraction ('Busy with urgency words') which merges with an only slightly heightened educated demotic: 'Try to speak and nearly succeed | Heal into time and other people'.

One of the many remarkable things about the Hughes of *Birthday Letters* is that he has turned his back on this masterful accommodation—not actually by abandoning the mix (the same ingredients are apparent), but by drastically adjusting the mix in favour of that 'only slightly heightened educated demotic', but mostly, now, in the form of narrative conversational address with a minimum of formal structuring. In 'The Rabbit Catcher', accordingly, the unassuming language of 'It was May. How had it started?' provides, so to speak, the key signature, and the key remains effectively the same even

---

[34] The conjunction, in the two cited Hughes poems, of language anxiety and medical imagery owes something specifically to *Four Quartets*. With the 'Words buckle... | Under the midriff...' of *Gaudete*, cf. 'Burnt Norton', V, 'Words strain, | Crack and sometimes break, under the burden, | Under the tension...'; and, for the medical connection, cf. 'East Coker', IV, 'The wounded surgeon plies the steel... | Our only health is the disease... | The whole earth is our hospital... | The fever sings in mental wires...'.

[35] 'The poetical language of an age should be the current language heightened, to any degree heightened and unlike itself, but not... an obsolete one': letter to Robert Bridges, 14 August 1879.

under, or against, sensuous-heightened tangents *en route* ('the open |
Blue push of sea-wind') and even under the Hughes-expressionist
violent simile ('poems, like smoking entrails'), at the end.

But that end (one can hardly call it 'closure') is also the high point
of allusion to Plath and her poem; his use of a violent simile, even,
alludes to hers. One might say there is an active correlation here,
then, between the richer Hughesian poetic and the allusive. On
reflection, though, it makes more sense to say that, in these poems,
allusion is a mode of linguistic enrichment in its own right, but, at
the same time, and paradoxically, an index of personal commitment.
To restate: if our expectation is that allusion exists to evoke a context
of particularities, as Plath's allusion to Shakespeare does, we will
often be surprised by Hughes. Allusions like the one to Hopkins in
his early 'Shells' seem to function chiefly as affirmations of a larger,
*impersonal* poetic tradition. And (with or without the miniature
colour-correction of her story in his story) Hughes's allusions to
Plath's 'Rabbit Catcher' in his 'Rabbit Catcher' again seem not to
evoke the particularities of her work beyond the extent to which these
are evoked already; and this is true, broadly, of the many allusions to
Plath's poetry in *Birthday Letters* as a whole. What these allusions
seem to do is something different again. They add an enriching level
of non-specific reference; they attest the unique particularity of
personal commitment—but, insofar as the personal is the private,
somehow without compromising the integrity of the personal even
here, as someone else's poetic particularity might threaten to do. And
in all this we need to bear in mind the peculiar *poetic* intimacy with
Plath (beyond the personal closeness) that the very existence of the
two 'Rabbit Catcher' poems attests. In Hughes's eyes, in particular, he
had been her 'midwife', they were 'like two feet', their 'telepathy' was
positively 'intrusive'; in hers, their 'impregnable togetherness' had
constituted an artistic, as well as a personal, ideal.[36]

---

[36] See, respectively, 'Suttee' (*CP* 1139); Hughes quoted in *The Manchester Guardian*, 23 March 1965; Hughes (1995: 77); Plath's Journals, in Kukil (2000: 294). Given
the overall scope of Hughes's allusive methods of writing, it could be argued that his
allusions to Plath represent an extreme example, rather than a separate category, of
intimacy: 'part of the excitement of reading [Hughes] is the sense that he is in urgent
conversation with a whole series of authors' (Tom Paulin in Gammage (1999: 147)).
But then again, that kind of 'urgent conversation' has many parallels in earlier poetry
(one thinks, say, of Pope's relation to Dryden, as elucidated by Ricks (2002: 9–42)),

Given that Plath is the usual addressee of the *Letters*, allusions to her are everywhere, and allusions to her poetry too. Besides direct references to poem titles, or equivalent, and meditations on her as writer, we have, more sharply—yet still without specific evocation— re-uses of her obsessive keywords, most obviously the ubiquitous 'Daddy' (title of one of her best-known poems), and then of signature Plath techniques. Typical here is Hughes's use of the close internal rhyming that figures so often in late Plath. Plath's 'Lady Lazarus', for instance, gives us 'the grave cave', 'the same place, the same face', 'a very large charge', 'I turn and burn',[37] and her 'Rabbit Catcher', likewise, 'my own blown hair' (2). Compare (random examples) from Hughes's collection: 'I assumed I was doomed', 'Shaking the snake awake', 'a flare of hair', 'You drummed on your thumb'.[38] But, then again, this particular technique was a feature of Hughes's writing, too, from the start: for instance, that early poem of 1957, 'The Horses', yields 'core tore'.[39] Pragmatically speaking, then, Hughes's technique here works the way the title works, and the violent simile works, in 'The Rabbit Catcher': it provides an enrichment *and* (or *because*) a shared point of reference. As even these examples suggest, it is difficult, and perhaps in the end unnatural, to separate his literary allusions to Plath from what (in ordinary

whereas Hughes's intimacy with Plath is altogether exceptional. Discussion of such issues is not assisted by the crudeness with which some readers of Hughes and Plath—or, usually, Hughes through Plath—have trivialized *BL* as 'manipulative and self-exculpatory'. That phrase is used—as a summary of unsympathetic responses— in the course of a sensitive discussion by Lynda Bundtzen in Gill (2006: 48). In the same collection, an otherwise intelligent piece by Diane Middlebrook offers a simple instance of the trivializing process by reducing Hughes's 'Rabbit Catcher' to a 'refutation' of Plath's: Middlebrook in Gill (2006: 167). Variants of such reductive responses are commonplace: '*Birthday Letters* is, effectively, a collection of poems in which Plath's poetry is translated by another poet' (Basnett (2005: 3); '*Birthday Letters* are [*sic*] a failure as a full record and therefore as poetry' (Raine (2007: 8). That 'effectively' and that 'therefore' would repay literary-theoretical scrutiny: an array of poets—from Vergil to T. S. Eliot—would be penalized by such logic.

[37] *SPCP* 244–6.

[38] From, respectively, 'The Lodger', 'The Rag Rug', 'Fairy Tale', and 'The God': *CP* 1123, 1132, 1146, 1165.

[39] *CP* 22. Likewise, close by in the same 1957 collection, 'feeds him seeds' ('Macaw and Little Miss': *CP* 20); and likewise, from Hughes's juvenilia, 'Only the lonely self ' and 'glazed crazed faces' ('The Recluse' and 'Initiation': *CP* 6 and 7). The two latter poems were written as early as 1948 (*CP* 1240).

circumstances) we would call personal allusions to their shared (or not shared) life; and it is in this light that one should read the remarkable presence of such allusions in his *Oresteia*.

In broad linguistic terms, Hughes's *Oresteia* must strike any reader familiar with his work as relatively respectful to the significant qualities (albeit not necessarily the denoted specifics) of the Greek original. To restate: it presents an idiom—or, as usual, a range of idioms—acceptably, if sometimes elusively, in touch with the bold elevatedness of the Greek. Linguistic anachronism, as noted,[40] is perceptible, but also muted. Conspicuously, Hughes shows a huge relish for the Aeschylean sense of physical Being—achieving an equivalent, even (sometimes) through such very un-Aeschylean techniques as concretized abstraction:

> Troy on its hill
> Cascades with blood, as under a downpour
> Of bodies from the heavens,
> Shattered and entangled with each other
> In every passage—mutilations,
> Amputations, eviscerations.[41]

The Aeschylean grasp of the physical world Hughes accommodates effortlessly to his own preoccupations: to his holism,

> There is no hope nor future
> For a land
> Whose mind is split
> Into two[42]

and to his language anxieties,

> We cannot live on words.
> Nothing can nourish us
> Except the exhalations
> Of the dead and the living blood[43]

---

[40] Above, p. 241.

[41] *O* 20: as often with Hughes's *Oresteia*, the words have no direct counterpart in the Greek—they spell out, in this case, what Aeschylus leaves implicit after *Agam.* 325. For the accumulated Latinate nouns, cf. Eliot, 'Coriolan', II: 'If the mactations, immolations, oblations, impetrations, | Are now observed . . .'

[42] *O* 192: expanded from Aesch. *Eum.* 981–5.

[43] *O* 187–8: replacing Aesch. *Eum.* 870–6.

and to his own primalism (and he invokes the very word):

> . . . the primal laws of the earth.[44]

As poetry, Hughes's *Oresteia* at its best (it *is* strikingly uneven) must be far and away the most compelling impression of Greek tragedy in English, though whether it works as drama may be an open question, not least because Hughes (as Terry Gifford and Neil Roberts once noted of *Gaudete*) is somehow unconcerned with the living quality of undisturbed lives, such as (in the Greek original) serves to humanize even the wild, god-centred landscape of Aeschylean tragedy.[45] Conversely, he does succeed in re-enacting the stark impersonality of the Greek, with its choral collectivity and its 'unified' characters (as Hegel called them).[46] And yet, remarkably, the force of this recreation of the great tragic impersonal depends partly on an informing of its language by reference (even protracted reference) to the intimate world of Plath and Hughes and *Birthday Letters*.

With the two 'Rabbit Catcher' poems, for instance, and with the personal penumbra that surrounds them, compare this, from the Iphigeneia episode in Hughes's *Agamemnon*:

> The prayers go up. Her father
> Gives the signal. Iphigenia
> Is hoisted off her feet by attendants—
> They hold her over the improvised altar
> Like a struggling calf.
> The wind presses her long dress to her body
> And flutters the skirt, and tugs at her tangled hair—
> 'Daddy!' she screams. 'Daddy!'—
> Her voice is snatched away by the boom of the surf.
> Her father turns aside, with a word
> She cannot hear. She chokes—
> Hands are cramming a gag into her mouth.
> They bind it there with cord, like a horse's bit.
>     . . .

---

[44] *O* 177: replacing Aesch. *Eum.* 676–7.

[45] Gifford and Roberts (1981: 156).

[46] Hegel, *Ästhetik*: Bassenge (1955: 1068–102). See briefly Silk and Stern (1981: 322–5).

> Now rough hands rip off her silks
>
> . . .
>
> Down across the beach, and over the surf.[47]

Think now of Hughes's poem: 'I *ripped* | The door open'; 'I found a snare . . . brown *cord*'; 'your doomed self, your tortured, crying | *Suffocating* self'. And, still more markedly, Plath's poem: 'The *wind gagging my mouth* with my own *blown hair,* | *Tearing off my voice,* and the sea, | *Blinding me with* . . . the lives of the dead'. Behold, then, the terrible humiliating pain of the young woman, beside the sea, and the helplessness of the man watching this terrible enactment of 'sacred ancient custom' (Hughes's phrase in his 'Rabbit Catcher', 55–6)—all in three versions: the Plath, the Hughes, and the Hughes–Aeschylus. There are, clearly, specific phraseological links between the three sequences—and not only between these three: the same kind of multiple connection is intermittent throughout the *Oresteia* and *Birthday Letters*, with Plath and her poetry as the third point of reference, the third cord, the third 'human contrivance'.[48] In the cited passage, Iphigeneia's 'Daddy! . . . Daddy!' sums it up.[49] There is no Daddy in either of the 'Rabbit Catcher' poems, but Daddy is a huge presence in Plath's late poems, as in her self-understanding generally—within which her German father Otto is equated (famously and infamously) with a Nazi and with death and with God ('Herr God', in 'Lady Lazarus') and indeed with Hughes too.[50] Most notoriously, in her poem 'Daddy' itself, we get:

> Daddy, I have had to kill you
>
> . . .
>
> Not God but a swastika

---

[47]   *O* 15: Aesch. *Agam.* 228–39.

[48]   It is characteristic of *BL* that words and phrases recur from poem to poem in, sometimes, quite different connections. A case in point, and a relevant case for the Iphigeneia sequence, is provided by the poem 'Error'. Here there is another 'cord', a 'stripping-off', 'fingers tearing', 'low tide', 'blood-water', 'crying soundlessly' (*CP* 1121–2)—but, this time, no overall sense of decisive cross-reference.

[49]   Aeschylus (*Agam.* 228) wrote *klêdonas patrôious*, approximately 'father's tellings'—'an extraordinary expression for "her cries of 'Father' "' (Page ad loc., in Denniston and Page 1957: 89).

[50]   *SPCP* 246.

> So black no sky could squeak through.
> Every woman adores a Fascist,
> The boot in the face, the brute
> Brute heart of a brute like you.
>
>            . . .
>
> If I've killed one man, I've killed two—
> The vampire who said he was you
> And drank my blood for a year,
> Seven years, if you want to know.[51]

(At the time of writing, this was now the seventh year since Hughes and Plath were married.)

The extraordinary idiom of equating or superimposing in that poem (Daddy = Fascist = vampire = Hughes) is itself a marked feature of *Birthday Letters*, both in terms of Plath's own specific equations and others as well. So Hughes can write,

> And I was your husband
> Performing the part of your father
> In our new myth.[52]

and

> your Daddy's
> Body full of your arrows. Though it was
> Your blood that dried on him.[53]

and

> Who was this alien joker
> Who had come to evict us,
> Sharing my skin, just as he shared yours . . . ?[54]

Compare, from Hughes's 'Rabbit Catcher' (69–70),

> Had you caught something in me,
> Nocturnal and unknown to me?

---

[51]  *SPCP* 222–4.
[52]  'Suttee': *CP* 1140.
[53]  'The Cast': *CP* 1159.
[54]  'The Lodger': *CP* 1125.

where the 'something' mutates into a strange unspecified 'it', which begins as a dark presence and ends as a *new* something, itself an equation of inspirational force and dead creature revived:[55] 'Those . . . | Fingers of your verse . . . | Felt it alive (73–5).'[56]

And compare passages like this, from Hughes's *Oresteia* (the Iphigeneia episode again),

> Avenging Artemis, who stands
> Casting the shadow of a great Queen.
> Then Clytemnestra's shadow
> Takes the shape of a sprawling murdered man.
> And the bloody footprints of Clytemnestra
> Become those of a sacrificed child[57]

and this,

> . . . I have done no more
> Than sacrifice myself—myself,
> Not only my daughter but also my daughter's father.[58]

---

[55] Seemingly artless in its conversational progression, the poem begins with an inconsequential 'It' and ends with an 'it' of fraught significance. Given the relationship, in this poem, between elusive unspecificity and proclaimed bafflement, one can be forgiven for pondering the mismatch—artistic, even moral—between the narrative of bafflement and the control implicit in these delicate organizational manoeuvres. The issue becomes more urgent when the control is seen to extend retrospectively to some of the 'innocent' detail of the poet's recollection. 'I simply . . . | Waited for you to come back to nature' (17–19): the potential irony of this 'back to nature' in the context of the 'natural' spectacle that so shocks Plath is activated by the image of pagan nature-worship ('smoking entrails', 75) at the end. Here, at least, the charge of 'manipulative and self-exculpatory' thrown at the Hughes of *BL* does need to be faced (see n. 36 above, and cf. n. 62 below). The artistic success of the collection overall is correlative to the sense that it finally achieves due perspective—the perspective (*mutatis mutandis*) of, say, an *Antony and Cleopatra*, as opposed to the poignant, but problematic, perspective of an Antony (or a Cleopatra).

[56] Plath's own identification, in her 'Rabbit Catcher', of Hughes/'him' with the Lawrentian catcher of rabbits in 'Love on the Farm' is yet another equation, both specific and representative, that might be said to seal the two poets' relationship in (is it cheap to say?) the blood of poetic life. Compare finally, then, Hughes's words, 'Fingers of your verse . . . | Felt it alive' (74–5), with, not so much anything in Plath's poem, as the words of her Lawrentian source: 'I let him finger there | My pulse of life'—and likewise Hughes's 'In those snares | You'd caught something. | Had you caught something in me . . . ?' (67–9) with Lawrence's 'I am caught in a snare' (n.5 above).

[57] *O* 10–11: expanded from Aesch. *Agam*. 151–5. The 'shadow' superimposition has a very direct equivalent in *BL*, in 'A Picture of Otto': 'Your ghost inseparable from my shadow' (*CP* 1167).

[58] *O* 14: expanded from Aesch. *Agam*. 214–16.

Both these equational gestures are read back into the Greek original. Meanwhile, though, right at the start of the *Agamemnon*, Hughes has already converted an Aeschylean hint of such an equation to a fuller version. Aeschylus' watchman invokes with awe Clytemnestra's indomitable purpose, speaking of 'the woman's man-purposing heart'.[59] Hughes adroitly expands this into

> Queen Clytemnestra—who wears
> A man's heart in a woman's body,
> A man's dreadful will in the scabbard of her body
> Like a polished blade. A hidden blade—

thus introducing both the equational and the self-allusive mode, with a further evocation of the 'moon's blade' at the start of his own 'Rabbit Catcher' (3).[60]

The three writings are linked in other ways besides. For a start, they share a characteristic and explicit fatalism. The very last poem ('Words') in Plath's last collection, *Ariel* (as published by Hughes), ends:

> From the bottom of the pool, fixed stars
> Govern a life.[61]

Elsewhere, in *Birthday Letters*, Hughes repeats and appropriates the words:

> Not dreams, I had said, but fixed stars
> Govern a life.[62]

---

[59] Aesch. *Agam.* 11: *gunaikos androbouion . . . kear.*

[60] *O* 3. In fact, earlier in the watchman's speech there are comparable echoes. 'Tethered on the roof of this palace | Like a dog', ' . . . the constellations | . . . | Slow as torture. | And the moon, coming and going—| Wearisome, like watching the sea | From a deathbed. Like watching the tide | In its prison yard . . . ' (*O* 3, expanding Aesch. *Agam.* 3–7): cf., from Hughes's 'Rabbit Catcher', 'Trailed after like a dog' (41) and (again) 'the moon's blade' (3), and, from Plath's 'Rabbit Catcher', 'extravagant, like torture' (10)—so that the first two similes in Hughes's *Oresteia* anticipate the larger allusions to the 'Rabbit Catcher' poems later on—and then, from the opening of 'Horoscope' in *BL*, 'You wanted to study | Your stars—the guards | Of your prison yard, their zodiac' (*CP* 1083).

[61] *SPCP* 270 (= Plath's *Ariel*, ed. Hughes (1965: 86) ).

[62] 'A Dream': *CP* 1119. Cf. numerous other poems in *BL*, such as 'Dreamers' (*CP* 1145–6) and the ends of '9 Willow Street' (cited below, p. 259) and 'The Pan' (*CP*

And fatalism is writ large in Hughes's *Oresteia*, following, but also rewording, Aeschylus, from the first play

> With these words, Agamemnon surrendered
> To necessity[63]

to the last:

> So God and Fate, in a divine marriage,
> Are made one in the flesh
> Of all our people . . . [64]

More fundamentally, the whole tragic configuration of the *Oresteia* aligns itself with the personal Hughes/Plath tragedy:[65] a family group (mother and father in conflict; son and daughter there too), a killing, a painful sequel, a hoped-for redemption—*Birthday Letters* traces this painful pattern from the first meeting of Ted and Sylvia, through her suicide, to the continuation of the line in the two children, in whose lifetime, perhaps, the beetle will 'roll her back into the sun'. And as in so much Greek tragedy (Aeschylus' trilogy included), there is an irresistible movement from innocence or ignorance, through premonitions, to the *pathos*, and to a state of understanding *after* the event—albeit Hughes, in *Birthday Letters*, has *not* reached that state, but is, rather, striving to reach out *towards* that state by the very act of writing and recording: the ignorance—and the premonitions—in his 'Rabbit Catcher' are representative.

At which point (if not before), one registers the fact that in *Birthday Letters* Hughes does repeatedly describe the marriage and

---

1090, 1121). The pervasiveness of fatalism in *BL* raises its own—artistic/moral—questions (cf. nn. 36 and 55 above). In a sympathetic review of *BL*, John Carey wrote: 'In [Hughes's] vision human beings have always been dwarfed by what he has called "the elemental power-circuit of the universe"—a coercive force variously identified with the laws of science, or the giant figures of classical [sic?] myth, or the brutal intensity of birds and animals. In this view of life . . . "responsibility" becomes a figment, valid only in the make-believe world of lawyers and moralists. We are moulded, directed and destroyed by cosmic forces beyond our control or understanding. Throughout *Birthday Letters*, this fatalism is relentlessly endorsed' (Carey 1998). Hughes's fatalism is, indeed, not invented in or for *BL*—but, within *BL*, it is not only 'moralists' who may want to query its implications.

[63]  *O* 14: Aesch. *Agam.* 218.

[64]  *O* 194: Aesch. *Eum.* 1045–6.

[65]  Following the precedent of Eliot's use of Aeschylus in *The Family Reunion*.

the relationship, along with Plath's life in its own right, as a drama: a conventional enough conceit, but deeply significant here. In his 'Rabbit Catcher' (36–7) we get,

> I was a fly outside on the window-pane
> Of my own domestic drama[66]

and elsewhere (with concomitant fatalistic overtones),

> I sleepwalked
> Like an actor with his script

and

> How could Fate
> Stage a scenario so symbolic
> Without having secreted the tragedy ending
> And the ironic death?[67]

A whole poem in the collection is given over to one particular development of the conceit—the poem 'Setebos', with plangent reference to *The Tempest* (along with Plath's own *Ariel*).[68] In this light one takes the point of a particularly disconcerting evocation of Greek tragic trauma in Hughes's 'Rabbit Catcher' (25):

> That day belonged to the furies.

There is, then, a huge network of cross-reference, a large subtext, linking *Birthday Letters*, Plath, and the *Oresteia*.[69] And if any confirmation for this subtext is still needed, it is provided by a poem in Hughes's very last collection: 'The Hidden Orestes', from *Howls and*

---

[66] The lines recall Tennyson's 'The blue fly sung in the pane' ('Mariana'), where—as again here—there is a hint of 'pain' in the 'pane'.

[67] 'The Table' and '9 Willow Street': *CP* 1133, 1090.

[68] *CP* 1128–9. In her journals, Plath herself wrote of the 'great, stark, bloody play acting itself out over and over again behind the sunny façade of our daily rituals': Kukil (2000: 456).

[69] Within Hughes's *Oresteia*, instances are most striking in, but not confined to, his *Agamemnon*. A single example from his *Choephori*: 'These demons are the decomposition | Of my mother's blood. | They are the wolves of her body, of her breasts, of her womb' (*O* 142: Aesch. *Cho.* 1054) as against this from 'Life After Death': 'As my body sank into the folk-tale | Where the wolves are singing . . . | For two babes, who have turned, in their sleep, | Into orphans | Beside the corpse of their mother' (*CP* 1161). At *Cho.* 1054 Aeschylus had, not 'wolves', but 'dogs' (*kunas*).

*Whispers* (published in late 1998). The eleven poems in this collection, like the eighty-eight in *Birthday Letters*, are centred on Hughes and Plath, who here (as there) are generally 'I' and 'you'. In this poem, though, 'you' is Electra and 'I' her befogged husband, trying and failing to keep up, as Hughes tries and fails in 'Rabbit Catcher' and elsewhere. In 'The Hidden Orestes', with transparent irony, Hughes represents himself as the husband that in Aeschylus Electra does not have (though she does have one in Euripides' *Electra*). In the Hughes poem, now, the wife is possessed by a killer spirit (spirit of revenge for the murder of her father, Agamemnon)—with that killer spirit itself equated with her brother, Orestes:

> Tragedies of the House of Atreus
> Exclude Electra's husband. Gossip has it
> He's a befogged buffoon. He can't make out
> What's eating his wife. Every woman
> Who sits in their home, no matter how friendly,                5
> She hates. Also, he's alarmed
> By the uncanny masculine voice
> That now and again, before she's aware of it,
> Bursts from between her lips
> With a demonic snarl                                           10
> That seems aimless, maybe
> While she watches a cricket, at dusk,
> Crawling in over the windowsill.
>
> He's not to know that Orestes
> Is padding up the long trail                                   15
> Like a black panther
> In inky darkness—the black velvet bagfull
> Of family emeralds. So he can't guess
> What incognito killer
> Pulls on her face, of a sudden,                                20
> At a knocking, and leaves their bed
> To let in the banshee, the death-shriek
> Of her own mother Clytemnestra.
> And he will never get clear
> How that body, murdered by Electra,                            25
> Comes to be her own. As if a tracker
> Had swerved onto the wrong spoor
> At the last moment. Or how the maternal Furies,

Hunting the guilty one, can be led
By Clytemnestra's ghost, carrying, fiery                    30
And furious as a torch, the corpse of Electra,
And coming for him.[70]

Almost as if Hughes had, precisely, set out to write a poem that spelled out and explained the relation of *Birthday Letters* to his *Oresteia*, we have, laid out before us, all the relevant ingredients: the Greek-tragic parallel, the family group, the wife in fraught relationship with the baffled husband, the supernatural superimpositions, the alien masculine voice taking the possessed wife over, the second superimposition whereby the body she kills becomes her own—and then the Furies, embodying the pain that this composite death leaves for the 'befogged buffoon' (3). The poem's detail is saturated with Hughes/Plath emblems. I note in particular the sardonic, punning colloquialism near the start: 'He can't make out | What's eating his wife'—compare 'The Dogs Are Eating Your Mother'.[71]

Uncanny 'voice', real language of men, current language heightened: the great problematic of poetic language. In his *Birthday Letters* and his *Oresteia*, generically unrelated and linguistically distinct, Hughes (who purportedly does not approach personal understanding) does approach a final intuitive solution to the language problem as it impinges on him, with allusion as the key. For his *Oresteia* (whose predominant idiom is, by his standards, a traditional one) allusion serves as a way of bringing the Greek tragic cycle into the here and now, while yet respecting the overt requirements of classical distance. For his *Birthday Letters*, located at the painful heart of his own here and now, personal honour prescribes a conversational

---

[70] *CP* 1175–6.

[71] *CP* 1168. Compare/contrast the famous last line of Plath's 'Lady Lazarus': 'And I eat men like air' (*SPCP* 247: n.72 below). Other notable connections between 'The Hidden Orestes' and *BL* involve the 'panther' (16: cf. the opening of 'Trophies', *CP* 1054, and also Plath's 'Pursuit', *SPCP* 22–3) and the 'emeralds' (18: cf. the 'treasure' at the end of 'Robbing Myself', *THCP* 1151, and the 'jewel' in the last line of the last poem in *BL*, 'Red', *CP* 1170). For the underlying analogy between Plath and Electra, cf. Plath's poem, 'Electra on Azalea Path' (*SPCP* 116–17) (theorized interestingly by Britzolakis (1999: 59–65), and her authorial comment on 'Daddy' (in a reading prepared for a BBC radio programme), cited by Hughes, editorially, in *SPCP* 293: 'Here is a poem spoken by a girl with an Electra complex.'

simplicity, and allusion serves as the necessary heightening factor, without compromising the personal.[72] For both works, the cross-reference is mutually enriching: it constitutes a heightening, both emotional and linguistic. This seems to me a remarkable composite achievement, among the most remarkable in Hughes's poetic career, and a distinctive achievement within twentieth-century poetry as a whole.[73]

[72] The *Oresteia* is not the only instance—but vastly the most significant and successful instance—of Hughes's mediating the Hughes/Plath 'tragedy' allusively within his late versions from the classics. Other instances are momentary or crude by comparison. For the momentary, see e.g. the last words of *Tales from Ovid* (1997), 'And the two lovers in their love-knot, | One pile of inseparable ashes, | Were closed in a single urn' (on Pyramus and Thisbe: *CP* 1042): cf. the end of Plath's 'Lady Lazarus', 'Out of the ash | I rise with my red hair | And I eat men like air' (*SPCP* 247). Much the crudest instance is the expansion of the Orpheus/Eurydice reference in Hughes's 1999 version of Euripides' *Alcestis* (pp. 22–3: Eur. *Alc.* 357–62)—a play which itself had a personal, Hughes-related significance for Plath: Middlebrook (2003: 284). Such connections are indeed in the public domain: 'In . . . the translations of the grand works of Western literature with which Hughes occupied himself toward the end of his life—Racine's *Phèdre*, *Tales from Ovid*, the *Alcestis* of Euripides—Hughes brings empathy to the theme of marriage under duress . . . and audiences were quick to intuit that a second passionate story—Hughes's own story—was being explored, inexactly, within the dynamics of a venerable classic' (Middlebrook 2003: xviii). Critical—and 'audience'—inattention to the one uniquely momentous instance of such 'exploration', in Hughes's *Oresteia*, can now, I hope, be remedied.

[73] For constructive comments, I am grateful to members of the audience at the 'Hughes and the Classics' conference at Edinburgh, 2005, and subsequent audiences at Comparative Literature Research Seminars at King's College London in 2006 and the University of North Carolina at Chapel Hill in 2007.

# 14

## The Hughes Version: Commercial Considerations and Dramatic Imagination

### Hallie Marshall

Ted Hughes wrote dramatic verse his entire career. While he found some measure of early success in writing dramatic verse for the radio, and for the BBC in particular, he had little success in writing for the stage.[1] Peter Hall, in his letter of rejection for *Difficulties of a Bridegroom*, a symbolic play based on alchemical concepts, wrote: 'Symbolic drama simply has to have a concrete basis, and this I don't believe has. It is a series of fascinating theatrical images which weary by their dexterity.'[2] Not until he was commissioned to produce a version of Seneca's *Oedipus* for Peter Brook did Hughes achieve any real theatrical success, and even then the critics' reviews were mixed and the production was short-lived.[3] This collaboration set the stage,

---

[1] Hughes's principal occupation and source of income during the 1960s was the dramatic verse that he was writing for the BBC. See both Middlebrook (2003: 135) and Feinstein (2001: 103–4).

[2] See Middlebrook (2003: 135–9) for both an outline of Hughes's interactions with Peter Hall and the Royal Shakespeare Company (RSC), and brief descriptions of *Difficulties of a Bridegroom* and other early unstaged dramatic work by Hughes.

[3] Hughes's play *The House of Aries* was given a staged reading at the Poet's Theatre in Boston in 1960, as was his play *The Calm* in 1961. Neither, however, received a full theatrical production. Hughes's translation of Seneca's *Oedipus* was his first theatrical work to receive a major production, and the first theatrical work to bring any substantive income. On the staged readings of Hughes's early plays see Middlebrook (2003: 136–7), and on his income from the *Oedipus* production, see Feinstein (2001: 158). Like most theatrical productions the contemporary reception of *Oedipus* by both audiences and critics has been largely overwritten by the memories of the luminaries involved, and the giant shadow cast on the production simply because of the involvement of figures such a Peter Brook, John Gielgud, and Ted Hughes. On Gielgud's experience of the production, see Morely (2002: 368–71). For a view from backstage, see Hallifax (2004: 243–4) and Lewis (1990: 38–40).

however, for the classical material that Hughes would return to at the end of his career, as well as his method of 'translation'.[4] This paper seeks to examine the place of Hughes's late plays within his literary output, as well as their place in the British tradition of verse translations of classical drama at the end of the twentieth century.

The last two decades of the twentieth century saw a rebirth of English verse translations and adaptations of classical plays by prominent poets. From the early 1980s it became common for major theatre companies to include at least one classical play in their season. Indeed, classical plays experienced such a vogue that, as Edith Hall has noted, in the first half of 1995 it was possible to see more Euripides than Shakespeare on the London stage.[5] One aspect of this revival has been that while there is a general vogue for ancient Greek drama, certain plays are more fashionable in given years. Some plays, such as *Oedipus Rex*, are of course mainstays and have been performed with some degree of regularity on the professional stage throughout much of the twentieth century. Other plays, however, despite having been rarely performed, may suddenly make frequent appearances on the stage within a very limited time period. For example, the seldomly performed *Philoctetes* received three major professional productions in three years between 1988 and 1991.[6] The 2004/5 theatre season saw the premiere of three new translations of *Hecuba*, two of which were major London productions.[7] While Hughes's late plays should be considered as a natural continuity of his lifelong interest in verse drama, the choice of plays should also be

---

[4] Keith Sagar has written of Hughes's translation method, 'As far as I know he was not fluent enough in any language to translate from it unaided. His method was to procure from someone else, often a friend, a crib—that is a straightforward literal prose translation, from which Hughes would then produce his "version". He would also, of course, read all the other translations he could get hold of.' See Sagar (2001).

[5] Hall (2004: 5).

[6] Kenneth McLeish's translation of *Philoctetes* was produced at the Donmar Warehouse in November 1988. Seamus Heaney's *The Cure at Troy* was produced by the Field Day Theatre Company in October 1990. Timberlake Wertenbaker's *Three Birds Alighting on a Field* was staged at the Royal Court Theatre in September 1991.

[7] The Foursight Theatre produced a new translation by John Harrison in October 2004. The Donmar Warehouse produced a new adaptation by Frank McGuinness in September 2004. The RSC produced a new translation by Tony Harrison in April 2005.

examined within this larger framework of the trends in the revival of classical drama on the British stage.

It is not clear why Hughes began late in his life to write so prolifically for the stage after a nearly twenty-year hiatus from dramatic verse, yet between 1994 and 2000 five new versions by Hughes of older works were staged.[8] It almost certainly had something to do with the repeated requests from directors for new versions of plays. He was the first writer approached by Jonathan Kent in 1991 for a new version of *Medea* for the Almeida Theatre.[9] In 1993, when he became director of the Young Vic, Tim Supple approached him to do a dramatic version of some Grimm folk tales.[10] In both cases Hughes declined, though he later expressed regret for having not done the plays.[11] Both directors, however, continued to inquire if he might be interested in doing new versions of particular plays. Supple suggested and Hughes agreed to do *Spring Awakening* in 1994, and then in 1995 Supple approached him to do a version of Lorca's *Blood Wedding*. While the chronology of the writing of the plays is not always clear, it appears that from 1994 until his death in 1998, Hughes worked steadily producing dramatic verse, some of it at the behest of others, and some by personal choice.[12]

The first version of a classical play by Hughes that was produced after his lengthy hiatus from dramatic verse was Racine's *Phèdre*, 'commissioned' by the relatively new Almeida theatre.[13] Hughes's

---

[8] *Spring Awakening* (1995), *Blood Wedding* (1996), *Phèdre* (1998), *The Oresteia* (1999), and *Alcestis* (2000). *Tales from Ovid*, adapted for the stage by Tim Supple, Simon Reade, and Ted Hughes, was staged in 1999.

[9] Personal conversation, Jonathan Kent.

[10] Personal correspondence, Tim Supple.

[11] Personal conversation, Jonathan Kent. Personal correspondence, Tim Supple.

[12] The chronology of composition, as opposed to production, appears to be: *Spring Awakening* (1994/5), *Alcestis* (1995–8), *Oresteia* (1995–8), *Blood Wedding* (1995/6), *Phèdre* (1997/8).

[13] Under the artistic direction of Jonathan Kent and Ian McDiarmid from 1990 to 2002, the Almeida Theatre grew from obscurity to a world-class theatre, or, in the words of Fiachra Gibbons, from 'backstreet fleapit' to 'a magnet for the biggest names on stage and screen' (*The Guardian*, 5 September 2001). Hughes's version of *Phèdre* was not exactly a commissioned play. According to Jonathan Kent, he wrote to Hughes inquiring as to whether he might be interested in doing a version of the play but, received no response. Two months later Hughes's response arrived in the mail in the form of a complete initial draft of the script; Jonathan Kent, personal conversation. See Sagar in this volume.

involvement in this production is relevant to this paper because of the other choices made by the theatre management and the director concerning the scheduling of performances and casting decisions. The choices made appear to have been, in part, an attempt to draw comparisons between this production and the National Theatre's 1975 production of the same play, adapted by Tony Harrison. Tony Harrison was first commissioned by the National Theatre in 1971 to do a verse translation of Moliere's *Misanthrope*.[14] The resulting production, staged in 1973, was a resounding success and Harrison was immediately commissioned to do a new translation of Racine's *Phèdre*. The resulting adaptation, *Phaedra Britannica*, was staged in 1975, and firmly established the National as a rival to the Royal Shakespeare Company (RSC) in the production of verse drama.[15] For both of the productions the central team remained the same; both were directed by John Dexter and both starred Diana Rigg, in the roles of Celimène and Phaedra respectively.[16]

The decision to cast Rigg as Phaedra in the Almeida Theatre production twenty-three years after she had first played the role in the National Theatre production is somewhat unusual. It could be argued that the casting decision represents an innovative take on the play, deliberately pointing to the textual uncertainty in the versions of Euripides, Seneca, and Racine regarding the age of Phaedra, rather than a deliberate attempt to invite comparisons between the Almeida production of Hughes's translation and the National's production of Harrison's *Phaedra Britannica*. Like John Dexter, director Jonathan Kent had an established relationship with Diana Rigg, having directed her in a production of Euripides's *Medea* for the Almeida Theatre in 1992, in *Mother Courage and Her Children* at the National Theatre in 1995, and in *Who's Afraid of Virgina Woolf?* for the Almeida Theatre in 1996. That argument becomes problematic,

---

[14] Harrison (2002: 3–110).

[15] Harrison (2002: 113–207). The rivalry between the RSC and the National Theatre in the early 1970s was fraught by a variety of tensions, not the least of which was the (not unfounded) fear that the National Theatre would be merged into the RSC. On the relationship between the National and the RSC, and the possibility of a merger, see Lewis (1990: 65–6, 70–2) and Goodwin (1983: 12–58, 154–5, and 166–9).

[16] Rigg won a London Theatre Critics Award for Best Actress in 1975 for her role as Phaedra in *Phaedra Britannica*.

however, when one has to account for the play that ran in repertoire with *Phèdre*: Racine's *Britannicus*. Not only did the Almeida Theatre run the plays in repertoire, but they printed a single programme for both plays, with the titles *Phèdre* and *Britannicus* printed in large bold letters one above the other, albeit using different fonts for each title. For those aware of the National Theatre's production of *Phaedra Britannica* the association between the productions seems unavoidable, though with twenty-three years between productions many people were surely unaware of, or had long since forgotten, the National Theatre's version of *Phèdre*.[17]

Jonathan Kent, director of the Almeida production, has said that the production choices were completely unrelated to the National Theatre's 1970s seasons: indeed, it never crossed his mind that there was an association.[18] Like all programming choices under his reign with Ian McDiarmid at the Almeida Theatre, the pairing of Racine's *Phèdre* and *Britannicus* was driven by artistic passion with no overarching plan to establish their company in relation to other major London theatres, past or present. Apparently Diana Rigg never mentioned during the course of the production that she had played the role of Phaedra before, though she had encouraged Kent in his choice of play. Given this, I am very reluctant to ascribe intent where the participants insist that there is none. The production of *Phèdre* by the Almeida is not alone in drawing associations, intentionally or unintentionally, between earlier productions of classical plays associated with Tony Harrison: every classical play or classically inspired play by Hughes in his late career was produced under such circumstances. And while many of those involved in these

---

[17] Gervais's 1999 article, discussing the Yorkshire poet Ted Hughes's version of *Phèdre*, briefly mentions the couplets of Lowell and Wilbur, but not fellow Yorkshire poet Harrison. He suggests that now that the Almeida has proven the theatrical merits of Racine in English: 'Perhaps even the National Theatre will do something when it can spare the time from all those musicals and revivals of J. B. Priestley.' This echoes *The Guardian* theatre critic Michael Billington's fairly constant criticisms of Trevor Nunn's programming choices during his time as director of the National Theatre (see especially Billington's articles in *The Guardian* 'Stage Fright', 10 October 2000, and 'Wanted: director with a taste for adventure', 18 April 2001 issue), but does not even hint that the National had ever staged Racine, let alone in an English verse translation by another major Yorkshire poet.

[18] Jonathan Kent, personal conversation.

productions stress that it was not a conscious choice to draw such associations, Jonathan Kent observed that Hughes himself would never have accepted that such things were mere coincidence.

In the mid-1990s Hughes also turned his hand to Aeschylus' *Oresteia*. Unlike his version of *Phèdre*, which was undertaken because of a direct suggestion from director Jonathan Kent, Hughes seems to have begun work on his version of the *Oresteia* on his own initiative without an immediate view to performance:

In October 1995 Hughes attended a performance of Steinbeck's *The Grapes of Wrath* at the Northcott Theatre, Exeter, and mentioned to members of the theatre management that he was working on the *Oresteia*. The theatre then commissioned the work. However, after the completion of Part I, the North-cott Theatre decided that it did not have the resources to mount a production of such magnitude.[19]

It appears that Hughes then approached the National Theatre in London, which commissioned the completion of his version. The National certainly had the resources to stage a monumental production on the scale of Aeschylus' trilogy, and it had, in fact, previously staged the *Oresteia* on a monumental scale with the 1981 Peter Hall production of Tony Harrison's translation. In the end, however, the production of Hughes's version was not large scale in any aspect. The production was directed by an up-and-coming director, Katie Mitchell, for the Cottesloe theatre, the smallest of the three theatres at the National, seating at a maximum only a quarter of those able to be seated in the Olivier. Nothing about Peter Hall's production had been subtle: it was a giant production meant to fill the cavernous space of the Olivier auditorium, and the translation itself pushed the boundaries of the English language. In contrast there was nothing large about the production of Hughes's version. Where Hall looked back to the theatrical traditions of the ancient Greeks for many of his ideas about staging the *Oresteia*, Mitchell looked instead to contemporary European theatre. While the productions had little in common, there were other aspects of the commissioning and production

---

[19] Keith Sagar, personal correspondence. It was also not the sort of production normally done by the theatre; from its opening in 1967 until 1998 the theatre had never produced an ancient play as part of its season.

process that shed some light on where this production fits into the artistic vision of the National Theatre in the late 1990s.

When Hughes's version of the *Oresteia* was 'commissioned' for production, Trevor Nunn was the Director of the National Theatre. Nunn had replaced Peter Hall as director of the RSC in 1968, and he stayed there until 1986; in 1997 he replaced Richard Eyre as director of the National Theatre. Given the close association of Nunn and Hall at the RSC it was inevitable that comparisons would be made again when Nunn took over at the National.[20] Hughes's version of the *Oresteia* appears to address those comparisons in a number of ways. The choice of play and the translator mark continuity with the artistic goals espoused by previous directors of the National: there is still a commitment to new translations of classics, and to theatrical works by prominent literary figures. Yet as can be seen in comparing the *Oresteia* productions, there are marked differences. Indeed, the publicity campaign drew attention to the fact that the production was going to be compared to a previous production: how else to advertise it but as a new National Theatre production of the *Oresteia*, with a new translation by Ted Hughes? As director Katie Mitchell said:

> People are inevitably going to make comparisons with Peter Hall's 1981 production at the National, though I don't know if they will mean very much. That was a unique and extraordinary group of people communicating the play and Tony Harrison's text in a very specific way, and I really respect what they did. But we're a very different group with a very different writer in Ted Hughes, and we're working in a very different time.[21]

For all those who came prepared to compare the productions, the only conclusion which could be drawn was that they were in every aspect entirely different. For anyone who was hesitant about making comparisons between the poetic language of Harrison and Hughes,

---

[20] It is clear that Nunn was conscious of the comparisons that would be drawn between the National under his reign and chose to make programming decisions that were a marked departure from previous directors. Among the choices he made was the decision not to commission new plays from a number of writers who had worked steadily at the National since the 1970s, the most prominent of which were David Hare and Tony Harrison.

[21] Katie Mitchell in conversation with Jonathan Croall.

the National did its best to encourage them, running Hughes's version of the *Oresteia* in repertoire in the Cottesloe theatre with a remount of Bill Bryden's production of Harrison's *The Mysteries*. The production of Hughes's version of the *Oresteia* clearly marked a new era for the National, fully aware of its history, but looking in new directions under Nunn.

Hughes's final classical play was the posthumously produced *Alcestis*. While *Phèdre* and the *Oresteia* were following in the footsteps of major productions at the National, *Alcestis* was apparently blazing a new trail. Despite having been performed at various schools and universities, *Alcestis* had not received a major production in the later half of the twentieth century, though it is perhaps known in the world of twentieth-century theatre for being T. S. Eliot's veiled model for *The Cocktail Party*. [22] The lack of productions of *Alcestis* is in itself not surprising. It is one of the problem plays that survive from antiquity, defying generic expectations and disturbing attempts at straightforward schematization. *Alcestis* was the fourth play in Euripides' tetralogy of 438, and therefore it ought to be a satyr play, yet it lacks a chorus of satyrs. Like many of the other problem plays, such as the tragedies with happy endings (*Helen* or *Iphigenia among the Taurians*), or those of uncertain authorship (*Rhesus*), *Alcestis* receives a proportionally small amount of scholarly attention, and even fewer outings on the stage, professional or otherwise. As Keith Sagar posed the question, 'Why then should Ted Hughes at the very end of his life have chosen this apparently undistinguished play on which to spend a large chunk of his increasingly precious time? Why not rather the *Bacchae*, the play which had meant more to him than any other and comes closest to his lifelong concerns?'[23] The parallel question is why would any major theatre company choose to produce this play as a central pillar in their season, even if classical

----

[22] Before the posthumous production of Hughes's version of *Alcestis* in 2000 there appear to have been only two professional productions of *Alcestis* in Britain: a 1924 production of Gilbert Murray's translation at Covent Garden, and a 1931 production of a translation by Richard Aldington at the Cambridge Festival Theatre. On performances of *Alcestis*, see the database of the Archive of Performance of Greek and Roman drama. For a brief discussion of versions of the Alcestis story from Euripides to Ted Hughes, see Parker (2003).

[23] See Sagar (2001).

drama is experiencing more popularity on the stage than at any time since antiquity?

The answer to the second question may help to answer the first. While most theatre companies would not consider producing an obscure classical play such as *Alcestis*, Northern Broadsides is not just any company in respect to the theatrical possibilities of obscure classical plays. The artistic director Barrie Rutter had starred in two plays by Tony Harrison that were built around the fragments of classical plays: *The Labourers of Heracles* and *The Trackers of Oxyrhynchus*.[24] He had also starred in the classically inspired play *The Kaisers of Carnuntum*. For an artistic director convinced that great theatre could be created out of the scant fragments of plays unperformed since antiquity, the decision to perform the complete, if somewhat unusual, *Alcestis* is not entirely radical. It was also a play whose performance Rutter had been contemplating for almost a decade. Tony Harrison had been planning to translate/adapt the play as part of a Heracles trilogy since at least the early 1990s, with Barrie Rutter playing Heracles in all three plays.[25] Harrison went so far as to begin an *Alcestis* notebook.[26] For reasons that are unclear the project was abandoned, and Harrison's translation quite literally shelved.[27] Rutter was already convinced that *Alcestis* was a viable

[24] *The Trackers of Oxyrhynchus* was built around the extant fragments of Sophocles' satyr play *Ichneutae*, while *The Labourers of Heracles* took its inspiration from the single extant line of Phrynichus' *Alcestis*. See Harrison (2004: 1–148) and (1996: 115–52).

[25] The press release for *The Labourers of Herakles* clearly stated that this play was part of Harrison's continuing work on the Heracles myth, which had begun earlier that year with the production of *The Kaisers of Carnuntum*. A brief hint of what the *Alcestis* production might have been is provided by Richard Eyre, who says that he and Harrison talked about doing the play in a Greek café; see Eyre (1997: 46).

[26] Harrison's method of working on a project always begins with his notebooks which he systematically fills as the project progresses with translations, sketches, images, and articles clipped from newspapers and magazines, academic articles, other poems, etc.

[27] Not only was the *Alcestis* production shelved, but it also marked the end of Harrison and Rutter's closely intertwined professional careers. Since the production of *The Kaisers of Carnuntum* in 1995 Rutter has worked on none of Harrison's new projects, though Northern Broadsides did productions of *The Mysteries* and *The Trackers of Oxyrhynchus*, in 1997 and 1998 respectively. According to Rutter, however, there are frequent discussions of possible future collaborations between Harrison and Northern Broadsides. Barrie Rutter, personal correspondence.

project, and one ideally suited to his talents and experience, and to the artistic mandate of Northern Broadsides.

Northern Broadsides had been established to perform primarily Shakespearean and classical plays in a northern voice, using regional dialects as opposed to the 'received pronunciation' historically privileged by the professional stage. The idea for Northern Broadsides originated in *The Trackers of Oxyrhynchus*, and Rutter characterized his experience of performing that play in a wool-combing shed in Salts Mill in a northern voice for a northern audience as his Damascus.[28] Yet after almost a decade in existence, the company's classical plays were strictly associated with Tony Harrison. The opportunity to produce Hughes's version of *Alcestis* helped to loosen that tie, while still remaining true to their artistic mandate. Since the production of *Alcestis* in 2000, Northern Broadsides has gone on to produce versions of Sophocles' *Oedipus* and *Antigone* by the Yorkshire poet Blake Morrison, whose play *The Cracked Pot*, an adaptation of Heinrich von Kleist's *Der Zerbrochene Krug*, they had staged in 1995. While maintaining their close association with classical translations and adaptations by Yorkshire poets, it has been nearly a decade since the company produced anything by Tony Harrison.

These are some of the more salient possibilities as to why Northern Broadsides produced Hughes's version of Euripides' *Alcestis*, though there are surely other factors: the personal, political, and artistic workings of any theatre are inherently nebulous. How Hughes came to decide to produce a translation of *Alcestis* is a separate, though perhaps related question, but one for which no certain answer is to be had. According to Barrie Rutter, Hughes, unsolicited, sent him an initial draft of his version in 1996.[29] Rutter expressed enthusiasm for staging the play with Northern Broadsides, and after some rewrites over the next two years Hughes delivered the final script to him in 1998.[30] According to the available evidence regarding the chronology of composition, *Alcestis*, was probably the first

---

[28] Barrie Rutter's biography on the Northern Broadsides website, via <www.northern-broadsides.co.uk>.

[29] Barrie Rutter, personal correspondence.

[30] Keith Sagar, in personal correspondence, has written that the only new material added after the completion of the initial script was the Heracles interlude in which the labours of Heracles are enacted and Prometheus is freed.

classical play Hughes began to work on after his long hiatus from dramatic verse.[31] It is not clear that he undertook the production of his own versions of either *Alcestis* or the *Oresteia* with the intent of seeing them on to the stage. Perhaps his interest in classical plays was sparked by the decision of his friend, Seamus Heaney, to produce his own version of Sophocles' *Philoctetes* in 1990.[32] Hughes had already begun looking at classical material, with four versions of *Metamorphoses* poems having appeared in the poetry collection *After Ovid* in 1995.[33] Ovid, however, cannot be the direct source of Hughes's interest in *Alcestis*, since Alcestis is absent from *Metamorphoses*. It is also possible that the idea of working on this particular play came not from any contact with classical material, but rather came to his mind as a result of his continuing work on what would become *Birthday Letters*. Hughes's version of *Alcestis* inevitably evokes biographical associations with Hughes's relationship with his first wife, Sylvia Plath. Perhaps one or more of these possibilities prompted Hughes to try his hand at producing his own version of *Alcestis*.

However Hughes came to choose the plays that he did, I would argue that in his final years he found the theatrical success that he had desired for much of his career by working within the framework of classical drama. The relative success of these plays was in its turn supported by the increased popularity of classical drama on the modern stage in the last two decades of the twentieth century, which greatly increased the commercial viability of these works, even when, or especially when, they were versions of infrequently produced plays. Regardless of the commercial and artistic considerations that might have gone into the programming selections of the theatre seasons in which they appeared, and regardless of the associations those programming choices might elicit, Hughes's classical plays evoke no one's style of poetry but his own. Not only is the poetic language and style recognizable as that of Hughes, but the plays are marked by his interest in symbolist drama and the hero quest, and none more so than his version of *Alcestis*.

[31] On the chronology of composition see Sagar in this volume.

[32] Heaney (1990).

[33] The versions of stories from Ovid's *Metamorphoses* which began with the four poems published in *After Ovid* was eventually expanded into Hughes's collection of twenty-four stories, *Tales from Ovid*. See Hofmann and Lasdun (1995).

*Alcestis* was the first classical play that Hughes began to work on when he returned to theatrical verse in the last years of his life, but it was the last of his three late career classical plays to be produced. None of Hughes's classical plays are translations: they are versions in which Hughes has hung his poetry over a recognizable pre-existing dramatic framework. In some cases there is both expansion and contraction in various parts of the pre-existing work—most notably the expanded emphasis on the suffering of Iphigenia, which resulted in Katie Mitchell putting the ghost of Iphigenia on stage in the National Theatre production.[34] In *Alcestis*, however, in addition to the expansion and contraction seen in other plays, there is large-scale interpolation of material not in the original. As Michael Walton observes:

Euripides' play, a brief 1163 lines in the Greek is adjusted and stretched with the introduction of five new characters. Two of them, Iolaus and Lichas, are the servants of Heracles who 'enact' the twelve labours. There is also a vision of Prometheus and God who converse with Heracles before the arrival of the talking vulture. The Vulture has two lines, one of which is 'Ah', the other 'No, I am alive and you are not free', before it bursts into flames when Heracles shoots an arrow at it. These are not to be found in Euripides.[35]

It is in these interpolations, I would argue, that we see Hughes return to his early interest in symbolist drama, incorporating it into a pre-existing non-symbolist dramatic framework.

There are early indications in Hughes's version of *Alcestis* of what aspects of the story he will emphasize and the possible interpolation of imagery closely associated with his own poetic imagination. The first large-scale expansion comes early in the play in a speech by Admetos, when reflecting on the impending death of Alcestis (*Al.* 357–62 [OCT]):

> εἰ δ' Ὀρφέως μοι γλῶσσα καὶ μέλος παρῆν,
> ὥστ' ἢ κόρην Δήμητρος ἢ κείνης πόσιν
> ὕμνοισι κηλήσαντά σ' ἐξ Ἅιδου λαβεῖν,
> κατῆλθον ἄν, καί μ' οὔθ' ὁ Πλούτωνος κύων

---

[34] For various responses to the onstage presence of Iphigenia in this production, see Walton (2005: 203–4), Hardwick (2005: 219–21), and, Rehm (2005: 355–8).

[35] Walton (2006: 189). The vulture also has an 11-line speech immediately upon entering describing how it plans to eat Prometheus' liver, which Walton has overlooked. Hughes *A* 74.

οὔθ᾽ οὑπὶ κώπῃ ψυχοπομπὸς ἂν Χάρων
ἔσχον, πρὶν ἐς φῶς σὸν καταστῆσαι βίον.

If I had the voice and music of Orpheus so that I could charm Demeter's daughter or her husband with song and fetch you from Hades, I would have gone down to the Underworld, and neither Pluto's hound nor Charon the ferryman of souls standing at the oar would have kept me from bringing you back to the light alive.[36]

Hughes inflates what was in Euripides' play a six-line passing reference to Orpheus into a nearly thirty-line summary of Orpheus' ill-fated journey into the underworld to retrieve his beloved wife Eurydice:

> I find myself
> Thinking about Orpheus—in the thick of all this.
> Thinking of the impossible.
> How he went down there,
> Into the land of the underworld, the dead land,
> With his guitar and his voice—
> He rode the dark road
> On the thumping of the guitar,
> A horse of music.
> He wrapped himself in his voice,
> Death-proof, a voice of asbestos,
> He went
> Down and down and down.
> You remember—
> He went for his dead wife
> And he nearly got her.
> Death let her go—on one condition.
> Orpheus almost saved her. But—
> He loved her too much, too helplessly.
> He made a little mistake.
> He made it out of love.
> A tiny error—unthinking—
> A glance. Think of it. Only a backward glance.
> And he had done what he should never have done.
> At the crucial moment.
> He lost her.
> Horrible.[37]

---

[36] All translations of Greek are from Kovacs (1994).
[37] A 29–30.

As Sagar notes, Hughes had purposefully avoided the Orpheus story for decades, except for a version for children written in 1970, despite its obvious applicability to his own life after the death of Sylvia Plath: Hughes wrote to Sagar saying it was 'too obvious an attempt to exploit my situation'.[38] However, at the end of his life, in the midst of another work derived from the ancient Greeks which was inevitably going to elicit biographical associations, Hughes includes the myth of Orpheus.

Soon after the expanded Orpheus reference, there is another interpolation which is a shorter but more radical expansion of the text of Euripides. In Euripides' play Admetos, in response to the plaintive cries of his son over the dead body of Alcestis, says (*Al.* 404 [OCT]) τὴν οὐ κλύουσαν οὐδ᾽ ὁρῶσαν, 'she does not hear or see'. In Hughes's text the child has been completely excised from the play, and following the choral announcement that Alcestis is dead, Admetos responds:

> Words!
> Don't you see what has happened?
> She dreamed of the great black bird
> With no eyes in its sockets
> That flew at her, and pecked her—[39]

The loss of the ability to hear is no longer present, and rather than losing sight Alcestis has entered the world of dreams where a large sightless black bird flew at her and pecked her. While this has no antecedent in Euripides, it does evoke Hughes's own poetry: one thinks of the Crow poems and their regular acts of dismemberment, as well the vulture from *Prometheus on his Crag*, which will return towards the end of the play.[40] While these interpolations early in Hughes's version are relatively minor, they are a clear indication that while Hughes may be working within the general dramatic framework of Euripides' play, he is reworking it to accommodate his own poetic and dramatic vision.

By far the largest interpolation in Hughes's version of *Alcestis* is the scene in which the labours of Heracles are enacted, which leads to the

---

[38] On Hughes and the myth of Orpheus, see Sagar (2000: 83–6); see also Sagar and Brown in this volume.
[39] *A* 32.      [40] *CP* 217–72 and 285–96.

freeing of Prometheus.[41] In Euripides' *Alcestis* the re-entrance of the drunken Heracles at line 773 marks the entrance of Heracles as comic buffoon, whose presence is expected on the comic stage, and seems to point the audience towards anticipation of the hitherto absent revelry characteristic of satyr plays.[42] The recapitulation of Heracles' labours in Hughes's version also introduces a new aspect of Heracles' character, pointing to the symbolic motif of the hero quest. As the scene in Hughes's version progresses it moves from its initial appearance of drunken revelry (*A* 60–2), to ritual enactment of the hero quest (62–9), to shamanic visions of the future (69–77). As the shamanic visions begin to appear to Heracles, the drunken revelry is also recast cast as part of the necessary ritual for ascent or descent along the *axis mundi* as Heracles calls out as he moves towards the celestial realm:

> Wait a minute. Give me a drink.
> Prometheus and the vulture![43]

And again:

> I see it! I see it.
> Give me another drink. I see it.
> Prometheus is there, on the crag.
> Look.[44]

Heracles' drinking is no longer behaviour inappropriate to a house in mourning, but a necessary action if he is to assume the shamanic ability to move between realms.

At the same time the line 'Prometheus is there, on the crag' immediately evokes Hughes's collection of twenty-one poems entitled *Prometheus on His Crag* which was written during the

---

[41] It should be noted that in Hughes's interpolated scene eleven of Heracles' twelve labours are acted out, though according to the timeline presented by Euripides and earlier in Hughes's own version, the events of *Alcestis* takes place when Heracles is on his way to Thrace to complete the eighth labour, taming the man-eating horses of Diomedes. See *Al.* 476–506 (OCT), Hughes *A* 37–40.

[42] For a discussion of the manifestation of various aspects of Heracles' character on the ancient stage, see Silk (1985). For the lack of expected revelry in *Alcestis*, see Marshall (2000: 229–38).

[43] *A* 71.        [44] *A* 72.

composition and production of the play *Orghast*.[45] In *Orghast* too, the central myth was the myth of Prometheus. In that play, Hughes also evoked the myth of Heracles slaughtering his family, dramatized in Euripides' *Heracles*, when the character Krogon slaughters his family, believing them to be evil birds.[46] This is significant because this myth is also evoked in Hughes's version of *Alcestis* and intertwined with the evocation of the myth of Heracles freeing Prometheus:

| | |
|---|---|
| IOLAUS: | You had a strange nightmare. |
| | A horrifying dream. Your dream became famous. |
| | You told it and they made a play about it. |
| | You're getting your dream mixed up with what |
| |     will happen. |
| | You're thinking of that play. |
| HERACLES: | What was that play? |
| | The madness of Heracles. Was that the title? |
| | What did I do in that play? |
| IOLAUS: | You did it in a dream. |
| HERACLES: | I see my wife. I see my dead wife. |
| | Who killed her? |
| IOLAUS: | It was not like that. |
| | You climbed a mountain. Remember?[47] |

Again, Hughes's chronology is confused in a number of ways. The slaughter of Heracles' family is generally positioned before his labours begin, though in Euripides' play the slaughter takes place as he returns home from having completed all twelve labours. Either way, the slaughter of his family is at a substantial remove from the freeing of Prometheus, which is not mentioned in Euripides' *Heracles*. It is in these chronological fissures, however, that we see most clearly the grafting of Hughes's poetic imagination onto the pre-existing dramatic framework.

---

[45] *Orghast* was a collaborative project between Hughes and Peter Brook and was performed at the Fifth Shiraz Festival in Iran in 1971. Building on a language created by Hughes for the production, the play was largely improvised around this language and central myths, and no text was published. For a discussion of the play, see Smith (1972).

[46] See Smith (1972: 98).

[47] *A* 70. See in this volume Sagar and Brown.

There are two important aspects of the Prometheus interlude, which extends for almost a hundred and forty lines. The first is the nature of the vulture. In *Orghast* Hughes envisioned the vulture as being female. As Hirschberg describes it, 'Hughes [was] once again transforming the myths surrounding Prometheus in a way that displaces the eagle as the bird of Zeus with an image of the devouring feminine projected in the form of a horrendous vulture.'[48] In *Alcestis* Hughes also uses female pronouns of the vulture, with Heracles saying:

> I have nailed her onto the sun with a laser
> More powerful than the sun.
> There she can blaze and glow and be consumed
> And shrivel to harmless atoms
> And vanish into the great good light. Prometheus!
> Your torturer is dead.[49]

Given the use of the female pronoun there is no reason to assume that Hughes had changed his mind about the nature of the vulture, which 'has the character of an overwhelming, devouring, demonic maternal force: the principle of nurturing gone terribly wrong.'[50] In Hughes's *Alcestis* Heracles frees Prometheus by twice shooting the vulture with his arrows, which is followed by the repetition of the line 'You are dead and Prometheus is free' four times in short order.[51] Hughes has described Prometheus as

fractured. He is at the crossroads of eternal life and ecstasy and temporal doom, pain, change and death. Conscious in eternity he has to live in time. And he cannot solve his dilemma. He hangs between heaven and earth almost torn apart, an open wound, immortal.[52]

In the act of freeing Prometheus, Heracles heals the wound and releases him from his captivity at these crossroads.

How this relates to the rest of Hughes's *Alcestis* is not readily clear, but some tentative steps can be made towards an understanding of how this interlude might function within the play. The imagery of the vulture eating away at the immortal Prometheus ought to be associated with the image of the large black bird flying at and pecking

---

[48] Hirschberg (1981: 130).    [49] *A* 75.    [50] Hirschberg (1981: 130).
[51] Hughes (1999: 75–8).    [52] See Smith (1972: 94).

Alcestis. The attack kills her because she is not an immortal. The reasons why both Alcestis and Prometheus are being attacked by these large black birds also links the characters: the attacks are in both cases the result of selfless sacrifice for others. Unlike the story of Orpheus, both of these stories end with the promise of hope, which is the message Hughes explicitly ends his *Alcestis* with, despite the fact that it is not in the original.[53] Hughes integrates the Heracles and Prometheus interlude into the *Alcestis* story by having Heracles make the claim that,

> Every labour so far has served
> Only to prepare me for this.[54]

In Hughes's play Heracles revels in his labours, and there is no sense of the compulsion of slavery under which he carries them out. When warned about the dangers of Diomedes' man-eating horses, Heracles responds:

> I've never refused a fight. To tell you the truth—
> I have to admit it—I like fighting.
> It seems to keep me healthy.[55]

Euripides has Heracles respond to the risk of the labour (*Al.* 487 [OCT]):

> ἀλλ' οὐδ' ἀπειπεῖν μὴν πόνους οἷόν τ' ἐμοί

> But all the same, I cannot decline these labours.

This indicates not that he relishes the task, but rather that he has no choice in the matter. For Hughes, through the imaginative scene of the re-enactment of Heracles' labours and the shamanistic scene of the freeing of Prometheus, coupled with the rescue of Alcestis from the underworld, the use of regenerative energies and a healing process are carried out at both the divine and human levels.

While this is by no means a complete examination of the ways in which Hughes imposes his poetic imagination into his version of

---

[53] Hughes's play ends with the line 'Let this give man hope.' *A* 103. Euripides' play ends with the far less optimistic (*Al.* 1163 [OCT]) τοιόνδ' ἀπέβη τόδε πρᾶγμα, 'Such was the outcome of this story.'
[54] *A* 81.     [55] *A* 40.

*Alcestis*, it does point to a number of ways in which Hughes's play develops its original. It is far more interested in mythic motifs or archetypes, such as Orpheus, than is the original play. Heracles is reimagined as a completely different character, with mantic qualities never ascribed to him in antiquity, and with different motives and different mechanisms for carrying out his difficult tasks, such as moving between realms. He becomes for Hughes a shaman, and this links him with Orpheus. But he is a shaman who reconfigures the world through violence, akin to Dionysus in the *Bacchae*. The insertion of Prometheus and the association of his punishment with the death of Alcestis, again reimagines the poetic symbolism of the play, particularly through the imagery of the dismembering vulture. This symbolism also introduces the idea of regeneration, which again is not associated with Euripides's original. In Euripides' play the tone of the ending is notoriously ambiguous, but Hughes affirms life with regeneration, healing, and restitution on a number of levels.

# 15

## Classics reanimated: Ted Hughes and reflexive translation

*Sarah Annes Brown*

Over the last few decades we have seen something of a return to the practices of the eighteenth century in that leading poets have chosen to display their art through the medium of translation, particularly translation of classical texts. Many of these translations are consciously updated, bearing clear traces of their creators' cultural context and political position. Thus Tom Paulin's *The Riot Act* (1985), a version of *Antigone*, is set in the early days of the Troubles in Northen Ireland and Tony Harrison's adaptation of *Lysistrata*, *The Common Chorus* (1992), is a response to the Greenham Common protests.[1] The translations of Hughes, by contrast, might at first seem comparatively 'neutral'. But any translation written by a poet as celebrated as Hughes, one moreover whose private life has been the focus of so much scrutiny, inevitably invites the reader to read the translation as an assertion of the translator's personality as well as a vector for the original poet's work.[2] The Poet Laureate will get top billing as it were, whereas the personality of the professional translator is subsumed by his source, becoming almost invisible.[3]

[1] See Hardwick (2000) for an extended discussion of the impact of the translator's cultural context on the act of translation.

[2] See Weissbort (2006: viii) on the 'Hughesian' quality of his translations.

[3] As Venuti (1995: 8) observes: 'The translator's invisibility is thus a weird self-annihilation, a way of conceiving and practising translation that undoubtedly reinforces its marginal status in Anglo-American culture . . . The typical mention of the translation in a review takes the form of a brief aside in which, more often than not, the transparency of the translation is gauged'.

Ted Hughes's many responses to classical texts avoid this invisibility by dramatizing the translator's relationship with his classical precursors and also his place within a wider literary tradition. I hope to demonstrate how Hughes makes his presence felt in his translations from the classics, how he appears to insert himself into the text in various ways. This is partly done, paradoxically, by also inserting the original author back into the poem. In a treatise on translation written in 1791 A. F. Tytler asserted that the translator 'must adopt the very soul of his author, which must speak through his own organs'.[4] This passive position as a kind of spirit medium or sibyl is countered if, as I would argue Hughes is doing in *Tales from Ovid,* the original poet is changed from an agent and creator into an interlocutor and object of scrutiny.

In the first poem of *Tales from Ovid,* 'Creation', Ted Hughes's translation of Ovid's opening invocation is subtly altered. When Hughes's narrator addresses the gods he inserts a line missing from the *Metamorphoses*: 'You did it for your own amusement'.[5] A little later Ovid's line *hanc deus et melior litem natura diremit* 'God—or kindlier nature—composed this strife' (1.21) becomes 'God, or some artist as resourceful, | Began to sort it out'.[6] The description of the power and artistry of the gods needs to be tweaked only a little to suggest the figure of Ovid the creating poet. Such adjustments combine to suggest that Hughes is both translating Ovid addressing the gods and, in the same breath, addressing Ovid himself. This coexistence of Hughes's own distinctive poetic persona with that of his model allows the translator autonomy and visibility.

In another slightly altered passage Hughes once again inserts a line with no equivalent in the *Metamorphoses*: 'descend *again,* be pleased to *reanimate* | This *revival* of those marvels'.[7] Even the reader who does not have Ovid's text to hand may detect the presence of the translator here in the insistent emphasis on repetition.[8] The marvels are the *Metamorphoses* of Ovid as well as the metamorphoses of the gods and Hughes is seeking inspiration from Ovid himself. There is a kind of contradiction here. On the one hand, if Hughes is indeed in some sense addressing Ovid in these lines, then he is inhabiting

---

[4] Tytler in Huntsman (1978: 212).     [5] *CP* 865.     [6] *CP* 866.
[7] *CP* 865, italics mine.     [8] See also Brown (1999: 13).

precisely the passive role prescribed by Tytler through treating his source text as a kind of heavenly muse. However, because an address to Ovid is, by definition, a swerve away from the original, Hughes's move is one of self-assertion as well as self-abnegation.

The association which Hughes's translation encourages us to trace between Ovid and the creating gods typifies a more general tendency for authors to become associated with numinous figures in their own works. We talk of a text's 'afterlife' as though it were a kind of ghost haunting the present, and fictional ghosts sometimes become associated with their creators. For example, Marjorie Garber makes a connection between the ghost of Hamlet's father and Shakespeare:

> The Ghost is Shakespeare. He is the one who comes as a revenant, belatedly instated, regarded as originally authoritative, rather than retrospectively and retroactively canonized, and deriving increased authority from this very instatement of authority backward, over time ... We know that Shakespeare played the part of the Ghost in *Hamlet*. What could not be foreseen, except through anamorphic reading, was that he would *become* that Ghost.[9]

Closer to Hughes is an example from *The Tempest*; Prospero's speech beginning 'Ye elves of hills, brooks, standing lakes and groves | And ye that on the sands with printless foot | Do chase the ebbing Neptune...' (5.1.33–5) closely follows Medea's similar invocation of supernatural beings in the *Metamorphoses*:

> dique omnes nemorum, dique omnes noctis adeste,
> quorum ope, cum volui, ripis mirantibus amnes
> in fontes rediere suos ...

> ... all ye gods of the groves, all ye gods of the night: be with me now. With your help when I have willed it, the streams have run back to their fountainheads ...

> *Metamorphoses* 7.198–200[10]

But whereas Prospero is about to renounce his magic Medea is determined to use her powers to destroy her enemies. Through this near quotation, particularly because it seems so incongruous, Shakespeare makes anyone who is familiar with the source summon Ovid to mind, through a kind of literary necromancy, and thus turns

---

[9] Garber (1987: 176).
[10] Translations of the *Metamorphoses* taken from Miller (1916).

Ovid into the subject as well as the original author of Prospero's assertion: 'graves at my command | Have waked their sleepers' (5.1.48–9). As Raphael Lyne puts it, there is 'a dead presence who is walking the stage at the very point that Prospero describes the graves opening, and that is Ovid'.[11] Similarly in Hughes's text, the mysterious gods of Ovid's opening lines are half-metamorphosed into the long-dead, almost legendary poet. In both examples, Ovid is translated into his own poem.

In another suggestive passage from the beginning of *Tales from Ovid*, concerned with each element finding its place at the beginning of the world's creation, Hughes again departs somewhat from the original. Ovid writes:

> quae postquam evolvit caecoque exemit acervo,
> dissociata locis concordi pace ligavit.

When thus he had released these elements and freed them from the blind heap of things, he set them each in its own place and bound them fast in harmony.

*Metamorphoses* 1.24–5

Hughes elaborates:

> He gave to each its place
> Independent, gazing about freshly,
> Also resonating—
> Each one a harmonic of the others,
> Just like the strings
> That would resound, one day, in the dome of the tortoise.[12]

This passage already has a potential metapoetic force in Ovid: it adumbrates the way the poem's tales are both self-sufficient and interrelated. But once translated it becomes a description of intertextual as well as intratextual links, of the relationship between the *Metamorphoses* and its many imitations and translations. Certainly there are special resonances in the translations of Ted Hughes which depend on the reader's sense of the original, and thus of the gaps between the two. A reader who comes to Hughes after Ovid hears a chord, not a single note.

---

[11] Lyne (2000: 159).     [12] *CP* 866.

This kind of double presence in the text, an impression of co-authorship, is a common feature of translation and may be achieved in various different ways. One of the most immediately identifiable markers of the translator as a visible presence is anachronism. A striking early example of this is the seventeenth-century poet George Sandys' rendition of Ovid's sly comment on the dwellings of the gods:

> hic locus est, quem, si verbis audacia detur,
> haud timeam magni dixisse Palatia caeli.

This is the place which, if I may make bold to say it, I would not fear to call the Palatia of high heaven.

*Metamorphoses* 1.175–6

> This glorious Roofe I would not doubt to call,
> Had I but boldnesse lent mee, Heaven's *White-Hall.*

Here the updated reference enriches the original partly because the gap between 'Palatia' and 'Whitehall' complements and extends the original Palatia/heaven pairing.[13]

Another variation is employed by the American poet Paul Blackburn. In his version of Guillem de Poitou's Provençal poem 'Ben vuelh que sapchon li pluzor' the collision of registers draws attention to the processes of translation:

> I would like it if people knew this song,
> a lot of them, if it prove to be okay
> when I bring it in from my atelier, all
> fine and shining:
> for I surpass the flower of this business,
> it's the truth, and I'll
> produce the vers (*sic*) as witness
> when I've bound it in rhyme.[14]

Here the remnants of a lexis which is both archaic and French are allowed to shine through Blackburn's obtrusive modernization.

The polyphonic effect Hughes creates in his translation of the elements passage, that sense of the translator's voice speaking

---

[13]  The Latin *Palatia* denoted the Roman imperial palace complex on the Palatine Hill.
[14]  Blackburn in Economou (1978).

alongside that of Ovid, just slightly out of sync or on a different note, is not an isolated occurrence. Hughes's voice contaminates other speakers in the poem as well as Ovid himself. Thisbe seems to escape from her Ovidian setting in order to remind us that she is now part of a larger, post-classical, literary landscape. She and Pyramus arrange to meet:

> Their rendezvous the mulberry tree
> Over the tomb of Ninus, *a famous landmark*.[15]

The last phrase is not in Ovid; we may infer that the 'landmark' is literary as well as geographical, 'famous' because it is immortalized as 'Ninny's tomb' by Shakespeare's Francis Flute, the bellows-mender. Thus rather than Ovid speaking through the organs of Hughes, to use Tytler's image, it is Hughes who makes use of Ovid's narrating persona to communicate a modern perspective. Thus Hughes's translation doesn't seem to seek to neutralize or erase the gap between himself and his source but rather to acknowledge the processes of reception, and the cumulative effects of a story's continued repetition.

Hughes's more pervasive and substantial alterations to Ovid's tale of Pygmalion similarly flag the translated status of his version. In his account of the myth, control seems to be wrested away from Pygmalion, and the creation of the statue is initiated by the spirit of the statue herself who comes to him in a dream:

> Though this dream
> Was not so much the dream of a perfect woman
> As of a spectre, sick of unbeing,
> That had taken possession of his body
> To find herself a life.
>
> She moved into his hands,
> She took possession of his fingers
> And began to sculpt a perfect woman.[16]

Ovid is traditionally associated with Pygmalion—writer and artist have a shared genius for simulating nature, for creation. By altering the story, making Pygmalion seem to be possessed by an existing female spirit, Hughes seems to indicate the difference between

---

[15] *CP* 1038, my italics.          [16] *CP* 965.

original composition and translation. As a 'spectre' she figures the original story waiting to be given new life in a fresh medium, to be translated rather than created.[17]

This sense of a pre-existing story is equally present in Hughes's translation of Racine's *Phèdre* (1677), itself a response to Euripides' *Hippolytus*. Here Hughes intensifies the characters' sense of their fame (or notoriety). For example, Phèdre seems to have a metatheatrical sense of being on show not present in the original French where her worry about self-betrayal is directed specifically at Oenone, her confidante:

> Je te laisse trop voir mes honteuses douleurs,
> Et mes yeux, malgré moi, se remplissent de pleurs.
>
> > (1.3.183–4)

I let you see too easily my shameful sorrow. And my eyes, in spite of myself, fill with tears.

> 'I can't hide it—everybody
> stares into my shame and its secret.
> I can't control this weeping.'[18]

Hughes's Hippolytus, like his Thisbe, apparently possesses an ana-chronistic awareness of his own (literary) reputation. Racine's 'C'est par-là [i.e. his 'haine des forfaits'] qu'Hippolyte est connu dans la Grèce' (4.2.1109), 'It is for that reason [i.e. his hatred of crime] that Hippolytus is known in Greece', becomes 'my aversion to it is a legend'.[19] The phrase 'is a legend' is scarcely a distortion of *connu*, but in the context of a speaker who is literally a legend, the idiom is hardly neutral.

Another slight shift creates the sense of an awareness in Theseus that he is a translation:

> De l'univers entier je voudrais me bannir.
> Tout semble s'élever contre mon injustice.
> L'éclat de mon nom même augmente mon supplice.
>
> > (4.7.1608–10)

I would like to banish myself from the entire universe. Everything seems to rise up against my injustice. The very splendour of my name increases my agony.

---

[17] My analysis of this section of *Tales from Ovid* is indebted to Garrett Jacobsen.
[18] D 9.       [19] P 54.

Even if I found another universe
This memory would be with me.
Everything proclaims what I have done.
My very fame blazes with my shame.[20]

Whereas Racine's Theseus is simply banished from the (only) universe, Hughes's Theseus entertains the possibility of finding an alternate universe, gesturing towards the translated text's transplantation into a very different, modern world.

Perhaps the most striking of such changes comes in Act III:

Je connais mes fureurs, je les rappelle toutes.
Il me semble déjà que ces murs, que ces voûtes
Vont prendre la parole, et prêts à m'accuser,
Attendent mon époux, pour le désabuser.

(3.3.853–6)

I know my furious outbursts, I remember them all. It seems to me already that the walls, that these vaults, are going to begin to speak and, prepared to accuse me, are waiting for my husband in order to undeceive him.

I have not forgotten my ravings.
Every gasp is still alive in me.
Even these walls remember them,
these ceilings are saturated with them,
Every room and passage in this palace
Is bursting to shout my secret
And accuse me. The air is quivering with it.

(*P* 43)

Here the passage is greatly intensified, and in Hughes (though not in Racine) the walls share with Phèdre the capacity for memory.[21] In the context of a performance, probably one which takes place on a stage which has witnessed other versions of Phèdre's story, the capacity to generate a metatheatrical charge through the allusion to the theatrical space's own 'memory' is intensified.

Many of Hughes's most substantial translations were of classical or neoclassical tragedies. In their earliest forms tragedies typically show humans as the victims of inexorable fate. However in later versions of the best-known tragic narratives literary tradition begins to reinforce

---

[20] *P*79.     [21] See Berry (2001: 220).

and even replace fate.[22] Just as we saw Ovid possibly turning into the very gods he invoked at the opening of the poem, so tragedians can in effect take over the gods' role as arbiters of fate, particularly in a modern, more secular, phase of a tragedy's afterlife. The protagonist falls less because the gods say he must than because Aeschylus or Sophocles wrote that it was so. In Hughes's translations the characters seem to have learnt from these processes—to know that their fates are written in books as well as in the stars. This quality is not of course Hughes's invention. Parallel effects are especially apparent in the plays of Seneca who, as a Roman playwright, was conscious of the cultural and temporal gap separating his own age from the Greek settings of most of his plays. A sense of belatedness is created by the Romanized atmosphere which pervades his *Medea* for example, as when the chorus (113) alludes to *Fescennina carmina*, a specifically Italian reference to a kind of fleering verse named after Fescennia, a small city on the Tiber. The metatheatricality is heightened by a persistent ambiguity in the play's many references to the past. These might either evoke Medea's personal past, her earlier life and particularly her horrific murder of her brother, or else her literary life as a tragic antiheroine.[23] Increasingly the heroine herself seems burdened with a sense of *déjà lu*, of acting a part written down for her and which she cannot escape. 'Medea nunc sum', 'now I am Medea' (910), she exclaims at the crisis, as though conscious of the role she must inhabit and aware of her own notoriety, almost as though for her, as for us, Medea (like Hughes's Hippolytus) was already a legend.[24] Similarly in many of Hughes's translations his characters' awareness of the future suggests that they have almost stepped out of their roles and have become metatheatrically aware of their drama as an unchanging and endlessly repeated cycle, *Groundhog Day* style.[25]

A similar quality is apparent in Hughes's translation of Seneca's *Oedipus*. This example is particularly striking because Jocasta is given

---

[22] See Eagleton (2003: 101–3). See also my introduction to Brown and Silverstone (2007).

[23] On the metatheatricality of the play see Boyle (1997: 122–33).

[24] Elizabethan and Jacobean revenge dramas, in particular *Hamlet*, offer a similarly metatheatrical type of tragedy, conscious of generic predecessors. A similar self-consciousness is present in many of Euripides's plays, in particular the recognition scene in *Electra*.

[25] *Groundhog Day* (1993) dir. Harold Ramis.

precise knowledge which, within the fiction of the play, she should not yet have. She seems to foretell both the deaths of Eteocles and Polyneices and her own imminent suicide. (In fact, despite the reference to 'ropes' here, Seneca's Jocasta, by contrast with Sophocles's, stabs rather than hangs herself.)

> when I carried my sons
> I carried them for death I carried them for the throne
> I carried them for final disaster when I carried my first son
> did I know what was coming did I know
> what ropes of blood were twisting together what bloody footprints
> were hurrying together in my body . . . [26]

The prescience of Hughes's Agamemnon is contaminated with a different kind of anachronistic knowledge. At the beginning of Aeschylus' *Agamemnon* we are reminded of the king's earlier sacrifice of Iphigenia after being advised by the seer Calchas that Artemis needed to be appeased. The chorus' account of Agamemnon's response to this news, as translated by Hughes, reveals a very heightened sense of his place within history, a detachment and sense of perspective not clearly present in the original:

Then the elder king spake and said: 'Hard is my fate to refuse obedience, and hard, if I must slay my child, the glory of my home, and at the altar-side stain with streams of a virgin's blood a father's hand.'

(Aeschylus, *Agamemnon* translated by Weir Smyth, vol. 2, ll. 205–10)

> If I obey the goddess, and kill my daughter—
> What do I become?
> A monster to myself, to the whole world,
> And to all future time, a monster—
> Weaving my daughter's bloody dress
> Like a turban. The King of cruelty
> Painting my royal palace afresh
> With her blood, the blood of Iphigenia.
> Perfuming my bath, after the battle,
> With the blood of Iphigenia.
> Filling the drinking cups of my family
> With the blood of Iphigenia—
> This is how I shall live on in men's minds.[27]

---

[26] *SO* 16–7.　　[27] *O* 13.

Agamemnon here describes the death of Iphigenia in terms which suggest a repeated action, mirroring the many performances and adaptations of Aeschylus' famous tragedy. The emphasis on memorial and on drinking her blood from cups is still more striking. It suggests on the one hand simply the horrific power of such a bloody deed but also the Christian sacrament of communion in which the blood of a sacrificed child is symbolically drunk.

A similar hint at Christianization can be found in Hughes's translation of Euripides' *Alcestis*. Apollo's opening speech is translated extremely freely by Hughes and the following lines have no equivalent in Euripides:

> Perhaps you have heard this story.
> The great god, the greatest of the gods,
> The maker of the atom,
> Is a jealous god.[28]

Two details here contribute to the sense that Hughes is responding to the complex processes of reception here—first, 'Perhaps you have heard this story' acknowledges the familiarity of the tragedy, secondly, the reference to the 'jealous god' inevitably imports the Judaeo-Christian tradition into the translation, acknowledging the difficulty of disentangling it from our reception of this or any other classical tragedy.

*Alcestis* is a particularly interesting case within Hughes's body of translations. I suggested earlier that the voices of Hughes and Ovid coexist in the narrative persona of *Tales from Ovid*. Similarly we are extremely aware of Hughes as a presence within *Alcestis* because of the resonances with his own biography. Whether or not the biographical record is accurate, and whatever Hughes's own intentions in translating *Alcestis*, the effect on the modern reader for whom 'Ted and Sylvia' is essentially a narrative, a modern myth, is to make him or her read Hughes's *Alcestis* through the lens of the translator's biography.[29] The curious remark he allegedly made to Helder Macedo, 'Helder, you must know it was either her or me' obtrudes into our response to a play which dramatizes a similarly stark

---

[28] *A* 1.

[29] There are comparable parallels with the story of Orpheus and Eurydice. See Bundtzen (2000).

dilemma.[30] Admetos, doomed to death by the gods, can evade his fate only by finding someone else to die in his place. Although his parents refuse to sacrifice their lives, his wife Alcestis agrees to become his replacement. However the play ends happily when Heracles intervenes to rescue her from death and she and Admetos are reunited.

Admetos is at best an equivocal figure. Although he regrets the loss of his wife he does not refuse her offer and is thus ultimately responsible for her death. Hughes's words to Helder almost sound like the confession of a murderer, as though in some way (like Admetos) he chose to sacrifice Plath to save himself. This suggestion of guilt and responsibility (exacerbated by his affair with Assia Wevill) encourages the reader to identify links between Hughes and Admetos. The reader of Feinstein's biography of Hughes may feel further encouraged to import it into a reading of his *Alcestis* by the description of Assia Wevill's response to Plath's suicide: 'her response to hearing the news—as Macedo remembers it—was to view Sylvia's suicide as an act of aggression against herself'.[31] This sketch of a passive-aggressive Plath may easily be mapped onto Alcestis for she seems fully conscious of the nobility of her actions and somewhat disdainful of her husband.[32]

Because it has animation at its heart *Alcestis* seems almost to invite translation or reinvention. Like the lines from *Phèdre* quoted above, its repetition has an inbuilt reflexive potential. The revival of Alcestis figures the revival of *Alcestis*. But in the case of Hughes's translation there is a further intertextual twist, an additional 'revival', for his *Alcestis* invites comparison (though this may not have been Hughes's intention) with Robert Browning's 'Balaustion's Adventure' (1871).

'Balaustion's Adventure' is a lengthy narrative poem set in the fifth century BC during the Peloponnesian War, a drawn-out conflict between Athens and Sparta, and derives from an account written in the first century CE by the Greek historian Plutarch in his *Life of Nicias*. Plutarch tells how the Sicilians helped a party of fleeing

---

[30] See Feinstein (2001: 165–6).

[31] Feinstein (2001: 145).

[32] In her review of the translation Kate Clanchy observes, countering suggestions of an affinity between Alcestis and Plath, 'Plath did not die to save her husband—indeed she may well have died partly to spite him', (2000: 50). But I would argue that Clanchy fails to acknowledge the potential for a spiteful reading of Alcestis' actions.

Athenians because they were so delighted by their knowledge of Euripides. Browning's poem is narrated by Balaustion, a young girl who is presented as an expert on Euripides. Most of the poem consists of her free rendition of *Alcestis* as a narrative (with commentary) rather than a drama, and typifies Browning's mastery of the dramatic monologue—his young female narrator may be compared with Pompilia, the heroine of 'The Ring and the Book' (1868–9).

Feinstein writes of Hughes and Plath: 'There can be few marriages between poets of such equal gifts in English literature.'[33] The Brownings were comparably well matched. Although Robert Browning's reputation has steadily maintained a lead over that of his wife, Elizabeth Barrett Browning was a celebrated poet in her own right, more famous than her younger husband when they first met, and a serious candidate for the Laureateship after Wordsworth's death. Although their marriage was very different from that of Hughes and Plath, both relationships captured the public imagination and both have been successfully dramatized as films. As Barrett Browning died of natural causes rather than through suicide, 'Balaustion's Adventure' does not invite an autobiographical reading in the same way as Hughes's *Alcestis* does. However some readers have detected a connection between Robert Browning's guilt following his marriage proposal to Lady Ashburton and Alcestis' anxiety that Admetos should never remarry.[34] But although Browning himself ensured that we should remember his wife when reading the poem, he does not highlight possible parallels between her and Alcestis. Instead, his use of the frame narrative distracts us from the affinities between Alcestis and Elizabeth Barrett Browning because Balaustion herself recalls Elizabeth's voice, in particular her autobiographical 'Aurora Leigh'. The connection is emphasized by the poem's epigraph which is taken from Barrett Browning's own poetic praise of Euripides in her poem 'The Wine of Cyprus':

> Our Euripides, the human
> With his droppings of warm tears,
> And his touches of things common
> Till they rose to touch the spheres.

---

[33]  Feinstein (2001: 62).
[34]  See Irvine and Honan (1974: 458–60).

Browning thus prepares the reader to identify Balaustion, a 'lyric girl' who loves Euripides, with his own dead wife.[35]

Browning in a sense occludes his own presence as the translator and poet here through his surrogate Balaustion. Like him she is a kind of translator—she is explicitly changing and altering Euripides, most obviously by changing *Alcestis* from a play to a poem. So where we might have said 'what is Robert Browning doing with Euripides?' we are more instinctively inclined to ask 'what is Balaustion doing with Euripides?' Self-conscious gestures which we would normally ascribe to the translator—of the same kind we saw in Hughes's *Alcestis*—are here ascribed to Balaustion, the internal translator or adaptor. Here for example she reflects on the way different poets can refashion myths, playing on the idea of poets as creating gods breathing new life into old stories about reviving, implicitly gesturing towards the reflexivity of *rewriting* a play about *reviving* a corpse.

> You, I, or anyone might mould a new
> Admetos, new Alkestis. Ah, that brave
> Bounty of poets, the one royal race
> That ever was, or will be, in this world!
> They give no gift that bounds itself and ends
> I' the giving and the taking: theirs so breeds
> I' the heart and soul o' the taker, so transmutes
> The man who was only a man before,
> That he grows godlike in his turn, can give—
> He also: shares the poets' privilege,
> Bring forth new good, new beauty, from the old.
>
> ('Balaustion's Adventure' ll.2415–25)

Thus it would seem that Browning is not making the expected move—representing his dead wife as the reanimated Alcestis—but is in fact reanimating Elizabeth in another sense by making her the model for his narrator. And Browning is not simply reanimating her—he makes *her* a reanimator, the figure of the self-conscious adapting poet bringing Euripides to life.

But we can still excavate submerged links between the active Balaustion and the more passive Alcestis. Balaustion, like Alcestis,

---

[35] Browning 'Balaustion's Adventure' l.186, edited by Dooley (1999).

cheats death through the intercession of Heracles, for she asks to be taken to the Sicilians' temple of Heracles that he may 'bid you set us free.' (234) The link is made still more explicit when Balaustion comments:

> For had not Herakles a second time
> Wrestled with Death and saved devoted ones? (258–9)

She is simultaneously saviour and saved, creator and artefact, and surrogate both for the living male poet and his dead wife.

Hughes's *Alcestis* is in some ways a more straightforward translation. The dramatic form is of course retained—there is no frame narrative. But although there is no important completely new character (such as Balaustion) the role of Heracles is enlarged by Hughes in by far the most prominent change to Euripides. In the middle of the play, after the servant's complaint about Heracles' behaviour as per Euripides, Hughes adds a long scene in which Heracles drunkenly acts out his labours with the help of servants. Heracles' speeches are raw, ebullient and full of references to animals—to the boars, birds, and bulls he subdued over the course of the labours. In his review of the translation David Gervais suggestively likens Hercules' speeches to 'a sort of knockabout *Crow*.'[36]

> Heracles grapples with the hydra
> That rises from the mud of the magma
> Out of which the round earth bubbled.
> Seven heads belch poison gas.
> Seven throats jet venom.
> And every head he crushes with his club
> Doubles into two new heads . . . [37]

> And here comes the crab, hydra's little brother,
> To help the hydra.[38]

Because this is all non-Euripidean material it seems more particularly Hughes's own voice and (tentatively) invites an identification between Heracles and Hughes. I have observed how gods and ghosts in texts can become identified with those texts' authors. Other surrogates are perhaps best suited to poets who are also translators

---

[36] Gervais (2001: 147).     [37] *A* 50.     [38] *A* 51.

and the role of Heracles, a reviver who brings the dead back to life, invites identification with his translator, here Hughes, who has revived this ancient play.[39] Hughes's Heracles seems to step outside the play-world partly because he instigates the non-Euripidean material, partly because he knows what will happen in the future, foretelling all his labours, even those which are not yet completed.

There may be a further reason for Hughes and Heracles to become identified at the point of the reception. Although she casts doubt on the anecdote, Elaine Feinstein alludes to a similar moment of revelry out-of-place following the death of Sylvia Plath:

Some time in February, Assia invited a number of people, including Lucas Myers, to come round and help cheer Ted up. Records were played but it was a far cry from the noisy party with bongo drums described by Plath's downstairs neighbour, Dr Thomas, who later wrote about the apparent callousness of such a gathering in a memoir.[40]

If Hughes is projecting himself as Heracles it may be because he prefers to identify himself as the saviour of Alcestis rather than identify with her husband Admetos who allows her to die in his place.[41] This identification between Heracles and poet translator is in a sense implicit in 'Balaustion's Adventure' for Browning 'revives' his wife in his poet heroine. But in Hughes's *Alcestis* this identification (if it is present) is problematic. According to some traditions Heracles killed his own wife and children in a fit of madness.[42] This action is not referred to by Euripides but intrudes uncannily into Hughes's additions to the text.[43] Heracles foretells the episode with horror but is distracted and soothed by Iolaus, his attendant. Both characters' weird prescience can of course be seen as a tacit comment on the text's translated, belated status. Iolaus explains to his master:

---

[39] The 'Medea' speech from *The Tempest* is again a useful analogue here. Prospero, who asserts that he is a reviver of the dead, has traditionally been associated with Shakespeare himself, a refashioner of old tales.

[40] Feinstein (2001: 166–7).

[41] Although Kate Clanchy's observation, (2000: 50), that Hughes makes Admetos considerably more sympathetic than he is in Euripides would be consistent with an identification between Hughes and Admetos.

[42] See for example Pausanias 9.11.2 and Apollodorus 1.183, 1.185.

[43] Heracles' madness was the subject of plays by Sophocles, Euripides, and Seneca.

> You had a strange nightmare
> A horrifying dream. Your dream became famous.
> You told it and they made a play about it.
> You're getting your dream mixed up with what will happen.
> You're thinking of that play.
> **Heracles:** What was the play?
> The Madness of Heracles. Was that the title?[44]

Both Heracles the character and Hughes the translator could be said to be using the reanimation of Alcestis (literal in Heracles' case, literary in Hughes's) as a way of deflecting their feelings of guilt (however undeserved) about the deaths of their own wives. Heracles' flash-forward to his tragic madness might suggest for the reader familiar with Hughes's biography the further horror in store for the poet following the loss of his wife. Assia Wevill killed herself and her daughter six years after Plath's suicide.[45]

The arts of biography and translation have something in common. Both make material available to a wider audience incapable of accessing the original. And both, in their different ways, are repetitions. In the case of Christine Jeff's biographical film *Sylvia*, the effect is similar to that I have identified in many translations of tragedies. The scriptwriter's invention (or selectivity) ensures that the characters seem to have an uncanny premonition of their own fate. In fact, inevitably, the celluloid Sylvia seems as devoted to death as Alcestis does at the beginning of her play. Soon after their first meeting Hughes recites to Plath lines spoken by Romeo to Juliet. The prolepsis of death is strengthened by the fact that these words are actually spoken when Romeo believes Juliet to be dead:

> Ah dear Juliet,
> Why art thou yet so fair? Shall I believe
> That unsubstantial death is amorous,
> And that the lean abhorred monster keeps
> Thee here in dark to be his paramour?
>
> (*Romeo and Juliet*, 5.3.101–5)

---

[44]  *A* 55–6. The play referred to here may be Seneca's *Hercules Furens* or Sophocles' *Trachiniae*.
[45]  For a recent extended account of Hughes's relationship with Wevill see Koren and Negev (2006).

Sylvia's apparent (over)determination to die is established in a conversation between her and a female friend in which she quotes from her poem 'Panther', referring to Hughes as a 'black marauder' and asserting that 'one day I'll have my death of him'. To see Gwyneth Paltrow acting the part of Plath is in a sense to see Plath rise from the dead like the shade of the dead poet in Hughes's translations. This revenant quality is impressed upon the viewer from the start, for the film's long opening shot is of Plath lying down as though dead until her eyes start open with the uncanny suddenness of a revived corpse. Like so many of Hughes's own tragic protagonists—Phèdre and Hippolytus, for example—this Ted and Sylvia seem to be re-enacting rather than just enacting their own private tragedy.

# 16

## Beyond tragedy: Ted Hughes, Racine, and Euripides

### David Gervais

> . . . a feeling of reconciliation that is painful, a kind of *unhappy blessedness* in misfortune.[1]
>
> (Hegel on *Romeo and Juliet*)

There is a sense in which Hughes's poetry always gravitated towards tragedy. From the outset, he saw nature as 'red in tooth and claw'. In 'Thrushes', for example:

> More coiled steel than living—a poised
> Dark deadly eye, those delicate legs
> Triggered to stirrings beyond sense—with a start, a bounce, a stab
> Overtake the instant and drag out some writhing thing.[2]

Sagar takes this as undermining the Wordsworthian creed of 'natural piety'. Even as a boy Hughes came closest to nature through such pursuits as hunting and fishing—to commune with it was to struggle with it.[3] Thus, in his haunting tale *The Rain Horse*, in *Wodwo*, the horse switches from a peaceable feature of the landscape into a relentless enemy of the man walking through it. It lunges blindly at

---

[1] In Paolucci and Paolucci (1962: 91).

[2] From *L*; *CP* 82–3.

[3] Compare Wordsworth's great poem 'Nutting' where, as a boy, he is dissuaded from violating a secluded bower by his sense of a 'spirit in the woods'. Hughes would have picked up the Shakespearian echoes in this scene (Angelo, Macbeth) though his later views on hunting etc. were closer to Wordsworth's than might be supposed.

him, overturning his complacent sense of closeness to his natural world. Far from being biddable, it resembles the maddened horses of Racine's Hippolyte. Nature, beautiful on the surface, is tragic at the core, inviting but implacable. Its final word is death.

This bias is plain in poem after poem in *The Hawk in the Rain* and *Lupercal*—it makes the early poetry original and exhilarating—but it is not in itself tragic. Tragic poetry does not usually confront death with such gusto. One might equally well describe the early poems as manichaean: hymns to nature that take pleasure not in its beauty but its darkness. Though Hughes writes from within the tradition of poets like Wordsworth and Hopkins and Lawrence, he is clearly revising it; he himself is shaped by more despairing, even nihilistic works like *The Waste Land* and the novels of Kafka and Beckett. Yet Hughes never settled for a bleakly secular vision; from the first, his poetry predicated the possibility of religious emotion, even though it rested on a foundation of modern *angst*. It was tragic mainly by virtue of what it excluded, its denial of hope. Such a mindset led on to tragedy but it was too fatalistic to be tragic itself. What distinguished Hughes from most of his contemporaries was that such a view (as in the vogue for existentialism) never satisfied him. In fact, his poetry came nearest to the tragic insofar as it included the possibility of religious vision. Thus, 'Thrushes' ends in a kind of fraught rapture:

> above what
> Furious spaces of fire do the distracting devils
> Orgy and hosannah, under what wilderness
> Of black silent waters weep.

Secular despair was never an option. In this respect, the poetry of T. S. Eliot struck Hughes as seminal. What moved him was not its despair but its struggle to rebuild a spiritual life on the basis of that despair:

In the twinkling of an eye. . . . the whole metaphysical universe centred on God had vanished from its place . . .

This emptiness was Eliot's starting-point. . . . It was as if only now, at this moment, mankind was finally born. For the first time in his delusive history he had lost the supernatural world . . . the infinite consolation, and the infinite inner riches. In its place he had found merely a new terror: the meaningless.[4]

Eliot rejoiced because he had to 'construct something upon which to rejoice'. The young Hughes, obsessed by the violence of nature, was in the same predicament. His lifelong fascination with the tragic poets—with Shakespeare, the Greeks and Racine—was part of this. It hinged not simply on the recognition of the tragic dimension in life but on the need to push tragedy beyond its own frontiers. How was it that the Ghost's warning was able to lead Hamlet through the soliloquies to his calm death? From the start, Hughes's interest in tragedy was indivisible from an interest in where it might take him to.

In this way, Hughes's tragic sense deepened as his poetry developed, partly in response to his own personal tragedies but, just as importantly, through his deepening interest in the tragic literature of the past. An early sign of this was his mythic reading of *Venus and Adonis* in *A Choice of Shakespeare's Verse*:

The Venus which [Adonis] refused became a demon and supplanted his consciousness. The frigid puritan, with a single terrible click, becomes a sexual maniac—a destroyer of innocence and virtue, a violator of the heavenly soul, of the very thing he formerly served and adored. Adonis has become Tarquin.[5]

Shakespeare's 'tragic equation' was more than just a way of facing the blackness of tragedy; its inner imperative was a quest to find a meaning in life once the tragic had been recognized. How could tragedy be accepted without its undermining the will to live? Hughes was to address this Nietzschean question exhaustively in *Shakespeare and the Goddess of Complete Being* (a crucial and underrated book) but it was already central for him by the 1960s. Take, for instance, a poem like 'Pibroch' in *Wodwo*:

> The sea cries with its meaningless voice
> Treating alike its dead and its living,
> Probably bored with the appearance of heaven
> After so many millions of nights without sleep,
> Without purpose, without self-deception.[6]

[4] *WP* 269–70.     [5] *WP* 114.     [6] *CP* 179–80.

Such cosmic blankness acts not as a drag but a spur:

> This is where the staring angels go through,
> This is where all the stars bow down.

The angels provide more than just a noble peroration to set against the grim landscape; they also suggest a means of transcending its unmeaning intensity. The poem may consciously espouse the tragic view of life but that is only its negative thrust: Hughes's real interest is in what positives might emerge from its negatives. Yet moving as 'Pibroch' is, there is something hectoring and didactic about it. A line like 'this is neither a bad variant nor a tryout' sounds too like an unintentional reminiscence of the more oracular parts of *Four Quartets*. It feels solemn, as if Hughes were pressing on his pen. A later poem like 'Dawn's Rose' in *Crow* is just as vivid without going into overdrive:

> A cry
> Wordless
> As the newborn baby's grieving
> On the steely scales.
>
> As the dull gunshot and its after-râle
> Among conifers, in rainy twilight.
>
> Or the suddenly dropped, heavily dropped
> Star of blood on the fat leaf.[7]

The tone here is more restrained, less portentous. It suggests that Hughes came closer to tragedy when he curbed his penchant for histrionics. The 'star of blood on the fat leaf' takes us by surprise. Its real meaning only dawns on us by delayed reaction. In the process, the crow's blood is transfigured into a 'star'.

Hughes's crow is a trickster rather than a tragedian. He delights in seeing through the protective veils of civilization to the horror at its heart, priding himself on being defiantly unpoetical. If his 'songs' are tragic it is, paradoxically, because they are couched in a tone of savage irony. They eschew tragic sublimity:

> While the bullfinch plumped in the apple bud
> And the goldfinch bulbed in the sun. . . .

[7] *CP* 239.

Crow spraddled head-down in the beach garbage, guzzling a
dropped ice-cream.

('Crow and the Birds'[8])

Such lines are not just grim but brazen. They go out of their way to
preclude the kind of nobility we get in tragedies like *King Lear* and
*Oedipus Rex*. Tragedy hits us whether we will or no. The comedy is a
way of insisting that it is inescapable. But if Hughes is intent on
getting underneath his reader's defences it is not simply in order to
shock. The real point of Crow's irreverence is that it invites us to
share in his indomitable spirit, his infinitely elastic gift for survival.
Far from being a mere naysayer, Crow is a kind of satanic Figaro: the
more perverse he is, the more we find him attractive. The book might
have been browbeating but it is, in fact, exhilarating. If it is tragic,
that is because it refuses to let tragedy wear it down. It is in this
respect, not simply out of fatalism, that Hughes can remind us of a
writer like Euripides. The elimination of sentiment makes way for
stronger emotions.

It may be that Hughes approached tragedy indirectly because
he could only express a Shakespearian-type tragic vision by steering
clear of the poetic register associated with Shakespeare's tragedies.
To have emulated Hamlet's soliloquies would have been fatal, stirring
up the ghosts of the poetic past. Crow soliloquizes in the voice of
Iago, not of Othello. In a culture epitomized by a play like *Waiting
for Godot*, tragedy naturally took the form of tragicomedy. It
could only express the tragic insights of a Euripides or a Racine by
reaching them in a subtly alienating way, by coming up on the inside.
Tragedy, once the most decorous of all literary forms, had to be
served raw.

In his later poetry Hughes found more severe means of evoking
suffering. The process begins, tentatively, in *Gaudete* and *Cave Birds*.
The first part of the former book reads like melodramatic farce, a
hyperbolical parody of life in an English village, but this modulates
into the terse poetic parables that enact the Reverend Lumb's transformation. Excess leads to whittled-down brevity. The poetic
journey is one of intensifying simplicity. Its holy grail is a bare,

---

[8] *CP* 210.

stark directness that is assertively unpoetical. There is no hint of a tragic style as such:

> Glare out of just crumpled grass—
> Blinded, I blink.
> Glare out of muddled clouds—
> I go in.
>
> Glare out of house-gloom—
> I close my eyes.
>
> And the darkness too is aflame.
>
> So you have come and gone again
> With my skin.[9]

Yet this trend is more than just a matter of style, a development in Hughes's verse. The eloquence of such lyrics derives not just from their diction but from the clarity with which the poetry unfolds the myth it recounts. The bare bones are as visible as the flesh and blood. This process is even more striking in *Prometheus on his Crag*, a sequence so denuded that its myth stands out like an x-ray, brutally explicit:

> What secret stays
> Stilled under my stillness?
> Not even I know.
>
> Only he knows—that bird, that
> Filthy-gleeful emissary and
> The hieroglyph he makes of my entrails
> Is all he tells.[10]

It is not going too far to conjecture that such effects were indebted to Greek tragedy, particularly Aeschylus. What Hughes found in the Greeks and sought to emulate was a poetry that pinned everything on the grandeur of unvarnished statement. This was something that his most revered modern masters—Yeats, Eliot, Lawrence—had all sought for before him. Like Hughes, Eliot had endorsed Lawrence's plea for 'a bare, rocky directness of statement':[11]

poetry which should be essentially poetry, with nothing poetic about it, poetry standing naked in its bare bones, or poetry so transparent that

---

[9] *CP* 375.    [10] *CP* 289.
[11] Quoted by Sagar (2000: 20).

we should not see the poetry, but that which we are meant to see through the poetry, poetry so transparent that in reading it we are intent on what the poem points at, and not on the poetry, this seems to me the thing to try for.[12]

Greek tragedy confirmed this project but Eliot's words would describe Racine equally well. One should never underestimate the extent to which Hughes's poetry pursued a dialogue with the poets who came before him.

*Cave Birds* is a powerful book but, to many readers, a curiously arcane one. Some of the poems strike home but others feel remote and elusive:

> Only a crumb of fungus,
> A pulp of mouldy tinder
> And you flare, fluttering, black out like a firework.
>
> Who are you, in the nest among the bones?
> You are the shyest bird among birds.
>
> 'I am the last of my kind.'[13]

We see the myth through a glass darkly and grope after its meaning. Hughes conceded as much himself: 'there's a funny atmosphere about [the poems]. . . . crabbed, dead, abstract.'[14] There is something quixotic about a myth in which the reader can only half share. It is notable that, after *Cave Birds*, Hughes rarely attempted the exposition of a myth of his own devising. Books like *Moortown* and *Season Songs* have an unspoken hinterland of myth behind them but their ostensible subject matter is palpable and accessible. When Hughes does return to myth, it is to myths with which the reader is already familiar from the classics. We can focus on the bare bones of their stories without feeling mystified or lost. Symbolism feels natural and the tragic ceases to run to bombast. Whatever one thinks of Hughes's translations, they are undoubtedly among his freest and most effortless works—his early poems often look rather strained beside them. Hughes's later verse (including *Birthday Letters*) depends on his knowing when to leave the story to speak for itself. The narrator of *Tales from Ovid*, for instance, is impressive precisely because of what

---

[12] Quoted by Sagar (2000: 21).          [13] *CP* 430–1.
[14] Quoted by Sagar (2000: 27).

he does not say, how little he needs to add to the tales themselves. Hughes has at last learnt to dispense with the portentous tragic voice we hear in a poem like 'Pibroch'.

It was only once he had reached this point that Hughes embarked on the translation of a work as alien and un-Shakespearian as *Phèdre*. He had long admired Racine and had once described hearing him at the Comedie Française as 'the closest thing . . . I have heard' to Peter Brook's Shakespeare:

> I felt I had glimpsed a whole greater existence of drama, one which our English stage has forgotten. Maybe this was how the rigid, stilted, masked actors of the Greek amphitheatre performed . . . [15]

Hence the difficulty of Hughes's task. *Phèdre* was not only the epitome of French classicism, it also stood for a radically different kind of theatre from that of his own master, Shakespeare. No play could have pressed him so far from his natural bent. Where Shakespeare's verse was wildly imaginative, 'a homely spur-of-the-moment improvisation', Racine's was impeccably polished.[16] Despite his experience as a poet, Hughes could hardly fall back on anything he himself had written as a model. What made Racine such a challenge was that there was nothing like his poetry in English. Hughes might feel an affinity with his tragic vision but the actual form it took, its flawless *alexandrine* couplets, must have seemed utterly foreign. In fact, Racine's tragic sense was itself markedly different from Shakespeare's. Hughes had long ago been struck by its ruthlessly undeviating darkness, its icy refusal to cling to straws. There is nothing in his tragedies to compare with Malcolm's optimistic epilogue to *Macbeth* or the visionary music that invades the stage at the death of Anthony. Phèdre dies in darkness, helpless and damned. Racine's endings rule out the fleeting glimpses of religious consolation that tease us in the ending of *Lear*. All this must have been clear to Hughes as soon as he picked up his pen. *Phèdre* is an English translator's Everest, as foreign in its spirit as in its form.

What Hughes encountered in it and in the *Hippolytus* was the drama of characters utterly possessed by Eros—'Vénus tout entière à sa proie attachée' ('Venus utterly pinned to her prey').[17] Most English tragedies

---

[15] *WP* 245–6.  [16] *WP* 105.
[17] Text from Picard's edition (1950) 759.

leave more room for dialogue and affection. Lady Macbeth is only incidentally in love; her real love is power; the infatuated Romeo and Juliet are not too carried away for romantic dalliance. Phèdre, by contrast, lusts after Hippolyte almost in spite of herself. She does not *choose* to love him; she is possessed by a god. Hughes had already fastened on this aspect of the myth in a long digression on the *Hippolytus* in *Shakespeare and the Goddess of Complete Being*:

[Euripides' Phaedra] recapitulates . . . the whole course of Aphrodite's feelings about Hippolytus—from before the Goddess's announcement of her revenge with which the play starts. Aphrodite's jealousy must originally have been love—becoming a jealous revenging frenzy (extreme in proportion to the love) only when it was rejected.[18]

What draws Hughes to the story is Phaedra's self-abandonment, a passion so exorbitant that it has no time for the more ideal feelings that complicate love in a play like *Othello*. This passion is as much religious as sexual. In Racine's famous phrase, she is the 'fille de Minos et de Pasiphaë' ('The daughter of Minos and of Pasiphae'). There is no escape from her tragedy: the gods have made it. Hughes was too steeped in Shakespearian tragedy not to see that *Phèdre*, by pushing suffering to extremes, was a different kind of tragedy from Shakespeare's. Whereas 'flights of angels' sing Hamlet to his rest, Phèdre simply returns to darkness.

   Hughes was invited by Jonathan Kent to translate Racine's play for the Almeida Company but he became bogged down in the task and eventually gave it up. It was only when Kent came back to him, at the end of his life, that he was able to produce the translation we now have (first performed at Malvern in 1998).[19] Only after that did he go on to write his free version of Euripides' *Alcestis* (posthumously staged at the Viaduct Theatre in 2000).[20] There is, however, a sense in which the two translations go together. To work on Racine was to work on Euripides too. Euripides was Racine's favourite tragic poet and *Phèdre* had been modelled on the *Hippolytus*. Between them, the two plays enabled Hughes to focus on many of his own most persistent concerns. After all, a writer as successful as he was did not

---

[18]  *SGCB* 69.        [19]  Sagar (2000: xxxiii).
[20]  For a fuller response to the play, see my review, Gervais (2001).

need to take on such an arduous commission unless he felt compelled to do so.

Many English-speaking poets have tried to translate Racine, not least because there is nothing like him in English. Robert Lowell, Richard Wilbur, Edwin Morgan, and Tony Harrison all made versions of his work. Invariably, they found it untranslatable. Racine's passion tends to come out seeming frigid and his elegance to appear dry and formal. When Harrison seeks to make it sound overtly poetic the result feels clotted and overwritten. Even a prosodist as delicate as Wilbur seems to drown in his own decorum. And translators who do manage to suggest Racine's *bienséance* fail to capture his brutal directness. In other words, even an English poet who believes in his task may lack the literary means to bring it off. Hughes himself was far too well-read not to have been aware of such pitfalls. For all the appeal of the Phaedra myth, he must have known that to translate Racine's play was a deliberate gamble, a kind of dare. It must have taken more than just an affinity for Racine's world-view to take it on. One presumes that Hughes knew all too well that any attempt to translate *Phèdre* was virtually doomed to failure.

It may be that, despite this, Hughes saw Racine as a kind of Yeatsian antitype, a confirmation of the rule of the attraction of opposites. His own verse is vigorous, outspoken, and rough, akin to the 'inspired signalling and hinting of verbal heads and tails' he found in Shakespeare, whereas Racine's is elegant and harmonious.[21] Racine may also be the most impassioned and intense of poets but his intensity has no equivalent in English. Even his most tremendous speeches unfold with an unruffled poise. For instance:

> Dans le fond des forêts allaient-ils se cacher?
> Hélas! ils se voyaient avec pleine licence.
> Le ciel de leur soupirs approuvaient l'innocence;
> Ils suivaient sans remords leurs penchants amoureux;
> Tous les jours se levaient clairs et sereins pour eux.
> Et moi, triste rebut de la nature entière,
> Je me cachais au jour, je fuyais la lumière.
> La mort est le seul Dieu que j'osais implorer.

---

[21] *WP* 105. 'Or did they hide it all in the forest? | Ah! They were free! | Heaven was pleased with their innocent affection. | Wherever their love led, they went light-hearted' etc. (*P*61) This is sayable, but its diction and music are vague beside Racine's.

Did they hide themselves in the depths of the forest? Alas! they met each other in complete freedom. Heaven approved the innocence of their passion and they pursued their affections without a trace of guilt—for them every day dawned clear and serene—whereas I, a sad outlaw from universal nature, hid myself away from the day and fled from the light. The only God that I dare to pray to is death. (Act IV scene vi)

It is hard to see how Hughes could capture effects like this: he did not have the requisite arrows in his quiver. A cynical critic might infer that a Hughesian *Phèdre* could never do more than turn a silk purse into a sow's ear. Yet this would be a shallow response to Hughes's interest in the play. A more fertile hypothesis is that he was attracted to Racine precisely because Racine had done things that he himself had not. In an interview he gave to Edgar Faas about *Crow* he spoke of 'songs with no music ... in a super-simple and a super-ugly language'.[22] This may seem informal beside Racine's formality but it cherishes the same sort of stark, single-minded directness. It is not inconceivable that Hughes turned with relief from the soliloquies of Hamlet and Macbeth (or from Shelley or Tennyson) to the razor-sharp directness of something like the end of *Andromaque*:

> Pour qui sont ces serpents qui sifflent sur vos têtes?
> A qui destinez-vous l'appareil qui vous suit ?
> Venez-vous m'enlever dans l'éternelle nuit ?
> Venez, à vos fureurs Oreste s'abandonne. (p. 300)

For whom are these serpents that are hissing above your heads? To whom do you destine the forces that accompany you? Are you coming to carry me away into eternal night? Come on then, Orestes yields himself up to your fury. (Act V scene v)

Orestes is impaled on his own words, without any freedom to elaborate them, in just the way Hughes's beleaguered Crow so often is.

It is quite plausible that his interest in Racine went hand in hand with his own modernist quest for simplicity, for the verbal bareness Eliot learnt from Lawrence. We know from Racine's criticism that Homeric simplicity was precisely what he sought in his own verse. Its style followed its function. Thus, he handed the completed manuscript of *Phèdre* to Boileau with the modest request

---

[22] Quoted by Sagar (2000: 127).

that he make any corrections to the verse that he saw fit. Just so, a good translation is as much a rewriting as a copy. We expect a Hughesian *Phèdre* to be as much of a poem by Hughes as by Racine. Yet it is still arguable that it is more than just an attempt to imagine an opposite. The more interesting possibility is that Hughes chose to translate *Phèdre* because of the common ground he shared with its author. Perhaps he turned to Racine because he was unable to find what he was looking for in English poetry? If this seems far-fetched it at least helps to explain why he chose to work on Racine in the first place.

Any English translation of *Phèdre* is bound to be a milestone. Racine's play figures not only as the epitome of French classicism but as the antithesis of Shakespeare. It is a double challenge, especially to a writer whose own poetry owed everything to Shakespeare. Hughes was always unusually frank on this score and even when he refers to his debt to other poets—to Hopkins or Lawrence or Eliot— we feel the presence of Shakespeare looming behind them. Yet his interest in Racine obliges us to qualify this impression. From the epilogue to *Gaudete* on, his poetry became increasingly succinct, as if he were trying to tear himself away from the Shakespearian profusion that had inspired his earlier work. A sequence like *Prometheus on his Crag* reveals a new, more severe sense of relevance. There is no time to be poetic. The story itself seems to swallow up any impulse to embellish it. Whether or not this is a positive development (readers differ) it is clearly related to Hughes's translations. In a translation (particularly of a play or a narrative poem) it is the action that is instrumental, not the (second-hand) language itself. Moreover, writers like Aeschylus seem to hew their poetry directly out of the myth itself rather than applying it descriptively. By this token, Hughes may have been trying to distance himself from Shakespeare. The decision to translate Racine was a more radical step than it seemed. Shakespeare is the great elaborator, drawing rich and subtle imagery out of the most ordinary language, whereas Racine worked within the most restricted vocabulary of any great poet in European literature (a mere 1200 words according to one estimate). Shunning the copious inventiveness of poets like Shakespeare and Victor Hugo, he sought for his effects in such things as tone of voice, decorum and consistency of diction. Where Shakespeare is constantly in pursuit of new meaning in familiar words, Racine concentrates his intelligence on *le mot juste*. Thus, in the preface to *Bérénice*, a play whose entire action enacts a single sentence from Suetonius, he urges his readers not to suppose 'qu'une pièce qui les touche et qui leur donne plaisir puisse être absolument contre les règles. La principale règle est de plaire et de toucher. Toutes les autres ne sont faites que pour parvenir à cette première' ('A play that moves and pleases them can go completely counter to the rules. The principal rule is to please and to move us. All the rest merely serve to help realize this first one').[23] Such singleness of ambition is the reverse of that of a play like *Hamlet* which sprawls and digresses in countless directions, from pathos to satire to farce, and has constantly to be pulled back by the soliloquies to its tragic core. But where *Hamlet* strives by 'indirections' to 'find directions out', *Phèdre* is utterly undeviating: there is not a single couplet in it that is not relevant to the whole play. An English reader like Hughes may have found such poetry unfamiliar but he can hardly have failed to recognize its beauty.

In fact, though Hughes's translation falls short of Racine's elegance, it is much more successful in evoking the headlong pace of his play. His verse is framed to allow no let-up in the tension:

> Everything I say makes my hair stand up.
> My life is so bloated with my crimes
> There's no reason for another. I stink
> Of incest and deceit. And worse—
> My own hands are twitching
> To squeeze the life out of that woman,
> To empty that innocent blood out of her carcase
> And smash her to nothing.
> Yet I stand here facing the sun.
> The light of heaven, my greatest ancestor,
> Is the father and ruler of the gods.
> The whole universe is full of my forbears.
>
> (P63[24])

---

[23] Racine in Picard (1950: 467). I discuss this in detail in (2007).
[24] *Birthday Letters* has the freedom of the later work but in many respects it belongs more with Hughes's earlier poetry than the translations; it is unfinished rather than new business.

This goes straight to the point, even if its fierce staccato lines seem too kinetic to be Racinian. The emotion feels unfettered, unchecked by any controlling rhythm. The original is both calmer and more relentless:

> Misérable! et je vis? et je soutiens la vue
> De ce sacré Soleil dont je suis descendue ?
> J'ai pour aïeul le père et le maître des Dieux;
> Le ciel, tout l'univers est plein de mes aïeux.
> Où me cacher ? Fuyons dans la nuit infernale.[25]

What a wretch! Yet I live and brave the light of this sacred sun from which I am myself descended; the father and master of the Gods is my forbear and the heavens, the entire universe, is peopled with my ancestors. Where can I go to hide? I must flee instead into the darkness of hell. (Act IV scene vi)

Racine is too serious to give way to his heroine's passion. He is impassive where Hughes is impassioned. Nevertheless, Hughes clearly relished Racine's intensity. Where his verse is specifically Hughesian is in its more informal idiom. Seeking for immediacy, he became colloquial:

> Oh God, what am I doing? What am I saying?
> I think I'm losing my senses.
> Me jealous?
>
> (*P*63)

This is informal despite its grand subject. On the other hand, it is more natural and matter-of-fact than the kind of directness one finds in *Cave Birds*. Somehow, Racine seems to have had the effect of freeing up Hughes's language. Some of his simplicity has rubbed off on his translator. Translation, that is, is also self-discovery. It taught Hughes something about the nature of poetry in general. To translate poets like Aeschylus and Ovid and Racine was to go to school to them, not simply to imitate them with unmoved accuracy. Eliot had approached Racine in much the same way:

... Racine's *Bérénice* represents about the summit of civilisation in tragedy; and it is, in a way, a Christian tragedy ... The dramatic poet who can engross

---

[25] Racine in Picard (1950: 791).

the reader's or the auditor's attention during the space of a *Bérénice* is the most civilised dramatist . . . [26]

What mattered was not just the poetry itself but that it suggested an alternative to Shakespeare. Without this example, Hughes's later verse might well have been quite different. Some readers still cling to the early, Shakespearian Hughes of *Lupercal* but, if they were to ponder his *Phèdre*, they might get more out of his later verse too.

When we think about Shakespeare, we often find ourselves thinking about specific moments in the plays, perhaps a single speech, but if we think of Racine it is the whole play that comes to mind. [27] Even at its most incandescent, the rhythm of *Phèdre* remains constant and regular. Each speech flows seamlessly into the next. But if this is one way of defining the classical it also suggests those qualities in the play that were likely to elude a translator like Hughes. The poet of *Crow* could be as direct as Racine but not as measured. Crow blurts his songs out under pressure, almost without thinking. Hughes (who is thinking) chooses to speak in that way. We sense that it is too late in the day and that things are too bad for there to be any time for airs and graces. Hughes's Phèdre is similar, desperate to get her troubles off her chest:

> Death was the only god I prayed to.
> I waited only for death.
> Nothing but gall sustained me, and tears.
> Surrounded by spies
> I did not even dare
> To unburden myself of my grief.

> (*P*62)

The verse is deliberately unliterary. Where Racine walks within the context of the myth, Hughes keeps trying to break out of it. His Phèdre suffers as Racine's does but she expresses her suffering in accents that recall the hysteria of Lady Macbeth. This is hardly surprising. Hughes was committed to creating a play in English and,

[26] Eliot (1964: 41–2).
[27] Stendhal (1823) and elsewhere writes constantly about the importance of 'moments' in Shakespeare (as opposed to acts or even speeches). He describes a different *kind* of theatre, a less stagey stage. The insight is valuable but English Shakespeare criticism has not pursued it far.

apart from Shakespeare, he had few other models to work from. However keen his desire to 'make it new' he was bound to fall back on Shakespeare in the end. Yet though his is an English *Phèdre*, it still takes from Racine a whole-hogging ferocity that none of Shakespeare's plays (save for *Timon*) possesses. If the verse is English, the tragic feeling itself is not. Like Racine's, the tragedy is more extreme and final. Hughes's poetry may be more frantic but his action is equally unremitting. It is as if he had tried to push his voice as far as it would go in one single direction. Ever since the death of Sylvia Plath, his poetry had sought to articulate an uninhibited cry of pain and, in his *Phèdre*, that aim was realized.

Yet the translation of a play cannot be judged simply on its style. What counts for more is how well it holds the stage. This is still too soon to tell but, in any event, most translations have only a limited lifespan. François-Victor Hugo's great complete Shakespeare was used as a reading text well into the twentieth century but, after the First World War, directors began to commission new performing texts of the plays. Even Constance Garnett and Scott-Moncrieff eventually came to look out-of-date. One presumes that Hughes would have realized that his *Phèdre* was for an age and not for all time. If any of his translations lasts longer it is more likely to be the *Tales from Ovid*. Yet this does not mean that the *Phèdre* was less important; on the contrary, it underlines how much Hughes invested in it. That said, it has to be noted that it does much more justice to some aspects of the play than to others. It has great force and simplicity but, like most translations of Racine, it lacks harmony and decorum. Its verse has a rough, improvised edge to it that feels stubbornly English:

> Before I could grasp what I'd seen
> I felt my face flame crimson—then go numb.
> My whole body scorched—then icy sweat.
> My eyes went dark.
> I could not speak. I could hardly stay upright.
> I knew then that the goddess had found me . . .
>
> (*P*13–14)

We hear Phèdre's cries of pain but we hear them as cries, not as poetry. In Racine, by contrast, her passion is intense precisely because it is never just raw passion. She never loses her dignity. The difference is crucial. It means that when Hughes's Phèdre flies into a rage she sounds too much like Hamlet or Othello going over the top. Simplicity and directness alone are not quite enough to do the job. In Racine, even at his most intense, they are refined by a kind of lyricism, a subtly *cantabile* music:

> Déjà je ne vois plus qu'à travers un nuage
> Et le ciel et l'époux que ma présence outrage;
> Et la mort, à mes yeux dérobant la clarté,
> Rend au jour, qu'ils souillaient, toute sa pureté.[28]

Already I can only see as far as through a mist, through the heavens and through the husband to whom my very presence is an outrage, and death, as it robs my eyes of their clarity, gives back to the daylight all the purity that they have sullied. (Act V scene vii)

Hughes misses such suave effects, not least because he makes no attempt to provide an equivalent for Racine's rolling heroic couplets. As a result, his version seems rather rushed. We no longer dwell on the heroine's every inflection and gesture, as if we were watching her tragedy in slow motion. Hughes's brusque, pared-down lines stick out and draw attention to themselves. This subverts our sense of the poem as a whole:

> Wretched victim of a divine vengeance!
> I detest myself
> More than you can ever detest me.
> You are right, the gods are watching me.
> Yes, the same gods
> Who have filled me with these horrible flames
> That are killing me ...
>
> (*P*33)

The very techniques that Hughes uses to bring out the energy and directness of the verse rebound against him, robbing the play of its composure. The translation is hot where the original generates its heat by remaining cool. Its rhythm controls the emotion rather than being dictated to by it. But to say this is simply to point to the uniqueness of Racine's verse. No doubt that is what Hughes himself

[28] Racine in Picard (1950: 802).

found by translating it. We translate great poetry to learn how to enjoy it better. It certainly required ambition and daring to seek to render *Phèdre* in English but it also required modesty and humility. Only a writer who understood this could be fit to undertake the task. What in the long run is most interesting about Hughes's attempt is that, at the height of his career, he was sufficiently self-effacing to devote himself to exploring a writer whose voice was so different from his own, to seek a new voice for himself not through self-expression but through the voice of another man.

The clearest indication that translating *Phèdre* was a formative experience for Hughes is that it enabled him to go on to write a very different play: his *Alcestis*. In fact, the new play is less of a departure from *Phèdre* than meets the eye. It is based on Euripides' play of the same name and Euripides was Racine's favourite among the Greek dramatists. Like Racine, Euripides was preoccupied by the way the god of love could take complete possession of his victims. Phèdre and Medea are putty in the hands of Eros whereas Juliet never runs out of poetry or Rosalind of wit; even Cleopatra at her most lovesick, always remains a tragedy-queen. In *Shakespeare and the Goddess of Complete Being*, Hughes has a long digression on the *Hippolytus* in which he focuses on the idea of love as an invasion of the entire being, an end in itself, untouched by idealism. The result is a particularly pure kind of tragedy, with no light at the end of the tunnel. Hughes's digression may well mark the inception of his interest in *Phèdre*. It also recalls the *Alcestis* since King Admetos in that play is utterly bound up in his love for his queen. As always, Euripides ensures that his characters have everything to lose and no means of defending themselves. It was not by chance that Hughes turned away from Shakespeare at this point. Hippolytus and Phèdre are in thrall to a divinity whereas, as Steiner puts it, Shakespearian tragedy is 'impartial, perhaps indifferent, in regard to God'.[29] Lear is just Lear, not a spiritual model like Antigone.[30]

---

[29] Steiner (1984: 303).

[30] Thus, Bradley compares Orestes with Hamlet but adds that what interests us in Hamlet is 'the whole personality . . . in his conflict, not with an opposing spiritual power, but with circumstances and . . . his own nature.' (1950: 374). Hegel revered Shakespeare but found Greek spirituality more congenial. The price of modern tragedy was that it was inevitably more secular. Bradley was troubled by this too.

Hughes's *Alcestis* differs from his *Phèdre* not in any diminution of
its debt to Euripides but in its daring decision to combine Euripidean
tragedy with two quite different sources, both of which he had long
been drawn to: Ovid's tale of Pygmalion in the *Metamorphoses* and
the statue scene in Shakespeare's *Winter's Tale*. Both stories imply
that tragedy can be reversed and that, like Alcestis herself, the dead
can be brought back to life. If tragedy is fully undergone, as Admetos
undergoes the loss of his wife, its victim may eventually glimpse a
redemptive and reconciling light to cancel out its darkness. Alcestis is
brought back to life, just as Hermione is in *A Winter's Tale*. This
ending is both Shakespearian and the antithesis of the ending of
*Phèdre*. Tragedy is less final than it seemed:

> **Admetos**
> We have taken the full measure of grief
> And now we have found happiness even greater.
> We have found it and recognised it.
>
> **Chorus 1**
> Incessantly the gods
> Manipulate the fortunes of mankind—
> Bringing great events
> To conclusions that were unexpected.
>
> **Chorus 2**
> Nothing is certain.
> What had seemed inevitable
> Comes to nothing.
>
> **Chorus 3**
> And now
> See how God has accomplished
> What was beyond belief.
>
> **Chorus 1**
> Let this give man hope.
>
> (*A*83[31])

At one level these lines may constitute Hughes's reply to Racine. It is
as if his study of Greek tragedy had opened up a way for him to go
beyond despair. The statue walks, Alcestis regains her voice, and
tragedy ceases to be the final word. Nor is this wishful thinking.

---

[31] Hughes also weaved the Orpheus myth into his *Alcestis* (22–3) as a pointer
towards the ending. He had excluded the story from his Ovid.

However one takes the play's final line—'Let this give man hope'—it is clear that Hughes could only have come out where he has done by reliving the dramas of Euripides and Racine.

On a personal level, the rebirth of Alcestis may be taken as Hughes's way of finally laying the ghost of Sylvia Plath, though his play is not personal in an intrusive way:

> Once you've contracted to write only the truth about yourself. . . . then you can too easily limit yourself to. . . . your conscious biography. Your own equivalent of what Shakespeare got into his plays is simply foregone.[32]

When Hughes finally unties the Gordian knot of his own 'tragic equation', the *catharsis* is of a kind in his readers can share. What arrests us theatrically is the sheer miracle of Alcestis brought back in the flesh. But the play is also the exposition of a myth of rebirth that goes a step further than the myths of *Crow*, *Cave Birds*, and the rest. This myth was always implicit in Hughes's poetry (at the end of *Gaudete*, for instance) but was only fully articulated at the end of his career, in *River*:

> Two gold bears came down and swam like men
>
> Beside us. And dived like children.
> And stood in deep water as on a throne
> Eating pierced salmon off their talons.
>
> So we found the end of our journey.
>
> So we stood, alive in the river of light
> Among the creatures of light, creatures of light.
>
> ('That Morning'[33])

It is worth noting how unusual such ecstatic exuberance is. The nearest thing I can think of to it is *Prometheus Unbound*. Failing that, the closest comparison must be with the headily lyrical choruses of Euripides himself. This is not to claim that Euripides was a direct influence on *River* (that is only secondary in any case); what is more significant is that it is possible to see Hughes as writing not just in an English but in a European tradition. By opening himself up to foreign influences he became a bigger poet himself. That is the true measure of what he gained from being a translator.

[32] Quoted in Sagar (2000: 57).     [33] *CP* 663–4.

With hindsight, Hughes had been moving towards this myth of rebirth from the start. His celebration of primitive energy already implied a Blakean faith in creativity. This impulse may be obscured by tragedy in his middle period, but despite that, a figure like Crow is always a survivor, even when he seems like an aggressive messenger of death. There is a sense in which Hughes was always a Lawrentian, someone for whom tragedy was no more than a halfway house, a prelude to religious emotion.[34] *Crow* could never be more than transitional. It is not surprising that Hughes never completed it. Perhaps his most resolved book was *River* which married visionary impulse with a casual freedom of manner:

> ecstacy dissolving
> In the mercy of water, at the start of the source,
> Devoured by revelation,
> Every molecule drained, and counted, and healed . . .
>
> ('The Gulkana'[35])

This is both hieratic and off-hand. It shows how instinctively Hughes felt his myth of creation. The sublime is made ordinary, with none of the straining after emotional effect of a poem like 'Pibroch'.

*Alcestis* has the same momentum. It is Hughes's equivalent to Lawrence's Phoenix symbol. The only difference is that, to make such restoration credible, Hughes needed to dwell more on the fact of death than Lawrence did. Yet his spiritual trajectory was already implicit in the 'animal' poems though it took him almost forty years to clarify it. Perhaps, even then, Hughes never completely realized the poetry he dreamed of. Looking at the way his *Alcestis* unfolds its myth it is not difficult to see what he was trying to say. The play is almost didactic or would be but for the knockabout antics of Heracles. Yet one should not confound the crowning significance it has for Hughes with its actual achievement as poetry. Alcestis' words are moving but it would be an exaggeration to see them as Hughes's final poetic testament:

---

[34] Lawrence wrote about tragedy and religion in many places, most notably (1936) and (1968). Hughes would certainly have read these essays; they are an important precedent for his own thought.

[35] *CP* 665–9.

**Admetos**
Pray, Alcestis.

**Alcestis**
What is that black river?
Do you see the river, the glitter
Brimming among the houses?
Somebody—who is it, Admetos?
Somebody out on the river shouting for me.

**Death's Voice**
Alcestis!

**Alcestis**
Shouting my name.
I hear the splash of an oar.

(A18)

This tragedy comes out where it aspires to come out but the poetry can sound oddly laconic. There is a hint of bathos in its purity; we hear no trumpets on the other side. Many readers will feel that *Crow* and *Cave Birds* give a fuller sense of Hughes's poetic gifts. It may even be that, in going beyond tragedy, he was trying to go beyond poetry itself. As Blake shows, prophecy and poetry can be uneasy bedfellows. One comes back, then, to Racine who did manage to keep them apart. After *Phèdre*, he retired from the stage to a life of respectable piety but when, in his last years, he returned with the biblical tragedy of *Athalie*, his tragic vision still vied with his sense of Christian hope. Only a poet with his iron control could make the two run together in harness. In *River*, on the other hand, we are conscious of a divide opening up between the poetry and what the poetry wants to make us feel. We may miss both the simplicity it aspires to and the kind of simplicity we get in Racine.

The rhapsodic lyricism of *River* is best seen as an attempt to go beyond words to something that words alone can never express. In poem after poem, Hughes seems to conclude (or simply end) in a sort of stunned ecstasy:

> And this is the liturgy
> Of earth's advent—harrowing, crowned—a travail
> Of raptures and rendings. Perpetual mass

Of the waters
Wells from the cleft.

('Salmon Eggs'[36])

Such poetry is almost intolerably vivid but it can also be elusive. How
do we pin down the emotion it conveys? The same poem:

> *Only birth matters*
> Say the river's whorls.

As in later Blake, the myth itself has to carry us through: the style
only takes us part of the way. One remembers that, ever since the
1960s, Hughes had insisted on the need to get beyond style:

. . . the very sound of metre calls up the ghosts of the past and it is difficult to
sing one's own tune against that choir. It is easier to speak a language that
raises no ghosts.[37]

One can read a poem like 'Pike' as an expression of personal style, as
one would 'To Autumn' or 'Among School Children', but *River* and
the *Alcestis* work differently. They expect us, as we read, to pledge our
faith to their religious vision. The reader has to become a kind of
adept. For all his startling sensuousness, Hughes always made
metaphysical claims on his readers and perhaps, by the end, his
metaphysics began to take over his poetry. Sometimes it seems as if
what he had to say was too important to him to stand simply as
poetry. He never lost his eagle eye for a dramatic phrase but there
were times when the scenario seemed more important to him than
the drama itself. That, however, is too grudging a verdict. It is surely
better to fail through overambition than (like Larkin?) to succeed
thanks to a lack of it. Hughes at least tried to stretch poetry to its
limits. One thinks of him as pressing against the boundaries of the
expressible, just as he himself saw poets like Hopkins and Whitman.
Moreover, for all his extravagances, he was never simply the literary
wild man that journalists liked to picture him as. He was far too
aware of the poetry of the past to be that simple-minded. If he was
sometimes overweening he could also be humble. One should not be
surprised that, at the height of his fame, he chose to go back to school

---

[36] *CP* 680–1.      [37] Sagar (2000: 127).

to Euripides and Racine, two of the most consciously literary poets in the entire European tradition. He may have sought a different kind of simplicity from Racine's but he understood why an immersion in the classical kind of simplicity was a necessary stage on his own journey. Poets must take their own way and to do so they need to know where the alternatives to it lead. If Hughes in the end aspired to go beyond poetry it was because he was so saturated in it.

# Works by Ted Hughes

**With abbreviations used in this volume.**

*A—Euripides. Alcestis* (London: Faber and Faber, 1999).

*BL—Birthday Letters* (London: Faber and Faber, 1998).

*CB—Cave Birds* (London: Faber and Faber, 1978).

*CP—Collected Poems,* ed. P. Keegan (London: Faber and Faber, 2003).

*CPC—Collected Plays for Children* (London: Faber and Faber, 2001).

*CSV—A Choice of Shakespeare's Verse* (London: Faber and Faber, 1971).

*DB—Difficulties of a Bridegroom* (London: Faber and Faber, 1995).

*DG—A Dancer to God: Tributes to T. S. Eliot* (London: Faber and Faber, 1992).

*EC—Eat Crow* (London: Rainbow, 1971).

*EN—Earth-Numb* (London: Faber and Faber, 1979).

*E-O—Earth Owl and other Moon People* (London: Faber and Faber, 1963).

*G—Gaudete* (London: Faber and Faber, 1977).

*HR—Hawk in the Rain* (London: Faber and Faber, 1957).

*L—Lupercal* (London: Faber and Faber, 1960).

*LTH—Letters of Ted Hughes,* ed. C. Reid (London: Faber and Faber, 2007).

*O—Aeschylus. Oresteia* (London: Faber and Faber, 1999).

*P—Racine. Phèdre* (London: Faber and Faber, 1998).

*PM—Poetry in the Making* (London: Faber and Faber, 1967).

*RC—Rain Charm for the Duchy* (London: Faber and Faber, 1992).

*SGCB—Shakespeare and the Goddess of Complete Being* (London: Faber and Faber, 1992).

*SO—Seneca's Oedipus* (London: Faber and Faber, 1969).

*SPCP—Sylvia Plath. Collected Poems,* ed. Ted Hughes (London: Faber and Faber, 1981).

*ST—Selected Translations,* ed. D. Weissbort (London: Faber and Faber, 2006).

*TO—Tales from Ovid* (London: Faber and Faber, 1997).

*TOa–Tales from Ovid. Adapted by Tom Supple and Simon Reade* (London: Faber and Faber, 1999).

*W–Wodwo* (London: Faber and Faber, 1967).

*Wedekind, F. Spring Awakening* (London: Faber and Faber, 1995).

*WP—Winter Pollen. Occasional Prose*, ed. W. Scammell (London: Faber and Faber, 1994).

# Bibliography

Adams, J. N. (1982), *The Latin Sexual Vocabulary* (London: Duckworth).

Aeschylus, *Works*, trans. H. Weir Smyth (1963), 2 vols (London: William Heinemann).

Aeschylus, *Prometheus Bound*, trans. J. Kerr (2005) (London: Oberon).

Ahl, F. (1984), 'The Art of Safe Criticism in Greece and Rome', *American Journal of Philology*, 105: 174–208.

Anderson, W. S. (1972), *Ovid's Metamorphoses Book 6–10* (Oklahoma: University Oklahoma Press).

—— (1997), *Ovid's Metamorphoses Book 1–5* (Oklahoma: University Oklahoma Press).

Appiah, K. A. (1993), 'Thick Translation', *Callaloo*, 16.4: 808–19.

Barchiesi, A. (2001), *Speaking Volumes: Narrative and Intertext in Ovid and Other Latin Poets* (London: Duckworth).

Barry, E. (ed.) (1973), *Robert Frost on Writing* (New Brunswick: Rutgers University Press).

Barth, K. (1958), *Church Dogmatics IV.2: The Doctrine of Reconciliation*, trans. G. W. Bromiley (Edinburgh: T. & T. Clark).

Bassenge, F. (ed.) (1955), Hegel, *Ästhetik* (Berlin: Europaische Verlagsanstalt).

Basnett, S. (2005), *Sylvia Plath: An Introduction to the Poetry*, 2nd edn. (Basingstoke: Palgrave).

Bate, W. J. (1963), *John Keats* (Cambridge, MA: Harvard University Press).

Beard, M. (2000), *The Invention of Jane Harrison* (Cambridge MA: Harvard University Press).

Bentley, P. (1998), *The Poetry of Ted Hughes: Language, Illusion and Beyond* (Harlow: Longman).

Berry, D. (2001), 'Rough Magic: Ted Hughes's translation of Jean Racine's *Phèdre*' in P. Tomlinson (ed.), *French Classical Theatre Today* (Amsterdam: Rodopi), 207–28.

—— (2002), 'Ted Hughes and the Minotaur Complex', *Modern Language Review*, 97.3: 539–52.

Bishop, N. (1994), 'Ted Hughes and the Death of Poetry', in K. Sagar (ed.), *The Challenge of Ted Hughes* (Basingstoke: MacMillan), 1–10.

Bloom, H. (1971), *The Ringers in the Tower: Studies in Romantic Tradition* (Chicago: The University of Chicago Press).

—— (1973), *The Anxiety of Influence* (Oxford: Oxford University Press).

Blumenberg, H. (2002), *Tenkning og Metafor* (Oslo: J. W. Cappelens Forlag).

Bömer, F. (1969–86), *P. Ovidius Naso, Metamorphosen: Kommentar* (Heidelberg: Carl Winter).

Boyle, A. J. (1997), *Tragic Seneca. An Essay in the Theatrical Tradition* (London: Routledge).

Braden, G. (1985), *Renaissance Tragedy and the Senecan Tradition: Anger's Privilege* (New Haven: Yale University Press).

Bradley, A. C. (1950), *Oxford Lectures on Poetry* (London: MacMillan).

Brandes, R. (1994), 'Hughes, history and the world in which we live' in K. Sagar (ed.), *The Challenge of Ted Hughes* (Basingstoke: MacMillan), 142–5.

Brett, R. L. and Jones, A. R. (eds.) (1963), Wordsworth and Coleridge, *Lyrical Ballads*, rev. edn (London: Methuen).

Britzolakis, C. (1999), *Sylvia Plath and the Theatre of Mourning* (Oxford: Oxford University Press).

Broadus, E. K. (1921), *The Laureateship: A Study of the Office of Poet Laureate in England with Some Account of the Poets* (Oxford: Clarendon).

Broege, V. (1972), 'Ovid's Autobiographical Use of Mythology in the *Tristia* and *Epistulae ex Ponto*', *EMC*, 16: 37–42.

Brook, P. (1998), *Threads of Time: A Memoir* (London: Methuen).

—— (1999) in N. Gammage (ed.), *The Epic Poise: A Celebration of Ted Hughes* (London: Faber and Faber), 154.

Brower, R. A. (ed.) (1959), *On Translation* (Cambridge, MA: Harvard University Press).

Brown, G. Mackay (ed.) (1987), *Four Poets for St. Magnus* (Breckness).

Brown, S. A. (1999), *The Metamorphosis of Ovid: From Chaucer to Ted Hughes* (London: Duckworth).

—— (2005), *Ovid: Myth and Metamorphosis* (London: Bristol Classical Press).

—— and Silverstone, C. (2007), *Tragedy in Transition* (London: Blackwell).

Browning, R. (1999), *The Complete Works of Robert Browning*, ed. A. Dooley *et al.*, 15 vols (Athens: Ohio University Press).

Bundtzen, L. K. (2000), 'Mourning Eurydice: Ted Hughes as Orpheus in *Birthday Letters*', *Journal of Modern Literature*, 23: 455–69.

—— (2006), 'Plath and Psychoanalysis: Uncertain Truths', in Gill, J. (ed.) *The Cambridge Companion to Sylvia Plath* (Cambridge: Cambridge University Press), 36–51.

Burgess, T. C. (1902), *Epideictic Literature* (Chicago: Chicago University Press), reprinted 1987 (New York and London: Garland).

Burkert, W. (1985), *Greek Religion* (Cambridge, MA: Harvard University Press).

Byrne, S. (ed.) (1997), *Tony Harrison, Loiner* (Oxford: Clarendon Press).

Cahoon, L. (1988), 'The bed as battlefield: erotic conquest and military metaphor in Ovid's *Amores*', *Transactions of the American Philological Association*, 118: 293–307.

Carey, J. (ed.) (1986), *William Golding: the Man and his Books* (London: Faber and Faber).

—— (1998), Review of Ted Hughes, *Birthday Letters*, in *The Sunday Times*, 27 January.

Carne-Ross, D. S. (1974), 'On looking into Fitzgerald's Homer', *New York Review*, 12 December.

Carson, A. (2006), *Grief Lessons: Four Plays by Euripides* (New York: New York Review Books).

Churchwell, S. (2001), 'Secrets and lies: Plath, privacy, publication and Ted Hughes', *Birthday Letters' Contemporary Literature*, 42.1: 102–48.

Clanchy, K. (2000), Review of *Alcestis*, *PN Review*, 26.4: 50.

Colvin, S. (1917), *John Keats: His Life and Poetry, His Friends, Critics and After-Fame* (London: MacMillan).

Corrigan, R. W. (ed.) (1990), *Classical Tragedy Greek and Roman: Eight Plays* (New York: Applause Theatre).

Coupe, L. (1997), *Myth* (London and New York: Routledge).

Cronin, M. (2006), *Translation and Identity* (London and New York: Routledge).

Dawe, R. D. (1993), *The Odyssey: Translation and Analysis* (Lewes: Book Guild).

Denniston, J. D. and Page, D. L. (1957), Aeschylus, *Agamemnon* (Oxford: Oxford University Press).

Derrida, J. (2004), *On Touching—Jean-Luc Nancy* (Stanford: Stanford University Press).

Diggle, J. (ed.) (1989), *Euripidis Fabulae, Tomus I* (Oxford: Oxford University Press).

Dillon, J. and Wilmer, S. E. (eds.) (2005), *Rebel Women: Staging Greek Drama Today* (London: Methuen).

Donoghue, D. (2000), *Words Alone: The Poet T. S. Eliot* (New Haven: Yale University Press).

Dougherty, C. (2006), *Prometheus* (London and New York: Routledge).

Dufallo, B. (2007), *The Ghosts of the Past: Latin Literature, the Dead, and Rome's Transition to a Principate* (Ohio: Ohio State University Press).

Dumezil, G. (1996), *Archaic Roman Religion*. Volume I (Baltimore: The Johns Hopkins University Press).

Eagleton, T. (1987), Review of Ted Hughes, *Gaudete, Stand*, 19: 78–9.

—— (2003), *Sweet Violence: The Idea of the Tragic* (Oxford: Blackwell).

Economou, G. (ed.) (1978), *Proensa: An Anthology of Troubadour Poetry*, trans. P. Blackburn (Berkeley: University of California Press).

Edmunds, L. (ed.) (1990), *Approaches to Greek Myth* (Baltimore: The Johns Hopkins University Press).

Eliade, M. (1951), *Le chamanisme et les techniques archaïques de l'extase* (Paris: Payot): trans. W. R. Trask, (1964) as *Shamanism: Archaic Techniques of Ecstasy* (London and New York: Routledge).

Eliot, T. S. (1923), 'The beating of a drum', *The Nation and the Athenaeum*, 34 (6 October).

—— (1960), *Selected Essays* (New York: Harcourt, Brace and World).

—— (1963), *Collected Poems 1909–1962* (London: Faber and Faber).

Eliot, T. S. (1964), *The Use of Poetry and the Use of Criticism* (London: Faber and Faber).

Euripides, *Alcestis and Other Plays*, trans. P. Vellacott (1953) (Harmondsworth: Penguin).

—— *Alcestis*, trans. R. L. Lattimore, in D. Grene and R. L. Lattimore (eds.) (1955), *The Complete Greek Tragedies*, vol. 5 (New York: Random House).

—— *Cyclops, Alcestis, Medea*, trans. D. Kovacs (1994) (Cambridge, MA: Harvard University Press).

—— *Hecuba: A New Translation*, trans. T. Harrison (2000) (London: Faber and Faber).

—— *Hecuba: A New Version*, trans. F. McGuinness (2004) (London: Faber and Faber).

—— *Alkestis* in *Grief Lessons: Four Plays by Euripides*, trans. A. Carson (2006) (New York: New York Review of Books).

Evans, H. B. (1983), *Publica Carmina: Ovid's Books from Exile* (Lincoln: Nebraska University Press).

Eyre, R. (1997), 'Tony Harrison the Playwright', in S. Byrne (ed.), *Tony Harrison, Loiner* (Oxford: Clarendon Press), 43–8.

Faas, E. (1980), *Ted Hughes: The Unaccommodated Universe, with Selected Critical Writings by Ted Hughes* (Santa Barbara: Black Sparrow).

Feinstein, E. (2001), *Ted Hughes: The Life of a Poet* (London: Weidenfeld and Nicholson).

Finley, M. (1968), *Aspects of Antiquity* (New York: Viking Press).

Firestone, E. R. (2001), 'Fritz Bultman's Actaeon Paintings: Sexuality, Punishment, and Oedipal Conflict', *Genders*, 34 <http://www.genders.org/g34/g34_firestone.html>, last accessed 3 November 2006.

Fitzgerald, R. (1961), *The Odyssey* (New York: Anchor Press).

Flanagan, H. (1943), *Dynamo* (New York: Duell, Sloane and Pearce).

Flower, N. (ed.) (1933), *The Journals of Arnold Bennett, vol. 3, 1921–1928* (London: Cassell).

Forbes Irving, P. M. C. (1990), *Metamorphosis in Greek Myths* (Oxford: Oxford University Press).

Fowler, D. P. (2000), *Roman Constructions. Readings in Postmodern Latin* (Oxford: Oxford University Press).

France, P. (2000), 'French: Classical Drama' in P. France (ed.), *The Oxford Guide to Literature in English Translation* (Oxford: Oxford University Press), 263–8.

—— (ed.) (2000), *The Oxford Guide to Literature in English Translation* (Oxford: Oxford University Press).

Fredrick, D. (1997), 'Reading broken skin: violence in Roman elegy', in J. Hallett and M. Skinner (eds.), *Roman Sexualities* (Princeton: Princeton University Press), 172–93.

Gadamer, H.-G. (1989), *Truth and Method*, 2nd edition (New York: Continuum).

Galinsky, G. K. (1975), *Ovid's Metamorphoses* (Oxford: Oxford University Press).

Gammage, N. (ed.) (1999), *The Epic Poise: A Celebration of Ted Hughes* (London: Faber and Faber).

Garber, M. (1987), *Shakespeare's Ghost Writers: Literature as Uncanny Causality* (London and New York: Routledge).

Gervais, D. (1993), 'Ted Hughes: an England beneath England', *English: The Journal of the English Association*, 52: 45–73.

—— (1999), 'Racine Englished', *Cambridge Quarterly*, 28: 181–9.

—— (2001), Review of *Alcestis*, *Agenda*, 38.1: 147–52.

—— (2002), 'Tragedy today: Ted Hughes's *Oresteia*', *Cambridge Quarterly*, 31: 139–54.

—— (2007), 'Tragedy and resignation: T. S. Eliot and *Bérénice*', *Cambridge Quarterly*, 36: 51–70.

Gielgud, J. (1999) in N. Gammage (ed.), *The Epic Poise: A Celebration of Ted Hughes* (London: Faber and Faber), 155.

Gifford, T. (1994), 'Gods of mud: Hughes and the post-pastoral', in K. Sagar (ed.), *The Challenge of Ted Hughes* (Basingstoke and London: Macmillan), 129–41.

—— (1995), *Green Voices: Understanding Contemporary Nature Poetry* (Manchester: Manchester University Press).

—— (2006), 'The Ecology of Ted Hughes: *Wolfwatching*—The Final Poetic Statement', in R. Schuchard (ed.), *Fixed Stars Govern A Life* (Across Academe 6, Academic Exchange, Emory), 37–45.

—— and Roberts, N. (1981), *Ted Hughes. A Critical Study* (London: Faber and Faber).

Gill, J. (ed.) (2006), *The Cambridge Companion to Sylvia Plath* (Cambridge: Cambridge University Press).

Goodwin, J. (ed.) (1983), *Peter Hall's Diaries* (London: Hamish Hamilton).

Gossett, S. (2004), *Perikles. William Shakespeare and George Wilkins* (London: Arden).

Graves, R. (1948, rev. 1966), *The White Goddess: A Historical Grammar of Poetic Myth* (London: Faber and Faber); amended and enlarged edition (1961) (New York: Farrar, Straus, and Giroux).

—— and Patai, R. (1964), *Hebrew Myths* (New York: Doubleday).

Griffith, M. (ed.) (1983), *Aeschylus Prometheus Bound* (Cambridge: Cambridge University Press).

Halifax, J. (1991), *Shamanic Voices: A Survey of Visionary Narratives* (London: Arkana).

Hall, E. (2004), 'Introduction', in F. Macintosh, P. Michelakis, E. Hall, and O. Taplin (eds.), *Agamemnon in Performance 458 BC to AD 2004* (Oxford: Oxford University Press), 1–46.

—— and Macintosh, F. (2005), *Greek Tragedy and the British Theatre 1660–1914* (Oxford: Oxford University Press).

Hallett, J. and Skinner, M. (eds.) (1997), *Roman Sexualities* (Princeton: Princeton University Press).

Hallifax, M. (2004), *Let Me Set the Scene: Twenty Years at the Heart of British Theatre, 1956 to 1976* (Hanover: Smith and Kraus).

Hardie, P. R. (2002*a*), *Ovid's Poetics of Illusion* (Cambridge: Cambridge University Press).

—— (2002*b*) 'Introduction', in P. R. Hardie (ed.), *The Cambridge Companion to Ovid* (Cambridge: Cambridge University Press), 1–10.

Hardie, P. R. (ed.) (2002*c*), *The Cambridge Companion to Ovid* (Cambridge: Cambridge University Press).

Hardwick, L. (2000), *Translating Words, Translating Cultures* (London: Duckworth).

—— (2003), *New Surveys in the Classics: Reception Studies* (Oxford: Oxford University Press).

—— (2005), 'Staging Agamemnon: the Languages of Translation', in F. Macintosh, P. Michelakis, E. Hall, and O. Taplin (eds.), *Agamemnon in Performance 458 BC to AD 2004* (Oxford: Oxford University Press) 207–21.

—— (2006), ' "Murmurs in the cathedral": the impact of translations from Greek poetry and drama on modern work in English by Michael Longley and Seamus Heaney', *Yearbook of English Studies*, 36: 204–15.

Hardwick, L. (2007a), 'Shades of Multi-lingualism in Modern Performances of Greek Tragedy' in Hardwick, L. and Gillespie, C. (eds.) *Classics in Post-colonial Worlds* (Oxford: Oxford University Press) 305–328.

—— (2007b), 'Decolonising the mind? Controversial productions of Greek drama in post-colonial England, Scotland and Ireland' in C. Stray (ed.), *Remaking the Classics: Literature, Genre and Media in Britain and Ireland since 1830* (London: Duckworth), 89–105.

—— (2008), 'Translated classics around the millenium: vibrant hybrids or shattered icons?', in A. Lianeri and V. Zajko (eds.), *Translation and the Classic: Identity as Change in the History of Culture* (Oxford: Oxford University Press), 341–66.

Hardwick, L. and Gillespie, C. (eds.) (2007), *Classics in Post-colonial Worlds* (Oxford: Oxford University Press).

Harrison, J. (1890), *Mythology and Monuments of Ancient Athens* (London: Merlin Press).

—— (1912), *Themis. A Study of the Social Origins of Greek Religion* (Cambridge: Cambridge University Press).

—— (1962), *Prolegomena to the Study of Greek Religion* (London: Merlin Press), reprinted from the 3rd edition of 1922 (Cambridge: Cambridge University Press).

Harrison, S. (2002), 'Ovid and Genre: The Evolutions of an Elegist', in P. R. Hardie (ed.), *The Cambridge Companion to Ovid* (Cambridge: Cambridge University Press), 79–94.

Harrison, T. (1990), *The Trackers of Oxyrhyncus* (London: Faber and Faber).

—— (1992), *The Common Chorus* (London: Faber and Faber).

—— (1996), *Tony Harrison: Plays 3* (London: Faber and Faber).

—— (1998), *Prometheus* (London: Faber and Faber).

—— (2000), *Laureate's Block* (Harmondsworth: Penguin).

—— (2002), *Tony Harrison: Plays 2* (London: Faber and Faber).

—— (2004), *Tony Harrison: Plays 5* (London: Faber and Faber).

—— (2005), *Euripides's Hecuba* (London: Faber and Faber).

Heaney, S. (1983), 'Hughes and England' in K. Sagar (ed.), *The Achievement of Ted Hughes* (Manchester: Manchester University Press), 13–21.

—— (1988), *The Government of the Tongue* (London: Faber and Faber).

—— (1990), *The Cure at Troy* (London: Faber and Faber).

—— (2002a), *Finders Keepers* (New York: Farrar, Straus, and Giroux).

—— (2002b), '*The Cure at Troy*: Production notes in no particular order', in M. McDonald and J. M. Walton (eds.), *Amid Our Troubles: Irish Versions of Greek Tragedy* (London: Methuen), 171–80.

—— (2004), *The Burial at Thebes* (London: Faber and Faber).

—— (2005), ' "Me" as in "Metre": Translating *Antigone*', in J. Dillon and S. E. Wilmer (eds.), *Rebel Women: Staging Greek Drama Today* (London: Methuen), 169–73.

Heath, J. (1992), *Actaeon, the Unmannerly Intruder: The Myth and its Meaning in Classical Literature* (New York: P. Lang).

Heidegger, M. (1993), 'What Calls for Thinking?' in D. Farrell Krell (ed.), *Basic Writings* (London and New York: Routledge), 365–92.

Heinz, D. (1995), 'The Art of Poetry', *Paris Review*, 134: 55–94.

Henderson, J. (1999), 'Ch-ch-ch-changes', in P. R. Hardie, A. Barchiesi, and S. Hinds (eds.), *Ovidian Transformations: Essays on the Metamorphoses and its Reception* (*Proceedings of the Cambridge Philological Seminar* Suppl. Vol. 23) (Cambridge: Cambridge University Press), 301–23.

Heubeck, A. *et al.* (1988–9), *A Commentary on Homer's Odyssey*, 2 vols (Oxford: Oxford University Press).

Hexter, R. (1993), *A Guide to the Odyssey: A Commentary on the English Translation of Robert Fitzgerald* (New York: Vintage).

Hill, D. E. (1985), *Ovid Metamorphoses I–IV* (Wiltshire: Aris & Phillips).

—— (1992), *Ovid Metamorphoses V–VIII* (Wiltshire: Aris & Phillips).

Hillis Miller, J. (1985), *The Linguistic Moment: From Wordsworth to Stevens* (Princeton: Princeton University Press).

Hinds, S. (1985), 'Booking the Return Trip: Ovid and *Tristia* 1', *Proceedings of the Cambridge Philological Seminar*, 31: 13–32.

—— (1998), *Allusion and Intertext: Dynamics of Appropriation in Roman Poetry* (Cambridge: Cambridge University Press).

Hirschberg, S. (1981), *Myth in the Poetry of Ted Hughes* (Dublin: Wolfhound).

Hoffman, D. (1992), 'Talking Beasts: The "Single Adventure" in the Poems of Ted Hughes', in L. M. Scigaj (ed.), *Critical Essays on Ted Hughes* (New York: G. K. Hall), 143–52 (originally published in *Shenandoah*, 19, Summer 1968, 49–68).

Hofmann, M. (1997), 'What Came After Ovid' (review of *TO*), *The Times*, 8 May.

Hofmann, M. and Lasdun, J. (eds.) (1994), *After Ovid: New Metamorphoses* (New York: Farrar, Straus, and Giroux).

Holes, C. (2000), 'The *Mu'allaqat*' in P. France (ed.), *The Oxford Guide to Literature in English Translation* (Oxford: Oxford University Press), 145–7.

Homer, *The Odyssey, with an English Translation by A. T. Murray* (1919) (London: Heinemann).

Homer, *The Odyssey*, trans. R. Fitzgerald (1961) (London: Doubleday).

—— *The Odyssey*, trans. A. T. Murray (1919) (London: Heinemann).

Hopkins, D. (2000), 'Latin: Ovid' in P. France (ed.), *The Oxford Guide to Literature in English Translation* (Oxford: Oxford University Press), 519–23.

Hopkins, K. (1954), *The Poets Laureate* (London: Bodley Head).

Hughes, Ted (1978), *Ted Hughes and R. S. Thomas read and discuss selections of their own poems* (Norwich Tapes).

Hughes, Ted (1980*a*), 'Ted Hughes and *Gaudete* (1977)', in E. Faas (ed.), *Ted Hughes: The Unaccommodated Universe* (Santa Barbara: Black Sparrow), 208–15.

—— (1980*b*), 'Henry Williamson', in Brocard Sewell (ed.), *Henry Williamson: The Man, the Writings* (Padstow: Tabb House), 159–65, reprinted from *Henry Williamson: A Tribute by Ted Hughes given at the Service of Thanksgiving at the Royal Parish Church of St Martin-in-the-Fields, 1 December 1977* (London: Rainbow Press, 1979), 9–16.

—— (1982), Radio Interview in Australia, transcribed by Ann Skea <http://ann.skea.com/ABC1.htm>.

—— (1986), 'Baboons and neanderthals: a rereading of *The Inheritors*', in J. Carey (ed.), *William Golding: The Man and his Books* (London: Faber and Faber), 161–88.

—— (1995), 'The Art of Poetry, No. 71', *The Paris Review*, 134: 55–94.

Huntsman, J. F. (ed.) (1978), *Essay on the Principles of Translation by Alexander Tytler* (Amsterdam: Benjamins).

Ingelbien, R. (1999), 'Mapping the misreadings: Ted Hughes, Seamus Heaney, and nationhood', *Contemporary Literature*, 40: 627–58.

Ingleheart, J. (2006*a*) 'What the Poet Saw: Ovid, the *error* and the theme of sight in *Tristia* 2', *Materiali e Discussioni*, 56: 63–86.

—— (2006*b*), 'Ovid's error: Actaeon, sight, sex and striptease', *Omnibus*, 52: 6–8.

Irvine, W. and Honan, P. (1974), *The Book, The Ring and The Poet: A Biography of Robert Browning* (London: Bodley Head).

Jacobs, F. R. (1983), 'Hughes and drama', in K. Sagar (ed.), *The Achievement of Ted Hughes* (Manchester: Manchester University Press), 154–70.

Jakobson, R. (1959), 'On linguistic aspects of translation', in R. A. Brower (ed.), *On Translation* (Cambridge, MA: Harvard University Press), 232–9.

Jong, I. J. F. de (2001), *A Narratological Commentary on the Odyssey* (Cambridge: Cambridge University Press).

Jung, C. G. (1963), *Memories, Dreams, Reflections*, ed. A. Jaffé, trans. R. and C. Winston (London: Collins and Routledge & Kegan Paul).

—— (1967), *Alchemical Studies. The Collected Works of C. G. Jung*, Vol. 13, trans. R. F. C. Hull (Princeton: Princeton University Press).

Kauffman, L. S. (1986), *Discourses of Desire: Gender, Genre, and Epistolary Fictions* (Ithaca and London: Cornell University Press).

Kennedy, D. (1993), *The Arts of Love: Five Studies in the Discourse of Roman Love Elegy* (Cambridge: Cambridge University Press).

—— (2002), 'Recent Receptions of Ovid', in P. R. Hardie (ed.), *The Cambridge Companion to Ovid* (Cambridge: Cambridge University Press), 320–35.

Kitto, H. D. F. (1961), *Greek Tragedy*, 3rd edition (London: Methuen).

Knox, B. (2000), 'Uglification', *The New Republic*, 17 and 24 April: 79–85.

Koren, Y. and Negev, E. (2006), *Lover of Unreason: Assia Wevill, Sylvia Plath's Rival and Ted Hughes's Doomed Love* (New York: Carol & Graf).

Krier, T. M. (1990), *Gazing on Secret Sights* (Ithaca and London: Cornell University Press).

Kristeva, J. (1986), *The Kristeva Reader* (Oxford: Blackwell).

—— (1987), *Tales of Love* (New York: Columbia University Press).

Kukil, K. V. (ed.) (2000), *The Journals of Sylvia Plath, 1950–1962* (London: Faber and Faber).

Kustow, M. (2005), *Peter Brook: A Biography* (London: Bloomsbury).

Lacan, J. (1977), *Écrits* (London and New York: Routledge).

—— (1998), *The Seminar of Jacques Lacan Book XX. On Feminine Sexuality: The Limits of Love and Knowledge. Encore 1972–1973* (New York: W. W. Norton).

Lahr, J. (1993), 'Inventing the enemy', *New Yorker*, October 18, 103–6.

Lawrence, D. H. (1936), *Phoenix. The Posthumous Papers of D. H. Lawrence*, ed. E. D. McDonald (London: Heinemann).

—— (1968), *Phoenix II*, ed. W. Roberts and H. T. Moore (London: Heinemann).

Lee, D. (1974), 'Translator's introduction' to Plato's *Republic* (Harmondsworth: Penguin).

Leonard, M. (2006), 'The uses of reception: Derrida and the historical imperative', in C. Martindale and R. Thomas (eds.), *Classics and the Uses of Reception* (Oxford: Blackwell), 116–26.

Lianeri, A. and Zajko, V. (eds.) (2008), *Translation and the Classic: Identity as Change in the History of Culture* (Oxford: Oxford University Press).

Lévinas, E. (1999), *Alterity and Transcendence* (New York: Columbia University Press).

Lewis, P. (1990), *The National. A Dream Made Concrete* (London: Methuen).

Logue, C. (1981), *War Music* (London: Cape).

—— (1999), *Prince Charming: A Memoir* (London: Faber and Faber).

Longley, M. (1995), *The Ghost Orchid* (London: Cape).

Loughlin, G. (1999), 'God's Sex' in J. Millbank, C. Pickstock, and G. Ward (eds.), *Radical Orthodoxy* (London and New York: Routledge), 143–62.

Lowell, R. (1959), *Life Studies* (London: Faber and Faber).

Luck, G. (1968), *The Latin Love Elegy* (London: Methuen).

Lyne, R. O. A. M. (1980), *The Latin Love Poets: From Catullus to Ovid* (Oxford: Oxford University Press).

Lyne, R. (2000), 'Ovid, Golding, and the "rough magic" of *The Tempest*', in A. B. Taylor (ed.), *Shakespeare's Ovid: The* Metamorphoses *in the Plays and Poems* (Cambridge: Cambridge University Press), 150–64.

—— . (2002), 'Ovid in English translation', in P. R. Hardie (ed.), *The Cambridge Companion to Ovid* (Cambridge: Cambridge University Press), 249–63.

MacCormack, S. (1981), *Art and Ceremony in Late Antiquity* (Berkeley: University of California Press).

Macintosh, F. (2000), *Programme Notes to Alcestis* (Halifax: Northern Broadsides).

Macintosh, F. Michelakis, P. Hall, E., and Taplin, O. (eds.) (2005), *Agamemnon in Performance 458 BC to AD 2004* (Oxford: Oxford University Press).

MacNeice, L. (1935), 'Translating Aeschylus', *Spectator*, 154 (10 May): 794, repr. in A. Heuser, (1987), *Selected Literary Criticism of Louis MacNeice* (Oxford: Clarendon Press), 7–10.

Mack, M. (ed.) (1967), *Alexander Pope: The Odyssey of Homer*, Books I–XII (London: Methuen).

Marais, E. (1973), *The Soul of the Ape* (Harmondsworth: Penguin).

Marshall, C. W. (2000), 'Alcestis and the problem of prosatyric drama', *Classical Journal*, 95: 229–38.

Martindale, C. and Thomas, R. (eds.) (2006), *Classics and the Uses of Reception* (Oxford: Blackwell).

McClatchy, J. D. (1998), 'Old Myths in New Versions', *Poetry*, 172: 154–65.

McDonald, M. and Walton, J. M. (eds.) (2002), *Amid Our Troubles: Irish Versions of Greek Tragedy* (London: Methuen).

Middlebrook, D. (1998), 'Poetic Justice for Sylvia Plath', *New York Times* (27 January).

—— (2003), *Her Husband: Hughes and Plath—A Marriage* (New York: Viking).

—— (2006*a*), 'The poetry of Sylvia Plath and Ted Hughes: call and response' in J. Gill (ed.), *The Cambridge Companion to Sylvia Plath* (Cambridge: Cambridge University Press), 156–71.

—— (2006*b*), 'Hughes, Plath, and the three caryatids' in R. Schuchard (ed.), *Fixed Stars Govern A Life*, Across Academe 6 (Emory: Academic Exchange), 47–56.

Millbank, J. Pickstock, C., and Ward, G. (eds.) (1999), *Radical Orthodoxy* (London and New York: Routledge).

Miller, P. A. (2004), *Subjecting Verses: Latin Love Elegy and the Emergence of the Real* (Princeton: Princeton University Press).

Miola, R. S. (1992), *Shakespeare and Classical Tragedy: The Influence of Seneca* (Oxford: Oxford University Press).

Mitchell, K. 'NT Education', available at <www.archive2.nt-online.org/? lid=2497>.

Monluçon, A.-M. (2006), 'En traduisant, en écrivant: la légende du rossignol chez Ovide et Ted Hughes', in V. Gely and A. Tomiche (eds.), *Littératures* (Clermont-Ferrand: Presses Universitaires Blaise Pascal), 285–303.

Moody, A. D. (1979), *Thomas Sterns Eliot: Poet*, 2nd edn (Cambridge: Cambridge University Press).

Morely, S. (2002), *John Gielgud, The Authorized Biography* (New York: Simon & Schuster).

Morgan, L. (2003), 'Child's Play: Ovid and his Critics', *Journal of Roman Studies*, 93: 66–91.

Moulin, J. (1995), 'History and Reason in the Work of Ted Hughes', <http:// www.uni-leipzig.de/~angl/hughes/download.htm>.

Moulin, J. (ed.) (2004), *Ted Hughes. Alternative Horizons* (London and New York: Routledge).

Murray, G. (1912*a*), *Four Stages of Greek Religion* (New York: Columbia University Press).

—— (1912*b*), 'Excursus on the Ritual Forms Preserved in Greek Tragedy', in J. Harrison, *Themis. A Study of the Social Origins of Greek Religion* (Cambridge: Cambridge University Press), 341–63.

Nagle, B. R. (1980), *The Poetics of Exile: Program and Polemic in the Tristia and Epistulae ex Ponto of Ovid*, Collection Latomus 170 (Brussels).

Nancy, J.-L. (1991), *The Inoperative Community* (Minneapolis and Oxford: University of Minnesota Press).

Nietzsche, F. *The Portable Nietzsche*, trans. W. Kaufmann (1971) (London: Chatto and Windus).

—— *The Birth of Tragedy Out of the Spirit of Music*, trans. S. Whiteside and M. Tanner (1993) (Harmondsworth: Penguin).

O'Brien, S. (1997), 'Skyfuls of fist and a shower of teeth' (review of *TO*), *Times Literary Supplement*, 4 July.

—— (1998), *The Deregulated Muse. Essays on Contemporary British and Irish Poetry* (Newcastle: Bloodaxe).

Ovid, *Metamorphoses*, trans. G. Sandys, K. H. Hulley, and S. T. Vandersall (eds.) (1970) (Lincoln: University of Nebraska Press).

Ovid, *Metamorphoses*, trans. F. J. Miller (1916), 2 vols (Cambridge, MA: Harvard University Press).

Paolucci, A. and Paolucci, H. (eds.) (1962), *Hegel on Tragedy* (New York: Anchor Books).

Parker, L. P. E. (2003), 'Alcestis: Euripides to Ted Hughes', *Greece and Rome*, 50: 1–30.

Parry, H. (1964), 'Ovid's *Metamorphoses*: Violence in a Pastoral Landscape', *Transactions of the American Philological Association*, 5: 268–82.

Paulin, T. (1985), *The Riot Act* (London: Faber and Faber).

—— (1992), *Minotaur: Poetry and the Nation State* (London: Faber and Faber).

Payne, H. (1978), 'Modernizing the ancients: the reconstruction of ritual drama 1870–1920', *Proceedings of the American Philosophical Society*, 122: 182–92.

Plath, A. S. (ed.) (1975), *Letters Home: Correspondence 1950–1963 by Sylvia Plath* (London: Faber and Faber).

Plath, S. (1965), *Ariel*, ed. Ted Hughes (London: Faber and Faber).

Plato, *Apology, Phaedo*, trans. H. Tredennick (1954), in *The Last Days of Socrates* (Harmondsworth: Penguin).

—— *Timaeus and Critias*, trans. H. D. P. Lee (1969) (Harmondsworth: Penguin).

—— *Symposium*, trans. W. Hamilton (1951) (Harmondsworth: Penguin).

Pound, E. (1954), *Literary Essays of Ezra Pound* (Norfolk, CN: James Laughlin).

Racine, J. *Oeuvres Complètes*, ed. Picard, R. (1950) (Paris: Gallimard).

—— (1985), *Phèdre* (Paris: Livre de Poche).

Raine, C. (2005), 'For better or for verse' *The Daily Telegraph*, 2 April.

—— (2007), 'Pursued by bears' [Review of C. Reid (ed.), *Letters of Ted Hughes*], *TLS* 5460 (23 November), 3–8.

Ramazani, J. (1993), '"Daddy, I have had to kill you": Plath, rage, and the modern elegy', *Publications of the Modern Language Association of America*, 108.5: 1142–56.

Reading, P. (1992), 'Turning on the water-works' [Review of *Rain-Charm for the Duchy and Other Laureate Poems*], *Sunday Times* (28 June), 13.

—— (1996), *Collected Poems*, 2 vols (Newcastle upon Tyne: Bloodaxe).

Rehm, R. (2005), 'Cassandra—the prophet unveiled', in F. Macintosh, P. Michelakis, E. Hall, and O. Taplin (eds.), *Agamemnon in Performance 458 BC to AD 2004* (Oxford: Oxford University Press), 343–58.

Reid, C. (sel. and ed.) (2007), *Letters of Ted Hughes* (London: Faber).

—— (2002), *Allusion to the Poets* (Oxford: Oxford University Press).

Roberts, N. (1985), 'Ted Hughes and the laureateship', *Critical Quarterly*, 27.2: 3–5.

—— (1999), 'Hughes, the laureateship and national identity', *Q/W/E/R/T/ Y: Littératures et Civilisations des Pays Anglophones*: 203–9.

—— (2006), *Ted Hughes. A Literary Life* (Basingstoke and London: Macmillan).

Robinson, C. (1989), *Ted Hughes as Shepherd of Being* (Basingstoke and London: Macmillan).

Russel, N. (1981), *Poets by Appointment. Britain's Laureates* (Poole: Blandford Press).

Sagar, K. (1975, 1978$^2$) *The Art of Ted Hughes* (Cambridge: Cambridge University Press).

Sagar, K. (ed.) (1983), *The Achievement of Ted Hughes* (Manchester: Manchester University Press).

—— (ed.) (1994), *The Challenge of Ted Hughes* (Basingstoke and London: Macmillan).

Sagar, K. (2000, 2006$^2$), *The Laughter of Foxes: A Study of Ted Hughes* (Liverpool: Liverpool University Press).

—— (2001), *Alcestis*, <http://keithsagar.co.uk/Downloads/Alcestis2.pdf>.

—— (2005), *Literature and the Crime against Nature* (London: Chaucer Press).

—— and Tabor, S. (1998), *Ted Hughes. A Bibliography 1946–1995* (London: Mansell).

Salzman-Mitchell, P. B. (2005), *A Web of Fantasies: Gaze, Image, and Gender in Ovid's* Metamorphoses (Columbus: The Ohio State University Press).

Sansom, I. (1998), 'I was there, I saw it', *London Review of Books* (19 February), 8–9.

Schuchard, R. (ed.) (2006), *Fixed Stars Govern A Life*, Across Academe 6 (Emory: Academic Exchange).

Scigaj, L. M. (ed.) (1992), *Critical Essays on Ted Hughes* (New York: MacMillan International).

Seneca, *Tragedies, Volume 2*, trans. J. G. Fitch (2004) (Cambridge, MA and London: Harvard University Press).

Shakespeare, W. *Antony and Cleopatra*, ed. J. Wilders (1995) (London: Arden).

—— *Pericles*, ed. S. Gossett (2004) (London: Arden).

Share, D. (ed.) (1998), *Seneca in English* (Harmondsworth: Penguin).

Sharrock, A. (2000), 'Latin: drama', in P. France (ed.), *The Oxford Guide to Literature in English Translation* (Oxford: Oxford University Press), 531–4.

Shaw, W. D. (1994), *Elegy & Paradox. Testing the Conventions* (Baltimore and London: The Johns Hopkins University Press).

Silk, M. S. (1985), 'Heracles and Greek Tragedy', *Greece & Rome*, 32: 1–22.

—— (1999), *Times Literary Supplement* 17 December, 16–17.

—— (2007), 'Hughes, Plath and Aeschylus: allusion and poetic language', *Arion*, 14: 1–33.

—— and Stern, J. P. (1981), *Nietzsche on Tragedy* (Cambridge: Cambridge University Press).

Skea, A. (2000), 'A Timeline of Hughes' Life and Work', in K. Sagar, *The Laughter of Foxes: A Study of Ted Hughes* (Liverpool: Liverpool University Press), xv–xxxiv.

Slavitt, D. R. (1994), *The Metamorphoses of Ovid Translated Freely into Verse* (Baltimore and London: Johns Hopkins University Press).

Smith, A. C. H. (1972), *Orghast at Persepolis* (New York: Eyre Methuen).

Solodow, J. (1988), *The World of Ovid's Metamorphoses* (Chapel Hill: The University of North Carolina Press).

Southam, B. C. (ed.) (1978), *'Prufrock', 'Geronion', 'Ash Wednesday' and Other Shorter Poems. A Casebook* (London: MacMillan).

Spivey, N. (1997), 'Metamorphosing still' (review of *TO*), *The Guardian*, 28 August.

Steiner, G. (1984), *Antigones* (Oxford: Oxford University Press).

—— (1998) *After Babel*, 3rd edn (Oxford: Oxford University Press).

Stendhal, (1823), *Racine et Shakespeare* (Paris).

Stevenson, A. (1989), *Bitter Fame: A Life of Sylvia Plath* (London: Viking).

Stothard, P. (2005), 'Hit me here, and here, and here', *Times Literary Supplement*, 15 April, 18.

Stray, C. A. (1998), *Classics Transformed* (Oxford: Clarendon Press).

Stray, C. A. (ed.) (2007), *Remaking the Classics: Literature, Genre and Media in Britain and Ireland since 1830* (London: Duckworth).

Struck, P. (2004), *Birth of the Symbol: Ancient Readers at the Limits of Their Texts* (Princeton: Princeton University Press).

Supple, T. (1999), in N. Gammage (ed.), *The Epic Poise: A Celebration of Ted Hughes* (London: Faber and Faber), 163–6.

Talbot, J. (2006), ' "I had set myself against Latin." Ted Hughes and the classics', *Arion*, 13.3: 131–61.

Taplin, O. (2002), 'Contemporary poetry and Classics' in T. P. Wiseman (ed.), *Classics in Progress* (Oxford: Oxford University Press), 1–19.

Taylor, A. B. (ed.) (2000), *Shakespeare's Ovid: The Metamorphoses in the Plays and Poems* (Cambridge: Cambridge University Press).

Timmerman, J. H. (1994), *T. S. Eliot's Ariel Poems: The Politics of Recovery* (Lewisburg, PA, London, and Toronto: Bucknell University Press).

Tissol, G. (1997), *The Face Of Nature* (Princeton: Princeton University Press).

Tomlinson, P. (ed.) (2001), *French Classical Theatre Today* (Amsterdam: Rodopi).

Turner, D. A. (1969), 'A Word about *Oedipus*', in T. Hughes, *Seneca's Oedipus* (London: Faber and Faber), 9.

—— (1990), *Oedipus* in R. W. Corrigan (ed.), *Classical Tragedy: Greek and Roman: Eight Plays* (New York: Applause Theatre).

Venuti, L. (1995), *The Translator's Invisibility: A History of Translation* (London and New York: Routledge).

Versnel, H. (1990), 'What's sauce for the goose is sauce for the gander: myth and ritual, old and new', in L. Edmunds (ed.), *Approaches to Greek Myth* (Baltimore: The Johns Hopkins University Press), 23–90.

Veyne, P. (1988), *Roman Erotic Elegy: Love, Poetry, and the West,* trans. D. Pellauer (Chicago: University of Chicago Press).

Vickery, J. (1966), *Myth and Literature* (Lincoln: University of Nebraska Press).

*Virgil, The Aeneid: A New Prose Translation,* trans. D. West (1991) (Harmondsworth: Penguin).

Wagner, E. (2000), *Ariel's Gift: A Commentary on* Birthday Letters *by Ted Hughes* (London: Faber and Faber).

Walcott, D. (1993), *The Odyssey: A Stage Version* (London: Faber and Faber).

Walder, D. (1987), *Ted Hughes* (Milton Keynes: Open University Press).

Walker, J. (2000), *Rhetoric and Poetics in Antiquity* (Oxford: Oxford University Press).

Walton, J. M. (2005), 'Translation or transubstantiation', in F. Macintosh, P. Michelakis, E. Hall, and O. Taplin (eds.), *Agamemnon in Performance 458 bc to ad 2004* (Oxford: Oxford University Press), 189–206.

Walton, J. M. (2006), *Found in Translation: Greek Drama in English* (Cambridge: Cambridge University Press).

Ward, D. (1973), *Between Two Worlds: A Reading of T. S. Eliot's Poetry and Plays* (London and Boston: Routledge and Kegan Paul).

Warner, M. (2000), *Monuments and Maidens. The Allegory of the Female Form* (Berkeley: University of California Press).

Watson, G. (ed.) (1962), John Dryden, *Of Dramatic Poesy, and Other Critical Essays,* vol. 1 (London: J. M. Dent).

Weissbort, D. (2000), 'Text types: poetry' in P. France (ed.), *The Oxford Guide to Literature in English Translation* (Oxford: Oxford University Press), 89–96.

—— (2006), *Ted Hughes: Selected Translations* (London: Faber and Faber).

Weissbort, D. and Eysteinsson, A. (eds.) (2006), *Translation—Theory and Practice* (Oxford: Oxford University Press).

Wheeler, A. L. (1924 and reprints), *Ovid: Tristia and Ex Ponto* (Cambridge, MA and London: Heinemann).

Wheeler, S. (1999), *A Discourse of Wonders* (Philadelphia: University of Pennsylvania Press).

Whitehead, A. (1999), 'Refiguring Orpheus: The possession of the past in Ted Hughes' *Birthday Letters*', *Textual Practice*, 13.2: 227–41.

Wilders, J. (1995), *Antony and Cleopatra by William Shakespeare* (London: Routledge).

Williams, G. D. (1994), *Banished Voices: Readings in Ovid's Exile Poetry* (Cambridge: Cambridge University Press).

Williamson, H. (1927), *Tarka the Otter* (London: Putnams).

Wilmer, S. E. (2007), 'Finding a post-colonial voice for Antigone. Seamus Heaney's *Burial at Thebes*', in L. Hardwick and C. Gillespie (eds.), *Classics in Post-colonial Worlds* (Oxford: Oxford University Press), 228–42.

Wiseman, T. P. (ed.) (2002), *Classics in Progress* (Oxford: Oxford University Press).

Worth, I. (1999), in N. Gammage (ed.), *The Epic Poise: A Celebration of Ted Hughes* (London: Faber), 156–8.

Yeats, W. B. (1903), *Ideas of Good and Evil* (London: Bullen).

—— (1962²), *A Vision* (London: MacMillan).

Ziolkowski, T. (2005), *Ovid and the Moderns* (Ithaca: Cornell University Press).

# Index